PLAYING WITH FIRE:
QUEER POLITICS, QUEER THEORIES

Edited by Shane Phelan

Routledge
New York & London

Published in 1997 by
Routledge
29 West 35 Street
New York, NY 10001
Published in Great Britain in 1997 by
Routledge
11 New Fetter Lane
London EC4P 4EE

Copyright © 1997 by Routledge
Printed in the United States of America

Judith Butler, "Critically Queer," originally appeared in *Bodies that Matter*, Routledge, 1993, and is reproduced with permission. Cynthia Burack, "True or False: The Self in Radical Lesbian Theory," originally appeared as "True or False: The Stratified Self in Lesbian Feminist Theory," in *Feminism and Psychology*, 3: 5 (1993): 329–344 and is reprinted with the permission of Sage Publications Ltd. Shane Phelan, "Lesbians and Mestizas: Appropriation and Equivalence," originally appeared in *Getting Specific: Postmodern Lesbian Politics* (University of Minnesota Press, 1994) and is reprinted with the permission of the University of Minnesota Press. Morris Kaplan, "Intimacy and Equality: The Question of Lesbian and Gay Marriages," origi-nally appeared in *The Philosophical Forum*, XXV:4 (1994): 333–360, and is reprinted with the permission of *The Philosophical Forum*. An earlier version of Lisa Bower's "Queer Problems/Straight Solutions: The Limits of a Politics of 'Official Recog-nition'" appeared in *Law & Society Review*, 28:5 (1994): 1009–1033, and is reprinted with the permission of the Law and Society Association. An earlier version of Anna Marie Smith's "The Centering of Right-Wing Extremism Through the Construction of an 'Inclusionary' Homophobia and Racism" originally appeared as "The Imaginary Inclusion of the Assimilable Immigrant and the 'Good Homosexual': the British New Right's Representation of Sexuality and Race" in *Diacritics*, 24:2, 3 (1994): 58–70, and is reprinted with permssion.

Library of Congress Cataloging-in-Publication Data
Playing with fire : queer politics, queer theories / edited by Shane Phelan.
     p.   cm.
    ISBN 0-415-91416-7 (c). —ISBN 0-415-91417-5 (pb)
    1. Gays—United States—Identity.   2. Lesbians—United States—Identity.   3. Gay men—United States—Political activity.   4. Lesbians—United States—Political activity.   5. Lesbian feminism—United States.
    6. Homosexuality—Political aspects—United States.   7. Homosexuality—United States—Philosophy.
I. Phelan, Shane
HQ76.3.U5P53   1996
306.76'6–dc20   95-51728
                                                             CIP

Contents

INTRODUCTION

Shane Phelan

In the last fifteen years sexuality has become central to modern politics, especially in the United States and Great Britain, to a previously unimaginable degree. The religious Right uses the specter of homosexual power in order to recruit and spur their armies to battle modernity. Overlapping battalions attack women's reproductive freedom—and increasingly endorse murder—in the name of life. Gay men argue with one another about whether assimilation or transgression is the road to freedom, and indeed about whether freedom is the goal. Lesbians debate sexual practices and political alliances, veering between identifying as women and as "homosexual/gay/queer." Vice presidents attack TV characters, and the TV characters answer back. The academic field of gay and lesbian studies is growing even as universities face an onslaught of conservative attacks.

Scholars in queer political theory, and in queer theory more generally, are playing with fire. Despite the anxiety of those who imagine that white heterosexual men and their civilization have been banned from the academy, women, racial and ethnic minorities, and sexual dissidents know that we have barely begun to pry open the doors. With the United States governed by the first Republican Congress since 1954, a Congress that seeks in many ways to return us to that time, we (the many "we's" so feared by that Congress) are not yet secure as equal citizens, much less as the powerful oppressors of conservative jeremiads. In such a time, publishing in lesbian and gay studies remains a risky business. Students continue to be discouraged by advisors when they pursue gay and lesbian research, scholars at all levels remain underfunded and undersupported, and university faculties continue to eye such studies as intellectually suspect.[1] Even to write in this field is playing with the fire wielded by the institutions we live within.

The last thirty years has been a time of huge controversy and upheaval, both in political/social theory and in political and cultural life. The primary names of the controversy in theory have been, first, poststructuralism and postmodernism in all their variety, and second, feminisms that range from the sweeping indictments of heteropatriarchal society laid down by early les-bian-feminists and continued by socialist feminists, to the modest "me-too-ism" of Betty Friedan and Naomi Wolf, to the critiques of white feminism by women of color. These currents have blended in the work of contemporary lesbian and gay theorists.[2] At the same time, hegemonic cultural and politi-cal forms in "the West" have been challenged by lesbian and gay activism, activism that has both drawn on and refused these theoretical strains. Queer Nation, ACT UP, OutRage! and the Lesbian Avengers are only a few of the constantly fluid groups that have used cultural forms such as visual and per-formance art to intervene in dominant political agendas in North America, Europe, and Australia.

These many discourses and movements share a profound confrontation with identities, both of persons and of communities. This confrontation is by no means a simple rejection of identity, but is a questioning, a challenge to the ontological and political status of sexuality, race, and gender. It emerges both in theoretical writing that directly addresses identities and in work that genealogizes and/or deconstructs them in practice. The debates over butch/femme identities, sadomasochism, transsexuals, bisexuals, and lesbians who sleep with men have all been enriched by postmodern chal-lenges to liberal/medical and lesbian-feminist narratives of identity. Questions of sexual identity also lead us to reconsider the possibilities and grounds of alliances between "straights" and "queers" as well as between men and women, and to reconsider legal and political strategies.[3] As a result of these debates, queer theory has begun to recruit political theorists. In the last five years a solid and growing group of new scholars has been mapping out a field, and their work is becoming increasingly important for scholars in other fields and for political activists.[4]

The first group of essays presented here, "Queer Identities," focuses on the question of sexual identities. The centrality of the category of identity is itself indicative of the changes in political theory over the last twenty-five years, and points to the role of new social movements in trans-forming politics. Feminist theory and queer theory have pointed to the fun-damental indeterminacy of identities—of inside/outside communities, of masculine/feminine, of homo/hetero/bi, of male/female, and of racial and ethnic categories. Ultimately, queer theory's target is identity itself—the assumption of unity or harmony or transparency within persons or groups. As Judith Butler notes in "Critically Queer," "if identity is a necessary error, then the assertion of 'queer' will be incontrovertibly necessary, but that assertion will constitute only one part of 'politics.' It is equally necessary, and perhaps also equally impossible, to affirm the contingency of the term." Butler's discussion of performativity elucidates gender as "the *effect* of a regulatory regime of gender differences in which genders are divided and hierarchized *under constraint*," and describes heterosexuality as part of that regulatory regime. Thus, rather than call for safe spaces for the assertion of "true" gay or lesbian identities, she argues for the disruption of sexual identities as part of a larger democratic project.

Butler's work is deeply informed by Lacanian psychoanalysis, as is much of current queer theory. Less central to queer theory, but prominent within feminist theory, is the object-relations tradition.[5] Cynthia Burack uses the work of D.W. Winnicott to trace the inadequacies of lesbian-feminist theory to the theory of the self that predominates in lesbian-feminist discourse, a theory that cannot account for the social constitution of selves as anything other than the imposition of facades covering "the true self." Ironically, she finds that lesbian-feminist accounts of the self strongly resemble some object-relations accounts, even as lesbian-feminists attack psychology as patriarchal; the problem then is not just one of historical confusion, but is also that "disclaimed assumptions are not subject to critique. The likelihood that ad hoc, usually comforting, conceptualizations of the self will be introduced is enhanced in such theories." In their search for "wholeness," she argues, lesbian-feminist theorists are led to deny the necessary limits and pains of human consciousness, and so to misidentify social problems.

Stacey Young extends the challenge to identity through her discussion of the treatment of bisexuality in queer theory and politics. Within a binary hetero/homo system, she argues, bisexuality can only be seen as "some of each," a sort of sexual *mestizaje*, rather than as a site of questions about the univocity of our sexual desires. Even as bisexuals are brought under the queer umbrella, they are erased. Indeed, many writers and activists use "queer" as a shorthand to cope with the lengthening list of sexual/political articulations—lesbians, gays, bis, transgendered people—without examining the hegemony of gays and lesbians within that articulation. Young uses bisexuality to further "queer" as a term within a discourse that we can describe, following Eve Sedgwick, as "universalizing." By this term, Sedgwick refers to a view in which the definition, demarcation, and deconstruction of the homosexual/heterosexual binary is not just an issue for those placed on the homosexual side (the minoritizing strategy) but is "an issue of continuing, determinative importance in the lives of people across the spectrum of sexualities."[6] By challenging the boundary lines as well as the content of the territories they mark, queer work calls each of us to attend to the uncertainties and incompletions in our identities.

In the United States, Canada, and Great Britain, the dynamics of sexual politics have been guided less by philosophical concerns than by the need to articulate desired changes within the language of liberal pluralism. In contrast to queer theory's challenge to identity, the first move in this articulation was the renewal of the biological/medical model in which homosexuality is genetic (and thus implicitly presocial). As a consequence, proponents argue, discriminating against "gays and lesbians" is no more legitimate than discrimination on the basis of race, parentage, or sex. After all, one cannot help what one is born with. Such strategies are designed to challenge popular understandings of homosexuality as a series of acts one chooses to perform—sinful acts, at that. In the medical model, it would be senseless cruelty to deny to people the one type of sexual pleasure for which they are designed and capable; it is akin to discrimination on the basis of race, ethnicity, or gender (also seen as essential, univocal attributes). This argument is used to support everything from simple antiviolence legislation to drives for same-sex marriage and partner benefits.

Such arguments have proved problematic in two ways. First, they fail to do justice to the fluidity and variety of sexual desire, fixing everyone as one or the other (or occasionally, as Young notes, as some of each). Second, facile analogies between the situation of queers and that of racial minorities is also politically misguided in that the analogization has alienated many people of color who feel that their history is being appropriated. As I argue in "Lesbians and Mestizas," facile equations inhibit coalition building and understanding about real differences. Rather than looking for "natural" alliances based on innate features, we should be working to forge links between movements against oppressions. Such linkages do not require appeals to something in our being; rather, they are premised on a shared understanding of social space and power.

The second section, "Queer Critiques," moves from questions of identity toward interventions in political theory and politics. Angelia Wilson describes her confusion about the articulation between queer theories of (non)identity and the seeming need in the political arena for a stable subject. She moves through Butler to the work of Ernesto Laclau and Chantal Mouffe, exploring the possibilities for a politics of articulation. She endorses Anna Marie Smith's view that "permanent problematisation" of identities must be balanced by "the realities of political systems where identities become significations of existence and of political claims." This balancing enables us to build coalitions around issues without naturalizing our identities. This project is exemplified by Smith's contribution to this volume, in which she examines the way that the British New Right seeks to contain emerging groups and identities by superficially endorsing the identities while refusing the actual persons who claim oppression on the basis of those identities and who seek equal public recognition. Her analysis leads us to see the issues that can link diverse groups against the dominant constructions of Euro/American identity as white, male, and heterosexual.

The next two contributions continue this movement between consolidation and problematization of identities. Gordon Babst responds to Michael Sandel's "communitarian dissent" of the *Bowers v. Hardwick* case, and argues that the language and theory of communitarianism will inevitably fail to protect gays and lesbians from social prejudice. Babst argues strongly for a renewed liberalism focused on individual rights and privacy claims. Gary Lehring critiques Jean Bethke Elshtain's 1982 article on homosexual politics, while also contesting views such as Babst's. As Lehring shows, gay liberation was radical partly for its rejection of fixed boundaries between gay and straight—its queerness. Since the 1980s, the liberationist project has been dismissed in favor of political visions simultaneously essentialist and assimilationist. In the 1970s gay liberation was the name of a major theoretical challenge to assimilation as well as minoritization. Early activists and writers argued that gay liberation could transform all sexual and gender relations; they argued against marriage and monogamy and against existing family structures.[7] Indeed, Lehring notes, their work is altogether too radical and anti-essentialist for many contemporary students.

In the final section, "Queer Agendas," three theorists who work on the boundary of political and legal theory critique the current legal/political situation of queers and offer strategies for future action. The heightened importance of identity within political theory has accompanied a profound rethinking of the liberal tradition. As the essays included here demonstrate, this rethinking is shaped by the demand for a more robust, yet more flexible, public sphere. Rather than reject rights discourse outright, however, an emerging group of queer scholars is working to transform our understanding of rights from trumps against society held by presocial individuals to practices that themselves frame and foster the constitution of identities. Like Babst, Paisley Currah takes aim at communitarian critics of liberalism who argue that individualist formulations of rights and current versions of identity politics both suffer from ontological and political deficiencies. She points toward conceptions of rights as social practices engaged in by mutually constituting persons. Currah agrees with Babst that communitarianism cannot provide ground for security or tolerance, and elaborates on the recent shift in legal strategies from "privacy" arguments based on essentialist understandings of sexuality to claims to equal citizenship in both the public and private aspects of our lives.

The shift from privacy to equality is mirrored in Morris Kaplan's argument for public recognition of private lives in his treatment of lesbian and gay marriage. As he argues, "even the most intimate associations between individuals are situated within a matrix of social relations and legal arrangements that both constrain and support them." Because of this need, "full equality for lesbian and gay citizens requires access to the legal and social recognition of our intimate associations." Kaplan argues that the right to marry is an essential element of equality, even if we do not endorse the current structure of marriages in patriarchal societies. His historical review of constitutional treatments on privacy illuminates the importance of this principle as well as an invigorated public sphere, and documents the ways in which privacy has been denied to queers even as we are commanded to keep our daily lives "private."

Against Currah, Babst, and Kaplan, Lisa Bower argues that strategies of "official recognition" are incapable of effecting major social change. Bound as they are to concepts already recognized by the state, such strategies work to contain queers as much as they open new ground. Bower uses the case of Karen Ulane, a transsexual who was fired after having sex reassignment surgery, to illustrate the limits of the law and the possibilities for articulating new identities. The question of Ulane's identity—as "woman" or as "transsexual"—and of her claim on that basis to discrimination in violation of Title VII of the Civil Rights Act of 1964 offers a window into the stakes and fears at work in the legal determination of identities. It also teaches us that premature attempts to find doctrinal solutions will close off the questions that are most basic and most important for real social change. Queer "cultural politics"—the transformation of public sensibilities and the creation of safe spaces within larger social formations—appears to present difficulties for queer political theory, as it veers between "the queer" and "the political," understood as the stable location of regulated identities. However, Bower suggests that these projects are not necessarily distinct, that the law is a terrain for cultural confrontation as well as doctrinal development. The tension is not between queerness and politics, but between queerness and the antipolitical search for closure. Thus, queer politics leads us to a new democratic project of alliances built not only, or not simply, on shared identities, but on communication across identities and spaces.

Although AIDS has been a major factor in gay and lesbian politics and communities since the early 1980s, it has barely begun to be a topic in political science and political theory. Voices such as Linda Singer's (a voice silenced too early by another epidemic) have been rare entrants on a stage generally occupied by theorists in other fields.[8] Within the discipline of political theory, AIDS remains understudied and undertheorized.

The queer strategy of cultural disruption is, as I mentioned at the opening, part of the reason for queer theory's advance in the humanities relative to political science and political theory. As the border between disciplines begins to be crossed, it will be new generations of political theorists who will enable us to be queer citizens, to queer citizenship, and to queer political discourse. Queer political theory brings together the recognition of the structures and patterns of electoral and legal politics with the imagination of new cultural forms and new political subjects. Across this bridge we may see not only the establishment of new research projects and designs, but the healing of the liberal arts from the surgery that has split their limbs into unrecognizable strangers.

Notes

1. On the state of lesbians and gays in political science, see Martha Ackelsberg, David Rayside, and Kenneth Sherrill, "Report of the Committee on the Status of Gays and Lesbians in the Profession," typescript.

2. On poststructuralism and postmodernism see Michel Foucault, *The History of Sexuality, vol I: An Introduction* (New York: Vintage, 1980) and *Power/Knowledge* (New York: Pantheon, 1980); Jacques Lacan, *Ecrits* (New York: W.W. Norton, 1978); Jacques Derrida, *Margins of Philosophy* (Chicago: University of Chicago Press, 1982); Jean Baudrillard, *Selected Writings*, edited by Mark Poster (Palo Alto: Stanford University Press, 1988); Jean-Francois Lyotard, *The Postmodern Condition* (Minneapolis: University of Minnesota Press, 1984); Richard Rorty, *Contingency, Irony, and Solidarity* (Cambridge: Cambridge University Press, 1989); Ernesto Laclau and Chantal Mouffe, *Hegemony and Socialist Strategy* (London: Verso, 1985). On feminism, see Charlotte Bunch, *Passionate Politics* (New York: St. Martin's, 1988); bell hooks, *Feminist Theory: From Margin to Center* (Boston: South End, 1984); Cherrie Moraga, *Loving in the War Years* (Boston: South End, 1983); Aida Hurtado, "Relating to Privilege: Seduction and Rejection in the Subordination of White Women and Women of Color," *Signs* 14/4 (1989: 833–55); Judith Butler, *Gender Trouble* (New York: Routledge, 1990) and *Bodies that Matter* (New York: Routledge, 1993); Teresa de Lauretis, *Technologies of Gender* (Bloomington: Indiana University Press, 1983) and *The Practice of Love* (Bloomington: Indiana University Press, 1993); and Linda Nicholson, ed., *Feminism/Postmodernism* (New York: Routledge, 1990).

3. Not all gays and lesbians identify as "queer," of course, nor are all queers homosexual. I use "queer" here to indicate, in Alexander Doty's words, "a quality related to any expression that can be marked as contra-, non-, or anti-straight." Alexander Doty, *Making Things Perfectly Queer: Interpreting Mass Culture* (Minneapolis: University of Minnesota Press, 1993), xv. Both an umbrella term and a particular inflection of nonstraight identity, "queer" in my usage includes lesbians, gays, bisexuals, transgendered people, and other "gender outlaws." On the linkage between heterosexism and "gender terrorism," see Kate Bornstein, *Gender Outlaw: On Men, Women, and the Rest of Us* (New York: Routledge, 1994).

4. See for example Shane Phelan, *Identity Politics: Lesbian Feminism and the Limits of Community* (Philadelphia: Temple University Press, 1989) and *Getting Specific: Postmodern Lesbian Politics* (Minneapolis: University of Minnesota Press, 1994); Joseph Bristow and Angelia R.

Wilson, *Activating Theory: Lesbian, Gay, Bisexual Politics* (London: Lawrence and Wishart, 1993); Mark Blasius, *Gay and Lesbian Politics: Sexuality and the Emergence of a New Ethic* (Philadelphia: Temple University Press, 1994); and Angelia R. Wilson, ed., *A Simple Matter of Justice?* (London: Cassell, 1995).

5.   See, for example, Jane Flax, *Thinking Fragments* (Berkeley: University of California Press, 1990).

6.   Eve Kosofscsky Sedgwick, *Epistemology of the Closet* (Berkeley: University of California Press, 1990), 1.

7.   See, for example, Karla Jay and Allen Young, eds., *Out of the Closets: Voices of Gay Liberation* (New York: Douglas, 1972; second ed., New York: New York University Press, 1992); and Dennis Altman, *Coming Out in the Seventies* (Boston: Alyson, 1981).

8.   Linda Singer, *Erotic Welfare: Sexual Theory and Politics in the Age of Epidemic*, edited and introduction by Judith Butler and Maureen MacGrogan (New York and London: Routledge, 1993). On AIDS politics see Cindy Patton, *Inventing AIDS* (New York: Routledge, 1990); Steven Seidman, *Embattled Eros: Sexual Politics and Ethics in Contemporary America* (New York: Routledge, 1992), ch. 4.

I. Queer Identities

1

Critically Queer

Judith Butler

Discourse is not life; its time is not yours.

Michel Foucault, "Politics and the Study of Discourse"

Eve Sedgwick's recent reflections on queer performativity ask us not only to consider how a certain theory of speech acts applies to queer practices, but how it is that "queering" persists as a defining moment of performativity.[1] The centrality of the marriage ceremony in J.L. Austin's examples of performativity suggests that the heterosexualization of the social bond is the paradigmatic form for those speech acts which bring about what they name. "I pronounce you ..." puts into effect the relation that it names. But where and when does such a performative draw its force, and what happens to the performative when its purpose is precisely to undo the presumptive force of the heterosexual ceremonial?

Performative acts are forms of authoritative speech: most performatives, for instance, are statements which, in the uttering, also perform a certain action and exercise a binding power.[2] Implicated in a network of authorization and punishment, performatives tend to include legal sentences, baptisms, inaugurations, declarations of ownership: statements which not only perform an action, but confer a binding power on the action performed. The power of discourse to produce that which it names is thus essentially linked with the question of performativity. The performative is thus one domain in which power acts *as* discourse.

Importantly, however, there is no power, construed as a subject, that acts, but only a reiterated acting that *is* power in its persistence and instability. This is less an "act," singular and deliberate, than a nexus of power and discourse that repeats or mimes the discursive gestures of power. Hence, the judge who authorizes and installs the situation he names (we shall call him "he," figuring this model of authority as masculinist) invariably *cites* the law that he applies, and it is the power of this citation that gives the performative its binding or conferring power. And though it may appear that the binding power of his words is derived from the force of his will or from a prior authority, the opposite is more true: it is *through* the citation of the law that the figure of the judge's "will" is produced and that the "priority" of textual authority is established.[3] Indeed, it is through the invocation of convention that the speech act of the judge derives its binding power; that binding power is to be found neither in the subject of the judge nor in his will, but in the citational legacy by which a contemporary "act" emerges in the context of a chain of binding conventions.

Where there is an "I" who utters or speaks and thereby produces an effect in discourse, there is first a discourse which precedes and enables that "I" and forms in language the constraining trajectory of its will. Thus there is no "I" who stands *behind* discourse and executes its volition or will *through* discourse. On the contrary, the "I" only comes into being through being called, named, interpellated (to use the Althusserian term), and this discursive constitution takes place prior to the "I"; it is the transitive invocation of the "I." Indeed, I can only say "I" to the extent that I have first been addressed, and that address has mobilized my place in speech; paradoxically, the discursive condition of social recognition *precedes* and *conditions* the formation of the subject: recognition is not conferred on a subject, but forms that subject. Further, the impossibility of a full recognition, that is, of ever fully inhabiting the name by which one's social identity is inaugurated and mobilized, implies the instability and incompleteness of subject-formation. The "I" is thus a citation of the place of the "I" in speech, where that place has a certain priority and anonymity with respect to the life it animates: it is the historically revisable possibility of a name that precedes and exceeds me, but without which I cannot speak.

Queer Trouble

The term "queer" emerges as an interpellation which raises the question of the status of force and opposition, of stability and variability, *within* performativity. The term "queer" has operated as one linguistic practice whose purpose has been the shaming of the subject it names or, rather, the producing of a subject *through* that shaming interpellation. "Queer" derives its force precisely through the repeated invocation by which it has become linked to accusation, pathologization, insult. This is an invocation by which a social bond among homophobic communities is formed through time. The interpellation echoes past interpellations, and binds the speakers, as if they spoke in unison across time. In this sense, it is always an imaginary chorus which taunts "queer!" To what extent, then, has the performative "queer" operated alongside, as a deformation of, the "I pronounce you . . ." of the marriage ceremony? If the performative operates as the sanction that performs the heterosexualization of the social bond, perhaps it also comes into play precisely as the shaming taboo which "queers" those who resist or oppose that social form as well as those who occupy it without hegemonic social sanction.

On that note, let us remember that reiterations are never simply replicas of the same. And the "act" by which a name authorizes or deauthorizes a set of social or sexual relations is, of necessity, *a repetition*. Let me, for the moment, cite Derrida:

> Could a performative utterance succeed if its formulation did not repeat a "coded" or iterable utterance, or in other words, if the formula I pronounce in order to open a meeting, launch a ship or a marriage were not identifiable as *conforming* with an iterable model, if it were not then identifiable in some way as a "citation"?. . . In such a typology, the category of intention will not disappear; it will have its place, but from that place it will no longer be able to govern the entire scene and system of utterance. (18)

If a performative provisionally succeeds (and I will suggest that "success" is always and only provisional), then it is not because an intention successfully governs the action of speech, but only because that action echoes a prior action, and accumulates the force of authority through the repetition or citation of a prior, authoritative set of practices. What this means, then, is that a performative "works" to the extent that it draws on and covers over the constitutive conventions by which it is mobilized. In this sense, no term or statement can function performatively without the accumulating and dissimulating historicity of force.

This view of performativity implies that discourse has a history[4] which not only precedes but conditions its contemporary usages, and that this history effectively decenters the presentist view of the subject as the exclusive origin or owner of what is said.[5] What it also means is that the terms to which we do, nevertheless, lay claim, the terms through which we insist on politicizing identity and desire, often demand a turn *against* this constitutive historicity. Those of us who have questioned the presentist assumptions in contemporary identity categories are, therefore, sometimes charged with depoliticizing theory. And yet, if the genealogical critique of the subject is the interrogation of those constitutive and exclusionary relations of power through which contemporary discursive resources are formed, then it follows that the critique of the queer subject is crucial to the continuing democratization of queer politics. As much as identity terms must be used, as much as "outness" is to be affirmed, these same notions must become subject to a critique of the exclusionary operations of their own production: for whom is outness an historically available and affordable option? Is there an unmarked class character to the demand for universal "outness"? Who is represented by which use of the term, and who is excluded? For whom does the term present an impossible conflict between racial, ethnic, or religious affiliation and sexual politics? What kinds of policies are enabled by what kinds of usages, and which are backgrounded or erased from view? In this sense, the genealogical critique of the queer subject will be central to queer politics to the extent that it constitutes a self-critical dimension within activism, a persistent reminder to take the time to consider the exclusionary force of one of activism's most treasured contemporary premises.

As much as it is necessary to assert political demands through recourse to identity categories, and to lay claim to the power to name oneself and determine the conditions under which that name is used, it is also impossible to sustain that kind of mastery over the trajectory of those categories within discourse. This is not an argument *against* using identity categories, but it is a reminder of the risk that attends every such use. The expectation of self-determination that self-naming arouses is paradoxically contested by the historicity of the name itself: by the history of the usages which one never controlled, but that constrain the very usage that now emblematizes autonomy; by the future efforts to deploy the term against the grain of the current ones, efforts that will exceed the control of those who seek to set the course of the terms in the present.

If the term "queer" is to be a site of collective contestation, the point of departure for a set of historical reflections and futural imaginings, it will have to remain that which is, in the present, never fully owned, but always and only redeployed, twisted, queered from a prior usage and in the direction of urgent and expanding political purposes, and perhaps also yielded in favor of terms that do that political work more effectively. Such a yielding may well become necessary in order to accommodate—without domesticating— democratizing contestations that have and will redraw the contours of the movement in ways that can never be fully anticipated in advance.

It may be that the conceit of autonomy implied by self-naming is the paradigmatically presentist conceit, that is, the belief that there is a one who arrives in the world, in discourse, without a history, that this one makes oneself in and through the magic of the name, that language expresses a "will" or a "choice" rather than a complex and constitutive history of discourse and power which compose the invariably ambivalent resources through which a queer and queering agency is forged and reworked. To recast queer agency in this chain of historicity is thus to avow a set of constraints on the past and the future which mark at once the *limits* of agency and its most *enabling conditions.*

As expansive as the term "queer" is meant to be, it is used in ways that enforce a set of overlapping divisions: in some contexts, the term appeals to a younger generation who want to resist the more institutionalized and reformist politics sometimes signified by "lesbian" and "gay"; in some contexts, sometimes the same, it has marked a predominantly white movement which has not fully addressed the way in which "queer" plays—or fails to play—within nonwhite communities; and whereas in some instances it has mobilized a lesbian activism (Smyth), in others the term represents a false unity of women and men. Indeed, it may be that the critique of the term will initiate a resurgence of both feminist and antiracist mobilization within lesbian and gay politics, or open up new possibilities for coalitional alliances that do not presume that these constituencies are radically distinct from one another. The term ought to be revised, dispelled, rendered obsolete to the extent that it yields to the demands which resist the term precisely because of the exclusions by which it is mobilized.

We no more create out of nothing the political terms which come to represent our "freedom" than we are responsible for the terms that carry the pain of social injury. And yet, neither of those terms are as a result any less necessary to work and rework within political discourse.

In this sense, it remains politically necessary to lay claim to "women," "queer," "gay," and "lesbian," precisely because of the way these terms, as it were, lay their claim on us prior to our full knowing. Laying claim to such terms in reverse will be necessary to refute homophobic deployments of the terms in law, public policy, on the street, in "private" life. But the necessity to mobilize the "necessary error of identity" (Spivak's term) will always be in tension with the democratic contestation of the term which works against its deployments in racist and misogynist discursive regimes. If "queer" politics postures independently of these other modalities of power, it will lose its democratizing force. The political deconstruction of "queer" ought not to paralyze the use of such terms, but, ideally, to extend its range, to make us consider at what expense and for what purposes the terms are used, and through what relations of power such categories have been wrought.

Some recent race theory has underscored the use of "race" in the service of "racism," and proposed a politically informed inquiry into the process of *racialization*, the formation of race (Omi and Winant; Appiah; Guillaumin; Lloyd). Such an inquiry does not suspend or ban the term, although it does insist that an inquiry into formation is linked to the contemporary question of what is at stake in the term. The point may be taken for queer studies as well, such that "queering" might signal an inquiry into (a) the *formation* of homosexualities (an historical inquiry which cannot take the stability of the term for granted, despite the political pressure to do so) and (b) the *deformative* and *misappropriative* power that the term currently enjoys. At stake in such a history will be the differential formation of homosexuality across racial boundaries, including the question of how racial and reproductive injunctions are articulated through one another.

If identity is a necessary error, then the assertion of "queer" will be incontrovertibly necessary, but that assertion will constitute only one part of "politics." It is equally necessary, and perhaps also equally impossible, to affirm the contingency of the term: to let it be vanquished by those who are excluded by the term but who justifiably expect representation by it, to let it take on meanings that cannot now be anticipated by a younger generation whose political vocabulary may well carry a very different set of investments. Indeed, the term "queer" itself has been precisely the discursive rallying point for younger lesbians and gay men and, in yet other contexts, for lesbian interventions and, in yet other contexts, for bisexuals and straights for whom the term expresses an affiliation with antihomophobic politics. That it can become such a discursive site whose uses are not fully constrained in advance ought to be safeguarded not only for the purposes of continuing to democratize queer politics, but also to expose, affirm, and work the specific historicity of the term.

Gender Performativity and Drag

How, if at all, is the notion of discursive resignification linked to the notion of gender parody or impersonation? If gender is a mimetic effect, is it therefore a choice or a dispensable artifice? If not, how did this reading of *Gender Trouble* emerge? There are at least two reasons for the misapprehension, one which I myself produced by citing drag as an example of performativity (taken then, by some, to be *exemplary*, that is, *the* example of performativity), and another which has to do with the political needs of a growing queer movement in which the publicization of theatrical agency has become quite central.[6]

The misapprehension about gender performativity is this: that gender is a choice, or that gender is a role, or that gender is a construction that one puts on, as one puts on clothes in the morning; that there is a "one" who is prior to this gender, a one who goes to the wardrobe of gender and decides with deliberation which gender it will be today. This is a voluntarist account of gender which presumes a subject, intact, prior to its gendering. The sense of gender performativity that I meant to convey is something quite different.

Gender is performative insofar as it is the *effect* of a regulatory regime of gender differences in which genders are divided and hierarchized *under constraint*. Social constraints, taboos, prohibitions, and threats of punishment operate in the ritualized repetition of norms, and this repetition constitutes the temporalized scene of gender construction and destabilization. There is no subject who precedes or enacts this repetition of norms. To the extent that this repetition creates an effect of gender uniformity, a stable effect of masculinity or femininity, it produces and destabilizes the notion of the subject as well, for the subject only comes into intelligibility through the matrix of gender. Indeed, one might construe repetition as precisely that which *undermines* the conceit of voluntarist mastery designated by the subject in language.[7]

There is no subject who is "free" to stand outside these norms or to negotiate them at a distance; on the contrary, the subject is retroactively produced by these norms in their repetition, precisely as their effect. What we might call "agency" or "freedom" or "possibility" is always a specific political prerogative that is produced by the gaps opened up in regulatory norms, in the interpellating work of such norms, in the process of their self-repetition. Freedom, possibility, agency do not have an abstract or presocial status, but are always negotiated within a matrix of power.

Gender performativity is not a matter of choosing which gender one will be today. Performativity is a matter of reiterating or repeating the norms by which one is constituted: it is not a radical fabrication of a gendered self. It is a compulsory repetition of prior and subjectivating norms, ones which cannot be thrown off at will, but which work, animate, constrain the gendered subject, and which are also the resources from which resistance, subversion, displacement are to be forged. The practice by which gendering occurs, the embodying of norms, is a compulsory practice, a forcible production, but not for that reason fully determining. To the extent that gender is an assignment, it is an assignment which is never quite carried out according to expectation, whose addressee never quite inhabits the ideal s/he is compelled to approximate.

This failure to approximate the norm, however, is not the same as the subversion of the norm. There is no promise that subversion will follow from the reiteration of constitutive norms; there is no guarantee that exposing the naturalized status of heterosexuality will lead to its subversion. Heterosexuality can augment its hegemony through its denaturalization, as when we see denaturalizing parodies which reidealize heterosexual norms without calling them into question. But sometimes the very term that would annihilate us becomes the site of resistance, the possibility of an enabling social and political signification: I think we have seen that quite clearly in the astounding transvaluation undergone by "queer." This is for me the enactment of a prohibition and a degradation against itself, the spawning of a different order of values, of a political affirmation from and through the very term which in a prior usage had as it final aim the eradication of precisely such an affirmation.

It may seem, however, that there is a difference between the embodying or performing of gender norms and the performative use of language. Are these two different senses of "performativity," or do they converge as modes of citationality in which the compulsory character of certain social imperatives becomes subject to a more promising deregulation? Gender norms operate by requiring the embodiment of certain ideals of femininity and masculinity, ones which are almost always related to the idealization of the heterosexual bond. In this sense, the initiatory performative, "It's a girl!" anticipates the eventual arrival of the sanction, "I pronounce you man and wife." Hence, also the peculiar pleasure of the cartoon strip in which the infant is first interpellated into discourse with "It's a lesbian!" Far from an essentialist joke, the queer appropriation of the performative mimes and exposes both the binding power of the heterosexualizing law *and its expropriability*.

To the extent that the naming of the "girl" is transitive, that is, initiates the process by which a certain "girling" is compelled, the term or, rather, its symbolic power, governs the formation of a corporeally enacted femininity that never fully approximates the norm. This is a "girl," however, who is compelled to "cite" the norm in order to qualify and remain a viable subject. Femininity is thus not the product of a choice, but the forcible citation of a norm, one whose complex historicity is indissociable from relations of discipline, regulation, and punishment. Indeed, there is no "one" who takes on a gender norm. On the contrary, this citation of the gender norm is necessary in order to qualify as a "one," to become viable as a "one," where subject-formation is dependent on the prior operation of legitimating gender norms.

It is in terms of a norm that compels a certain "citation" in order for a viable subject to be produced that the notion of gender performativity calls to be rethought. And it is precisely in relation to such a compulsory citationality that the theatricality of gender is also to be explained. Theatricality need not be conflated with self-display or self-creation. Within queer politics, indeed, within the very signification that is "queer," we read a resignifying practice in which the desanctioning power of the name "queer" is reversed to sanction a contestation of the terms of sexual legitimacy. Paradoxically, but also with great promise, the subject who is "queered" into public discourse through homophobic interpellations of various kinds *takes up* or *cites* that very term as the discursive basis for an opposition. This kind of citation will emerge as *theatrical* to the extent that it *mimes and renders hyperbolic* the discursive convention that it also *reverses*. The hyperbolic gesture is crucial to the exposure of the homophobic "law" which can no longer control the terms of its own abjecting strategies.

To oppose the theatrical to the political within contemporary queer politics is, I would argue, an impossibility: the hyperbolic "performance" of death in the practice of "die-ins" and the theatrical "outness" by which queer activism has disrupted the closeting distinction between public and private space, have proliferated sites of politicization and AIDS awareness throughout the public realm. Indeed, an important set of histories might be told in which the increasing politicization *of* theatricality for queers is at stake (more productive, I think, than an insistence on the two as polar opposites within queerness). Such a history might include traditions of cross-dressing, drag balls, street walking, butch-femme spectacles, the sliding between the "march" (NYC) and the parade (SF); die-ins by ACT UP, kiss-ins by Queer Nation; drag performance benefits for AIDS (by which I would include both Lypsinka's and Liza Minelli's in which she, finally, does Judy);[8] the convergence of theatrical work with theatrical activism;[9] performing excessive lesbian sexuality and iconography which effectively counter the desexualization of the lesbian; and tactical interruptions of public forums by lesbian and gay activists in favor of drawing public attention and outrage to the failure of government funding of AIDS research and outreach.

The increasing theatricalization of political rage in response to the killing inattention of public policy-makers on the issue of AIDS is allegorized in the recontextualization of "queer" from its place within a homophobic strategy of abjection and annihilation to an insistent and public severing of that interpellation from the effect of shame. To the extent that shame is produced not only as the stigma of AIDS, but also of queerness, where the latter is understood through homophobic causalities as the "cause" and "manifestation" of the illness, theatrical rage is part of the public resistance to that interpellation of shame. Mobilized by the injuries of homophobia, theatrical rage reiterates those injuries precisely through an "acting out," one which does not merely repeat or recite those injuries, but which deploys a hyperbolic display of death and injury to overwhelm the epistemic resistance to AIDS and to the graphics of suffering, or a hyperbolic display of kissing to shatter the epistemic blindness to an increasingly graphic and public homosexuality.

Melancholia and the Limits of Performance

Although there were probably no more that five paragraphs in *Gender Trouble* devoted to drag, readers have often cited the description of drag as if it were the "example" which explains the meaning of performativity. The conclusion is drawn that gender performativity is a matter of constituting who one is on the basis of what one performs. And further, that gender itself might be proliferated beyond the binary frame of "man" and "woman" depending on what one performs, thereby valorizing drag not only as the paradigm of gender performance, but as the means by which heterosexual presumption might be undermined through the strategy of proliferation.

The point about "drag" was, however, much more centrally concerned with a critique of the truth-regime of "sex," one which I took to be pervasively heterosexist: the distinction between the "inside" truth of femininity, considered as psychic disposition or ego-core, and the "outside" truth, considered as appearance or presentation, produces a contradictory formation of gender in which no fixed "truth" can be established. Gender is neither a purely psychic truth, conceived as "internal" and "hidden," nor is it reducible to a surface appearance; on the contrary, its undecidability is to be traced as the play *between* psyche and appearance (where the latter domain includes what appears *in words*). Further, this will be a "play" regulated by heterosexist constraints though not, for that reason, fully reducible to them.

In no sense can it be concluded that the part of gender that is performed is therefore the "truth" of gender; performance as bounded "act" is distinguished from performativity insofar as the latter consists in a reiteration of norms which precede, constrain, and exceed the performer and in that sense cannot be taken as the fabrication of the performer's "will" or "choice"; further, what is "performed" works to conceal, if not to disavow, what remains opaque, unconscious, unperformable. The reduction of performativity to performance is, therefore, a mistake.

In *Gender Trouble*, I rejected the expressive model of drag which holds that some interior truth is exteriorized in performance, but what I failed to do is to refer the theatricality of drag back to the psychoanalytic discussions that preceded it, for psychoanalysis insists that the opacity of the unconscious sets limits to the exteriorization of the psyche. It also argues, rightly I think, that what is exteriorized or performed can only be understood through reference to what is barred from the signifier and from the domain of corporeal legibility.

It would have been useful as well to bring forward the discussion of gender melancholia into the discussion of drag, given the iconographic figure of the melancholic drag queen. Here one might ask also after the disavowal which occasions performance and which performance might be said to enact, where performance engages "acting out" in the psychoanalytic sense.[10] If melancholia in Freud's sense is the effect of an ungrieved loss (a sustaining of the lost object/Other as a psychic figure with the consequence of heightened identification with that Other, self-beratement, and the acting out of unresolved anger and love),[11] it may be that performance, understood as "acting out," is essentially related to the problem of unacknowledged loss.

Where there is an ungrieved loss in drag performance (and I am sure that such a generalization cannot be universalized), perhaps it is a loss that is refused and incorporated in the performed identification, one which reiterates a gendered idealization and its radical uninhabitability. This is, then, neither a territorialization of the feminine by the masculine nor an "envy" of the masculine by the feminine, nor a sign of the essential plasticity of gender. What it does suggest is that the performance allegorizes a loss it cannot grieve, allegorizes the incorporative fantasy of melancholia whereby an object is phantasmatically taken in or on as a way of refusing to let it go.

The analysis above is a risky one because it suggests that for a "man" performing femininity, or for a "woman" performing masculinity (the latter is always, in effect, to perform a little less, given that femininity is often cast as the spectacular gender), there is an attachment to, and a loss and refusal of, the figure of femininity by the man, or the figure of masculinity by the woman. Thus it is important to underscore that drag is an effort to negotiate cross-gendered identification, but that cross-gendered identification is not the paradigm for thinking about homosexuality, although it may be one. In this sense, drag allegorizes some set of melancholic incorporative fantasies that stabilize *gender*. Not only are a vast number of drag performers straight, but it would be a mistake to think that homosexuality is best explained through the performativity that is drag. What does seem useful in this analysis, however, is that drag exposes or allegorizes the mundane psychic and performative practices by which heterosexualized genders form themselves through the renunciation of the *possibility* of homosexuality, a foreclosure which produces a field of heterosexual objects at the same time that it produces a domain of those whom it would be impossible to love. Drag thus allegorizes *heterosexual melancholy*, the melancholy by which a masculine gender is formed from the refusal to grieve the masculine as a possibility of love; a feminine gender is formed (taken on, assumed) through the incorporative fantasy by which the feminine is excluded as a possible object of love, an exclusion never grieved, but "preserved" through the heightening of feminine identification itself. In this sense, the "truest" lesbian melancholic is the strictly straight woman, and the "truest" gay male melancholic is the strictly straight man.

What drag exposes, however, is the "normal" constitution of gender presentation in which the gender performed is in many ways constituted by a set of disavowed attachments, identifications which constitute a different domain of the "unperformable." Indeed, it may well be that what constitutes the *sexually* unperformable is performed instead as *gender identification*.[12] To the extent that homosexual attachments remain unacknowledged within normative heterosexuality, they are not merely constituted as desires which emerge and subsequently become prohibited. Rather, these are desires which are proscribed from the start. And when they do emerge on the far side of the censor, they may well carry that mark of impossibility with them, performing, as it were, as the impossible within the possible. As such, they will not be attachments that can be openly grieved. This is, then, less *the refusal* to grieve (a formulation that accents the choice involved) than a preemption of grief performed by the absence of cultural conventions for avowing the loss of homosexual love. And it is this absence which produces a culture of heterosexual melancholy, one which can be read in the hyperbolic identifications by which mundane heterosexual masculinity and femininity confirm themselves. The straight man *becomes* (mimes, cites, appropriates, assumes the status of) the man he "never" loved and "never" grieved; the straight woman *becomes* the woman she "never" loved and "never" grieved. It is in this sense, then, that what is most apparently performed as gender is the sign and symptom of a pervasive disavowal.

Moreover, it is precisely to counter this pervasive cultural risk of gay melancholia (what the newspapers generalize as "depression") that there has been an insistent publicization and politicization of grief over those who have died from AIDS; the NAMES Project Quilt is exemplary, ritualizing and repeating the name itself as a way of publicly avowing the limitless loss.[13]

Insofar as the grief remains unspeakable, the rage over the loss can redouble by virtue of remaining unavowed. And if that very rage over loss is publicly proscribed, the melancholic effects of such a proscription can achieve suicidal proportions. The emergence of collective institutions for grieving are thus crucial to survival, to the reassembling of community, the reworking of kinship, the reweaving of sustaining relations. And insofar as they involve the publicization and dramatization of death, they call to be read as life-affirming rejoinders to the dire psychic consequences of a grieving process culturally thwarted and proscribed.

Performativity, Gender, Sexuality

How then does one link the trope by which discourse is described as "performing" and that theatrical sense of performance in which the hyperbolic status of gender norms seems central? What is "performed" in drag is, of course, *the sign* of gender, a sign which is not the same as the body which it figures, but which cannot be read without it. The sign, understood as a gender imperative, i.e., "girl!" reads less as an assignment than as a command and, as such, produces its own insubordinations; the hyperbolic conformity to the command can reveal the hyperbolic status of the norm itself, indeed, can become the cultural sign by which that cultural imperative might become legible. Insofar as heterosexual gender norms produce inapproximable ideals, heterosexuality can be said to operate through the regulated production of hyperbolic versions of "man" and "woman." These are for the most part compulsory performances, ones which none of us choose, but which each of us is forced to negotiate. I write "forced to negotiate" because the compulsory character of these norms does not always make them efficacious. Such norms are continually haunted by their own inefficacy; hence, the anxiously repeated effort to install and augment their jurisdiction.

The resignification of norms is thus a function of their *inefficacy*, and so the question of subversion, of *working the weakness in the norm*, becomes a matter of inhabiting the practices of its rearticulation.[14] The critical promise of drag does not have to do with the proliferation of genders, as if a sheer increase in numbers would do the job, but rather with the exposure or the failure of heterosexual regimes ever fully to legislate or contain their own ideals. Hence, it is not that drag *opposes* heterosexuality, or that the proliferation of drag will bring down heterosexuality; on the contrary, drag tends to be the allegorization of heterosexuality and its constitutive melancholia. As an allegory that works through the hyperbolic, drag brings into relief what is, after all, determined only in relation to the hyperbolic: the understated, taken-for-granted quality of heterosexual performativity. At its best, then, drag can be read for the way in which hyperbolic norms are dissimulated as the heterosexual mundane. At the same time these same norms, taken not as commands to be obeyed, but as imperatives to be "cited," twisted, queered, brought into relief as heterosexual imperatives, are not, for that reason, necessarily subverted in the process.

It is important to emphasize that although heterosexuality operates in part through the stabilization of gender norms, gender designates a dense site of significations that contain and exceed the heterosexual matrix. Whereas it is important to emphasize that forms of sexuality do not unilaterally determine gender, a noncausal and nonreductive connection between sexuality and gender is nevertheless crucial to maintain. Precisely because homophobia often operates through the attribution of a damaged, failed, or otherwise abjected gender to homosexuals, that is, calling gay men "feminine," or calling lesbians "masculine," and because the homophobic terror over performing homosexual acts, where it exists, is often also a terror over losing proper gender ("no longer being a real or proper man" or "no longer being a real and proper woman"), it seems crucial to retain a theoretical apparatus that will account for how sexuality is regulated through the policing and the shaming of gender.

We might want to claim that certain kinds of sexual practices link people more strongly than gender affiliation (Sedgwick, 1989), but such claims can only be negotiated, if they can, in relation to specific occasions for affiliation; there is nothing in either sexual practice or in gender to privilege one over the other. Sexual practices, however, will invariably be experienced differentially depending on the relations of gender in which they occur. And there may be forms of "gender" within homosexuality that call for a theorization which moves beyond the categories of "masculine" and "feminine." If we seek to privilege sexual practice as a way of transcending gender, we might ask at what cost the *analytic* separability of the two domains is taken to be a distinction in fact. Is there perhaps a specific gender pain that provokes such fantasies of a sexual practice that would transcend gender difference altogether, in which the marks of masculinity and femininity are no longer legible? Would this not be a sexual practice paradigmatically fetishistic, trying not to know what it knows, but knowing it all the same? This question is not meant to demean the fetish (where would we be without it?), but it does mean to ask whether it is only according to a logic of the fetish that the radical separability of sexuality and gender can be thought.

In theories such as Catharine MacKinnon's, sexual relations of subordination are understood to establish differential gender categories, such that "men" are those defined in a sexually dominating social position, and "women" are those defined in subordination. Her highly deterministic account leaves no room for relations of sexuality to be theorized apart from the rigid framework of gender difference, for kinds of sexual regulation which did not take gender as their primary objects (i.e., the prohibition of sodomy, public sex, consensual homosexuality). Hence, Gayle Rubin's influential distinction between sexuality and gender in "Thinking Sex" and Sedgwick's reformulation of that position have constituted important theoretical opposition to MacKinnon's deterministic form of structuralism.

My sense is that now this very opposition needs to be rethought in order to redraw the lines between queer theory and feminism.[15] For surely it is as unacceptable to insist that relations of sexual subordination determine gender position as it is to separate radically forms of sexuality from the workings of gender norms. The relation between sexual practice and gender is surely not a structurally determined one, but the destabilizing of the heterosexual presumption of that very structuralism still requires a way to think of the two in a dynamic relation to one another.

In psychoanalytic terms, the relation between gender and sexuality is in part negotiated through the question of the relationship between identification and desire. And here it becomes clear why drawing lines of causal implication between these two domains is as important as keeping open an investigation of their complex interimplication. For if to identify as a woman is not necessarily to desire a man, and if to desire a woman does not necessarily signal the constituting presence of a masculine identification, whatever that is, then the heterosexual matrix proves to be an *imaginary* logic which insistently issues forth its own unmanageability. The heterosexual logic which entails that identification and desire are mutually exclusive is one of the most reductive of heterosexism's psychological instruments: if one identifies *as* a given gender, one must desire a different gender. On the one hand, there is no one femininity with which to identify, which is to say that femininity might itself offer an array of identificatory sites, as the proliferation of lesbian femme possibilities attests. On the other hand, it is hardly descriptive of the complex dynamic exchanges of lesbian and gay relationships to presume that homosexual identifications "mirror" or replicate one another. The vocabulary for describing the difficult play, crossing, and destabilization of masculine and feminine identifications within homosexuality has only begun to emerge within theoretical language: the nonacademic language historically embedded in gay communities is here much more instructive. The thought of sexual difference *within* homosexuality has yet to be theorized in its complexity.

Performativity, then, is to be read not as self-expression or self-presentation, but as the unanticipated resignifiability of highly invested terms. The film *Paris is Burning* has been interesting to read less for the ways in which the drag performances deploy denaturalizing strategies to reidealize whiteness (hooks) and heterosexual gender norms than for the less stabilizing rearticulations of kinship that the film offers. The drag balls themselves at times produce high femininity as a function of whiteness and deflect homosexuality through a transgendering that *reidealizes* certain bourgeois forms of heterosexual exchange. And yet, if those performances are not immediately or obviously subversive, it may be that it is rather in the *reformulation of kinship*, in particular, the redefining of the "house" and its forms of collectivity, mothering, mopping, reading, becoming legendary, that the appropriation and redeployment of the categories of dominant culture enable the formation of kinship relations that function quite supportively as oppositional discourse within that culture. These men "mother" one another, "house" one another, "rear" one another, and the resignification of the family through these terms is not a vain or useless imitation, but the social and discursive building of community, a community that binds, cares, teaches, shelters, and enables. This is doubtless a task that any of us who are queer need to see and to know and to learn from, a task that makes none of us who are outside of heterosexual "family" into absolute outsiders to this film. Significantly, it is here in the elaboration of kinship forged through a resignification of the very terms which effect our exclusion and abjection, a resignification that creates the discursive and social space for community, that we see an appropriation of the terms of domination that turns them toward a more enabling future.

How would one ever determine whether subversion has taken place? What measure would one invoke to gauge the extent of subversion? From what standpoint would one know? It is not simply a matter of situating performances in contexts (as if the demarcation of context is not already a prefiguring of the result), of gauging audience response, nor of establishing the epistemological ground from which one is entitled to "know" such effects. Rather, subversiveness is the kind of effect that *resists calculation*. If one thinks of the effects of discursive productions, they do not conclude at the terminus of a given statement or utterance, the passing of legislation, the announcement of a birth. The reach of their signifiability cannot be controlled by the one who utters or writes, since such productions are not owned by the one who utters them. They continue to signify in spite of their authors, and sometimes against their authors' most precious intentions.

It is one of the ambivalent implications of the decentering of the subject to have one's writing be the site of a necessary and inevitable expropriation. But this yielding of ownership over what one writes has an important set of political corollaries, for the taking up, reforming, deforming of one's words does open up a difficult future terrain of community, one in which the hope of ever fully recognizing oneself in the terms by which one signifies is sure to be disappointed. This not owning of one's words is there from the start, however, since speaking is always in some ways the speaking of a stranger through and as oneself, the melancholic appropriation of a language which one never chose, which one does not find as an instrument to be used, but which one is, as it were, used by, expropriated in, as a continuing condition of the "one," the ambivalent condition of the power that binds.

Notes

1. The following is indebted to Eve Sedgwick's "Queer Performativity," published in the first issue of *GLQ*. I thank her for the excellent essay and for the provocations, lodged in her text and perhaps most poignantly in earlier drafts, which have inspired this essay in important ways. A different version of this essay is published in Judith Butler, *Bodies that Matter* (New York: Routledge, 1993).

2. It is, of course, never quite right to say that language or discourse "performs," since it is unclear that language is primarily constituted as a set of "acts." After all, this description of an "act" cannot be sustained through the trope that established the act as a singular event, for the act will turn out to refer to prior acts and to a reiteration of "acts" that is perhaps more suitably described as a citational chain. Paul de Man points out in "Rhetoric of Persuasion" that the distinction between constative and performative utterances is confounded by the fictional status of both: ". . . the possibility for language to perform is just as fictional as the possibility for language to assert"(129). Further, he writes, "considered as persuasion, rhetoric is performative, but considered as a system of tropes, it deconstructs its own performance"(130–31).

3. In what follows, that set of performatives that Austin terms illocutionary will be at issue, those in which the binding power of the act appears to be derived from the intention or will of the speaker. In "Signature, Event, Context," Derrida argues that the binding power that Austin attributes to the speaker's intention in such illocutionary acts is more properly attributable to a citational force of the speaking, the iterability that establishes the authority of the speech act, but which establishes the nonsingular character of that act. In this sense, every "act" is an echo or citational chain, and it is its citationality that constitutes its performative force.

4. The historicity of discourse implies the way in which history is constitutive of discourse itself. It is not simply that discourses are located *in* histories, but that they have their own constitutive historical character. Historicity is a term which directly implies the constitutive character of history in discursive practice, that is, a condition in which a "practice" could not exist apart from the sedimentation of conventions by which it is produced and becomes legible.

5. My understanding of the charge of presentism is that an inquiry is presentist to the extent that it (a) universalizes a set of claims regardless of historical and cultural challenges to that universalization or (b) takes an historically specific set of terms and universalizes them falsely. It may be that both gestures in a given instance are the same. It would, however, be a mistake to claim that all conceptual language or philosophical language is "presentist," a claim which would be tantamount to prescribing that all philosophy become history. My understanding of Foucault's notion of genealogy is that it is a specifically philosophical exercise in exposing and tracing the installation and operation of false universals. My thanks to Mary Poovey and Joan W. Scott for explaining this concept to me.

6. Theatricality is not for that reason fully intentional, but I might have made that reading possible through my reference to gender as "inten-

tional and nonreferential" in "Performative Acts and Gender Constitution." I use the term "intentional" in a specifically phenomenological sense. "Intentionality" within phenomenology does not mean voluntary or deliberate, but is, rather, a way of characterizing consciousness (or language) as *having an object*, more specifically, as directed toward an object which may or may not exist. In this sense, an act of consciousness may intend (posit, constitute, apprehend) an *imaginary* object. Gender, in its ideality, might be construed as an intentional object, an ideal which is constituted but which does not exist. In this sense, gender would be like "the feminine" as it is discussed as an impossibility by Cornell in *Beyond Accommodation*.

7. In this sense, one might usefully construe the performative repetition of norms as the cultural workings of repetition-compulsion in Freud's sense. This would be a repetition not in the service of mastering pleasure, but as that which undermines the project of mastery altogether. It was in this sense that Lacan argued in *Four Fundamental Principles of Psychoanalysis* that repetition marks the failure of subjectivation: what repeats in the subject is precisely that which is not yet mastered or never masterable.

8. See Román.

9. See Kramer; Crimp and Rolston; and Sadownick. My thanks to David Román for directing me to this last essay.

10. I thank Laura Mulvey for asking me to consider the relation between performativity and disavowal, and Wendy Brown for encouraging me to think about the relation between melancholia and drag and for asking whether the denaturalization of gender norms is the same as their subversion. I also thank Mandy Merck for numerous enlightening questions that led to these speculations, including the suggestion that if disavowal conditions performativity, then perhaps gender itself might be understood on the model of the fetish.

11. See "Freud and the Melancholia of Gender" in *Gender Trouble*.

12. This is not to suggest that an exclusionary matrix rigorously distinguishes between how one identifies and how one desires; it is quite possible to have overlapping identification and desire in heterosexual or homosexual exchange, or in a bisexual history of sexual practice. Further, "masculinity" and "femininity" do not exhaust the terms for either eroticized identification or desire.

13. See Crimp.

14. This may be a place in which to think about performativity in the sense outlined here in relation to the notion of performativity offered by Ernesto Laclau in *New Reflections on the Revolution of Our Time*. This convergence has been usefully explored by Anna Marie Smith.

15. Toward the end of the short theoretical conclusion of "Thinking Sex," Rubin returns to feminism in a gestural way, suggesting that "in the long run, feminism's critique of gender hierarchy must be incorporated into a radical theory of sex, and the critique of sexual oppression should enrich feminism. But an autonomous theory and politics specific to sexuality must be developed"(309).

Bibliography

Appiah, Anthony. "The Uncompleted Argument: Du Bois and the Illusion of Race." In *"Race," Writing and Difference,* edited by Henry Louis Gates, Jr., 21–37. Chicago: University of Chicago Press, 1986.

Butler, Judith. *Gender Trouble: Feminism and the Subversion of Identity.* New York: Routledge, 1990.

———. "Performative Acts and Gender Constitution." In *Performing Feminisms,* edited by Sue Ellen Case, 270–82. Baltimore, MD: Johns Hopkins University Press, 1991.

Cornell, Drucilla. *Beyond Accommodation: Ethical Feminism, Deconstruction, and the Law.* New York: Routledge, 1992.

Crimp, Douglas. "Mourning and Militancy." *October* 51 (Winter 1989): 97–107.

Crimp, Douglas, and Adam Rolston, eds. *AIDS Demo Graphics.* Seattle: Bay Press, 1990.

De Man, Paul. "Rhetoric of Persuasion." In *Allegories of Reading,* 119–31. New Haven: Yale University Press, 1987.

Derrida, Jacques. "Signature, Event, Context." In *Limited Inc.,* edited by Gerald Graff. Translated by Samuel Weber and Jeffrey Mehlman, 1–24. Evanston, IL: Northwestern University Press, 1988.

Guillaumin, Colette. "Race and Nature: The System of Marks." *Feminist Studies* 8 (1988): 25–44.

hooks, bell. "Is Paris Burning?" *Z* (June 1991): 60–64.

Kramer, Larry. *Reports from the Holocaust: The Making of an AIDS Activist.* New York: St. Martin's, 1989.

Laclau, Ernesto. *New Reflections on the Revolution of Our Time.* London: Verso, 1990.

Lloyd, David. "Race Under Representation." *Oxford Literary Review* 13 (Spring 1991): 62–94.

Omi, Michael, and Howard Winant. *Racial Formation in the United States: From the 1960s to the 1980s.* New York: Routledge and Kegan Paul, 1986.

Román, David. "'It's My Party and I'll Die If I Want To!': Gay Men, AIDS, and the Circulation of Camp in U.S. Theatre." *Theatre Journal* 44 (1992): 305–27.

———. "Performing All Our Lives: AIDS, Performance, Community." In *Critical Theory and Performance*, edited by Janelle Reinelt and Joseph Roach, 208–21. Ann Arbor: University of Michigan Press, 1992.

Rubin, Gayle. "Thinking Sex: Notes for a Radical Theory of the Politics of Sexuality." In *Pleasure and Danger*, edited by Carole S. Vance, 267–319. Boston: Routledge and Kegan Paul, 1984.

Sadownick, Doug. "ACT UP Makes a Spectacle of AIDS." *High Performance* 13.1, no. 49 (1990): 26–31.

Sedgwick, Eve Kosofsky. "Across Gender, Across Sexuality: Willa Cather and Others." *South Atlantic Quarterly* 88 (1989): 53–72.

———. *Epistemology of the Closet*. Berkeley: University of California Press, 1990.

Smyth, Cherry. *Lesbians Talk Queer Notions*. London: Scarlet, 1992.

Spivak, Gayatri Chakravorty. "In a Word: Interview with Ellen Rooney." *differences* 1.2 (Summer 1989): 124–56.

2

True or False:
The Self in Radical Lesbian
Feminist Theory

Cynthia Burack

Retrieving Psychoanalysis

Lesbian feminist social theorists have responded to psychoanalytic theory in a variety of ways, some through rejection or critique, some through selective appropriation or reconceptualization. Three well-known radical lesbian feminist social theorists, Mary Daly, Janice M. Raymond, and Sarah Lucia Hoagland, have rejected the usefulness of psychoanalytic theory for lesbians.[1] Daly, Raymond, and Hoagland construct an account of lesbian selfhood and subjectivity that assumes the internalization of social rules, relations, and prohibitions that are harmful to lesbians. At the same time, their account denies lesbian feminism any kind of psychological discourse. The account of the self that emerges from these radical lesbian feminist works is a "false self" account that is psychologically and politically insubstantial.

The false self account of radical lesbian feminism is inadequate for two reasons. First, the false self account of identity as internalization itself disguises a disclaimed psychological discourse. The mere existence of a disclaimed inquiry into the psychological processes of identity formation calls into question the rejection of psychology within radical lesbian feminist theory. In fact, the similarities between the radical lesbian feminist false self account and the false self concept developed within psychoanalytic theory belies the synoptic radical lesbian feminist dismissal of all psychological discourses and practices. A comparison of D.W. Winnicott's relational psychoanalytic version of a false self account of identity to the radical lesbian feminist version demonstrates this affinity.

31

The second reason that a false self account of identity in lesbian feminism is inadequate is political. The false self account fails to provide a theoretical foundation for some of the political goals and aspirations expressed by many lesbians (and other feminists), and it precludes the expression of others. A relational psychoanalytic reading reveals the lesbian feminist false self account of identity to be one-dimensional, but not merely this. Relational psychoanalysis also provides ways of reconceptualizing identity that recognize the transformative possibilities of common political action for the self and that are more compatible with the ethical and political ideals propounded by lesbian feminist theorists.

There are predictable objections to the way I frame the debate. Many would argue that a psychoanalytic strategy needlessly "psychologizes" social theory (and lesbians) in a way that vindicates the concerns of those very theorists who purged lesbian theory of psychology in the first place. There are certainly other perspectives—from which a critic might mount objections to the self that prevails in some lesbian theory without dragging discourse about lesbian life "back" into the psychological framework from which it has escaped.

Nevertheless, it is possible to recognize psychoanalytic theories as discourses of power, constructed (and constructing) through practices of exclusion and discipline, and not dispense with them. The requisite stance toward such theory should be contingent, skeptical, and perhaps playful. Indeed, a conception of theory-creation itself as adult play is consistent with the work of Donald Winnicott. My argument is not that we *must* use psychoanalytic theory to analyze the identity constructions of lesbian feminist theorists; it is, more conservatively, that a relational psychoanalytic theory can illuminate relational and group issues, many only tangentially connected to sexual orientation, that are of interest to lesbian feminists. Certainly relational psychoanalysis can be used to interrogate the self that radical lesbian feminist theorists characterize as "false."

The False Self in Lesbian Theory

Many radical lesbian feminists, including Daly, Raymond, and Hoagland, characterize psychological and psychoanalytic theories and practices as tools that facilitate the progressive penetration, exposure, and manipulation of the self. As tools, psychoanalytic theories and practices are wielded to attack, bare, transform, and—importantly—construct interior, private, layers of the self. When the use of psychology is successful, it helps both to create and to continually perpetuate false layers of a stratified female/lesbian self in accordance with the patriarchal standards of womanhood. Hence, it is the instrument by which a lesbian is kept from her true self. This reading of psychology and psychoanalysis is consistent with the account of the self that emerges from the work of lesbian theorists such as Daly, Raymond, and

Hoagland: the lesbian self consists of a true "core" surrounded by corrupted layers of internalized patriarchal conditioning, exploitative ideology, and self-hatred—all reinforced by psychology.

Mary Daly begins *Gyn/Ecology* with a statement that reveals the pervasiveness of patriarchy and its repercussions for women's identity:

> this [patriarchal] colonization [does not] exist simply "outside" women's minds, securely fastened into institutions we can physically leave behind. Rather, it is also internalized, festering inside women's heads, even feminist heads.[2]

What emerges from the process of internalization is a self that is split, divided by a fault line between true and false. Throughout the text, Daly distinguishes the "Self" (or "authentic center") from the "imposed/internalized false 'self.'"[3] The true Self is a "deep reality"; it is "genuine," the "real Source." False selves, on the other hand, represent "patriarchally imposed, Self-denying masks."[4]

A similar account of true and false selfhood pervades other radical lesbian feminist works. Janice Raymond echoes Daly in theorizing about the "original woman," the "passionate," "deepest" self. The "original integrity" of a woman can be violated by the later strains of heterosexualism that learning and coercion implant, but it is not substantially altered. This is true for Sarah Hoagland as well, as she quotes Mary Daly in the course of a discussion in support of lesbian separatism. For Hoagland, "paring away the layers of false selves from the Self" requires a psychic separation from internalized heterosexist and male-aggrandizing propaganda.[5]

For those who ground lesbian theory in such a view of identity, the conclusion that the true self is obscured by the false layers around it is really merely a first step. The goal implied by this analysis is obvious: through struggle the layers can be successively removed (or "peeled" away, in a favored metaphor) to reveal the true self below. Thus, for Daly one goal of the feminist is to "burn away the internalized false selves, so that she *is* deeper within her Self and outside the State of Possession."[6] The "conditioning" and "heterosexism" that lesbians have internalized is, according to Hoagland, difficult to "unravel":

> just because something is conditioned doesn't mean it can be changed or that it can be changed quickly or even in a lifetime. We are aware of how long it takes to unravel aspects of our own conditioning. In fact, whatever battle wounds we have will remain with us during our lifetimes, at the very least as scars.[7]

Yet the sustained use of images of "unpeeling" and "unraveling" is itself testimony to the kind of task to which these theorists exhort lesbians. The struggle is to remove the harmful—socialized, victimized—layers of the self in order to discover that which is true. However long held, integrated, comfortable, or even useful, the false self is not really a part of the self. It is formed through compliance to pernicious demands originated outside the self, and therefore is counterfeit.

The false self account has not gone uncriticized by feminists. Philosopher Jean Grimshaw characterizes this self (after Ibsen) as an "onion":

> Ibsen's Peer Gynt compared his quest for identity to the process of peeling layers off an onion; but after shedding all the "false selves," he found that there was nothing inside, no "core."[8]

Grimshaw continues that the "spatial metaphors" in the story of Gynt fit with the accounts of the self that she analyzes with one exception: in the feminist theories she has selected, "there *is* assumed to be a 'core.'" The problems associated with conceptualizing a core or true self will be addressed below, but these are not the only problems with false self accounts.

Jean Grimshaw's critique exposes the fact that false self accounts construct a potentially punitive philosophic model of authenticity. She fears that a standard of authenticity could be used to marginalize those whose personal quest for "unravelling" has stalled before disclosing the true core beneath the false layers of socialized selfhood. Grimshaw's fear of the uses to which a false self account of authenticity might be put is vindicated in work by legal theorist Ruth Colker. Colker writes that she formerly identified herself as lesbian, and suggests that she now identifies as bisexual. What is interesting is Colker's (obviously also recent) contention that women who identify themselves as exclusively "lesbian" cannot be authentic, as they have already eliminated the possibility that intimate relations with men might constitute some aspect of their authenticity.[9]

Colker's argument regarding lesbian authenticity reveals a serious limitation of false self accounts: they are easily deployed to create standards of "true" or authentic ways of being, some of which can even be hostile to lesbian identity. For Colker, such standards of authenticity are not troublesome; she defends them as consistent with feminism. In addition, she provides a particularly lucid defense of the false self account. She writes:

> I believe that we have an authentic self because assuming that we do *not* have an authentic self makes no sense to me. For example, through our feminist work, we try to peel away social influences that limit our authenticity or freedom. If we are successful in our attempts to peel away those influences what would be left? It only makes sense for me to assume that what would be left would be our authentic selves.[10]

Indeed, she does not merely clarify the terms of the false self account; she argues that *only* such a model of the self is consistent with feminist theory and politics.

> We need some measuring rod through which we can construct a critique and be confident that we can more fully develop our human potential or, again, our feminist struggles would make no sense.[11]

Although Jean Grimshaw's discomfort with the spatial metaphors in feminist discussions of authenticity is well founded in a number of respects, one aspect that she does not address is the implication that a "core" self must be perceptibly different from the harmful and painful layers that surround it. If this were not so, how would we recognize the boundary between true and false? Indeed, Colker writes unapologetically of the "good"—"peaceful, loving, compassionate"—selves that lie "within us."[12] Although she acknowledges that women are unlikely to peel away enough of the social layers of conditioning and harmful influences to actually "discover" what lies behind them, she insists that such a core exists, and that its nature is benevolent; "if our authentic self were not a good self then there would be no reason to try to uncover it."[13]

The False Self in Psychoanalytic Theory

A discourse of true and false self is not unknown to mainstream psychoanalytic psychology; neither is the similarity to radical lesbian feminist accounts merely linguistic. Affinities exist between the psychoanalytic and the radical lesbian-theoretical concepts of the false self, but divergences are also present, and it is these differences that expose the facile and defensive radical lesbian feminist "psychology."

The concept of the false self has an interesting history. Most scholars associate it with either the work of American psychiatrist R.D. Laing, who popularized it, or British psychoanalyst D.W. Winnicott.[14] Richard Chessick points out its derivation from Kierkegaard's concept of "shut-up-ness," explicated in *The Concept of Dread,* but this precursor is only tenuously related to the later, and more spiritually agnostic, psychodynamic speculations.[15]

Although lesbian theorists have shown virtually no interest in employing the psychoanalytic object relations tradition of which Winnicott is a representative, other feminist theorists have used it to create an influential body of theory.[16] Among feminist theorists Winnicott himself has been popular for, among other reasons, his willingness to engage issues regarding the impact of external (intimate and social) relations on the self. Political theorists have recognized in Winnicott's analytic thought ways of bridging the theoretical gap between an exclusive focus on individual, internal life (characterized by much psychology and psychoanalytic theory), and social and communal concerns.[17] This interest in the mutually constitutive nature of the self and of various social relations is, in fact, exemplified in his account of the false self.

What does Winnicott understand by the false self? On one end of a tacit continuum of "normal" to ill-health, Winnicott emphasizes that in psychic health every person displays (and experiences) some aspects of falseness that are indispensable tools for living in a world of others. Because particular mores and modes of civility are (more or less) required, this variety of false self is a ubiquitous, indeed, an ordinary, aspect of mental and social development and functioning. There are, however, more disturbing kinds of falseness of the self with which Winnicott is more concerned.

At the opposite end of a continuum of falseness is the false self that results from the severest interruptions of "the process of becoming a person." Most generally, it is the conforming self that comes into existence in disruptive circumstances from which the person cannot escape. More particularly, Winnicott writes of the false self as a function of the child's relations with a mother—Winnicott uncritically assumes the biological mother's responsibility for child care—who intrudes upon and stymies the child's own responses. The consequence of these dynamics is a rigid and defensive set of reactions to external reality that does not challenge or subvert the demands to which one is subjected.

Winnicott's interest in the mother-child dyad is regarded as a refreshing departure from, for example, Freud's virtually exclusive interest in the father-son pair. It is nonetheless true that the preoccupation with the mother fixes the blame for dysfunction on her, and by extension, on women. If this were all that could be said of Winnicott's theory of development, it would not be a useful source for alternative feminist readings of identity formation. In this case, even his relative indifference to the inculcation of gendered characteristics would not suffice to differentiate him from other psychological experts. However, placing the concept of falseness in the context of his theory of transitional space opens up the possibility of a false self account that is not exhausted by descriptions of inadequate early child-rearing by mothers.

For Winnicott, the process of becoming "real" (a true self) is one that begins in earliest childhood, but that continues throughout life. The process requires, at a minimum, nonintrusive and nonretaliative relations with proximate and significant others. But more, it requires the construction and continuation of an "intermediate area of experiencing" that is neither "inner" reality nor objectively "outer," and therefore consensually shared. In this transitional space "illusion" and play thrive, and the emerging self is not rigidly imposed upon to recognize, internalize, and act in accordance with the reality of more powerful others.[18]

> [The transitional space] is an area that is not challenged, because no claim is made on its behalf except that it shall exist as a resting-place for the individual engaged in the perpetual human task of keeping inner and outer reality separate yet interrelated. . . .[19] In playing, and perhaps only in playing, the child or adult is free to be creative.[20]

Making the theory of transitional space relevant for social theory is a matter of recognizing its life-span implications. As Winnicott makes clear, the self must continually create its own subjectivity by testing the "survival" of others' boundaries; self and others must be able to tolerate, and even affirm, productions and assertions of otherness without either retaliation or collapse of those boundaries. This is not, however, a placid and easy pluralism. The self is not one with itself, and psychic complexity added to the disruptions and "normal difficulties of life" remain sufficient even in the best of circumstances to thwart any attempt to situate and define the self once and for all. Moreover, there is no point in development when the necessary features for psychic health can be said to have been consolidated, or a true self completed:

> Integration of a personality does not arrive at a certain time on a certain day. It comes and goes, and even when well attained it can be lost through unfortunate environmental change.[21]

The capacity to tolerate the multiple incongruities presented by different interpretations of reality—within and between selves—is one developmental achievement at which Winnicott aims. That capacity in turn facilitates the ability to forge from diverse visions of reality new forms of art, religion, and intellectual life. Winnicott insists that psychic development requires an overcoming of belief in a strict dichotomy of inner and outer reality; it requires acceptance of a "paradox"—that there exists another kind of reality which is neither exclusively internal nor external. When others fail to tolerate one's own creativeness and play, the inability to maintain transitional space is virtually assured. The consequence is some degree of a reactive and defensive system that problematizes the progress of connection with others and maturation of the self: "the resolution of paradox leads to a defence organization which in the adult one can encounter as true and false self organization."[22]

For Winnicott, as for the radical lesbian theorists, the existence of a false self presumes a true self. Yet the similarity of language is misleading, especially as it imputes to Winnicott a perspective of the self as made up of definitive and concrete layers. Winnicott does write frequently of the "relation" between true and false aspects of the self: the false self "defends" and "protects" the true. But unlike the lesbian account, Winnicott means by true self a set of potentials or possibilities that may or may not be realized—the "human individual's capacity for creative living"—and not a complete and functioning (or "core") self.[23]

The uniqueness to which lesbian theorists allude as "true," "original," or "genuine" depends, for Winnicott, upon the installation and maintenance of facilitating environments. He is particularly interested in the emotional environment of childhood, and the quality of the "mothering" that prevails there. But it is consistent to translate this concern into a broader defense of open-ended and nonauthoritarian social and political spaces. It is, in fact, a central argument of Winnicott's that such spaces can be partially reconstructed in adult experience even if they were missing or inadequate in early life. The self may be able to be healed in some respects, yet the healing does not return the self to a preexistent wholeness. The unique "true" self always remains to be created.

Limitations of the False Self Account

Unfortunately, in protecting lesbian identity from the assaults of psychologists (as well as religious moralizers and bigots of all descriptions), radical lesbian feminists have often constructed a profoundly essentializing and individualizing account of lesbian selfhood. Thus, while many feminists have labored to theorize about the problems and possibilities associated with diverse forms of intimate and social relations, these radical lesbian theorists foreclose even a discussion of developmental issues, including the ways in which aspects of relations come to be internalized as part of the self. The true lesbian self, it seems, is not relational; it is, instead, a classical liberal self—indivisible and rational, a product first of nature and then, ideally, of voluntaristic choice. The lesbian feminist theorists who employ a false self account deliberately construct a self that, but for its having acquired layers of patriarchal conditioning, could be described as having been "born directly into adulthood."[24]

Because lesbians are understood to possess an essential true self, theorizing about the possible significance for social and political life of processes of individual (psychological) development is precluded. Conditioning and ideology are seen as being laid down on an already existing self in sedimentary layers, in a way that fails to represent the active nature of even processes of internalization and defense. We are presented with the image of mind as an archaeological dig whose strata are successively exposed under the tools of the persistent excavator. This solution is understandable as a way of avoiding the interventions of experts and the normalizing effects of psychological theory, especially in interpreting the origins of lesbian desire. On the other hand, it involves significant costs because it also avoids attention to the dialectical play between experience and the passions and defenses of the self. The lesbian (true) self is protected by this strategy, but not merely in ways that lesbian theorists acknowledge. Surrendered as well are opportunities for theorizing about the psychological and social effects of loss, isolation, and traumatic experience on the self. Here psychodynamic theories can be useful even though they might disagree among themselves and demand further scrutiny and development.

Through the false self account radical lesbian theorists assert a vision of the "true" self as unified, coherent, and accessible to introspection, a vision about which many other feminists (and nonfeminists) are increasingly skeptical. To the extent that many feminist theorists have exposed just this shortcoming of mainstream (male) political theory and linked it to the privileging of masculine identity and the denigration and exclusion of women, the radical lesbian feminist position is a troubling retrogression.

Moreover, as Norma Alarcón suggests, feminist theorists of color have implicated the presumed "true" self in the oppression and marginalization of women of color by white women.[25] Angela Harris marks out a similar consequence of unintended totalizing (white women's) identities in the work of Robin West and Catharine MacKinnon.[26] Theories of "true" authentic self-hood—even if they only theorize barriers between unique, individual selves and deleterious experience—are not innocuous. They can easily be assimilated to conclusions about the "nature" of groups that foster theoretical and political exclusions.

The problematic dimensions of the false self account of lesbian identity are many, but consider just two: the purported (or at least strongly implied) essential goodness of the (true) self, and the failure of the true/false identity configuration to provide a foundation for feminist struggles to transform identity. In both of these areas, a relational psychoanalytic reading of a false self concept broadens the range of theoretical vision. A psychoanalytic analysis can encourage attention to external pressures and influences on the development of self; unlike the lesbian theory examined here, a psychoanalytic analysis can address the processes of identity formation that concern the *interaction* of self and world. It is in this respect that a relational psychoanalytic perspective moves beyond the limitations implicit in a false self account of identity.

The lesbian false self account encourages a virtually inescapable conclusion of an essential core of self that is "good"—unpolluted by patriarchal socialization, heterosexual ideals of femininity and relational patterns, and unwanted unconscious desires, including "intractable emotional responses or retrograde erotic fantasies."[27] Unfortunately, feminist theorists have often reinforced this view of women's "nature" by failing to theorize adequately such aspects of female experience as psychic aggression and other "disagreeable passions." As I have argued elsewhere, the construction of theory by feminists that is inattentive to certain modalities of women's psychic and emotional experience constrains and shapes the ways in which social theory can respond to women's interests, relations, and agency.[28] The costs of a simplistic and one-dimensional account of women as "good" are great, even when they provide protection from other, more frightening, stories about women's (or lesbians') "nature."

Winnicott has often been read by feminists as proposing an account of human nature that deemphasizes aggression and painful internal conflict in healthy development. This reading attends to one dimension of Winnicott's thought, but ignores another that has implications for theorizing about individual development and social relations. A more subtle reading suggests that the maintenance of a sense of being real requires a constant negotiation of ambivalence toward aspects of the self and others. This is because the self whose feelings and relations are not determined through compliance to external demands must freely create those relations and suffer their psychic consequence. Unconscious fantasies of ambivalence—love and hate—toward intimate and social others are the "price to be paid" for the capacities associated with becoming a "true" self. For Winnicott, this self is not unitary and "good"; it is conflicted and defended, and therefore unstable and indeterminate.

A second problem with the lesbian false self account is that it cannot accommodate significant transformations of the self, even though theorists often assume (and prescribe) such change in relation to political and ethical ends. Within the context of a false self account of identity, it makes sense to conceive of change as the self's attempts to rid itself of falseness, to recover its original wholeness and goodness. Indeed, this is what theorists prescribe. This conceptualization is, in fact, inconsistent with many of the most searching and nuanced accounts of identity transformation in lesbian and feminist thought. Examples from the work of Victoria Davion and Minnie Bruce Pratt suggest more fruitful positions toward identity and transformation.

Victoria Davion explores the relationship between feminism and "radical change" through a consideration of the role of moral commitments in feminist identity.[29] Against the view that integrity demands the possession of "unconditional commitments," Davion proposes an argument that she believes is more consistent with feminist (self and social) transformation. Her view holds that feminists anticipate that intellectual and social struggle will give rise to new understandings of the self, of others, and of social "reality"; hence, as understandings change so will (and must) the moral commitments associated with them. To believe otherwise is to deny that multiplicitous selves can have integrity. It is, in short, to constrain the personal transformation that is at the heart of feminism.

Davion's skepticism regarding unconditional commitments is particularly interesting because she locates it in the ethics of Sarah Hoagland. While Davion reads Hoagland's call for change accurately, Hoagland's account of the self simply cannot accommodate such open-ended transformation. One example clarifying the contradiction between a false self account and the ethical and political aspirations of radical lesbian feminism emerges in Hoagland's discussions of lesbian separatism.

By "separatism" Hoagland refers to a wide range of commitments and behaviors; these include refusal to engage in heterosexual relationships, "exit" from social institutions and practices that demand "feminine" and altruistic behavior of women, and membership in women-only groups, communities, and social spaces. Questions remain, however: is the removal of self-hatred, subordinating beliefs, feminine consciousness, and all that constitutes the false self sufficient for the creation of distinctively lesbian communities? Is the realization of (good, nonconflictual) true selves necessary and sufficient for the development of an alternative ethics and politics of lesbian life? Hoagland's answer departs significantly from the false self account, and invokes a need for experimentation, relational transformation, and invention:

> If we are to form an enduring community . . . it will not be on the basis of
> a rich tradition nor of what we find here. . . . If we are to form an empow-
> ering community, it will be on the basis of the values we believe we can
> enact here: what we bring, what we work to leave behind, and what we
> develop as we engage with each other. *If we are to transform subculture to
> community, it will be on the basis of what we create, not what we find.*[30]

Here Hoagland concedes that even strategies of separatism do not merely
enact the latent aspects of true selves. Her vision of lesbian political life is
inconsistent with her defensive and nonrelational account of the self.

Not only is the false self account exposed as inconsistent with relational
and transformational forms of politics, but a false self account can also
operate to preclude the development of more sophisticated and empirically
accurate conceptualizations of political life. This problem is evident in
Hoagland's many discussions of conflict in *Lesbian Ethics*.

Conflict is, for Hoagland, a remediable problem, but it is virtually exclusively associated with men, male philosophy, and masculine institutions and
practices. When the problem of conflict is contingently identified with
women and lesbians, it is in the context of lesbians engaging in capitalist
economic relations[31] and of lesbians practicing flawed forms of lesbian community.[32] In the latter case, Hoagland's brief consideration of Susan
Krieger's *Mirror Dance* is telling; she suggests that the book's focus is "lesbian community as it now exists."[33] The implication, supported by arguments throughout the text, is that properly constructed lesbian communities
need not be obstructed by conflicts over rights, interests, power, sexual (or
other) practices, relationships, culture, or beliefs.

There is also no intimation that conflict itself might be understood and
practiced as personally and politically useful. Conflict is not depicted as a
potentially enlightening and transformative process of learning about the self
and others. For example, Hoagland rejects the view—which she identifies
exclusively with Hegel's master-slave dialectic—that individuals create
boundaries in part through conflict.[34] Instead, the focus is on the elimination
of conflict and on the interaction of preexisting selves.

Contrast Hoagland's understanding of true selfhood and conflict with
Minnie Bruce Pratt's transformational autobiographical essay "Identity: Skin,
Blood, Heart." Pratt tells the story of her continuous attempts to confront
and change her own racism and anti-Semitism by relating a series of encounters with her self—her preconceptions and prejudices, but also her fear,
silence, and comfortable ignorance. Pratt's essay is provocative because she
does employ the language of "falseness" that is intrinsic to so many lesbian
texts:

> As I've worked at stripping away layer after layer of my false identity,
> notions of skin, blood, heart based in racism and anti-Semitism, another
> way I've tried to regain my self-respect, to keep from feeling completely
> naked and ashamed of who I am, is to look at what I have carried with me

from my culture that could help me in the process . . . [and] buried under the layers, I discovered some strengths.[35]

Yet Pratt's version of falsity of the self competes with a more prominent voice in the story—a voice that denies the true/false configuration of identity in favor of a recognition of, and imperative toward, constant self-creation. Hence, Pratt writes of "a positive process of recreating ourselves, of making a self that is not the negative, the oppressor," and of "find[ing] new ways to be in the world."[36] It is instructive that Pratt concurs with Daly and others that oppressive demand and relations are internalized by women, yet differs in her understanding of the significance of this for feminist thinking about identity.

> I have learned that as the process of shaping a negative self identity is long, so the process of change is long, and since the unjust world is duplicated again every day, in large and small, so I must try to recreate, every day, a new self striving for a new just world. What do we *do* to create this new self?[37]

For Pratt, the problem is not merely that the prejudices and simplistic designs of the culture in which she lives have settled *in* her, gathering in sedimentary layers, and awaiting a final removal. She confronts her own collusion, the ways in which conformity has enhanced her comfort, as much as she directs anger at social oppression and its conspicuous agents. Nancie Caraway interprets Pratt's struggle as a realization that "the 'wholeness' of the self involves an inescapably protean encounter with others."[38] The "'wholeness' of the self" does not preexist relations with others, however malign or constructive, but is itself, ironically, a process.

Juxtaposing wholeness and process lends itself to political, and not just to personal, theorizing. Envisioning the self as a process, rather than an entity to be protected, is necessary, as Shane Phelan argues, to the possibility of a "local politics" of coalition-building and action.[39] Here politics is understood not just as a consequence of preexisting goals and legitimations, but as incremental struggles for (daily and plural) justices. The self who engages in these forms of politics with others is transformed by new knowledge, new relations, and new perspectives on her own position with regard to the others whose subjectivity she now confronts. Many radical lesbian feminists whose thought reflects a false self account would agree to these political goals; it is merely that the compatibility between the goals and their account of identity is uneasy and unexamined.

In fact, examining incompatibilities between accounts of identity and political ideals helps to clarify the distinction between theorists such as Hoagland who employ a false self account and theorists such as Pratt who subvert it. Pratt (and this is true of Audre Lorde as well) undermines her own adoption of false self language by consistently delegitimizing its terms.[40] On the other hand, Hoagland, Raymond, and Daly consistently hew to a false self account of identity even when they demand a more relational account of community. The false self account thus goes unremarked, and the fit between the conception of identity it constructs and the politics it grounds is left unchallenged.

Unlike the false self account of radical lesbian theorists, the psychoanalytic account of Winnicott can accommodate radical change of identity. For Winnicott, false aspects of the self are enacted to protect a nascent self—that which has not yet come into existence—as a set of potentials for increasing integration, mastery, and creativeness. The self is not a datum, but an open field of possibility. Winnicott was little interested in specifying the outcomes of relational configurations and moral dilemmas, preferring to delineate the kinds of environments and structures that "hold" and support the self in its unpredictable contacts with the world.

It is in theorizing the constant creation and negotiation of identity—personal and collective—that the relational psychoanalytic paradigm is potentially most useful for lesbian feminists. Winnicott can advance our understanding of the ways in which groups perform functions of symbolically "holding" members through the development of group cultures and shared interpretations of social realities.[41]

Other relational theories can help us to begin to investigate the psychodynamics of conflict and group fragmentation, collective anxieties over leadership and group boundaries, and the erotics of group membership as they apply to lesbian communities and organizations.[42] The notion of the self as plural and relational is consistent with an emphasis on groups: it is through relations with others—and the meanings of class, race, gender, culture, and sexuality that they convey—that the self is constructed as a conflicted and unstable site of transformation. It is continuing relations with others that enhance or thwart individual efforts to realize the kind of personal and political transformation of which Pratt writes. Psychoanalytic theorists have generally ignored the possibilities that are latent in so much relational theory, including race and class as constitutive aspects of subjectivity.[43] Addressing just these kinds of political concerns, Elizabeth Abel suggests that a relational psychoanalytic perspective is more useful to feminists than the more popular Lacanian perspective.

> Introducing the category of the social into Lacanian discourse requires a deliberate intervention, since this discourse collapses the social into a symbolic register that is always everywhere the same.[44]

This insensitivity of Lacanian theory is connected to its inability to distinguish an analysis of groups and group relations from its analysis of the production of individual subjectivity. This is not to suggest that group theory can entirely displace individual theory; any responsible psychological theory of groups refers ultimately to the psychology of individuals. It is just that relational psychoanalysis, in its emphasis on constellations of defenses and the ongoing creation of the self through relational struggle, adapts to the ways in which individuals use groups to accomplish, and defend against, developmental tasks. Relational theory lends itself to theorizing about the ways in which individuals are lifelong sites and agents of reality construction, defense, and group negotiation. The political implications are many: individuals use groups to satisfy needs for authority, to identify and respond to threats and enemies, and to inform conceptions of the good society.

There are also explicit ethical implications and admonitions inscribed within much relational psychoanalysis that belie the charge of psychology's ethical vacuousness that is frequently leveled by lesbian feminists.[45] Like other relational theorists, Winnicott would not have regarded all possible psychic and relational outcomes as morally equivalent. He believed, for example, that capacities to sustain ambivalence and concern are essential for productive intimate and social relationships. It is not surprising that these very capacities are deeply implicated in feminist movements toward self-transformation.

Unlike representatives of other psychoanalytic perspectives, relational theorists (including Winnicott) have speculated little about the etiology and significance of male homosexuality or lesbianism.[46] More broadly, Winnicott does not champion adjustment as the goal of individual development; just the opposite: he contends that "freedom from symptoms" of trauma, stress, and anxiety is not necessarily a sign of psychic health because the smoothly functioning false self "can very easily be mistaken for health."[47] In expressing concern that the false self might be mistaken for the "whole person," and in arguing that "compliance is a sick basis for life,"[48] Winnicott does not ally himself with the disciplining of lesbians as the synoptic dismissal of psychology and psychoanalysis would suggest. Here is a progressive theoretical moment of which lesbians can avail themselves.

Conclusion

Lesbian feminists have been rightly fearful of the disciplinary discourses that have labelled lesbians as perverts, deviants, introverts, or examples of immature or arrested development. Exposing the abuses of the intellectual discourses of psychology and psychoanalysis is an undeniably urgent goal. Even so, an unqualified refusal to seek insights within the disparate psychological traditions does not contribute to the construction of knowledge. It is always *possible* that some insight will be useful, even if it must be disconnected and reclaimed from a mass of assumptions that reflect ideological views of women and/or lesbians. Reevaluation and reconstruction, not unqualified refusal, are important tasks of feminist critique.

Social and political theories do employ psychological assumptions, either explicit or covert. Certainly, the lesbian feminist theories that denounce psychology and psychoanalysis make assumptions about the nature of lesbian identity and the ways in which pernicious aspects of reality are integrated into the self. The problem with psychological assumptions that are made and then disclaimed by social and political theorists is that disclaimed assumptions are not subject to critique. The likelihood that ad hoc, usually comforting, conceptualizations of the self will be introduced is enhanced in such theories.

In fact, the psychoanalytic perspective advanced here is consistent with provocative arguments about the construction of the self by lesbian and straight feminists. Lesbian feminist theorists such as Minnie Bruce Pratt, Maria Lugones, and Audre Lorde, among many others, resist the temptation to neatly repudiate even those aspects of identity about which they are ambivalent. What these theorists share is a project of social critique that requires a critical exegesis of the self. The understanding of the self (and one-self) that emerges is one that acknowledges the self as a site of multiple social meanings, hierarchies, resistances, and strategic (if unconscious) complicities; it is most often expressed in theoretical analysis of the race, ethnic, class, sexual orientation, or other components of identity creation. This perspective of transformational multiplicitous selfhood does not require psychological support or foundations, yet it can be reconciled fruitfully with attention to psychodynamic struggle and the emergence of personal identity.

Through attention to the affinities between relational psychoanalytic accounts of the self and transformational feminist accounts we can recover the histories of particular theories of subjectivity and understand the meanings that they have carried in other theoretical systems. If our arguments about lesbian identity, resistance, and community are not utterly unique, we can learn much about our own ideas by investigating their intellectual provenance and implications. At the least, an awareness of the ways that lesbian thought and psychological discourses intersect can help to restrain the pynoptic—and at times inaccurate—dismissals of mainstream thought that sometimes pass unnoticed in lesbian writing.

Many lesbian feminist theorists would argue that the introduction of psychology is unnecessary and oppressive—a continuation of female socialization and gender role requirements, compounded by coercive heterosexuality. On its face, given the continuing biases of psychoanalytic theory regarding the relative merits of hetero- and homosexuality, this argument is compelling. Psychology is not so easily excluded, however. Psychological assumptions lurk within the discourse of social theory, and these assumptions can be evaluated by those who would judge the usefulness of theories.

Certainly it is not necessary to translate every concern, every concept, of lesbian or feminist theorizing into psychological terms. Yet it is also unwise to preempt the possibility of accommodation between the various psychologies and lesbian feminist ideas. When theorists such as Ruth Colker and Janice Raymond write of the need for feminists to heal the "brokenness" of the self in a hostile world, it is easy to feel an affinity with such a goal. It is possible, however, that the brokenness to which such scholars refer is inescapable, and must itself be used as a basis for identity construction and politics. Such a conviction need not evoke dispair. It does, however, demand a more critical posture toward the accounts of the self in lesbian theory and a receptiveness to those that probe the consequences of relations and that challenge closure.

Notes

I would like to thank Jyl Josephson, Laree Martin, Shane Phelan, and Diana Zoelle for their critical comments on earlier drafts of this paper, which was originally presented at the annual meeting of the American Political Science Association in Washington, D.C., in September 1993.

1. Mary Daly, *Gyn/Ecology: The Metaethics of Radical Feminism* (Boston: Beacon Press, 1978); Janice M. Raymond, *A Passion For Friends: Toward a Philosophy of Female Affection* (Boston: Beacon, 1986); Sarah Lucia Hoagland, *Lesbian Ethics: Toward New Value* (Palo Alto, California: Institute of Lesbian Studies, 1988). Work by Daly, Raymond, and Hoagland is not the only source of a "false self" account, which can also be found in the work of Jeffner Allen, Nett Hart, and Julia Penelope. See Jeffner Allen, *Lesbian Philosophy: Explorations* (Palo Alto, California: Institute of Lesbian Studies, 1986) and Nett Hart, "Lesbian Desire as Social Action," in *Lesbian Philosophy and Cultures,* edited by Jeffner Allen (New York: State University of New York Press, 1990). In her contribution to the *Lesbian Philosophy and Cultures* volume, "The Lesbian Perspective," Penelope employs a false self account, but is more ambiguous than the other theorists about the prescriptive stance usually associated with it.

2. Daly, *Gyn/Ecology,* 1.

3. Ibid., 26.

4. Ibid., 27.

5. Hoagland, *Lesbian Ethics,* 61.

6. Daly, *Gyn/Ecology,* 370.

7. Hoagland, *Lesbian Ethics,* 95.

8. Jean Grimshaw, "Autonomy and Identity in Feminist Thinking," in *Feminist Perspectives in Philosophy,* edited by Morwenna Griffiths and Margaret Whitford (Indianapolis: University of Indiana Press, 1988), 93.

9. Ruth Colker, "Feminism, Sexuality, and Authenticity," in *At the Boundaries of Law: Feminism and Legal Theory,* edited by Martha Albertson Fineman and Nancy Sweet Thomadsen (New York: Routledge, 1991), 146–47.

10. Ruth Colker, "Feminism, Sexuality, and Self: A Preliminary Inquiry Into the Politics of Authenticity," in *Boston University Law Review* 68, 220.

11. Ibid., 221.

12. Ibid., 220.

13. Ibid.

14. Laing and Winnicott address the concept of the "false self" in a number of works. See R.D. Laing, *The Politics of Experience* (New York: Pantheon, 1967) and *The Divided Self: An Existential Study in Sanity and Madness* (London: Penguin, 1969); D.W. Winnicott, *The Maturational Processes and the Facilitating Environment: Studies in the Theory of Emotional Development* (New York: International Universities Press, Inc., 1965), *Playing and Reality* (London: Tavistock, 1971), and *Through Paediatrics to Psychoanalysis* (New York: Basic, 1975).

15. Richard Chessick, *A Dictionary For Psychotherapists: Dynamic Concepts in Psychotherapy* (New York: Aronson, 1993); Soren Kierkegaard, *The Concept of Dread,* translated by Walter Lowrie (Princeton: Princeton University Press, 1957).

16. The best known of those who have used Winnicott's ideas are Nancy Chodorow, Jessica Benjamin, and Jane Flax. See Nancy Chodorow, *The Reproduction of Mothering: Psychoanalysis and the Sociology of Gender* (Berkeley: University of California Press, 1978) and *Feminism and Psychoanalytic Theory* (New Haven: Yale University Press, 1989); Jessica Benjamin, *The Bonds of Love: Feminism, Psychoanalysis, and the Problem of Domination* (New York: Pantheon, 1988); Jane Flax, *Thinking Fragments: Psychoanalysis, Feminism, and Postmodernism in the Contemporary West* (Berkeley: University of California Press, 1990).

17. See, for example, James M. Glass, *Private Terror/Public Life: Psychosis and the Politics of Community* (Ithaca, New York: Cornell University Press, 1989); Jane Flax, "The Play of Justice: Justice as a Transitional Space," in *Political Psychology* 14, 2; Cynthia Burack, *The Problem of the Passions: Feminism, Psychoanalysis, and Social Theory* (New York: New York University Press, 1994).

18. For another use of Winnicott's concept of transitional space see Beverly Burch's examination of the psychodynamics of lesbian relationships. Beverly Burch, *On Intimate Terms: The Psychology of Difference in Lesbian Relationships* (Urbana and Chicago: University of Illinois Press, 1993).

19. Winnicott, *Playing and Reality,* 2. The essays collected in this volume are cited by many scholars as central in positioning Winnicott as a social theorist.

20. Ibid., 53.

21. Winnicott, *Through Paediatrics to Psychoanalysis*, 205.

22. Winnicott, *Playing and Reality,* 14.

23. Ibid., 68.

24. This phrase is drawn from Susan Moller Okin's critique of Alasdair MacIntyre. Her point is not an explicitly psychological one, but rather alludes to the inattention in mainstream political thought to women's historical role in child-bearing and child-rearing. Susan Moller Okin, *Justice, Gender, and the Family* (New York: Basic Books, 1989), 56.

25. Norma Alarcón, "The Theoretical Subject(s) of *This Bridge Called My Back* and Anglo-American Feminism," in *Making Face, Making Soul: Creative and Critical Perspectives by Women of Color,* edited by Gloria Anzaldúa (San Francisco: Aunt Lute Foundation, 1990).

26. Angela P. Harris, "Race and Essentialism in Feminist Legal Theory," in *Feminist Legal Theory: Readings in Law and Gender,* edited by Katherine T. Barlett and Rosanne Kennedy (San Francisco: Westview Press, 1991).

27. Ruth Perry, Book Reviews: *Feminism and Psychoanalytic Theory, Thinking Fragments: Psychoanalysis, Feminism, and Postmodernism in the Contemporary West, Refiguring the Father: New Feminist Readings of Patriarchy,* in *Signs* 16, 3, 597–603.

28. Burack, *The Problem of the Passions.* Specifically, feminist social theory of Carol Gilligan, Jessica Benjamin, Nancy Chodorow, and Dorothy Dinnerstein is analyzed.

29. Victoria M. Davion, "Integrity and Radical Change," in *Feminist Ethics,* edited by Claudia Card (Lawrence, Kansas: University of Kansas Press, 1991).

30. Hoagland, *Lesbian Ethics,* 155 (emphasis added).

31. Ibid., 79–81.

32. Ibid., 232–33.

33. Ibid., 232.

34. Ibid., 235–36.

35. Ibid., 61.

36. Ibid., 59.

37. Ibid., 64. On Pratt and the idea of the false self see also Biddy Martin and Chandra Talpade Mohanty, "Feminist Politics: What's Home Got to Do with It?" in *Feminist Studies/Critical Studies,* edited by Teresa de Lauretis (Bloomington: University of Indiana Press, 1986).

38. Nancie Caraway, "The Riddle of Consciousness: Racism and Identity in Feminist Theory," in *Women in Politics: Outsiders or Insiders?* edited by Lois Lovelace Duke (Englewood Cliffs, New Jersey: Prentice Hall, 1993), 23. Diana Fuss notes the "tension between the notions of 'developing' an identity and 'finding' an identity" in lesbian theory, but suggests a Lacanian deconstructive approach as a way of confronting the political demand for a unified lesbian identity. Diana Fuss, *Essentially Speaking: Feminism, Nature, and Difference* (New York: Routledge, 1989).

39. Shane Phelan, "(Be)Coming Out: Lesbian Identity and Politics," in *Signs* 18, 4.

40. For an analysis of the uses and subversions of the "jargon of authenticity" in the work of Audre Lorde, see Shane Phelan, "The Jargon of Authenticity: Adorno and Feminist Essentialism," in *Philosophy and Social Criticism* 16, 1.

41. C. Fred Alford, *Melanie Klein and Critical Social Theory: An Account of Politics, Art, and Reason Based on Her Psychoanalytic Theory* (New Haven: Yale University Press, 1989).

42. See, for example, W.R. Bion, *Experiences in Groups and Other Papers* (London: Routledge, 1989) and R.D. Hinshelwood, *What Happens in Groups: Psychoanalysis, the Individual, and the Community* (London: Free Association, 1987).

43. There are signs that this may be changing. As of this writing the National Psychological Association for Psychoanalysis (NPAP) has established a Center for the Psychoanalytic Study of Social Trauma, and the Association for the Psychoanalysis of Culture and Society (APCS) has established a Politics Area Committee. Both the NPAP Center and the APCS are dedicated to the study and amelioration of problems such as racism, anti-Semitism, homophobia, and the social roots of violence.

44. Elizabeth Abel, "Race, Class, and Psychoanalysis? Opening Questions," in *Conflicts in Feminism,* edited by Marianne Hirsch and Evelyn Fox Keller (New York: Routledge, 1990), 185.

45. For one such argument, see Celia Kitzinger and Rachel Perkins, *Changing Our Minds: Lesbian Feminism and Psychology* (New York: New York University Press, 1993), especially chapter 2.

46. Noreen O'Connor and Joanna Ryan, *Wild Desires and Mistaken Identities: Lesbianism and Psychoanalysis* (New York: Columbia University Press, 1993), 14.

47. Winnicott, *The Maturational Processes and the Facilitating Environment: Studies in the Theory of Emotional Development*, 101–102.

48. Winnicott, *Playing and Reality,* 65.

3

Dichotomies and Displacement: Bisexuality in Queer Theory and Politics

Stacey Young

Queer theory and queer politics continue to exhibit a marked silence around bisexuality. This silence is perhaps more complete in theory than in politics, given the nature of the theoretical enterprise. The solitude in which theory, in the final instance, is produced—despite its being shaped fundamentally through the collective processes of reading, teaching, studying, attending conferences, and so on—gives the author greater control than the activist over what issues make it onto her agenda.

In queer politics, the silence has occasionally been interrupted by vocal skirmishes, sometimes initiated by bisexuals, sometimes not. Until recently, these skirmishes have typically involved a swift conquest and subsequent banishment of the topic of bisexuality and, on occasion, of bisexuals.[1] This scenario has, in many cases, given way to another, in which "bisexual" is added to the title of an organization or event. In some cases, that addition has then been overturned: the word has been added only to be removed (and, sometimes, added again later). Very occasionally, the addition of "bisexual" has been followed by the addition of "transgendered."[2]

Silence can take many forms, however, and for all the name changes, queer politics has yet to reflect any real transformation in analyses or agendas: "queer" is usually used interchangeably with "lesbian/gay;" challenges to AIDS-related homophobia remain silent about the demonization of bisexual men ("stealth killers") in mainstream/heterosexist AIDS discourses; calls for civil rights are typically framed in terms of "lesbian and gay" rights;

biphobia continues to find crude expression among some lesbians and gay men; and—in part, but not entirely, because of these factors, lesbian/gay political organizations and bisexual ones still operate largely in isolation from one another. By and large, bisexuality continues to be avoided or dismissed.

On paper, we see a similar phenomenon: when bisexuality is mentioned at all in writings about queerness that aren't specifically about bisexuality, it is often in the form of being tacked on to one or more of the innumerable iterations of "lesbian and gay" one finds in a given book or article—and then not mentioned again. Very rarely is it actually discussed, explored, or articulated as a queer identity alongside "lesbian" and "gay."

These silences are extremely curious; the critical stance that leads us to investigate other sexualities should, it would seem, lead us to investigate this one, but this has not been the case. Figuring out why can certainly aid us in our understanding of bisexuality. Such an enterprise is necessary: bisexuals, like lesbians and gay men, are queer, are part of queer movements and communities, and are subject to oppression on the basis of their sexuality. They make conscious choices about their sexuality that lie beyond those acceptable within the institution of heterosexuality. Investigations of queer politics and queer realities are incomplete without looking at bisexuality, in terms both of its consonance with lesbianism and male homosexuality and its difference from them.

But discerning the reasons for so much silence around bisexuality can do more than simply begin to fill those silences; it can assist us in our interrogations of other sexualities as well. This is because attention to bisexuality—and, in particular, to what the silences surrounding it can tell us—can reveal the costs to queer theory and politics of these lacunae, and can prod our thinking about sexuality in general in new directions—specifically, those suggested by what we discover when we look at bisexuality.

Bisexuality's heuristic value in the analysis of other sexualities stems not from any status it enjoys as a "universal" or "more complete" sexuality than lesbianism, male homosexuality, or heterosexuality. Ironically, its value has to do with the fact that it has been only marginal to the process by which other queer identities have been constructed. Queer identity politics has necessarily involved constructing definitions of queer identities whose content is characterized by the reversal of constructions of heterosexuality. While this has facilitated coherence among queers and an oppositional stance toward heterosexism, it has also had the effect of closing off certain avenues of inquiry into queer sexuality—avenues which, should we wander them, may expand our understanding of the consequences of narrowing our focus. These consequences are costly not only to bisexuals but to lesbians and gay men as well.

To put this another way: lesbian and gay identity and experience are coming to be the subject of intense and insightful scrutiny in the burgeoning field of queer theory. This produces both insight and restriction, for, as certain "truths," experiences, and realities begin to be articulated, others, not having been explored, recede to the margins and become eclipsed, while an accepted body of knowledge (and an accepted body of questions and unknowns) comes to govern discourse—and to preclude other questions, acknowledgment of other unknowns, and construction of other knowledges.

This paper begins to examine, through the lens of bisexuality, how the requisites of identity politics and the binarisms at the center of those requisites structure (and limit) queer theories and politics. It argues that beginning the work of theorizing bisexuality can assist us in articulating bisexual realities and bisexual politics, in theorizing lesbianism and male homosexuality, and in constructing political practices that can more effectively subvert existing power structures.

Reasons for "Bisexual Avoidance"

One reason some people avoid or dismiss bisexuality has to do with the garden variety (which is not to say simple) revulsion of prejudice. Some people, queer and heterosexual, respond to bisexuals directly through the phobic filter of stereotypes. They want nothing to do with people who are cast, variously, as indiscriminate, disease-ridden, unwilling to commit, promiscuous, opportunistic, apolitical, in a phase, cowardly, and deceitful.

Another factor in queer silence around bisexuality is the fact that silence tends to breed silence, and the relative lack of bisexual theory no doubt impedes those who don't think much about bisexuality from acknowledging it as an important analytic category. The phenomenon is somewhat circular, of course: queer institutions, milieux, collectivities, and intellectual enterprises have certainly reduced the costs to bisexuals, along with other queers, of pursuing same-sex desire, and have assisted efforts to analyze that pursuit in terms of homophobia and heterosexism. However, they have not been particularly conducive to the development of specifically *bisexual* political and theoretical analyses—nor in helping queers of any orientation (including bisexuals) to identify what might be gained from such analyses. Publishing and other forms of communication are mediated through highly politicized institutions. Editors of queer publications sometimes reject manuscripts about bisexuality on the grounds that it lies beyond their publication's scope, or because "we haven't decided yet what we want to do about covering this issue."[3] Conference organizers often ghettoize all papers on bisexuality into a few panels on the subject, rather than adopting a more integrative approach.[4] And so on.

This relative lack of theoretical work on bisexuality is compounded by a general lack of attention among queer theorists to the bisexual theory and writing that does exist—which is in turn compounded by the fact that most of this work has been published in collections specifically of work on bisexuality. Collections of this sort are often overlooked in queer studies, given the equation, in most instances, of "queer" with "lesbian and gay."

A fourth consideration contributing to lesbian and gay resistance to taking bisexuality seriously is the propensity on the part of some bisexual activists and writers to posit bisexuality as somehow superior to all other sexualities, claiming that it is "universal," that it transcends boundaries between genders and between sexualities, that it escapes the "limitations" of "monosexuality." These grandiose and patronizing claims, though by no means common to all bisexuals, have augmented existing antipathies toward bisexuals and have fueled resistance among lesbians and gay men to viewing bisexuals as part of queer communities and bisexuality as a legitimate and necessary subject of inquiry for queer theorists.

Beyond stereotypes, the relative paucity of work on bisexuality, the lack of attention to the work that has been done, and condescension on the part of some bisexuals, there are more complex reasons for lesbians' and gay men's silences around bisexuality—reasons that have to do with identity politics and its requisites, as well as with the intransigence of the homo/hetero dichotomy, its importance to identity politics, and its force in structuring our theorizing about sexuality. When we look at the status of bisexuality in queer politics in light of the exigencies of identity politics in general, we begin to see how these factors combine in certain strategies (dismissal, avoidance, displacement) that ultimately obscure not just bisexuality, but also a host of other identities that differentiate queers from one another, as well as a range of lesbian and gay experience.

Identity Politics

The question of what one calls oneself, how one identifies one's sexuality—and why it matters—is bound up in identity politics as it has been practiced by various social movements in this country since the 1960s (including the Civil Rights, Black Power, women's, homophile, and gay movements). Despite these movements' differences—in goals, targets, participants, and tactics—and despite increasingly sophisticated analyses of identity, identity-based political movements have generally shared a common set of assumptions about the relationships between identity, ideology and behavior, political commitment and trustworthiness. These assumptions include the notions that

- people who belong to the same identity group have more or less the same political analysis of (at least) the oppression they share (e.g., that all women share a feminist analysis of women's status);
- that form of oppression supersedes all others for all members of the group (e.g., that people of color are primarily concerned with racism, queers are primarily concerned with homophobia and heterosexism—the overlap between the categories gets lost behind this assumption);
- identity group members are always each other's natural allies, and can be trusted politically simply because they share an identity (e.g., all women are "sisters," all queers can be counted upon to resist homophobic practices);

- those in the "oppressor" group all benefit directly, consciously, and equally from their subordination of the "oppressed" group, and thus are rarely or never allies of the oppressed (e.g., all men, regardless of race, class, etc, enjoy higher status and more power than do all women; there's no such thing as a heterosexual ally to queer movements); and so forth.

These assumptions in turn originate from two grounding binary constructions:

(1) The binary split between "us" and "them"

- Identity politics movements represent people who share a common identity and who are oppressed as a group on the basis of that identity by people who share a different, "opposite" identity. There are only two main groups, for all practical purposes, and they are easily distinguishable from each other: we know who belongs in which group (e.g., blacks and whites, women and men, homosexuals and heterosexuals).

(2) The binary split between active oppressors and active resisters

- Members of the privileged group are complicit with those power structures, and will work actively to maintain them should they be threatened. Members of the oppressed identity group naturally resist the power structures that facilitate their oppression and that confer privileges upon those who belong to the other, opposite, oppressing identity group; unless they are suffering from extreme self-hatred, they feel solidarity with others who share their identity and they act accordingly. Hence, oppressed people need only mobilize "our own kind" in order to strengthen our movements and achieve our goals.

On the basis of these dichotomies, identity politics has freighted the question of identity with the baggage of legitimacy: one's claim to being a member of a given identity category is gauged by one's political analysis and political commitments, which in turn are assumed to be evident in one's personal practices. Identity is seen as preceding the individual: individuals base their claims to membership in a particular identity category on the content of that category as it has been constructed.

Lived reality, though, inevitably exceeds identity categories. Where the political stakes of the constructions of those identity categories are highest, this excess can sometimes be perceived as a form of treason, expressed in such terms as "Uncle Tom" or "oreo cookie," "male-identified" or "closety"; explained as "false consciousness," "internalized oppression," or "self-hatred"; or rejoined with expressions of doubt about the legitimacy of an individual's claim to inclusion in a given category. In some cases, individuals find themselves called upon to prove the legitimacy of their claims to a certain identity by others within the identity category who doubt that legitimacy; most often, they defend their claims to legitimacy in a way that upholds the fiction that identity categories are discrete, their membership self-evident (a fiction belied, of course, by the need to prove membership in the first place). That is, they are likely to formulate their claims to legitimacy in terms of their congruity with the established discursive content of the identity in question.

But not always. Theory and practical politics increasingly seek to problematize these very assumptions, challenge these binarisms, and call into question the assumed links between what one practices, what one calls oneself, how one views the world, and what political commitments one makes. Particularly strong within feminist movements, these challenges to established notions about what characterizes the subjects of a particular movement have also emerged within queer movements. Some queer or queer-inspired organizations (such as Queer Nation and ACT UP) have reflected these challenges in some of their actions and agendas. ACT UP New York, for example, has had active Women's Issues and Majority Outreach caucuses that were able to steer substantial portions of the organization's activity in the direction of addressing the concerns of women and people of color—pressuring the Centers for Disease Control to base its definition of AIDS on clinical factors that are more relevant to women's experience of the disease, for example, and setting up needle exchange programs to meet the HIV-prevention needs of injection drug users, who disproportionately come from communities of color.

But these actions did not come about without significant struggle—nor do they reflect the end of that struggle. And there are certainly many more examples of activists and intellectuals presuming to speak on behalf of whole categories of subjects but doing so from a limited—and usually dominant—perspective that represents the experiences and interests of only a relatively privileged few. Thus, for example, we hear white queer activists say that racism isn't their issue, while male activists complain, when called upon to explain the mostly male membership of their organizations, that "women can come—they just won't; it's not like we keep them out." Or we read political theory that paints a two-dimensional, homogenizing portrait of queers:

> for lesbians and gay men, [sexuality] is *the* principle [of identity]. It is on the basis of their sexuality that they are subjected to domination . . .

thus

> the part of themselves that [lesbian and gay people] have had to pay most attention to ethically, and that hence centers the way they live their lives, is their sexuality and their erotic relationships.[5]

The fact is that no matter how compelling are the challenges to homogenizing constructions of "lesbians and gay men"—constructions that reduce them to a unitary group with identical interests—the impact of these challenges is often startlingly limited, even among those most receptive to them. Those who have worked politically within identity politics movements will recognize the tenacity of reductive, homogenizing binary notions of who a movement's constituents are, even among people who are intellectually persuaded by challenges to them. (One of the most common—and most devastating—manifestations of these assumptions is an unwillingness to work sincerely to establish coalitions with people who share political goals even as they inhabit different subcultures.) These notions are difficult to uproot not because they are "true" or compelling on a rational level: candid observation turns up many counterexamples, more than enough to call those assumptions into question. Rather, as Derrida and so many others have argued, they are difficult to uproot because the binary structures of thought they represent are so ingrained, and are constantly reinforced. (Consider, for example, the widespread, automatic acceptance enjoyed in our society by such commonsense pronouncements as "There are two sides [read: only two] to every story," and that those two are necessarily each other's opposite.)

In a way, the continued theoretical and practical efforts to complicate categories of identity that so often get figured homogeneously testify to the resilience of the homogeneous constructions of identity categories. That is, the challenges are continually made necessary by the strength and resilience of constructions that (inevitably) fail to take account of a range of experience, and that exert some disciplinary force over individuals' lives. The challenges continue precisely because the governing binarisms are so intransigent.

Identity Categories: Uses and Limitations

Challenges to identity politics-based assumptions of homogeneity among those represented by a given identity category have resulted in the proliferation of terms of difference. For example, the category "homosexuals"—the subjects on whose behalf queer movements have sought to pursue progressive change—has been complicated both by historical and political shifts (which brought the terms "gays" and "queers" into use); and by the articulation of the ways that a queer person's interests are shaped not only by her/his position vis-à-vis the social organization of sexuality, but also by her/his position vis-à-vis the social organization of race, class, gender, ethnicity, nationality, and so forth. In political practice, this complication has enhanced, in particular, the visibility of women in queer collectivities. It has also spawned an abundance of terms that seek, in ever-increasing degrees of specificity, to define the totality of people's (salient) identities. Thus we get terms like "white, heterosexual, middle-class women," "Jewish lesbian," and "working-class gay men of color." These terms reflect what Eve Sedgwick calls the "tiny number of inconceivably coarse axes of categorization" that we have available to us and that, in the end, still leave us mired in descriptions that obscure their variable content and relevance, such that "even people who share all or most of our own positionings along these crude axes may still be different enough from us, and from each other, to seem like all but different species."[6]

One of the political consequences of this proliferation can be seen in one form of dismissal or avoidance of bisexuality: In debates over whether to add "bisexual" to the titles of "lesbian and gay" organizations and events, a common response is "Why stop at adding 'bisexual' to the title of this event?" In other words, why not be all-inclusive? And yet, it is at this point that so many people balk, sometimes because they recognize, when faced with the task of making language more accurately reflect the diversity of social reality, that that diversity is impossible to capture fully in language. This impossibility of being truly representative, however, seems contrary to the stated premises of so much recent important activity directed at expanding rights and representation to "include everyone": even as we might recognize the impossibility of representing "everyone," we still feel that we must represent "someone."

A dilemma thus takes shape: identity categories (including "bisexual") seem to be simultaneously indispensable to and restricting of our political projects. When these and other identity categories are invoked to represent the subjects in whose names political movements are launched, the implicit or explicit demarcations that serve to distinguish these subjects as a group (and to identify what might be the project of a movement advanced in their name) automatically work to secure exclusion at the very moment that they appear to facilitate inclusion. The dilemma centers around the paradoxical relationship between the desire to represent categories of subjects as such for political purposes, and the desire to avoid the exclusions that seem inevitably to take place when one seeks to identify and define the content of such categories. In practice, it is not uncommon for people to opt for the status quo—that is, "lesbian and gay"—as a way to deal with the conflicting demands of inclusiveness and expediency.

Challenges to identity politics' assumptions have sought to move the debate to a different level by contesting the ostensible content of established identity categories. Sometimes the critique is that they are over- or under-inclusive, as in Greta Christina's effort to define "lesbian":

> Is a lesbian: a woman who only fucks other women? That would include bi women who're monogamously involved with other women. A woman who doesn't fuck men? That would include celibate straight women. A woman who would never get seriously involved with men? Rules out lesbians who've been married in the past. A woman who never has sexual thoughts about men? That excludes dykes who are into heavy and com-

plex gender play, who get off on gay men's porn, or who are maybe just curious.

Christina goes on to make the point that the category "bisexual women" includes desires, behaviors, and identifications that are so disparate as to defy any coherent representation:

> For me, being bi means I mostly like to fuck women, and I also like to fuck men. For Joan, it means that she's attracted to both men and women, regardless of who she is or isn't humping. For Sandra, it means that she only gets serious about women, but is willing to fuck men for fun as well. Marta, who's been monogamously married to a man for some time, says she's bi because she's been involved with women in the past and is still attracted to them. Rachel, on the other hand, is sexual almost entirely with women, but occasionally likes to tie men up and dominate them—she also calls herself bi. The key factor can be who you're attracted to, who you're willing to sleep with, who you're actually screwing, who you fall in love with. And the key factor is different for each woman. It's very hard to pin down.[7]

Moreover, there's a certain amount of overlap in sexual practices between the categories "lesbians" and "bisexual women"; this overlap might be represented by the examples of a lesbian who sleeps with men on occasion and a bisexual woman who is monogamous with her woman lover. All of these examples illustrate the impossibility of defining all the possible meanings that can attach to a particular identity category.

Yet the categories' limitations have to do not simply with their content being over- or under-inclusive, but with the ways that their content shifts depending on who employs them, in what contexts, and so on. Critics of identity categories argue persuasively that these categories, far from signifying discrete and coherent groupings of individuals, in fact function as representational fictions that do violence to differences between people, as well as to individuals' own internal complexities, in order to secure an appearance of coherence among all those who "belong" to a given category. Biddy Martin discusses this phenomenon when she writes of efforts at "boundary control," those explicit attempts to impose a stable content that is supposed to describe or define all members of a given category. Specifically with regard to efforts from within to control the boundaries around the category "lesbian," Martin writes:

> A friend of mine recently referred to these efforts at boundary control as "purification rituals," and they do seem to involve efforts to rid the category "lesbian" of anything messy, anything like its inevitable internal differences or our own irreducible heterogeneities. . . . The amount of work required to keep the category intact exposes its ultimate instability and its lack of fixed foundations.[8]

These "rituals" themselves, Martin notes, when they are conducted from within the category, are part and parcel of the intense high-stake struggles that characterize the construction of identities.[9]

Purification rituals take many forms, including the more subtle form of insisting that we retain for political purposes constructions of subjects—lesbians, women, and so forth—that, through their denial of internal instability, retain and impose meanings that work to marginalize certain kinds of individuals those subject categories are supposed to represent. This is a political strategy that is destined to fail, according to Martin:

> The question is whether the perceived need for uniformity, complete autonomy and authenticity is the best way to challenge heterosexism and misogyny, or an effective strategy to defend against annihilation. . . . Whatever the intent of these efforts to render lesbianism internally coherent and stable, discipline and control are the effects. Unruly sexual fantasies, desires, pleasures and practices, *but also more complex analyses of social realities, are sacrificed to investments in identity.*[10] [emphasis added]

Often, of course, explicit efforts to control boundaries are not even necessary, because the process by which individuals group themselves and articulate their supposed shared identity is one that involves suppressing the possibility of internal contradictions. Sometimes this process takes place consciously: people will discipline their own desires and behaviors in order to fit acceptable categories, rather than place themselves outside of them or have to challenge them—like one gay man who told me that he called himself bisexual for a while, and had lovers of both sexes, but then decided that he had to choose, and that he did so because "nobody likes bisexuals." Biphobia rendered bisexuality an inviable choice for him.

Judith Butler describes this process as the "juridical definition" of subjects:

> The question of "the subject" is crucial for politics . . . because juridical subjects are invariably produced through certain exclusionary practices that do not "show" once the juridical structure of politics has been established. In other words, the political construction of the subject proceeds with certain legitimating and exclusionary aims, and these political operations are effectively concealed and naturalized by a political analysis that takes juridical structures as their foundation. *Juridical power inevitably "produces" what it claims merely to represent . . .*[11] (emphasis added)

In other words, while categories such as "lesbian" or "bisexual" are often employed as ontological givens—as if their "truth" lay beneath their cultural construction and need only be revealed and mobilized—the categories themselves make sense only within a paradigm that emphasizes some behaviors, desires, or analyses, reduces others, and ignores still others altogether in order to appear natural and self-evident.

Complexity, Instability, and the Status of Bisexuality

What's so interesting about this, of course, is that *while lesbianism, male homosexuality, and male and (especially) female heterosexuality may have been explored and theorized at greater length than bisexuality thus far has been, those other sexualities are by no means less complex or more stable than bisexuality, not even in terms of object choice.* Certainly there are many lesbians and heterosexual men who sleep only with women, many gay men and heterosexual women who sleep only with men. However, as categories, these identities also include, for example, gay men who occasionally sleep with women; lesbians who are in long-term relationships with men; and countless heterosexuals who form short- or long-term sexual relationships with people of the same sex. The stability that these categories seem to represent with regard to object choice is, in many cases, a fiction. Likewise, while some bisexuals have multiple male and female partners, others are fairly constant in the gender of their partners, or are in long-term, monogamous relationships—and thus may have less variability in the gender of their partners than some people expect when they hear the term "bisexual," with all that it seems to connote.

This is not to imply that identity categories are empty or useless (even as descriptive terms) simply because they don't mean the same thing to everyone, or because their content is unstable. But I do want to challenge both the notion that identity categories represent epistemological certainties, and the notion that the uncertainties that do exist are located primarily at what we think of as the boundaries that demarcate one category from another. This view of sexual object choice among members of identity categories—the view of a stable center with flux relegated to the margins—obscures the degree to which uncertainty and variability may be closer to a rule than an exception. It also does a great deal to maintain the homosexual/heterosexual binarism.

If variability is as prevalent in most or all categories as it seems to be when we investigate those categories typically associated, in discourses on sexuality, with stability and certainty (i.e., lesbianism and male homosexuality), *why, then, does the mention of bisexuality in particular raise the specter of unrepresentability in ways that the mention of other identities does not?*

If we begin to investigate this phenomenon, I believe we will learn a great deal about some of the ways that homosexual/heterosexual dichotomies function at the levels of discourse and identity construction, and specifically how bisexuality is made to stand in for multiplicity and complexity, and is then banished together with all of that multiplicity in order to restore the appearance of a stable, binary world.

The example of the title of recent national queer studies conferences is a good place to begin this investigation.

*****

"Pleasure/Politics: 4th Annual Lesbian, Bisexual and Gay Studies Conference," held at Rutgers in the fall of 1991, was the first time that "bisexual" was included in the conference title.[12] When the organizing committee for the fifth annual conference decided to remove bisexual from the title, changing it back to "Lesbian and Gay Studies" after "Bisexual" had been included only once, even they seemed unable to articulate what was at stake. Even at the moment of enacting this change, the organizing committee stated, "We have decided that we are not ready to change the title at this point." This statement came in a form letter the organizing committee sent to those who wrote to protest the removal of "bisexual" from the conference title. It was also the gist of one of the organizers' discussions, at the fouth annual conference, of the fifth annual conference's title—a discussion that accompanied the circulation of a flyer announcing "Lesbian and Gay Studies Conference #5: Untitled. (ca. 1991)" The flyer included three columns of nouns and adjectives organized under the headings, "titles," "subtitles," and "entitlements." The terms "lesbian," "gay," and "bisexual" all appeared in the "subtitles" column (along with a number of other terms—see Figure 1), but only "lesbian" and "gay" appeared in what was, in fact, the title of the conference—contrary to what the word "untitled" might be meant to suggest. (In later correspondence, the word "untitled" was dropped altogether, and along with it the pretense that "Fifth Annual Lesbian and Gay Studies Conference" was not, in fact, the title of the conference.)

Several events took place simultaneously with the appearance of "bisexual" in the conference title. These simultaneous events included: the claim on the part of the organizing committee that they were choosing not to change the conference title even as they were changing it back to what it had been before; the claim that the conference was untitled, even as the title was the subject both of change and of claims that it was not the subject of change; the compilation and circulation of an extensive list of nouns and adjectives representing a number of potential differences within queer collectivities; and, finally, the distribution (to those who wrote to protest the change) of a form letter from the organizing committee expressing the sentiment that "this question about the conference and bisexuality itself should be important areas of discussion at the conference."

It is striking that the organizing committee represented their actions as a decision not to change when, in fact, they were changing the title, claiming not to be changing it, and claiming that there was no title. It is equally striking that the issue of whether "bisexual" should appear in the conference

Lesbian and Gay Studies Conference #5.

Untitled. (ca.1991)

TITLES	SUBTITLES	ENTITLEMENTS
Ablebodiness	Bisexual	Bodies
Age	Dyke	Canons
Class	Faggot	Communities
Education	Gay	Cultures
Ethnicity	Heterosexual	Families
Gender	Homosexual	Fashions
Generation	Invert	Histories
Language	Lesbian	Images
Nationality	Pervert	Institutions
Occupation	Queer	Laws
Race	Sodomite	Narratives
Region	Straight	Properties
Religion	Transsexual	Rights
Sex	Transvestite	Subjects

1-3 November 1991

At Rutgers University.
Sponsored by Rutgers and Princeton Universities.
Deadline for papers on all topics is 31 May 1991.
For information, contact Monica Dorenkamp or Beryle Chandler at:

Center for the Critical Analysis of Contemporary Culture (CCACC)
Rutgers, The State University of New Jersey
8 Bishop Place
New Brunswick, New Jersey 08903
(908) 932-8678 FAX: (908) 932-8683

title, and the sentiment that "bisexuality itself" (whatever that might mean) should be an important area of discussion at the conference, first inaugurated, and then came to stand in for, a discussion of a whole range of identities, practices, and differences (represented on the flyer) that, if taken into account, would have a profoundly destabilizing effect on the categories "lesbian" and "gay"—categories that have been retained, one can only conclude, as signifiers of the stability that is so much in question at the moment. In other words, *the destabilizing effects of all these points of difference were displaced onto bisexuality* by the committee's call for a discussion of bisexuality specifically, rather than of all the sexualities and other identifications represented by the terms listed on the flyer. In this way, not only is the homosexual/heterosexual dichotomy sustained; but also, crucial questions of race, ethnicity, class, and gender are suppressed. That is, as long as queer studies and other queer entities marginalize or suppress questions of, for example, race, then the terms "lesbian" and "gay" will continue to carry racialized connotations that implicitly reinforce the hegemony of whiteness in queer collectivities.

The message of the committee's actions seems to be that there is something uniquely destabilizing about bisexuality, whereas the categories "lesbian" and "gay" are more stable; and that once you throw bisexuality in, everything is up in the air: too complicated, unstable, impossible to define. But these conclusions make sense only if the heterosexual/homosexual binarism and the resistance to multiplicity go unchallenged. The fact is, of course, that everything is already complicated and unstable; definitions are always partial and provisional. The removal of "bisexual" while lesbian and gay remain, and the suppression of the other terms on the conference flyer from this call for discussion, are symptomatic of the way that the heterosexual/homosexual binarism is still so central to how we think, and of an abiding, generalized resistance to grapple with multiplicity and resist boiling several things down to two. This dogged adherence to binarisms arises from the apparent stability they seem to represent.[13]

And stability—or rather, its appearance—seems to be what is at stake when bisexuality is made to stand in for complexity in general, and when both bisexuality and complexity are then dismissed.

*****

This phenomenon of displacement and avoidance is clearly evident in other recent debates surrounding the question of what to call queer collectivities (such as communities and movements, organizations, pride marches, and academic conferences).[14] Many queer collectivities are choosing to add "bisexual" alongside "lesbian and gay" to their titles. This addition is double edged. On the one hand, it represents a long-overdue recognition of the presence of bisexuals in queer communities and queer political struggles, and of a burgeoning bisexual movement. On the other hand, adding "bisexual" alongside "lesbian and gay" can perpetuate the notion that the titles we give our organizations are inclusive—that they define the full spectrum of possible sexualities. That is, the addition somehow ratifies the notion that, by coming up with the right string of subject signifiers, we can reach a full solution to the problem of exclusion in representation. (That the term "queer" is less susceptible to this interpretation is one of its most appealing aspects.) Despite being double edged, however, the addition of "bisexual" to the names of queer organizations and events does signal an important step both toward addressing biphobia and, potentially, toward opening up our thinking beyond the homo/hetero binarism.

But we're also seeing another phenomenon: the removal of "bisexual" soon after it has been added to the titles of certain queer entities. The national queer studies conference is one example. The Northampton Pride March is another: "bisexual" was added to the march title one year, only to be voted out the following year by members of the local lesbian communities who organized precisely for that purpose, arguing that the presence of "bisexuality" in the march title rendered lesbians invisible. (They also voted bisexuals off the march steering committee.)[15]

Again, what is so interesting about this series of events is the particular capacity that acknowledgments of bisexuality seem to have for unsettling things, and the fact that that capacity seems to revolve around the anxiety of not knowing with which term in a binary opposition someone is aligned.[16] Moreover, bisexuality becomes the magnet for problems—in this case, the relative invisibility of lesbians within queer communities—that certainly stem from sources other than the assertion of a bisexual presence, and that would certainly persist even if bisexuals took the suggestion of some lesbians in this case to "go off to form their own community."

*****

These practical examples of displacement and avoidance surrounding bisexuality find parallels in the emerging field of queer theory. This field's otherwise careful and insightful projects are nonetheless practically uniform in leaving the homosexual/heterosexual binarism undisturbed—to the detriment of our understanding of sexuality and power. Two works will serve as brief examples here.

At the end of her groundbreaking study *Epistemology of the Closet*, Eve Sedgwick points out that, thus far, discussions of bisexuality don't "signal any movement at all on two analytic blockages as old as the century: the transitive/separatist question about gender identity, and the minoritizing/universalizing question about sexual definition" (251). This is because, in her examples, these discussions figure bisexual men as both effeminate and masculine, and as both a tiny minority and a potentially vast cross section of the population.

It seems more than a little odd that Sedgwick begins and abruptly ends her discussion of bisexuality in the last three pages of her study. Her virtual silence on bisexuality and the shortcomings of discussions of it begs explanation, given her laser-like attention to ambiguities and shortcomings in homosexual and ostensibly heterosexual representation. While it is true that most, if not all, discussions of bisexuality to date are in fact characterized by precisely the blockages she identifies, it may also be the case that further probing will reveal bisexuality to be not only an important subject of inquiry in itself but also a useful heuristic when it comes to looking at the general phenomenon of sexuality and its structuring within hetero/homo binarisms. For example, one way to expand on Sedgwick's work would be to turn her critique of the heterosexual/homosexual binarism to questions of its disciplining effects on people who would choose partners of either or both sexes, in addition to the effects on those who would choose partners only of their own sex.

There are no doubt other insights to be gleaned by addressing what Sedgwick's silences around bisexuality mean for her work in terms of some of the holes those silences produce, some of the subjects the silences allow to be glossed over. But what does it mean that after she tirelessly (and splendidly) interrogates queerness in representations of heterosexuality and homosexuality, for hundreds of pages, she then tacks bisexuality literally onto the end of her study, concluding (apparently without the need to demonstrate, as she does so thoroughly throughout the rest of her discussions) that what she has said about homosexuality in these portrayals applies to bisexuality as well? After plumbing the depths of matters overlooked to tease out insightful readings of queerness in canonical texts, is she simply "overlooking" bisexuality? And, if so, can this be due to anything more or less than the paralysis that takes hold when we try to contemplate more than two (binary) terms at one time?

Similar obfuscations operate in Mark Blasius's *Gay and Lesbian Politics: Sexuality and the Emergence of a New Ethic*. In his book, Blasius claims to articulate an experience universal among queers—the coming out process—from a perspective that is

> not primarily that of a category of subjective identity (the author's lived experience as a gay man of middle-class European American ancestry—although it has obviously been informed by it). Rather, I have tried to *create* perspective from the analytical category of *sexuality:* one that applies to all lesbians and gay men regardless of other differences. (6)

Blasius goes on to argue for an "ethic of reciprocity," which he says characterizes not only queer sexual relationships, but political ones as well. Lesbians and gay men, he says, have developed

> an erotics that integrates the pleasure of the other into one's own pleasure, an ethic of erotic reciprocity. As such, it is the creation of equality within and by means of sexual relationships. This can lead toward social equality (as it has to some degree with lesbian and gay communities—that is not to say there is no class, racial or ethnic, and age stratification there, merely that erotics offers a bridge across these divisions). . . . (125)

Replete with galloping generalizations and totalizing constructions of lesbianism and male homosexuality, Blasius's book manages to avoid engaging with the whole range of complicated and often painful differences that sometimes divide queers. The passage above represents a rare nod to those differences—one that he declines to follow with any real focused discussion of the implications of those differences for queer politics.

Blasius makes another nod that he does not follow up—this time to bisexuality and the homosexual/heterosexual binarism:

> the contemporary lesbian and gay movement, *to the extent that it incorporates bisexuals and transgendered people,* de-essentializes the sexual binary (male/female) itself, the "keeper" of heterosexuality.[17] (emphasis added)

Elsewhere, he asserts:

> The March on Washington document: (1) through the inclusion of bisexuals, challenges the teleological grounding of sexuality as an instinct; . . . [and] by the inclusion of transgender and cross-gender as a component of the freedom of expression of sexual identity, eliminates dimorphic biological sex or gender as the ground of what sexuality is at all.[18]

At first glance, these textual moments may seem to be unrelated. However, Blasius's project in this book is to limn that which is unique to lesbian and gay experience, and universal to lesbians and gay men, and to set that against heterosexuality. Given this project, and given his momentary acknowledgment of the potential for attention to bisexuality and transgenderism to upset sexual and gender binarisms, it may well be the case that he retains his own binary construction of queer and heterosexual experience only by failing to follow his own vague assertions about bisexuality and transgenderism to their logical conclusions.

In other words, Blasius's argument, which is an enthusiastic capitulation to the heterosexual/homosexual binary, can barely contain itself. If Blasius were to look fully at the challenges he claims bisexuality poses for that binary, it is unlikely that he could retain it intact. And once the homosexual/heterosexual binary raveled, he would no longer have any need to construct a homogenizing account of queers or to suppress the racial, class, gendered, or ethnic—let alone sexual—differences that often divide us from one another.

This is not to say that bisexuality is the "magic bullet" for totalizing constructions of sexuality. It is simply to say that bisexuality, brought into theoretical play, might exert enough pressure on those constructions to disrupt, irreparably, *sexually homogenized* accounts of queers. Doing so might in turn make way for disrupting the homogenization that takes place around race, gender, class, and other sources of difference that are so often suppressed in the service of constructing a coherent subject of queer theory and politics.

What Is to be Done?

I have argued here that queer theory and politics can gain from paying greater attention to bisexuality and its relation to the binarisms embedded in queer identity politics. This is true both in terms of exploring the largely uncharted territory of bisexual identity, bisexual theory and other bisexual writings, and bisexual politics; and in terms of using bisexuality heuristically, to find out what it can tell us about other queer identities, experiences, theories, and politics. What follows is a brief discussion of what these enterprises might entail.

Theorizing about bisexuality

Examining the ways the heterosexual/homosexual binarism structures theories about bisexual lives will entail, first of all, moving beyond the tendency in some bisexual theory to claim that bisexuality transcends this opposition. We should certainly examine the potential for some manifestations of bisexuality to *subvert* this opposition, just as we should examine the potential for various manifestations of lesbianism, male homosexuality, and male and female heterosexuality to subvert it. We should not, however, claim that the very existence of bisexuality—or of anything—*transcends* this opposition. We also need to look at how some of the theoretical work on bisexuality makes the mistake of accepting the premise that bisexuality embodies complexity and other sexual identities do not—a premise whose implications are both homophobic and biphobic. Just as we have come to recognize that lesbian relationships are in some way structured by the same gender divisions that structure the rest of society—they don't transcend those divisions, though they may in some cases work to subvert them—we need to recognize that bisexuality is imbricated in the homo/hetero binarism that structures the rest of society—it does not transcend that dichotomy, though it may in some cases work to subvert it. Our task should be to interrogate this imbrication with an eye to how it might be transformed—not to circumvent that difficult work as if by fiat.

A good way to begin theorizing about this imbrication of bisexuality in the heterosexual/homosexual binarism is by looking at examples of how that opposition gets mapped onto bisexuality in ways that construct bisexuality as a combination of heterosexuality and homosexuality, rather than as an identity unto itself; and the related phenomenon of some bisexuals referring to their "straight side" and their "lesbian/gay side." We need to explore the consequences of labels that identify, where bisexuals are concerned, the genders of the people in the relationship but not their sexualities, whereas the terms "lesbian," "gay," and "heterosexual" can signify both. That is, what are the consequences of the erasure of bisexual identity that takes place when bisexuals' relationships are labeled "lesbian" or "gay" if our partners are the same sex as us, or "heterosexual" if they are not?

For example, common among bisexuals is the experience of seeing our relationships to queer communities shift according to whether our lovers are the same sex as us. The pressures that bring about these shifts can take many forms and issue from many sources, but many of them certainly stem from a homosexual/heterosexual dichotomy that breaks people into respective "camps," assigns individuals to one or the other depending on how the gender of one's partner compares with one's own, and, on the same basis, derives conclusions about one's complicity with or resistance to homophobic oppression. The disciplining effects of such an arrangement are complex and extensive, not only for bisexuals but for lesbians, gay men, and heterosexuals as well (as in the example, above, of the gay man who chose not to identify as bisexual and to restrict himself to male partners because "nobody likes bisexuals"; or when bisexuals stay in the closet as such in queer contexts; or when lesbians and gay men feel discomfort, guilt, or fear at being found out for having sexual feelings toward members of the other sex; etc.). While they are not as calamitous, perhaps, as societal exhortations to heterosexuality, the disciplining effects of an enforced appearance of uncomplicated homosexuality need to be investigated to a much greater extent than they have been thus far in queer theory.

A second undertaking of bisexual theory, and of queer theory in general, should be to examine how projects celebrated by some bisexuals, such as the Kinsey Scale and Fritz Klein's Sexual Orientation Grid, reinscribe the heterosexual/homosexual opposition by continuing to characterize sexual orientation and identity solely in terms of gender. The Kinsey Scale places individuals on a continuum from zero (exclusively heterosexual) to six (exclusively homosexual), based on their sexual behavior (conceived nar-

rowly as genital sexual encounters leading to orgasm) as adults. Klein's tax-
onomy is a step up from conceptualizations like Kinsey's and others that
hinge completely on sexual *behavior* with respect to the gender of one's
partner. In Klein's method, one maps one's sexuality using Kinsey's numbers (zero to six) on a grid that charts gender preference in the past, present
(defined as "in the past year"), and "ideal future goal," with respect to sexual
and social attraction, sexual fantasies, and self-identification, along with sexual behavior (which nonetheless remains unspecified).[19] While both these
taxonomies accommodate the possibility of bisexuality, they retain an
approach to sexuality that focuses exclusively on gender in object choice.
Theoretical work on any sexual identity is more likely to gain from an
approach that takes into account the sort of wide-ranging array of sexual
differences, some relating to gender and some not, that Eve Sedgwick
advances in *Epistemology of the Closet*. In her study, Sedgwick proposes a
number of other differences to be considered as a way to refine our theoretical inquiries into sexuality. These factors include, among others, the different meanings to different people of identical "genital acts"; the different
degrees of importance different people attach to the psychic and/or physical
aspects of sex; and the degree to which different people feel that their
response to a sexual act, object, context, or role is innate or chosen.

Third, it will be theoretically useful to explore instances in queer praxis in
which the homo/hetero binarism seems to enable lesbians and gay men to operate under a double standard, denouncing bisexuality in the very terms to which
they strenuously object when used by homophobes to denounce lesbians and
gay men. For example, it bears investigating the discursive relationship that
emerged in debates surrounding the title of the "1993 March on Washington for
Lesbian, Gay and Bi Rights." In these debates, "bisexual" was constructed as
carrying sexual connotations that were too overt, and much more so than "lesbian" or "gay"; hence, the representation of bisexuals in the title of the march
was made conditional upon bisexuals accepting the designation "bi" over "bisexual."[20] What does it mean for the sexual liberation of lesbians and gay men, as
well as that of bisexuals, that this kind of internalized sex-phobia—so frequently
and devastatingly marshaled against all queers—was in this instance, at least,
mobilized against bisexuals from within a queer movement? What can this discursive incident reveal about the status and function of bisexuality in queer
movement politics?

Theorizing through bisexuality

Any theoretical work on sexuality in general would be greatly enhanced
by an examination not only of what bisexuality means for bisexuals, but of
how it functions in larger discourses around sexuality as well. Besides the
function I have identified here—that of standing in for complexity and insta-

bility—what other functions does bisexuality perform in discourses on sexuality? When does it get invoked, and how? When and why does it disappear, and with what effects? What other issues seem to attach to it, what questions does it perennially raise? What complications that appear when we theorize bisexuality actually exist for, but are obscured in theories about, lesbianism, male homosexuality, and male and female heterosexuality?

For example: how can theorizing the multiple closets bisexuals inhabit complicate a discussion of the closets gay men and lesbians inhabit? One of the closets bisexuals occupy is that which homophobia creates—that is, the closet produced by the need of some bisexuals to conceal same-sex desire, behavior, etc., in relation to heterosexist institutions and individuals, for the same reasons that some lesbians and gay men also need to do so. Another closet bisexuals inhabit is created specifically by biphobia within queer communities, such that bisexuals sometimes "pass" as gay or lesbian, concealing their bisexuality, in ways that are similar to the imperative some lesbians and gay men feel to conceal, in relation to queer communities, sexual interaction with or desire for members of the other sex.

Additionally, bisexuals sometimes "pass" as lesbians or gay men among heterosexuals for a number of reasons, including the sense that, in some situations, correcting a straight person's assumption that one is lesbian or gay with the statement, "I'm not lesbian/gay, I'm bisexual" is more likely to fuel homophobia than to combat it (because of the heterosexist construction of bisexuality in some discourses). Like the ways in which many lesbians and gay men feel the need in queer contexts to "closet" sexual desire for members of the other sex, they may also inhabit this closet—for reasons similar to bisexuals'—among heterosexuals, that is, to combat the heterosexist assumption that even queers are really straight at heart.

In some arguments against including bisexuals in queer collectivities, these closets are constructed as being primarily the province of bisexuals—a construction that works to isolate bisexuals, characterizing them as untrustworthy; and that also works to flatten the experiences of some lesbians and gay men, to keep them in these closets, and to simplify the complex negotiations they must make with regard to sexuality, identity, and power.

Theorizing bisexuals' multiple and complex relationships to the closet could begin to clarify bisexual realities. But it could also illuminate some of the hidden aspects of lesbian/gay experience, identity construction, and politicization, by looking at how lesbians and gay men feel they need to represent themselves—to other queers and to heterosexuals—and to what extent that coincides with their views of themselves, their own experiences, their identities.

Related to discourses about closets is the issue of heterosexual privilege: thus, another fruitful area of investigation would be the discursive relationship between bisexuality and heterosexual privilege, and what that relationship reveals or obscures (and with what effects) about important realities in the lives of bisexuals, as well as those of lesbians and gay men, who also, of course, can occupy myriad positions in relation to heterosexual privilege.

These are just some of the questions that emerge from a strategy of theorizing *from* bisexuality—that is, theorizing bisexual lives—and theorizing *through* bisexuality to gain insights into the construction and deployment of other sexualities as well. This strategy has a great deal to offer queer theory and politics.

Notes

My thanks to Linda Nicholson, Trevor Hope, and Kim Christensen for helping me to clarify some of the ideas I present here, and to Shane Phelan for her comments on earlier versions of this article.

1. For example, the 1990 pride march in Northampton, Massachusetts, was preceded by a bitter struggle in which members of the lesbian community organized to remove "bisexual" from the march title and bisexuals from the steering committee.

2. One example is a students' organization at Cornell University that over the past decade has gone from being called the Cornell Lesbian and Gay Coalition to the Cornell Lesbian, Gay and Bisexual Coalition to the Cornell Lesbian, Gay, Bisexual and Transgendered Coalition.

3. I encountered the latter response from the editorial board of *OUT/LOOK: National Lesbian & Gay Quarterly* when I submitted a piece on bisexuality to that journal in 1991. OUT/LOOK's Spring 1992 issue featured its first and only article on bisexuality, whose inauspicious title, "What do Bisexuals Want?" was followed by a "debate" between Ara Wilson and Carol A. Queen (the latter a bisexual woman) over the legitimacy of bisexuals' claims to inclusion in queer movements.

4. The Fourth Annual Lesbian, Bisexual and Gay Studies (Harvard, 1990) and the Fifth Annual Lesbian and Gay Studies (Rutgers, 1991) conferences are cases in point: at these conferences, papers concerning bisexuality were clustered in two or three panels, regardless of their topic, while bisexuality went unrepresented—even unmentioned—in more general panels on such topics as "new directions in queer theory." Moreover, conference organizers sometimes neglect to ensure at least a nominally bi-positive setting even for these panels. For example, organizers for the Fifth Annual conference assigned the job of moderator of a panel on bisexuality to Martin Duberman, who, at the beginning of the session, felt compelled to inform the audience, "I'm not bisexual. I've never had a bisexual impulse in my life."

5. Mark Blasius, *Gay and Lesbian Politics: Sexuality and the Emergence of a New Ethic* (Philadelphia: Temple University Press, 1994), 82, 204.

6. Eve Kosofsky Sedgwick, *Epistemology of the Closet* (Berkeley/Los Angeles: University of California Press, 1990), 22.

7. Greta Christina, "Drawing the Line: Bisexual Women in the Lesbian Community," in *On Our Backs: the magazine for adventurous lesbians* (May–June 1990), 14–15.

8. Biddy Martin, "Sexual Practice and Changing Lesbian Identities," in Michele Barrett and Anne Phillips, eds., *Destabilizing Theory: Contemporary Feminist Debates* (Stanford: Stanford University Press, 1991), 97–9

9. Ibid., 99.

10. Ibid., 98. Moreover, as Martin points out, these rituals reflect the relatively disadvantaged positions of those who conduct them. She writes: "I would suggest that they are also ritualistic efforts to deal with what is experienced as loss, and exhibit all the forms of denial that accompany unresolved losses. Surely the perceived need for uniformity, authenticity and firm, separate foundations in a world outside of heterosexuality operates as a defence against the continued marginalization, denial and prohibition of women's love and desire for other women".

11. Judith Butler, *Gender Trouble: Feminism and the Subversion of Identity* (New York: Routledge, 1990), 2.

12. "Bisexual" reappeared in the title of the national queer studies conference held in Iowa in November 1994.

13. Eve Sedgwick argues (in *Epistemology of the Closet*) that it is the appearance of a secure boundary demarcating the terms in the homo/hetero binarism that is at stake in the physical and symbolic violence directed at queers so routinely in our culture. Leslie Feinberg's novel, *Stone Butch Blues* (Ithaca, NY: Firebrand Books, 1992), painfully illustrates the violence with which this appearance of stable binarisms is relentlessly enforced with respect to lines of gender and sexuality in the lives of butch lesbians.

14. Calling them "queer" is, of course, one option, and a good one. Some people balk at this, both out of concern that the term might not be the most intelligible and effective one for intervening in certain institutional settings, and out of a sense that there has been too much homophobic hatred and violence associated with the term for it to be reclaimed, for its meanings to be sufficiently transfigurable. My own view is that "queer" can be a very useful term, both because of its association with

the reemergence of radical, antihomophobic direct action activism; and because its meaning is both sufficiently intelligible and sufficiently ambiguous to encompass a wide range of nonhegemonic sexualities without needing to impose rigid definitions on them, or to mark fixed boundaries that determine what is and isn't queer.

Of course, as with any term, "queer" lends itself to multiple and sometimes contradictory interpretations and uses. All too often, "queer" is used interchangeably with "lesbian" and "gay." In these cases, the use of "queer" doesn't seem to result in the articulation of sexualities other than "lesbian" and "gay." "Queer"'s potential to articulate and advance an expanded view of what constitutes a nonhegemonic and potentially subversive sexuality depends on how it is used. Certainly, when it is implicitly equated only with "lesbian/gay," it doesn't expand much of anything. When it is explicitly equated with "lesbian/gay" only, as in the case of a few Queer Nation chapters in the United States and Canada that reportedly exclude self-identified bisexuals, its use can be simply reactionary. There are, however, many examples of the term "queer" initiating or representing a progressive expansion of how we think about sexuality, politics, and the subversion of sexual hegemony and repression.

15. For an in-depth discussion of these events, see Stacey Young, "Bisexuality, Lesbian and Gay Communities, and the Limits of Identity Politics," in *Bisexual Politics: Queries, Theories, and Visions,* edited by Naomi Tucker (Binghamton, NY: Haworth Press, 1995).

16. Of course, it comes up when people raise the issue of other sexual minorities within the queer community as well, particularly when the sexual minorities in question explicitly blur the lines of the male/female binarism—transgenderists, transsexuals, cross-dressers. Just as bisexuals blur the lines of (homo/hetero) sexual binarisms, those who blur the lines of gender binarisms evoke the anxiety of not knowing.

17. Blasius, *Gay and Lesbian Politics,* 125–26.

18. Ibid., 174.

19. For a discussion of Kinsey and Klein, see Amanda Udis-Kessler, "Appendix: Notes on the Kinsey Scale and Other Measures of Sexuality" in *Closer to Home: Bisexuality and Feminism,* edited by Elizabeth Reba Weise (Seattle: Seal Press, 1992), 311–18.

20. This debate was covered in *Gay Community News* in the spring of 1992.

4

Lesbians and Mestizas: Appropriation and Equivalence

Shane Phelan

Early models of oppressions as additive have increasingly given way to an understanding that oppression and resistance are lived as unities, and that another way of understanding the cumulative effects of multiple oppressions must be formulated. The Combahee River Collective described oppressions as "interlocking," stating that "the synthesis of these oppressions creates the conditions of our lives."[1] More recently, Gloria Anzaldúa's concept of the "new mestiza" illuminates a view of multiple oppression as the site of a new consciousness, a consciousness with a heightened appreciation of ambiguity and multiplicity. The effect of interlocking systems of power is to prevent a secure singular identity. This is not a weakness, but a strength; only such a dislocation can provoke the awareness of possibilities and the tolerance of ambiguity that she sees as requirements for real social change.

Anzaldúa's work on the new mestiza intersects two disparate discussions about lesbian identity. The first is the discussion, largely among white gay men, of sexuality as ethnicity. The second, more "lesbian" usage, refers less to "the facts" about sexuality and more to mestiza consciousness, a possibility of thought that might prove fruitful for all people. In this second conversation, the mestiza appears as an "inappropriate/d other," as one who challenges existing categories by her refusal or inability to fit within them.[2] After addressing the first discussion, I will return to the question of mestiza position and consciousness as a model for feminist theory. Lesbianism is a locus of social oppression, but not one that is simply analogous to race. The simple analogy, and a politics built on the theory that all oppressions are the same because they share a pattern of inequality, is culturally imperialist. The image of the mestiza has tremendous power and attraction for many white lesbians, but we cannot for that reason simply adopt it as our own. Nonetheless, Anzaldúa's vision and description provide an ontological account of coalitional identity politics that is sorely needed.

Race and Ethnicity

In their work on *Racial Formation in the United States From the 1960s to the 1980s*, Michael Omi and Howard Winant describe the paradigms by which races have been constructed and understood in the United States. The dominant paradigm, which they term "ethnicity-based" theory, seeks to describe race as a social grouping rather than a biological one. Ethnicity theory bypasses race in favor of culture, or, more accurately, it rewrites racial difference as equivalent to other cultural and historical group differences. In this theoretical frame, blacks in the U.S. are an ethnic group in the same way as Italian-Americans. Omi and Winant note the Euro-American bias of this equation, both for its rejection of any distinctive difference between "white" ethnic groups and "black" or other racial groups, and also for the treatment of blacks as a single ethnic group without acknowledgement of either the tribal differences before enslavement or regional differences in the United States.

The central concerns of ethnicity theory desribed by Omi and Winant are the "incorporation and separation of 'ethnic minorities,' the nature of ethnic identity, and the impact of ethnicity on politics."[3] The ethnicity model is the research paradigm of liberal politics. Founded in a rejection of biological racial theory, the ethnicity paradigm spoke to the experience of European immigrants, with their dilemmas of assimilation and "getting ahead" versus maintaining cultural identity. Cultural identity became a "private" matter, irrelevant to one's work and legal position. This conceptualization's affinity with liberalism is clear. In a liberal world, we are united by laws and, secondarily, by economic interdependence, but culture is irrelevant to the public sphere.

This blindness, or impoverishment, in liberal visions of the polity produces a number of reactions. The most faithful child of this vision of ethnicity is what Daniel Bell has labeled "the new ethnicity." The "new ethnicity" has changed the conception of ethnicity from something private and simply affective to a bifurcation between an explicitly political identity, aimed at the state and interest-group politics, and an "expressive" moment of "community." Bell suggests that the new ethnicity can be seen as either "the emergent expression of primordial feelings" or as "a 'strategic site,' chosen by disadvantaged persons as a new mode of seeking political redress in the society."[4] In fact, the two are not exclusive; as a reaction to the impersonal bureaucratic political and social culture of the late-twentieth–century U.S., ethnic identity provides a site for community and interpersonal relations. The feelings expressed may not be "primordial" in the sense of a stable if unacknowledged complex of attachments and values, but they are quickly rearticulated and experienced as such. The new ethnicity may be clearly political, but it is also a response to cultural impoverishment.

A second response to the narrowness of liberalism is the rejection of the ethnicity paradigm in favor of visions that allow for the force of culture as a binding element in human life. Omi and Winant identify class theory and nation theory as the primary paradigms of critical work on race. Class theory seeks to understand race in terms of the "social allocation of advantage and disadvantage," in economic terms, while nation-based theories focus on "cultural autonomy and the right to self-determination" as a people.[5]

Both of these theories gained a certain strength from the historical conditions of people of color in the United States. Segregation, whether official or not, forced the development of institutions and identities for people wholly overlooked or excluded from white definitions of the U.S. and its institutions of culture and power. White recognition of the "activities and institutions" of people of color relied upon their resemblance to white ones; "truly indigenous activities and institutions qualitatively distinct from majority values" (that is, ones that did not simply translate into the cultural language of the dominant society), remained invisible and thus bereft of hegemonic legitimation.[6]

Segregation and poverty lent themselves to two contrasting images of race. Mario Barrera describes how the focus on poverty among Chicanos led many to adopt a Marxist analysis in which all Chicanos were by definition part of the working class.[7] This argument has always run up against the political reality that the call for class unity "has amounted in practice to an argument that nonwhites give up their racially based demands in favor of 'class' unity on white terms."[8] In contrast, the argument for nationhood has relied upon the idea of a homeland, locating racial oppression within a narrative of national oppression and colonialism. The political consequence has generally been separatist, focusing on the development of "indigenous" organizations and institutions and the reclamation of culture. This has led both to culturally strong, vital communities and to political marginalization, as mainstream politicians learned that these groups often will not participate in any event. More dangerously, members of such nationalist communities often became "consumers of their own culture,"[9] and saw this consumption as political activity sufficient unto itself. In this way, nationalism and capitalism intertwine.

Before moving on to consider whether sexuality "is like" ethnicity, it is important to underscore that the ethnicity model does not simply describe something, "ethnicity," that is out in the world, but is rather one articulation of differences. Its historical links to liberalism have made it a powerful articulation for interest-group politics in the form of the "new ethnicity." As an articulation that serves primarily to assimilate and pacify rather than to bring differences into the sphere of critical recognition, however, it is questionable whether ethnicity is an adequate paradigm for any radical social movement.

Sexuality as Ethnicity

Ethnicity has provided a powerful self-understanding for many whites from nondominant groups, such as Southern and Eastern Europeans.[10] It has spoken to the experience of people whose aim truly has been assimilation, and who have felt the pain of successful assimilation in the loss of historical identification. It has also been one powerful model for liberal feminism, with its agenda of assimilation into the male public world. Racial metaphors, on the other hand, have provided a different ground for political imagination. Race in the U.S. has been the mark of the unassimilable, the "truly different." As a result, movements defined "racially" have vacillated between the poles of assimilation and nationalism in a manner unavailable to "ethnic minorities."

The project of gay/lesbian liberation was conceived in the United States along the lines of ethnic or racial politics, largely because that seemed politically effective.[11] The impact of the Civil Rights and Black Power movements on the U.S. political imagination made them ripe for imitation. The white feminist movement as well as the gay and lesbian movements appropriated not only the (often contradictory) arguments for civil rights and for group pride but also the descriptions and metaphors of position; as Kobena Mercer has described the situation in Britain, "[b]lack pride acted as metonymic leverage for the expression of 'gay pride' just as notions of 'brotherhood' and 'community' in black political discourse influenced the assertions of 'global sisterhood' or 'sisterhood is strength.'"[12] The large component of cultural nationalism in radical lesbian/gay politics is a result of this "racial" articulation.

Ethnic and racial articulations of sexuality have coexisted in uneasy balances in various cities for almost fifty years now. Both, however, have revolved around the same axis of essentialism that leads to so much confusion and pain. While they are politically efficacious in their hold on popular imagination and their implicit political prescriptions, they must be carefully negotiated if lesbians and gays are to avoid simple imitation of some of the worst features of those articulations.

Treating sexuality as ethnicity requires a certain amount of essentialism.[13] By this I mean that sexuality must come to seem as much a matter of "primordial affinities and attachments" as ethnicity does to most Americans.[14] Sexuality, specifically sexual object choice, must come to be seen as given and stable over the lifetime of an individual. This stability, in turn, should then be described as resting upon or resulting from a sexual identity, a persistent attribute beyond "behavior." This interpretation of sexuality in fact coincides with prevailing United States characterizations, in which people "really are" heterosexual or homosexual (though homosexuality is a regrettable, hopefully curable, condition). Sexual activity does not inevitably dictate sexual identity—one may occasionally engage in "lesbian sex" while identifying as a heterosexual—but generally such a person is presumed by both lesbians and gays and heterosexuals to be in a state of denial about the "truth" of their identity.

Barbara Ponse describes the heterosexist "principle of consistency" that links sex assignment, gender identity, gender role, sexual object choice, and sexual identity. Through this linkage, "female" comes to be equated with "woman," which in turn is linked to "heterosexual" (in this case, attraction to men). Thus, a lesbian is not "really" a woman. Her gender identity ("woman") conflicts with her sexual identity ("lesbian"), and this conflict is resolved through the stereotype of the "masculine" lesbian as the "real" lesbian.[15]

Ponse argues that, far from rejecting this principle of consistency, lesbians adopt a corresponding "gay trajectory" of lesbian identity formation that "functions as a biographic norm" among white lesbians.[16] The trajectory moves from "a subjective sense of being different from heterosexual persons" that is attributed to attraction to women, to "an understanding of the homosexual or lesbian significance of these feelings." The third stage is acceptance of a lesbian identity—"coming out." On this basis, the individual searches for a community and for lesbian sexual and emotional relationships. As Ponse notes, any one of these elements is sufficient to establish the belief among lesbians that a woman is "lesbian," whether she acknowledges it or not. Lesbian explanations of sexual identity conform to what Omi and Winant term the rule of "hypo-descent" in race categorizing.[17] In racial theory, hypo-descent is the rule that "even a little" makes one "really" one race or another, usually a stigmatized one. The lesbian corollary to this is the belief that "even a little" lesbian sexual desire makes one "really" a lesbian, as though desire (and race) were discreet entities, categorized by nature. Thus, both the heterosexual and the lesbian stories assume a fixed reality about one's "true" sexual identity, and seek explanations for deviations and anomalies.

This assumption has been increasingly problematic for lesbians. The room for lesbians within white feminism, even the sanctioning of lesbian relationships as "feminism in action," has provided a means for many white women to identify as lesbians on the basis of political and affective ties rather than sexual activity.[18] Such choices, however, have given a different twist to essentialism among white feminist lesbians. Here, the essentialism is less about lesbianism as object choice than it is about male and female natures and heterosexual relations. Early arguments about "sleeping with the enemy" presumed a monolithic male nature and a correspondingly unambiguous feminist politics. Lesbians, in this interpretation, are the ones who leave the world of (male or patriarchal) nature for the realm of (female or feminist) freedom.[19]

Notions of primordial affinities have not, however, been sufficient in themselves to establish an ethnic articulation of sexuality. The second element of the ethnic model is having a culture and a history. Some lesbians and gay men have worked at establishing historical linkages and claiming ancestors as part of the project of "ethnicizing" sexuality. For example, Judy Grahn has argued that "Gay (sic) culture is ancient and has been suppressed into an underground state of being," but that it nonetheless is "continuous."[20] To make her point, Grahn moves across continents, time, and sexual desires. She includes as ancestors women who had sex exclusively with men, but who defy modern white stereotypes of "feminine" behavior.[21] For Grahn, the early feminist slogan that "feminism is the theory, lesbianism is the practice" is transformed into "acting in ways that feminists now celebrate makes one a lesbian." Thus, the lesbian appropriation of unconventional women described by Ponse is extended by Grahn across time and culture.

Grahn's project belies her experience of growing up in a lesbophobic, medicalized society. For her, the decisive marker of lesbianism in the past is gender-role inversion. As Scott Bravmann has noted, Grahn's project ignores the fact that non-European societies do not always assign and link gender and sexuality as European and Euro-American ones do: thus the berdache, interpreted by Euro-Americans as "homosexual," is defined (within those Native American cultures where berdache is an institution) not by "sexual orientation" but by a different alignment between biological sex and social gender than the prevailing one.[22] The "recovery" work of writers such as Grahn amounts to colonization of other cultures for the service of a contemporary, largely Euro-American, movement. In so doing, this work treats the other cultures and contemporary lesbians incompletely. The centrality of inversion belies a prefeminist, medicalized understanding of homosexuality. In extending this alignment of gender and desire to other cultures, it misrepresents them as well.[23]

The creation of a history is part of an effort to justify our lives. "Successful" justification will not be a matter of demonstrating longevity, however; Jewish, Christian, and Muslim fundamentalists all agree that sodomy was practiced at Sodom. Nor will the demonstration that "homosexuality is a way of being," rather than a "behavior," be sufficient to end oppression.[24] Medicalization was precisely that demonstration, but it has not served lesbians and gays well. Even the argument that there is and has been a "culture" will not stop the "cultural war" of the Right; Europeans and Euro-Americans (including white women, gay men, and some lesbians) have proved willing, and even zealous, to destroy other cultures.[25] The New Right is perfectly willing to talk of a "gay culture," and to accuse its members of destroying the United States. Invented traditions will not do the work of politics for us. This does not mean that any attempts to treat the past and honor heroes are mistaken. It does mean that such attempts must always be modest, aware of their limitations and possible pitfalls.

Postmodern Ethnicity

Postmodernism works to deconstruct not only lesbian claims to ethnicity, but the general category of ethnicity itself. In this postmodern theorists are not alone, but are joined by the whole range of "social constructionists" who have called into question the view of ethnicity as primordial rather than strategic or functional. In the latter view, known variously as "circumstantialist," "optionalist," or "social constructionist," ethnicity is "a strategic possibility peculiarly suited to the requirements of political and social mobilization in the modern large-scale state."[26] Ethnicity becomes a matter of "putative" rather than "absolute" ascription,[27] distinguishable from voluntary affiliation not in kind but in degree.

The conceptual opposition of voluntary association and absolute ascription rests on liberal models of society in which one is either the agent of voluntary association (that is, with no necessary pressure beyond "subjective affinity") or one is fixed in social space by factors beyond one's control. Marx's exposure of the ideological functions of this opposition within capitalism did not enable him to overcome it in his own thought, and Marxism has for a century oscillated between voluntarism and various determinisms. Thoroughly challenging this model requires that we question the idea of "society" as a "founding totality of its partial processes,"[28] and work instead on describing social relations as articulatory practices that produce and/or modify the identities of individuals. "Ethnicity" then can be seen as one such articulation, a "construction of nodal points which partially fix meaning."[29]

With such a view, the question can no longer be stated, "Is lesbianism analogous to ethnicity?" Instead, the question is, "What are the implications of such an analogy? What sort of relations are established through this articulation of lesbianism?"

As developed by writers such as Grahn, the ethnic model has little to offer feminist lesbians. This is so for several reasons. First, the articulation often relies on an essentialist view of lesbianism, a view that I challenged in the preceding section. This essentialism may speak to the experience of lifelong lesbians, but it cannot adequately address the desires and understandings of those who came to women later in life. Second, the ethnicity model relies fundamentally on a medicalized view of sexuality, in which sexual object choice and gender identity are "naturally" aligned. Finally, this articulation enacts a "natural" identity with gay men, an identity that many feminist lesbians would challenge. This is perhaps the reason why so few lesbians have involved themselves in the ethnicity debates at all. As lesbians and gays move into open political battles in the U.S., however, the ethnic analogy appears more commonly, and thus deserves discussion. I will argue later that we do not need this analogy to argue for civil rights. If we do not need the ethnic paradigm for civil rights, and given its dangers of cultural nationalism and essentialism, then we can and should dispense with it.

Lesbianism: A New Mestizaje?

There is another "racial" articulation that has been attractive to many white lesbians. This is the vision of the mestiza described most notably by Gloria Anzaldúa. In *Borderlands/La Frontera*, Anzaldúa describes and enacts mestiza history and consciousness.[30] The history of the U.S. Southwest, of Aztlan, is a history of conquest upon conquest, of Indian mixing with Spaniard, Anglo, and Afro-American. In this, it resembles the rest of the U.S., indeed of the American continents. The distinctive feature of the Southwest is the survival of indigenous people as distinct peoples, and simultaneously as mixtures, as living history of rapes and slaughters and loves and memories. This demarcation, which is always shifting, is evident even in the names used to delineate heritage: *Chicano* has implications quite contrary to those of *Spanish-American* or *Mexican-American*, and, as John Garcia notes, "one's ethnic label choice may vary with the social setting."[31] Anzaldúa's self-labeling as a Chicana marks her off as politically radical, proud of her border existence, seeking neither the purity of Indian ancestry nor the privilege of the Spanish, but instead looking for distinctive values in mestiza history.[32]

Anzaldúa's lesbianism prevents her full or easy assimilation into Chicana culture, just as her ethnic heritage marks her within white lesbian communities. She compares the two exclusions, treating them as bridges instead:

> As a *mestiza* I have no country, my homeland cast me out; yet all countries are mine because I am every woman's sister or potential lover. (As a lesbian I have no race, my own people disclaim me; but I am all races because there is the queer of me in all races.)[33]

In many ways, Anzaldúa's formulation might be read as a reification of lesbian identity; references to "the queer of me," statements that lesbians have "no race" *qua* lesbians, might appear to reinstate "modern" universalist notions of identity. That is not Anzaldúa's meaning here, however. She does not state that she "is" raceless, but that her "own people" reject and deny her. She retains a link to "all races" through her connections with other lesbians. This is clarified in a later essay, when she states that "Though the deepest connections colored dykes have is to their native culture, we also have strong links with other races, including whites. Though right now there is a strong return to nationalist feeling, colored lesbian feminists in our everyday interactions are truly more citizens of the planet."[34] This is not simply a matter of the good will of lesbian feminists, but instead reflects that "white culture and its perspectives are inscribed on us/into us."[35]

Perhaps the most important lesson for white lesbians to learn from Anzaldúa's discussion is the rejection of "ontological separatism." The heterosexist rejection of lesbians as belonging somewhere else, usually to an enemy, is matched by a separatist vision in which lesbians are not "really" of the world in which they were raised and encountered their pain and isolation. Ontological separatism is distinct from certain political separatisms that focus on the need for a moment of separation to build and reinforce threatened identities. Where the latter treats separatism not as a final solution but as part of a movement toward general social change, the former describes separatism as an acknowledgement of the fundamental and permanent differences between men and women (or lesbians and everyone else) that make common action impossible.[36]

The mestiza has moments of separation, but the more fundamental aspect of mestizaje is the dual inability ever to fully separate or fully belong. If "belonging" requires exclusion of the other(s), the mestiza can only belong by sacrificing part of herself; and in this case, then not all of her has lived to belong. Whatever survives is not mestiza so much as part of a person. Separation likewise is a denial of her own reality, of elements of her life that remain meaningful. As a consequence, the mestiza focuses on blending, on inclusion rather than exclusion. This blending is not simply transcendence of conflict and opposition, but internalization of the struggle. Mestizas belong even where "their own people" deny it, through their connections to actual others.[37]

Thus, mestiza identities are paradigmatic of postmodern social ontology, in which social identities are treated as "the meeting point for a multiplicity of articulatory practices, many of them antagonistic."[38] Mestizaje is not an essence, but is the very transgression of essence, a "point of departure, a mark of difference, allowing for the expression of other differences."[39] Mestizas "juggle cultures" with "plural personalit[ies]."[40] This is not a valorization of dissociation or multiple personality syndrome, as some critics have charged. The multiplicity of the mestiza is not simply internal fracture, a failure to build an integrated personality, but is a socio-historical reality. Against those who would have mestizas "choose" one aspect of their lives, one culture over others, Anzaldúa insists that all of her "personalities" are part of her integrated self. This is evident in Anzaldúa's writing, in which the "we" shifts from page to page, meaning sometimes queers, sometimes Chicano/as, sometimes feminists. Her contextualization of this shifting "we" removes the possibility of reading her statements as simple calls for unity, instead calling on us to acknowledge all of her locations at once and equally.

This does not mean that Anzaldúa is "postmodern," or that every aspect of the mestiza is replicated and captured by poststructuralist theory. The belongingness of the mestiza for Anzaldúa is not simply a matter of choice, of voluntary affiliation, but of history and social density. In that evocation of history and rebellion, and in her political commitment, she is allied with Michel Foucault. She is not simply "Foucaultian," however, as if reading Foucault would tell us what Anzaldúa thinks. She retains a sense of the mystery at the heart of being that vanishes from Foucault's later work. In that recognition of mystery she is on the same path as Lyotard, Nancy, and Derrida, but she provides a more forceful alliance of strong politics and philosophical humility than do they. Her recognition of the incompleteness of every identity and every project does not lead her to inaction, to continual deferral of politics as has been the case for so many poststructuralists or postmodernist thinkers.[41] Rather, it leads her to a "radical acceptance of vulnerability,"[42] in Gayatri Spivak's terms. The mestiza is defined by her shifting territories and incomplete identifications, but the instability and incompleteness of the territories and identifications does not render them less "real" than more unitary ones. They point to the historical, rather than ontological, nature of all territories and identities.

As lesbians, we (both white lesbians and lesbians of color) are often denied by our families or our communities, cut off from major social institutions, but the fact of our birth and life within those communities and cultures is not so easily erased within us. We may be defined as other, but in fact we are always here, always present before those who would deny us. Lesbianism does not locate us as members of one culture who are trapped by birth or circumstance in an alien land. As Iris Young explains, difference "is not absolute otherness, a complete absence of relationship or shared attributes,"[43] but exists within a field of discourse that provides the system of relationships of same/other, similar/different. To the extent that white middle-class lesbians refuse difference and insist on otherness, on absolute exclusion, we replicate the prevailing structures of domination.

Rather than being marginal, rather perhaps even than being liminal, lesbians are central to the societies that repudiate them. We are not accepted as lesbians, but this is insufficient to demonstrate that there is a somewhere else we really belong. It is tempting to think that we must fully belong somewhere, but the temptation must be resisted.[44] The ideal of full and uncomplicated belonging rests on the ideal of the unitary, harmonious self, thus demanding that we seek out and eliminate the obstacles to this harmonious unity.

This does not mean that there is not, will not be, or should not be any such thing as "lesbian culture." Lesbian cultures are becoming a social reality; the question is not whether to build lesbian cultures, but what sort of cultures we want to build.[45] The historical development of lesbian communities alerts us to the fact that there is no one such thing as "lesbian culture" for all of us to belong to; rather, there are many lesbian cultures or subcultures. "Lesbian culture" cannot be a monolith or a totality that encompasses all of our lives, and this is a strength. We must recognize and retain our positions in the dominant society, both as a group and as individuals, or we risk losing important parts of our selves as well as any possibility for political intervention.

Interpretation and Appropriation

There are two straightforward arguments to be made for the legitimacy of the use of the mestiza concept to describe white lesbian lives. The first is that Anzaldúa understands mestizaje in this way, and that therefore such a use is simply faithful to her intent. This argument is easily dismissed by a reading of her later references to mestizas. In her 1988 plenary address to the National Women's Studies Association, Anzaldúa refers repeatedly to "mestiza lesbians" and "mestiza queer persons."[46] She contrasts these people with "white lesbians," the people with whom mestizas must make alliances. For Anzaldúa, it seems, mestizaje is a racial or ethnic category. Though mestizas may also be lesbians, mestizaje is used by Anzaldúa as a racial, not a sexual, category.

The second, more complex, argument rests on the analogy between lesbianism and mestizaje as loci of oppression and oppositional culture. This is the position that, whether Anzaldúa intended lesbianism to be understood as mestizaje, it is proper to use it this way. There are several elements to such an argument. First, we must argue that appropriation of an author's ideas in a way they may not endorse is "fair" in public academic relations. This is usually assumed in cases where the relevant authors are from dominant groups.[47] But does Anzaldúa's position as a lesbian of color change the rules here?

Several feminist authors have begun writing about the limits of white women's interpretation of the texts of women of color, but there has been less discussion about the appropriate use of those texts for analysis of white women's lives.[48] This gap is primarily due to the hegemonic position of white feminist theory, which leads white women too often to read the work of women of color as anthropology, as learning about others, rather than using these texts for introspection. Thus, for instance, virtually all feminists now acknowledge that our analyses must allow for the effects of race and class in the lives of those who have been marked as inferior within those structures, but white feminists too often fail to examine the effects of race on white women or of class on middle- or upper-class white women.[49]

Feminists then need to discuss how much or in what ways the theory of women of color can be used by white women in our descriptions of our situations. I don't think that there will be a blanket answer to this problem. Kobena Mercer distinguishes, for example, between the appropriation involved in the "White Negro," a figure representative of white alienation from middle-class white culture, embodied most fully in Elvis Presley and Mick Jagger, and the identification of Jean Genet with the Black Panthers and Palestinian freedom fighters. The first operates from a basis of unconsciousness and rejection, an unconsciousness that leads to appropriation rather than political solidarity. Genet's position is rather one that "does not attempt to master or assimilate difference but which speaks from a - position of equality as part of a shared struggle to decolonize models of subjectivity."[50]

This example suggests that the first imperative is that identification should always acknowledge the differences between the social location of the original author and that of the user. This acknowledgement includes the willingness to listen and be corrected for one's mistakes, for, as Trinh T. Minh-ha puts it,

> hegemony works at leveling out differences and at standardizing contexts and expectations in the smallest details of our daily lives. Uncovering this leveling of differences is, therefore, resisting that very notion of difference which defined in the master's terms often resorts to the simplicity of essences.[51]

Resistance to the "leveling of differences" requires a careful attention to the details of history and daily life that produce particular positions and consciousnesses. This must be balanced by a recognition that such details will never fully account for any position or consciousness, that "differences do not only exist between outsider and insider," but also "within the outsider herself, or the insider herself."[52]

One of the consequences of the recognition of difference has been the argument that white women should not presume to interpret the work of women of color, because such interpretation is always an appropriative act performed from a hegemonic position. This argument founders both theoretically and politically. It is not possible to read without interpretation; such a distinction relies on positivistic notions of reading that cannot be sustained. The political consequence of the injunction is to reinforce the gap, to freeze white women into their privilege and its accompanying narrowness, by locking the doors of otherness against them. Such a politics bars any hope of common understanding.[53]

Moving from the idea of "difference," which all too often lends itself to such unbridgeable gaps, toward specificity of locations or "identity points," allows us to acknowledge inequalities of power and position (as well as differences not so easily captured in a linear frame of measurement) while through that very acknowledgment discovering and articulating the linkages between us.[54] Specificity provides the ground for commonality without sameness, and so allows for the possibility of antihegemonic appropriation.

As currently used, mestizaje refers to a historical experience of oppression and resistance, of living within and also transgressing categories of race that structure domination within the United States. It does not refer to any mixing of cultures or identities, but to the specific history of Aztlan. In the United States, this politically important distinction is endangered by white appropriation. The United States is the land of the melting pot, within certain narrow limits. The very term "white" is justifiable largely because Christian European-Americans have succeeded in melting into something of a stew, rather than retaining a central focus on the nations from which they or their ancestors emigrated. What, then, is to prevent white heterosexual males from adopting the label of mestizo and claiming equality of position with Chicana lesbians?[55] What is to prevent the total demolition of mestizaje into a useless category? The political danger of conceptualizing white lesbians as mestizas lies not in the interpretation of lesbian identity and politics but in making an imitation that obscures relevant distinctions in racial battles, and thereby failing as allies.

Someone might take this point into account without abandoning the concept entirely. They might do this by describing clearly the differences between ethnicity and race in the U.S., differences that define the limits of the melting pot's ingredients. When this is done, we see that "white" people in the U.S. are often "mutts," but that their differing ethnic "roots" do not provide a basis for current oppression; they are not publicly relevant, but are now simply matters of affective resonance. This can be seen most clearly in the observation that the law of hypo-descent does not apply among whites; we do not debate about whether someone is "really" Hungarian or French or English, as we routinely do about whether someone is "really" black or Native American or Jewish or Hispanic. The essentialism that marks racial discourse off from ethnicity discourse also serves to mark the politically important from the "private." The mestizaje lived by Anzaldúa is an experience of conflict precisely because one of her "elements" is privileged over another, and consequently her positioning among those elements has direct consequences for her life. This inequality of position, and the racism that defines the two (or more) positions as discrete, concrete entities (such as "blood"), is what produces the unique dynamism of her mestiza identity and politics. This dynamism is missing from the "mutthood" of white men whenever their melting has been produced without strain.

For example, my brothers have ancestors who are English, Dutch, Ashkenazi Jew, and whatever else may have gone into long lines of life in North America. These distinctions were often relevant for their ancestors, the hub of political struggle between Dutch and English in New York, the source of pain for Jews in twentieth-century U.S. society, etc. However, these distinctions have not entered into their consciousness as anything more than interesting stories of their ancestors. Raised as Episcopalians, with English last names, they have lived not as mestizos but as "Americans" with no hyphens. I have shared in that mutthood, but somewhat differently. Through my bond to my grandmother, I identified with the Jews more strongly than with the Anglos for a long time. This produced personal tension, but there were no societal effects—no one excluded me from hotels or clubs or made anti-Semitic remarks about me, as they had to my grandmother and my mother. Thus, my "roots" did not automatically place me in a mestiza position.

Lesbianism, however, forced that tension into my life. In heterosexist society, as in racist society, one must be one or the other(s)—there is no room for sexual mutthood. Laws of hypo-descent apply here, as they do in racial discourse. Those who identify as lesbian and experience themselves through that self-conception live in a constant either/or situation: either one is "in the closet," passing for straight and experiencing the loss of self that that entails, or one is "out" and facing the consequences in the harrassment, economic deprivation, threat of violence, and loss of family support that so often follow.

This is still not enough for mestizaje, however. Most fundamentally, lesbianism is a difference that most of us can choose to manifest or not. While needing to hide is oppressive, being able to hide still marks lesbians off from racially defined groups. Anzaldúa acknowledges the pain of heterosexism and homophobia, but she ranks this pain below what she experiences when white women seem to rank racism below sexism as an issue, when she feels, "after all our dialogues and struggles, that my cultural identity is *still* being pushed off to the side, being minimized by some of my so-called allies who unconsciously rank racism a lesser oppression than sexism."[56] "Lesbian cultures" in which white women predominate have too often provided a place in which the experience of mestizaje is avoided, not celebrated. Lesbians of color are "world-travellers" in such lesbian cultures, as they are among heterosexuals of their various races.[57] As Anzaldúa describes it, being a mestiza has to do with the integration of difference as a daily lived reality, and not simply with "belonging" to multiple and seemingly opposed groups.

Historically, white feminists in the U.S. have articulated their oppression along lines borrowed from movements of racial liberation. In so doing, they have sometimes failed to explore the particulars of white women's oppression as such, instead linking prematurely to frameworks developed in other struggles. A central moment of getting specific is the description and theorization of our own positions. We need not, and cannot, abandon analogy and metaphor (those crucial tools of political struggle), but we must not allow these to take the place of consideration of the ways in which race, class, gender, and sexuality (among others) *all* inflect *all* of our lives. Appropriating mestizaje does not serve to build alliances; it serves to convince mestizas that white women don't get it, that white women are blind to their own privilege and oblivious to the force of history. Our alliances cannot be built by grafting ourselves onto others' identities. The process of democratic articulation is not one of equation, or even of simile, but is one of linkage between disparate elements. Such linkage must recognize those disparities, or it simply renews colonization.

Mestiza Consciousness

Rather than appropriating the position of the mestiza, white middle-class lesbians can learn from Anzaldúa's discussion of mestiza consciousness. The power of mestiza consciousness lies in the refusal of dualisms and boundaries that have worked to limit and separate us, from one another and from the fullness of ourselves. Mestizas, Anzaldúa tells us, cope by "developing a tolerance for contradictions, a tolerance for ambiguity."[58] This tolerance allows for the acceptance of conflict as necessary and fruitful, rather than threatening. In this, Anzaldúa is in sharp contrast to theorists such as Nancy Hartsock, who repudiates an "agonistic" world view as essentially male.[59] Hartsock's gender dualism, in which women are fundamentally cooperative and community-oriented and men are disposed to individualism and domination, continues the tradition of either/or thinking that Anzaldúa is struggling against. Anzaldúa does not deny the fundamental asymmetry of power between men and women, nor does she call for a romantic politics of reconciliation, but she does insist on understanding the lives of men of color within the context of oppression that makes them potential allies as well as opponents.

The idea of mestizaje has been an avenue for white women to develop a new understanding of alliance. This theory developed through the 1980s and into the 1990s into visions that blend the abstractions of poststructuralist theory with the "theory in the flesh" that Anzaldúa and Moraga brought forward in their collection, *This Bridge Called My Back.*[60] It is the theme and the politics of bridging that is so crucial for white lesbians now. This lesson may be learned without resorting to appropriations of mestizaje; indeed, such appropriations are a refusal to bridge.

In discussing the theory implicit in *This Bridge,* Alarcón argues that "the theory of the subject of consciousness as a unitary and synthesizing agent of knowledge is always already a posture of domination."[61] She indicts Anglo-American feminists for their continued refusal or inability to truly grasp the meaning of this, arguing that the continual return to the unitary subject limits the possibilities for solidarity with feminists of color. This drive for unity extends to the idea of "reclaiming" an identity; such reclamation "means always already to have become a subject of consciousness" capable of simply authorizing or denying a given identity.[62] Alarcón argues that "to be oppressed means to be disenabled not only from grasping an 'identity,' but also from reclaiming it," because the force of oppression works not simply to disadvantage some on the basis of a given identity, but creates and disintegrates identities themselves. On this basis, she urges her readers to treat consciousness "as the site of multiple voicings" that "transverse consciousness and which the subject must struggle with constantly." Refusing this consciousness in favor of a unitary, stable self is described as a "refusal to play 'bridge,'" which is "the acceptance of defeat at the hands of political groups whose self-definition follows the view of self as unitary, capable of being defined by a single 'theme.'"[63]

While she refrains from adopting the poststructuralist language of "subject positions" or "deconstructive identities," Anzaldúa's "new mestiza" does not transcend race but transgresses it, refusing to collude in the homophobic demands of some Chicana/os or in the racist invisibility that is too much a part of white lesbian communities. Anzaldúa and Alarcón agree that such a position involves forsaking the safety of the familiar or the stable for flux and struggle. Yet both recognize that only this renunciation makes change possible. They agree with Bernice Johnson Reagon that coalition politics is not about nurturance, but is about stretching past the limits of comfort and safety to the work that needs to be done.[64]

It is this ambiguous, simultaneous recognition of alliance and opposition, friendship and alienation, support and betrayal that makes mestiza consciousness so important. One of the lessons of the past twenty-five years of lesbian organizing is that communities and identities built on the expectation that "we" will only be allies, friends, and supporters of each other will inevitably fail. With such expectations, conflicts can only be understood as betrayal, and opposition can only mean exclusion.

Mestiza consciousness moves away from false oppositions between reform and revolution, separatism and coalition, and the like. These distinctions, while seemingly clear when written down in analytic fashion, are in fact of little use politically. The reform/revolution split has operated within a Marxist paradigm of history that is too thoroughly modernist, too monolithic, and too antidemocratic to be truly helpful. The separatism/coalition divide has similarly been the product of totalizing theory at its worst, the analytic intellect run wild. Both of these dualisms force us to unsatisfactory choices that we need not make, and rarely in fact make in political life. Mestiza consciousness honors the complexity of political life.

The history of nationalist movements is one of internal strife and the failure of self-criticism, and thus of eventual irrelevance or cooptation.[65] The strength of mestiza consciousness is a result of its multiplicity and ability to sustain contradiction and ambiguity, and this includes the ability to withstand conflict and misunderstanding. The revolutionary force of the mestiza is the ability to refuse the reifications of cultural nationalism without abandoning the nation entirely, and to provide links to class-based movements without becoming subsumed within them. Because she never simply "is" any one element of her blended being, the mestiza cannot be captured in the oppositions that are presented as inevitable; class *or* nation, sex *or* race, or any other reified opposition. The mestiza does not dispute the historical or contemporary reality of these designations, but she does operate constantly to undermine their unitary solidities.

To the extent that any lesbian politics, separatist or not, relies upon the fiction of a unitary self and its autonomy, that politics will fail to do justice to the multiplicity of mutually irreducible struggles and "identity points" at which we live our lives. As Jacquelyn Zita describes it, "claiming a lesbian identity often diffuses into difference, once its locations are made physical, real, and lived."[66] This is the linkage between the ethnic experience of mestizaje and the experience of white lesbians who were raised and live in a heterosexual world; not ethnicity, an ascribed identity, but the specific differences that preclude any settled unity.

Notes

1. Combahee River Collective, "A Black Feminist Statement," in *All the Women Are White, All the Blacks Are Men, But Some of Us Are Brave: Black Women's Studies*, edited by Gloria T. Hull, Patricia Bell Scott, and Barbara Smith (New York: The Feminist Press, 1982), 13.

2. See Trinh T. Minh-ha, ed., "She, The Inappropriate/d Other," *Discourse* 8 (1986/7).

3. Michael Omi and Howard Winant, *Racial Formation in the United States From the 1960s to the 1980s* (New York: Routledge and Kegan Paul, 1986), 15.

4. Daniel Bell, "Ethnicity and Social Change," in *Ethnicity: Theory and Experience*, edited by Nathan Glazer and Daniel Patrick Moynihan (Cambridge: Harvard University Press, 1975), 169.

5. Omi and Winant, *Racial Formation*, 52.

6. Vine Deloria, Jr., "Identity and Culture," in *From Different Shores: Perspectives on Race and Ethnicity in America*, edited by Ronald Takaki (New York and London: Oxford University Press, 1987), 97.

7. Mario Barrera, "Chicano Class Structure," in *From Different Shores*.

8. Omi and Winant, *Racial Formation*, 33.

9. Deloria, "Identity and Culture," 100.

10. I exclude Jews here, first because Jews are not all European, and secondly because even Ashkenazim (European Jews) do not agree on whether they are "white" or not. The status of Jews is a wonderful example of the instability of racial articulations, as well as of the extreme discomfort that such instability causes many (i.e., anti-Semitism).

11. I do not want to equate ethnicity and race here. As Omi and Winant make clear, the ethnicity paradigm for understanding race has been liberal at best, reactionary at worst, in its implications. For more discussion see Omi and Winant. For a sweeping discussion of the sexuality-as-ethnicity debates see Steven Epstein, "Gay Politics, Ethnic Identity: The Limits of Social Constructionism," *Socialist Review* 93/94 (May/August 1987).

12. Kobena Mercer, "'1968': Periodizing Politics and Identity," in *Cultural Studies*, edited by Lawrence Grossberg, Cary Nelson, and Paula Treichler (New York: Routledge, 1992), 434.

13. See Epstein, "Gay Politics, Ethnic Identity," 13–15.

14. This phrase is that of Harold Isaacs in "Basic Group Identity: The Idols of the Tribe," in Glazer and Moynihan, *Ethnicity*, 30.

15. Barbara Ponse, *Identities in the Lesbian World* (Westport, CT: Greenwood, 1978), 24–29.

16. Ibid., 124–133.

17. Omi and Winant, *Racial Formation*, 60.

18. For examples, see Celia Kitzinger, *The Social Construction of Lesbianism* (London and Newbury Park: Sage, 1987).

19. I have in mind here especially the work of Mary Daly, and also Adrienne Rich's 1980 argument. See Mary Daly, *Gyn/Ecology* (Boston: Beacon, 1978) and *Pure Lust* (Boston: Beacon, 1982); Adrienne Rich, "Compulsory Heterosexuality and Lesbian Existence," *Signs* 5/4 (Summer 1980), 631–60.

20. Judy Grahn, *Another Mother Tongue: Gay Words, Gay Worlds* (Boston: Beacon, 1984), xiii, xiv.

21. See for example pp. 139–44, where Grahn derives the epithet *bulldyke* from the Celtic queen Boudica, without any evidence that Boudica slept with or desired women; Boudica's claim to ancestral status is her independence and strength.

22. Scott Bravmann, "Invented Traditions: Take One on the Lesbian and Gay Past," *NWSA Journal* 3/1 (Winter 1991), 86.

23. Matters are no less complex when the subjects of appropriation are modern whites who did not choose the identity of lesbians. Adopting independent women as heroes or inspirations is not problematic; adopting them as ancestors is. Each adoption amounts to a retrospective redefinition of these people into terms that were not available to them, or that were available and were rejected.

24. Grahn, *Another Mother Tongue*, xiv.

25. See, for example, Kathleen M. Blee, *Women of the Klan: Racism and Gender in the 1920s* (Berkeley: University of California Press, 1991), and Randy Shilts, *Conduct Unbecoming: Gays and Lesbians in the U.S. Military* (New York: St. Martin's, 1993). While Shilts does not document active racism among gays and lesbians, his subjects almost uniformly desire to serve in the U.S. military, finding no difficulty with its mission as a colonizing force.

26. Peter K. Eisinger, "Ethnicity As A Strategic Option: An Emerging View," *Public Administration Review* 38/1 (Jan./Feb. 1978), 90.

27. See Donald L. Horowitz, "Ethnic Identity," in Glazer and Moynihan, *Ethnicity*, 114.

28. Ernesto Laclau and Chantal Mouffe, *Hegemony and Socialist Strategy: Towards a Radical Democratic Politics* (London and New York: Verso, 1985), 95.

29. Ibid., 113.

30. Gloria Anzaldúa, *Borderlands/La Frontera: The New Mestiza* (San Francisco: Spinsters/Aunt Lute, 1987).

31. John A. Garcia, "Yo Soy Mexicano . . .: Self-Identity and Socio-demographic Correlates," *Social Science Quarterly* 62/1 (1981), 89.

32. Garcia found that *Chicano* was generally used by younger respondents and those with higher education levels than other groups, and was virtually absent among those born in Mexico.

33. Anzaldúa, *Borderlands,* 80.

34. Anzaldúa, "Bridge, Drawbridge, Sandbar, or Island: Lesbians-of-Color Haciendo Alianzas," in *Bridges of Power: Women's Multicultural Alliances*, edited by Lisa Albrecht and Rose M. Brewer (Philadelphia: New Society Publishers, 1990), 222.

35. Ibid., 223.

36. Ontological separatism is most often espoused in writing by women who do not always publicly identify as separatists, for example, Mary Daly and Sonia Johnson. For descriptions of and arguments for what I am calling political separatism, see K. Hess, Jean Langford, and Kathy Ross, "Comparative Separatism," in *For Lesbians Only*, edited by Sarah Lucia Hoagland and Julia Penelope (London: Only Women Press, 1988), 125–32; Bette S. Tallen, "Lesbian Separatism: A Historical and Comparative Perspective," in *For Lesbians Only*, 132–45; and Sarah Lucia Hoagland, *Lesbian Ethics: Toward New Value* (Palo Alto, CA: Institute of Lesbian Studies, 1988).

37. See Norma Alarcón, "The Theoretical Subject(s) of *This Bridge Called My Back* and Anglo-American Feminism," in *Making Face, Making Soul/Haciendo Caras*, edited by Gloria Anzaldúa (San Francisco: Aunt Lute Foundation, 1990); Cherrie Moraga, "A Long Line of Vendidas," in *Loving in the War Years* (Boston: South End, 1983).

38. Laclau and Mouffe, *Hegemony*, 138.

39. Jacquelyn N. Zita, "Lesbian Body Journeys: Desire Making Difference," in *Lesbian Philosophies and Cultures*, edited by Jeffner Allen (Albany: State University of New York Press, 1990), 342.

40. Anzaldúa, *Borderlands*, 79.

41. See Nancy Fraser, *Unruly Practices: Power, Discourse, and Gender in Contemporary Social Theory* (Minneapolis: University of Minnesota Press, 1989), ch. 4; Gayatri Chakravorty Spivak, *The Post-Colonial*

Critic: Interviews, Strategies, Dialogues, edited by Sarah Harasym (New York: Routledge, 1990), 13.

42. Spivak, *The Post-Colonial Critic*, 18.

43. Iris Marion Young, *Justice and the Politics of Difference* (Princeton: Princeton University Press, 1990), 98.

44. "There are at least two ways in which lesbianism has been isolated in feminist discourse: the homophobic oversight and relegation of it to the margins, and the lesbian-feminist centering of it, which has had at times the paradoxical effect of removing lesbianism and sexuality from their embeddedness in social relations." Biddy Martin and Chandra Tolpade Mohanty, "Feminist Politics: What's Home Got to Do with It?" in *Feminist Studies/Critical Studies*, edited by Teresa de Lauretis (Bloomington: Indiana University Press, 1986), 203.

45. Ann Ferguson makes a similar argument about the conditions of existence for lesbians in her response to Adrienne Rich, "Patriarchy, Sexual Identity, and the Sexual Revolution," in *Feminist Theory: A Critique of Ideology*, edited by Nannerl O. Keohane, Michelle Z. Rosaldo, and Barbara C. Gelpi (Chicago: University of Chicago Press, 1982), 147–61. See also Ann Ferguson, "Is There A Lesbian Culture?" in *Lesbian Philosophies and Cultures*, edited by Jeffner Allen (Albany: State University of New York Press, 1990), 82.

46. Anzaldúa, "Bridge, Drawbridge, Sandbar, or Island."

47. In these cases, the question is not whether it is fair to the cited source to use their ideas, but whether such use does not constitute cooptation or colonization by privileging the work of such authors.

48. Nancy Caraway, *Segregated Sisterhood* (Knoxville: University of Tennessee Press, 1991).

49. I am extending this only to white women because middle-class members of other racial groups are often extremely conscious of where their class locates them in their communities; unlike in white communities, middle-classness is not unremarkable among people of color.

50. Mercer, "'1968,'" 434. On this problem, see also Catharine Stimpson, "'Thy Neighbor's Wife, Thy Neighbor's Servants': Women's Liberation and Black Civil Rights," in *Woman in Sexist Society: Studies in Power and Powerlessness*, edited by Vivian Gornick and Barbara K. Moran (New York: Basic Books, 1971), 622–657.

51. Trinh T. Minh-ha, "Not You/Like You: Post-Colonial Women and the Interlocking Questions of Identity and Difference," in *Making Face, Making Soul/Haciendo Caras*, 372.

52. Ibid., 375.

53. Ibid.

54. I recognize that this is not so simply the case for différance, but différance suffers from the temptation to evade location rather than spec-
ify it, producing an "antiessentialism" that is politically anemic. For the
concept of "identity points," see Teresa de Lauretis, "Feminist Studies/
Critical Studies: Issues, Terms, and Contexts," in *Feminist Studies/
Critical Studies*, 9.

55. I thank Iris Young for this question.

56. Anzaldúa, "Bridge, Drawbridge, Sandbar, or Island," 218.

57. For the notion of "world-travelling," see Maria Lugones, "Playfulness,
'World'-Travelling, and Loving Perception," *Hypatia* 2/2 (1987).

58. Anzaldúa, *Borderlands*, 79.

59. Nancy C. M. Hartsock, *Money, Sex, and Power: Toward a Feminist
Historical Materialism* (Boston: Northeastern University Press, 1983).

60. Cherríe Moraga and Gloria Anzaldúa, *This Bridge Called My Back:
Writings by Radical Women of Color* (New York: Kitchen Table Women
of Color Press, 1983).

61. Norma Alarcón, "The Theoretical Subject(s) of *This Bridge Called My
Back* and Anglo-American Feminism," 364.

62. Ibid.

63. Ibid., 365.

64. Bernice Johnson Reagon, "Coalition Politics: Turning the Century," in
Home Girls: A Black Feminist Anthology, edited by Barbara Smith (New
York: Kitchen Table Women of Color Press, 1983), 356–68.

65. See Omi and Winant, *Racial Formation*; Adolph L. Reed Jr., "Black
Particularity Reconsidered," *Telos* 39 (Spring 1979), 71–93.

66. Zita, "Lesbian Body Journeys," 329.

II. Queer Critiques

5

Somewhere Over the Rainbow: Queer Translating

Angelia R. Wilson

In the summer of 1992 I attended a gay and lesbian conference at the University of London. As one of the first of such conferences in Britain, the high level of attendance reflected the diverse interests in gay and lesbian studies emerging in this country. However, many of the sessions focused on literary criticism. While perhaps this should have been unsurprising given the vast contribution literary criticism has made in gay and lesbian studies, it was nevertheless disconcerting. The lack of representation on the agenda by gay and lesbian activist groups in London was, for this student of politics, shocking. Admittedly my annoyance at the seemingly depoliticized event was slightly parochial: Judith Butler and Eve Kosofsky Sedgwick had not as yet become required reading for political theorists. A similar concern, however, was voiced in the final plenary session where Butler had stunned the audience with streams of impenetrable prose. The allotted time allowed for only one question, which was posed by one of the most respected literature academics in Britain. He asked why, when the conference had intended to be interdisciplinary, Butler chose to utilise highly theoretical language that was unfamiliar, if not inaccessible, to academics from such varied fields. Her response was something along the lines of "this is how I write, deal with it." While I sympathise with her response given the situation, it also characterises the difficulty of translating, or negotiating between, the often exclusive practice of theorising and the inclusive potential of political action.

As a theorist I would agree with Diana Fuss that political theory and political action are not necessarily separate exercises, but a few questions consistently arise in my mind as I read "postmodern" or more specifically "queer" theory (Fuss, 1991). My thoughts here may go against current trends or be considered simplistic. And they are; since for all my pretensions to be a theorist, I cannot seem to rid myself of the question, "where is all this getting us?" So to those readers who are beyond such parochial anxieties, you may wish to stop here, but I ask you to continue, if only to humour yourself. I do not believe that I am the first theorist to ask such a basic question. In fact, I have heard political theorists well versed in modernity whisper similar bewilderment at the impenetrable works of those who have become the deities of postmodern theorising (Foucault, Derrida, Lyotard, Rorty, et al.). And, when I sometimes find myself surrounded by queer theorists rejoicing with missionary zeal at the radicalism of considering sexuality as a performance with the potential of disrupting the entire gender/sex binary of the western world, I too have wanted to believe. Unfortunately, however, even in my euphoria over this limitless potential, I find myself wanting to ask, "yes let's do it, but tell me again, how exactly?"

Even among queer theorists, I do not stand alone. There are those theorists who have noticed the gap between queer theory and the practicalities of political activism. For example, Frank Mort's recent essay entitled "Essentialism Revisited" rehearses the current landscape of queer theory that has posited varied subjectivities as a replacement for the essentialised gay, or gay and lesbian, identities associated with the gay movement of the 1960s and 1970s (1994). He concludes the article not on a pessimistic note questioning the progressiveness of queer discourse, but with an acute awareness of the canyon between queer theory and mainstream politics. "Formal political culture," writes Mort, "is still almost exclusively organised around fixed epistemologies, conceived within what is in reality an early twentieth-century system of political representation. A cornerstone of this structure remains the fiction of a fixed and stable political self" (Ibid., 220). Given that fixation around a stable political self, the multi-subjectivities proposed by queer theory may be, in the least, difficult to communicate to those who operate daily on the assumptions of a coherent self. Mort's purpose, in his own words, is "to inject a more urgent sense of the political realities facing the pluralist project" (Ibid., 221). He adds, "there needs to be further thought given to the issue of translating what are a sophisticated set of intellectual concepts into *the language of politics*" (Ibid.). Mort's point strikes at the heart of my concern with queer theory, specifically with the unrealised potential of queer theory. In order to address this I want to rehearse briefly the sexual identities that are manifesting themselves in queer theory and queer politics. Doing so will highlight the disruptive potential claimed by queer theory but as yet unrealised, or not translated, by queer activism. Working on the assumption that theorising is a form of activism, my intervention here is directed at the practicalities of the translation process—a point that I do not believe we as queer theorists have addressed sufficiently. Therefore in the second section of this chapter I will consider a unique approach to the difficulties of articulating multi-subjectivities in a political framework premised upon a coherent self.

We Assumed

Since the 1969 Stonewall riots the "gay (and lesbian) movement"—as it was originally labeled and continues to be referred to—has been built upon one premise: the division between "us"—the homosexual—and "them"—the heterosexual "other." This is not to say that "we" have not been reminded, from the beginning, of internal differences both of multi-subjectivities and of multi-political positionings. As Sheila Jeffreys has so aptly noted in her text *Anticlimax,* gay men embracing the freedom of post-Wolfenden Britain rarely considered the way in which the "sexual revolution" continued to objectify and discriminate against women (1990). The "we" of the early gay liberation movement was seen by many lesbians as a bastion of white gay men who in the least ignored lesbian feminism or in the extreme were misogynists. And when lesbians claimed their role as a valid and strong part of the "movement," "gay and lesbian" identity politics served to solidify the "us" versus "them" political positioning. Jeffrey Weeks comments on the role that sexual identity plays in gay and lesbian politics:

> The preoccupation with identity cannot be explained as an effect of a peculiar personal obsession with sex. It must be seen, more accurately, as a powerful resistance to the organising principle of traditional sexual attitudes, encoded in the dominant and pervasive heterosexual assumption of the sexual tradition. . . . Modern gay identities, whether they are the out-growth of essential internal characteristics (which I do not believe to be the case) or of complex socio-historical transformations (which I think is more likely), are today as much *political* as personal or social identities. They make a statement about the existing divisions between permissible and tabooed behaviour and propose their alteration. (1985, 189, 201)

Identity politics has been personally affirming for those previously demonised by the sex/gender norm while at the same time politically challenging that norm. The power of such oppositional politics, as Weeks suggests, "subverts the absolutism of the sexual tradition" (ibid.). In addition, the image of a coherent gay "community," or a gay and lesbian constituency, continues to be a strong political position, or tool, for activists. Appeals on the part of this supposed gay and lesbian community are commonplace within the political discourse of both traditional lobbying groups such as Stonewall or the National Gay and Lesbian Task Force in the U.S. and the more radical action-oriented groups (like OutRage!).

Within a historical/political context, the emergence of "queer" can be seen as a progressive realisation of difference. For example, Weeks comments on the assumption of a coherent gay community in the days of the

Gay Liberation Front (GLF): "although it would have been heresy to say so at the time, it turned out that homosexuality was not a stable basis on which to build a large-scale movement; a host of conflicting class, cultural, sexual, political and social allegiances tugged in increasingly divergent directions" (1977, 205). "Queer," then, attempts to redress the presumed stability of 'identity' in the early political movement. According to Cherry Smyth's *Queer Notions,* queer refers to a range of sexualities: "Queer means to fuck with gender. There are straight queers, bi-queers, tranny queers, lez queers, fag queers, SM queers, fisting queers in every single street in this apathetic country of ours" ("Queer Power Now" leaflet in Smyth, 1992, 17). The challenge to the "gay and lesbian community" posed by "queer" theory is interesting in at least two aspects: it creates new possibilities for reinterpreting what it means to be "nonheterosexual" and, as a result, it also creates new possibilities for rearticulating the language of politics. However, queer activism in Britain has yet to come to terms with these possibilities. While queer theory has undoubtedly enfranchised previously marginalised, or suspect, sexual citizens, queer activism as manifest in radical action politics continues to rely heavily upon the assumed coherent constituency of the "gay and lesbian community."

For example, OutRage!—which professes itself to be "queer"—specifically defines itself in relation to "lesbians and gay men" fighting "homophobia"; very familiar terminology indeed. In a recent article, Peter Tatchell, the most nationally recognised member of OutRage! (and the most vocal) uses the term "queer" interchangeably with "gay and lesbian." He writes that "the problem is heterosexual supremacism and homophobia, not queer dissent. As lesbian and gay people, we are valuable in our own right" and that assimilation means "us giving up the unique and enriching aspects of our lesbian and gay lifestyle and community" (1995, 12). While this assumption of community is at once problematised and assumed by those of us writing about sexual politics, Tatchell leaves no doubt about the characteristics, or perhaps limits, of the "community" to which he refers:

> Compared to most straight people, for example, lesbians and gay men are more willing to transgress the traditional boundaries of masculinity and femininity. As a result, gay men tend to be less macho and more in touch with their emotions. This gives them a sensitivity and creativity that has enabled queers to make a disproportionate contribution to the arts and the caring professions. Lesbians are usually less reliant on men and more independent and assertive than their hetero sisters. Hence their pioneering contribution to women's advancement in previously all-male occupations. (Ibid., 13)

So much for a broadening of identities. The people in the above "community" are so blatantly a part of the stereotypes associated with gay men and lesbians, I wonder who exactly is doing the defining here. Surely the potential of queer theory has been lost in this interpretation.

Queer Potential

Closer examination of queer theory, such as that delineated in Judith Butler's *Gender Trouble,* brings into focus more clearly the political potential of queer politics. Identity, as Butler reasons, is not necessary to oppositional politics. "The foundationalist reasoning of identity politics" she writes, "tends to assume that an identity must first be in place in order for political interests to be elaborated and, subsequently, political action to be taken. My argument is that there need not be a 'doer behind the deed,' but that the 'doer' is variably constructed in and through the deed" (1990, 142). In this now familiar text, both sex and gender are considered to be "regulatory fictions that consolidate and naturalise the convergent power regimes of masculine and heterosexist oppression" (Ibid., 33). Sex and gender, as a "performatively enacted signification . . . can occasion the parodic proliferation and subversive play of gendered meanings" (Ibid.). And as such sex and gender, or the parodying of sex norms, have subversive political potential. "The loss of gender norms would have the effect of proliferating gender configurations, destabilising substantive identity, and depriving the naturalising narratives of compulsory heterosexuality of their central protagonists: 'man' and 'woman.' The parodic repetition of gender exposes as well the illusion of gender identity as an intractable depth and inner substance" (Ibid., 146). Sex and gender are performance, an acting out of social scripts about sexual behaviour through both speech acts and nonspeech or appearance. The way in which traditional scripts are to be challenged is by acting, if you will, out of character; suggesting through speech or appearance that those scripts are unsuited to expressing the fluidity of sexuality.

More specifically, Butler questions the identity categories presumed to be foundational to feminist politics, "those deemed necessary in order to mobilise feminism as an identity politics" (Ibid., 147). She argues at the end of the text that since identity is contextually defined within a particular system of signification, those trapped in that system can only redefine it by repeating it "through a radical proliferation of gender, *to displace* the very gender norms that enable the repetition itself" (Ibid., 148). "The deconstruction of identity is not the deconstruction of politics; rather, it establishes as political the very terms through which identity is articulated" (Ibid.). With identity—or a set of identifiable subjects—no longer the defining point for political positioning, politics becomes a practice of parodying the very constraints of identity.

> The task here is not to celebrate each and every new possibility *qua possibility,* but to re-describe those possibilities that *already* exist, but which

> exist within cultural domains designated as culturally unintelligible and impossible. If identities were no longer fixed as the premises of a political syllogism, and politics no longer understood as a set of practices derived from the alleged interests that belong to a set of ready-made subjects, a new configuration of politics would surely emerge from the ruins of the old. Cultural configuration of sex and gender might then proliferate or, rather, their present proliferation might then become articulable within the discourses that establish intelligible cultural life, confounding the very binarism of sex, and exposing its fundamental unnaturalness. (Ibid.)

According to Butler the deconstruction of identity "establishes as political the very terms through which identity is articulated." The interpretation of Butler's "gender trouble" has taken queer theorists, as well as queer activists, onto some fairly difficult terrain. By focusing on identity construction as a political act, one which can be self-initiated, Butler's theory appears to be empowering, but those who stress transgressiveness of performing, creating, identity, run the risk of ignoring the social, political, and economic context which can affect identity construction.

For example, British television has become central in portraying "gay and lesbian life" to the public through gay-friendly programs—for example: "Gay Time TV," an evening television magazine program; "DYKE TV," similar but broadcast late at night, allowing for more salacious stories; and regular interviews with OutRage! member Peter Tatchell. Unfortunately, many of these focus on transgressive identities and sexual practices rather than discrimination in a social or political context. As a result, many gay men and lesbians do not identify with the images created on screen. Smyth notes this tension between recognising multi-subjectivities and locating a political constituency: queer activism is "torn between affirming a new identity—'I am queer'—and rejecting restrictive identities—'I reject your categories'" ("Outlook," quoted in Ibid.) Interestingly, in his recent book *State of the Queer Nation*, Chris Wood, a founder of the London-based OutRage! reflects upon how the potential inclusivity promised by queer theory has been mutated by queer activism into elitism:

> It (queer) allows for the perpetual deconstruction of identity, the pursuit of antiideology (itself a crude ideological position), the raising-up of iconoclasm. The "mundanity" of gay, with its utopian ideology, is replaced with an identity rich in contradiction and obscure in meaning and purpose, that allows for cultural and political introspection and the maintenance of the cult of perfection. So nebulous is the meaning of queer that those who claim to be so use the term in a masonic fashion. Only those who are queer know its sensibilities. The mass of homosexuals are excluded from this secretive dialogue, their own desires and pursuits devalued. (1995, 31)

Similarly, in Smyth's text she points to the difficulties of emphasising sex and gender over other aspects of identity: "At its most successful, queer art represents a vigorous challenge to the normalisation of positive images and a radical recognition of pluralities, in a style that flaunts conventions. At its worst, it is the shock tactics of a new generation of lesbians and gays who, in transcending the old categories of sexuality and gender, ignore issues of sexual inequality, class and race" (1992, 48). Black activist Helen (charles) expresses concern over what exactly is on offer in queer politics: "Getting identities together is pretty complex already (I speak for myself), and although I'm not unhappy with the fragmented possibilities of my own cultural identity, I wonder at the thought that maybe the next thing on the agenda will be the suggestion that 'Nigger' should be transported from the British playground and placed into a reverse-discourse theory and practice" (1993, 102). Clearly the interpretations of queer on offer are failing to communicate its political potential even to those it may claim to represent. As such "queer" not only risks ignoring other structures of oppression, it also may fail to articulate the political significance of gender performance, or posturing, itself.

The potential of the politics of transgression may become not only limitless but pointless. Leading British sociologist Elizabeth Wilson comments on the Foucaultian notion of transgression as "the crossing of a boundary—a going further" that produces a new boundary that must also be transgressed. She writes, "what you then have is a transgressive spiral which at least in theory is interminable . . . from that point of view, transgression can define no final goal, and there can never be any final mastery" (1993, 110). Wilson worries that the aesthetic attraction of transgression may be a substitute for politics; "We transgress in order to insist that we are there, that we exist, and to place a distance between ourselves and the dominant culture. But we have to go further—we have to have an idea of how things could be different, otherwise transgression ends in mere posturing. In other words, transgression on its own leads eventually to entropy, unless we carry within us some idea of transformation" (Ibid., 116). Queer theorist Clare Hemmings comments that although "Wilson has reminded us that 'transgression' may be translated other than in terms of transgressive transformation . . . we may have to take that risk" (Ibid., 136). Although Hemmings is willing to risk such (mis)interpretation, I am not. Transgression for its own sake may be personally enjoyable, but as a political tactic its message is too important to leave to interpretation by the "heterosexual other." If we are to establish "as political the very terms through which identity is articulated" then surely we must be clear about that message. And in so doing we must be sensitive to the collage of identities—racial, economic, religious—that individuals struggle to balance in understanding themselves.

Queer A(e)ffection

An approach to politics and political activism that incorporates an understanding of multi-subjectivities can be found in the works of Chantal Mouffe and Ernesto Laclau. Their important intervention into postmodern theory, *Hegemony and Socialist Strategy,* outlines an interpretation of a new radical democracy in which diverse social movements build "chains of articulation" (1985). In her text *Rights of Passage,* Didi Herman relates these chains of articulation that "create mechanisms and processes whereby the 'other' is identified *with,* and the interests of individual groups are seen to be shared by all" to gay and lesbian "interest group" politics. Commenting on how lesbian and gay rights claims need to move beyond that specificity of essentialised, particularly biologically determined, identities, she writes: "Lesbian and gay struggle, in legal arenas and elsewhere, ought to be broad, encompassing, and inclusive. Individuals are made up of complex identities, some often contradictory. When we argue for rights as a fixed 'minority,' claiming that we were 'born this way,' we simultaneously imply that our demands 'stop here'" (1994, 148). Herman argues that rights claims made by gay men and lesbians do not necessarily challenge other sets of social relations, particularly those of race or economic class. "On the contrary," she continues, "these hierarchies are reproduced within lesbian and gay communities" (Ibid.). As noted previously, this is precisely what the quotation from Smyth identifies as "a new generation" that "ignores" issues of "inequality, class and race," one which is built upon in Tatchell's characterisation of "gay men" and "lesbians."

A similar interpretation of Laclau and Mouffe's model is espoused by Anna Marie Smith in her essay "Hegemony Trouble." Contrasting their approach with Butler's, Smith notes that Butler "promotes the permanent problematisation of 'identity' through subversive appropriations" and that Laclau would agree that "every dislocation of a hegemonic space opens up possibilities which had been relegated to the residual sphere of the unthinkable" (1994, 232). However, Smith argues that Laclau moves beyond this by recognising that identity claims construct spaces that give us a sense of location within a partially bounded order and whose "incomplete frontiers operate simultaneously as the defences against disruption and the limits of our freedom" (Ibid.). She adds, "we cannot remain in the non-spacialisable moment outside all identity claims: every subversion of a hegemonic space depends on the resources of marginalised spaces, and the defence of the possibilities which are opened up through subversion depends in turn on the construction and reinforcement of alternative spaces" (Ibid.). So Laclau and Mouffe "offer a double analysis of the politics of identity: the ways in which all identities are always open to problematisation, subversion, parody, and so on, and the ways in which the political terrain is always simultaneously respacialised through new articulations or identity claims" (Ibid.). The impact of this approach on political activism is clear for Smith: "The permanent problematisation approach may be a useful response to the representation of white gay maleness as a hyper-sexual excess, but it may have limited value for lesbians, bisexual women and gay men of colour who are struggling against erasure" (Ibid.). In short, problematisation has its uses. It enables us continually to challenge the voice, or voices, that claim to represent "the community." But it is in the proclamation of identities that voices of difference are heard.

So as an answer to the *Trouble* caused by Butler's approach to "gay and lesbian" or "sexual" activism, the Laclau-Mouffe project both enables the problematisation of socially enforced identities *and* recognises the realities of a political system where identities become significations of existence and of political claims. Recalling Mort's concern that we rearticulate these rather sophisticated theories of multi-subjectivity into a language of politics—a politics dominated by modernity's coherent self—Smith's interpretation seems to allow for utilising identity politics while simultaneously problematising the situatedness of any one identity. This allows for identity claims while challenging us to see the identity-signification system for what it is: politically necessary and politically dangerous.

It is important to note here that this approach is not the same as a traditional model of coalition politics. Smith in particular is adamant on this point: "a hegemonic bloc does not involve the mere combination of pre-constituted elements" (1994, 224). Pointing again to the approach espoused by Laclau and Mouffe, she comments that "articulations do not operate outside of, or in addition to pre-constituted identities; identities, and the social itself, are nothing but the effects of articulation" (Ibid.). A similar argument has been made by Shane Phelan in her text, *Getting Specific:* "Doing a better identity politics does not mean finding the best definition of our identities so as to eliminate problems of membership and goals; it means continual shuffling between the need for categories and the recognition of their incompleteness" (1994, 154). Instead of coalition politics based on coherent identities, Phelan challenges us to ask "not whether we share a given position but whether we share a commitment to improve it, and whether we can commit to the pain of embarrassment and confrontation as we disagree" (Ibid., 156).

While Smith understands Laclau and Mouffe to offer space for these chains of articulation, she believes they do not pay enough attention to differences that can emerge within struggles. For example, "where lesbians are confronted with an utterly non-negotiable wall of sexism from gay men, the consolidation of our lesbian struggles may in fact depend on the pursuit of a different, and equally impossible, goal: the organisation of an autonomous lesbian space" (Ibid., 225). Smith points to June Jordan's analysis of coalitions: "I would say about coalitions what I said about unity, which is what for? This issue should determine the social configuration of politics" (Ibid.). The answers to that question, according to Phelan, must be a result of *getting specific* about the issues which concern us, communicating the differences, and recognising that political positioning results from a signification system that demonises, or privileges, on the basis of coherent identities

(1994). At the same time it will guard against coalitions that disregard the reformulation of oppressive hierarchies for the sake of political expediency. As Herman warns, lesbian and gay communities focused only on "their" issues can overlook other struggles, even the race and class issues within its own struggle.

In forging these chains of articulation, specific issues can be translated across categories of oppression. More specifically, the articulation process can actually break down the "us" against "them" binarism that has so defined gay and lesbian, and now queer, politics. As Jordan notes, mutual understanding about specific issues must be the compelling reason for making connections. I am not advocating "identification with the oppressor" or "assimilation" but communication: communication that goes beyond mere posturing and recognises multi-subjectivities as well as multi-structures of oppression.

Rearticulating: The Language of Politics

I noted in the opening section that my primary concern here was with the way in which the potentiality of queer theory has yet to be realised in queer activism. Above I have highlighted one theoretical framework that recognises both the need to cause trouble—that the dislocation of hegemonic space opens up new possibilities—and the need to assert identities within structures of oppression. In the final section I want to consider the way in which this model can be seen to inform activism.

First, as Smith notes, identities do play a significant role in positioning oneself in relation to the varied forms of oppression. Quite obviously this will remain the case in gay and lesbian politics as we articulate rights claims to the "heterosexual other." Equally, however, the need to recognise multi-subjectivities should inform those activist groups that claim to be representative. The elitism that increasingly is manifesting itself in gay and lesbian, and now in queer, politics must remain suspect. Diversity of identities must necessitate chains of articulation, not reflect familiar hierarchies of oppression.

Second, as noted by Smith, while Laclau and Mouffe accept that the dislocation of a hegemonic space opens up possibilities which had been unthinkable, they balance this re-spacialisation with an understanding of the "ways in which the political terrain is always simultaneously re-spacialised through new articulations or identity claims" (1994, 233). Such a re-spacialisation of the political terrain must incorporate a range of "political" activities. In her interesting account of the power of the state, "An Engaged State: Sexuality, Governance, and the Potential for Change," Davina Cooper argues that the pervasive nature of the state must be challenged from the "inside" as well as the "outside":

> We spend a lot of time on the left denouncing and condemning the strategies of others, arguing their approaches are too reformist, ultra-leftist,

Leninist, Trotskyist or Stalinist to succeed. Yet on what basis can such judgements be made? Rarely do we really know what the outcomes of particular projects might be, which will be effective, which will fail and what will befall as a result. Would we, then, be better off positively pursuing a pluralist approach to political strategy, inside and outside of the state, one that recognises the uncertainty and contingency of possible achievements, and the precarious status of prediction? (1993, 214)

Cooper is quick to note that she is not arguing for "any one privileged positioning" but for "the need to face and contest the pressures that exist, which place social forces in a hierarchy of legitimacy and political status" (Ibid.). In recognising the diverse terrain of the state, and engaging with each, the possibilities for change move beyond the "revolution versus reformation" debate. Furthermore, such interventions can enable the translation of multi-subjectivities into the political framework based on the coherent self. In short, "we're here, we're queer" can, and should, be shouted in the halls of government as well as in the streets.

Finally, Mort's directive—that we articulate multi-subjectivities into the language of politics—carries with it the assumption that we must speak a language of politics that has defined parameters, defined rules of articulation. It is, however, the closed process of signification found in such articulations that are the target of Butler's criticism. Again there is a gap between the potential of "queering" such a signification process and the translation offered, or not, by queer activists. More recently in "sexual" politics activists have increasingly avoided the references to liberation that marked the early days of the movement—references strongly dependent upon a coherent identity politics—and instead have utilised the familiar language of justice, freedom, and equality. Each of these, however, acts as a very specific signifier within a given political system. And the meaning of these concepts is often taken for granted (see assertions from Stonewall brochures of working toward "equality," "justice," and "freedom"; and similar pamphlets from OutRage! and Tatchell, 1992).

In his latest essay, "Why do Empty Signifiers Matter to Politics?" Laclau argues that the role of empty signifiers in politics is to show themselves as the interruption or breakdown of the process of signification. It could be that as the multi-subjectivities within "sexual" politics articulate their political claims in the language that has traditionally been associated with modernity's coherent subject, new possibilities emerge that both rearticulate those concepts in potentially "queer" ways and expose modernity's signification system to be, as Butler would argue, "fundamentally unnatural." In short, the very fact that those who are making those claims are doing so from multi-subject positions will inevitably affect the kind of justice, equality, or freedom that can be realised.

Given Smith's interpretation of the Laclau-Mouffe model, the way in which multi-subjectivities are exposing themselves through the proliferation of assumed identities traditionally associated with gay and lesbian politics encourages visibility and articulation of multi-political positionings. In addition, the connections that are made between groups focus on issues while continuing to strategically utilise the "us" versus "them" of identity politics. These factors, along with the shift in political language, provide space to rearticulate political signifiers. In so doing, it may be possible to draw attention to the unnaturalness of modernity's articulations of both a coherent self and justice, freedom, and equality "for all." Translating the potentiality of queer theory, of multi-subjectivities, cannot be left up to interpretation by "the other." Instead, if that potentiality is to be realised, the articulation process must be more intentional, more connected to the varied structures of oppression, and more committed to the communication of specific issues resulting from those oppressions.

A version of this paper was presented at the Political Studies Association (UK) conference in April 1995 and can be found in the conference proceeding published by the PSA, Belfast. I am grateful to David Owen and David Evans for their comments.

Bibliography

Bristow, Joseph and Angelia R. Wilson (1993) *Activating Theory: Lesbian, Gay, and Bisexual Politics* (London: Lawrence and Wishart).

Butler, Judith (1990) *Gender Trouble* (London: Routledge).

(charles) Helen (1993) "Queer Nigger: Theorizing White Activism" in Bristow and Wilson (1993).

Cooper, Davina (1993) "An Engaged State: Sexuality, Governance, and the Potential for Change" in Bristow and Wilson (1993).

Fuss, Diana (1991) "Inside/Out," *InsideOut: Lesbian Theories, Gay Theories* (New York: Routledge).

Hemmings, Clare (1993) "Resituating the Bisexual Body" in Bristow and Wilson (1993).

Herman, Didi (1994) *Rights of Passage: Struggles for Lesbian & Gay Legal Equality* (Toronto: University of Toronto Press).

Jeffreys, Sheila (1990) *Anticlimax: A Feminist Perspective on the Sexual Revolution* (London: The Women's Press).

Laclau, Ernesto, ed. (1994) *The Making of Political Identities* (London: Verso).

Laclau, Ernesto (1994) "Why do Empty Signifiers Matter to Politics?" in Weeks (1994).

Laclau, Ernesto and Chantal Mouffe (1985) *Hegemony and Socialist Strategy: Towards a Radical Democratic Politics* (London: Verso).

Mort, Frank (1994) "Essentialism Revisited? Identity Politics and Late Twentieth-Century Discourses of Homosexuality" in Weeks (1994).

Mouffe, Chantal (1993) *The Return of the Political* (London: Verso).

Mouffe, Chantal, ed. (1992) *Dimensions of Radical Democracy* (London: Verso).

Phelan, Shane (1994) *Getting Specific* (Minneapolis: University of Minnesota Press).

Phelan, Shane (1989) *Identity Politics: Lesbian Feminism and the Limits of Community* (Philadelphia: Temple University Press).

Smith, Anna Marie (1991) "Hegemony Trouble: The Political Theories of Judith Butler, Ernesto Laclau, and Chantal Mouffe" in Weeks (1994).

Smyth, Cherry (1992) *Queer Notions* (London: Scarlet).

Studzinski, Kristina (1994) *Lesbians Talk: Left Politics* (London: Scarlet).

Tatchell, Peter (1995) "Age of Consent: Equality Is not Enough," *Rouge,* issue 20, 12–14.

Tatchell, Peter (1992) *Europe in the Pink: Gay and Lesbian Equality in the New Europe* (London: Gay Men's Press).

Wilson, Angelia R., ed. (1994) *A Simple Matter Of Justice?* (London: Cassell).

Wilson, Elizabeth (1993) "Is Transgression Transgressive?" in Bristow and Wilson (1993).

Weeks, Jeffrey (1991) *Against Nature: Essays on History, Sexuality and Identity* (London: Rivers Oram).

Weeks, Jeffrey (1977) *Coming Out* (London: Quartet Books).

Weeks, Jeffrey, ed. (1994) *The Lesser Evil and the Greater Good: The Theory and Politics of Social Diversity* (London: Rivers Oram).

Weeks, Jeffrey (1985) *Sexuality and Its Discontents* (London: Routledge).

Wood, Chris (1995) *State of the Queer Nation* (London: Cassell).

6

The Centering of Right-Wing Extremism Through the Construction of an "Inclusionary" Homophobia and Racism

Anna Marie Smith

The term "homophobia" must be invested with new meaning. It is usually defined as a feeling of dread or horror toward homosexuality, a strong aversion against it, and a desire to distance oneself from it. The homophobia model suggests that official anti-lesbian and gay campaigns take the form of a one-dimensional exclusion. From this perspective, there appears to be no relation whatsoever between official bigotry and the constitution of lesbian and gay identities: the struggle remains a simple "us" versus "them" situation. When put to the test, however, this model fails to account for some of the most important aspects of actual homophobic formations.

The deployment of anti-lesbian and gay rhetoric and policies by Margaret Thatcher's Conservative Party in Britain in the late 1980s is a case in point. The Thatcherites launched their antipromotion of homosexuality campaign in the midst of a full-scale moral panic around homosexuality. Opinion polls found that homophobic attitudes peaked in 1987,[1] while the popular media was virtually saturated with extremely homophobic representations of the AIDS phenomena at this time.[2] Even in this context, however, Thatcherite homophobia did not take the form of a one-dimensional exclusion. Instead of aversion, the Thatcherites exhibited a symptomatic obsession and fascination with homosexuality. Instead of constructing a singular "us" versus "them" frontier, they made every effort to represent themselves as the "tolerant" centrists who were mediating between two extremist camps: the vociferous parents' groups, violent queer-bashers, and the whole "moral" backlash on one side, and the flaunting, disease-spreading, child-seducing queers and their corrupt socialist allies on the other.

These aspects of Thatcherite homophobic discourse were not accidental: they were central to Thatcherism's overall hegemonic representational strategy. A political project may obtain hegemonic status through the organization of consent without ever constructing an easily identifiable majority bloc of unequivocal supporters. A "consenting" bloc can be quite heterogeneous, embracing both enthusiastic believers and reluctant voters who are resigned to the notion that there is no alternative. Extensive opinion poll data demonstrate, for example, that many Conservative Party voters actually preferred Labour's policies throughout the 1980s. When asked why they did not vote for Labour, these voters responded that the Conservative Party was more "fit to govern" and that Thatcher was a "strong" leader who once again made the British proud to be British.[3] Voters are not rational actors who sort out their preferences on a set of issues and then cast their votes accordingly. Like all social agents, voters make decisions based on images and identifications; Lacanian models of misidentification and disavowal ("I know very well that Labour has better policies, but, nevertheless, I'm going to vote Conservative") are much better suited to political analysis than rational choice.[4]

The hegemonic organization of consent does not depend on actual approval for actual policies; it depends instead on the transformation of a particular political project into an imaginary. Insofar as this transformation takes place, a given project becomes thoroughly normalized: it ceases to appear as one possible alternative among many and begins to operate like a horizon. In other words, it establishes the rules and limits of the entire political agenda. The contingent and historical dimensions of the hegemonic project's vision of the social order are increasingly concealed such that this vision becomes increasingly accepted as the only possible social order. There are many risks involved for a hegemonic authoritarian project when it articulates homophobic strategies, for its hegemonic status would be jeopardized if it began to appear extremist to the majority of voters: it must always occupy an imaginary "middle ground."

Even the most opportunistic right-wing leaders must always be concerned about their "prime ministerial" or "presidential" appearance. For example, the political career of Newt Gingrich, the current Speaker of the U.S. House of Representatives, will always be hampered by his "unpresidential" radical right-wing image. By contrast, Bob Dole, in 1996 the Republican Presidential candidate, has been much more successful in articulating extreme right-wing positions while maintaining a "centrist" appearance. From a progressive perspective, the "middle ground" occupied by authoritarian hegemonies and leaders is, of course, quite far to the right. The "middle ground" appearance must nevertheless be constantly reconstructed, for the majority of the intolerant misidentify as "tolerant." They want to be reassured—especially in the midst of national crises and popular panics—that they are supporting moderate leaders who are cautiously but firmly leading the country toward a sound recovery. The aims of the intolerant are contradictory: they want official permission to unleash their bigotry, and, at the same time, they want to congratulate themselves on their "moderate," "liberal democratic" values.

A hegemonic authoritarian project must provide the necessary structures for these contradictory identifications. A total exclusion of a demonized figure may weaken the authoritarian project's claim to universality. It must pretend to accommodate virtually every legitimate social element; it must appear to be utterly unaffected by the multiplication of new social differences. At the same time, it must pursue populist strategies. It must mobilize and reproduce the reactionary forces that provide its political momentum. It must also drag the political center so far to the right that the conservative elements within the centrist and center-left parties become more prominent and move their parties to the right. This in turn contributes to the increasing alienation among the voters who traditionally support the center-left and leftist parties, such as progressive lesbians and gays, workers, blacks, and feminists. Ultimately, the authoritarian populism of the new right and the neoconservatives is itself contradictory since it depends simultaneously on the permanent mobilization of a small cadre of right-wing voters and the virtual disenfranchisement of the majority of the electorate.[5] In the United States, for example, evidence of the advance of authoritarian populism should be sought not only in the electoral victories of Reagan and Bush in the 1980s and the Republicans in the 1994 congressional elections, but also in low voter turnouts and the increasing sense of political alienation.

The deployment of the imaginary assimilable "other" allows authoritarian populism to resolve some of these contradictions in at least a partial manner. By constructing the imaginary figure of the assimilable homosexual—the "good" gay man or lesbian who knows his or her proper place: the closet—and by pretending to include this figure within the Thatcherite vision of the social order, the That-cherites were able to transform their homophobic extremism into a tolerant, moderate, and *inclusionary* discourse.

The New Racism, Multiculturalism, and Immigration

Before investigating these representational maneuvers, however, it should be noted that Thatcherite homophobic discourse borrowed extensively from the new racism. By the late 1980s, new racism metaphors and logic had become so thoroughly integrated into the sedimented background of right-wing political discourse in Britain that they operated as a hegemonic normalizing structure. The new racism shaped and legitimated the Right's mobilizations around immigration policies, law and order issues, equal opportunity programs, multiculturalism, and central government/local government relations. When the Thatcherites reiterated aspects of new racism discourse in their attack against the dangerous queer, they set into motion a whole set of powerful demonization tactics.

For the Thatcherites, the Left's greatest crime was its "social engineering" programs: its promotion of putatively anti-British concepts such as socialism, multiculturalism, and lesbian and gay rights. The Right invented many different political crises around homosexuality in the 1980s, ranging from a vicious smear campaign against a gay man during his unsuccessful election bid as a Labour Party candidate for a Parliamentary seat, to attacks against local government socialists who supported lesbian and gay positive-image campaigns, debates on safer sex education programs, and campaigns against lesbian and gay parenting. The most important moment in the Conservatives' homophobic discourse, however, was the passage of Section 28 of the 1987–88 Local Government Act. Section 28 was not aimed against a set of practices, such as sexual acts, or a class of persons, such as homosexuals; it prohibited the "*promotion of homosexuality*" by local governments.

In their parliamentary speeches on the Local Government Bill, 1987–88, the Conservative supporters of Section 28 unanimously agreed that sexuality is not fixed biologically at birth and that virtually every child and teenager is vulnerable to sexual corruption through "improper" sexual education. Many precedents for this representation of the homosexual as a seducer figure can be found within official discourse on sexuality, dating back to the 1957 Wolfenden Committee Report on homosexuality and prostitution and the nineteenth-century discourse of the sexologists.[6] The official representation of heterosexual "normalcy" as vulnerable to homosexual perversion either reflected nineteenth-century "common sense" discourse in the first place or has now become thoroughly normalized on an everyday level, for gay men are commonly stereotyped as predatory seducers who aim to pervert young children. Section 28 therefore owes its coherence in part to official and popular homophobic traditions.

There is, however, nothing in the traditional demonization of gay men as predators and seducers that links the promotion of homosexuality specifically to leftist "social engineering" by local governments. The precedent for that specific articulation lies within racial discourse, namely the 1980s debate on multiculturalism. Thatcher's own statements demonstrate the extent to which the promotion of the homosexuality crisis was manufactured with direct reference to the multiculturalism debate. At a Conservative Party conference in October 1987, Thatcher explicitly attacked progressive teachers in local government-controlled schools for politicizing the curricula. She ridiculed the inclusion of multiculturalism in the schools by suggesting that the notion of "anti-racist maths" was absurd. She then declared, "Children who need to be taught to respect traditional moral values are being taught that they have the inalienable right to be gay."[7]

The multiculturalism debate took various forms, such as the controversies about black studies programs, critical approaches to the teaching of imperial history, and the actual quantitative "imbalance" of black, Asian, and white children in locally administered schools. In each case, the Thatcherites represented the identity of the white British schoolchildren as vulnerable to corruption through illegitimate black and Asian influences and leftist "social engineering." From a radical perspective, some of the "multiculturalism" initiatives were already highly suspect. Beverly Bryan, Stella Dadzie, and Suzanne Scafe argue that black studies and multiculturalism were often used in secondary schools as a form of social control: the new curricula were supposed to placate black parents and educators who were concerned about the miseducation of black students. They make the important distinction between multicultural curricula, which emphasize cultural differences, and antiracist curricula, which emphasize the analysis of power relations.[8] From the Thatcherites' perspective, however, even the most timid step in the direction of multiculturalism constituted an illegitimate politicization of the classroom by socialist local governments. Regardless of actual skin pigmentation, parenting, and apparent "normalcy," the white child was viewed by the Thatcherites as a fragile being who needed protection from these subversive elements; her true identity had to be actively produced through proper teaching.

The logic of the right-wing response to the multiculturalism debate was borrowed in turn from the new racism movement. Analysts of British race relations trace the emergence of the new racism back to the late 1960s, when Enoch Powell's racist immigration campaign became tremendously popular. A profound shift took place in right-wing discourse on race in this moment: racial intolerance was reconstructed around arguments about cultural difference. "Race" was defined by the New Right as a cultural category: it was structured around language, rituals, traditions, and values rather than physical features alone. The new racists articulated race and national identity together so thoroughly that the differences between them virtually disappeared. At the same time, they recoded their racial exclusions within the "progressive" discourse of cultural relativism.[9] New racism discourse claimed to recognize the legitimacy of the racially "other" cultures of the south Asian and Afro-Caribbean populations within Britain.[10]

Imperial racism, by contrast, had erected Eurocentric cultural standards such that the colonized were equated with a total lack of culture. For the colonizing "settler," the "native" did not have a different culture; she was, instead, the enemy of all culture. Fanon writes:

> As if to show the totalitarian character of colonial exploitation the settler paints the native as a sort of quintessence of evil. Native society is not simply described as a society lacking in values. It is not enough for the colonist to affirm that those values have disappeared from, or still better never existed in, the colonial world. The native is declared insensitive to ethics; he represents not only the absence of values, but also the negation of values. He is, let us dare to admit, the enemy of values, and in this sense he is the absolute evil.[11]

The colonized "native" during the imperial era could only obtain "culture" by submitting to the assimilatory process of Europeanization—by adopting the customs, dress, language, and value system of the white European "settler," and, above all, by attending a European university.

By the late 1960s, this explicitly imperialist Eurocentrism had become more or less taboo in official circles as white Europeans engaged in a collective repression of their heritage.[12] Racists such as Powell feigned a respect for the cultures of the Asians and Afro-Caribbeans within Britain, thereby erasing from view the power relations that had structured the exploitative relations between the white British and the colonized for centuries. The new racists refused to claim that the racial "others" were inferior; they were, quite simply, different. Powell himself, for example, consistently argued that he was not a racist because he did not claim "that one race is inherently superior to another."[13] By avoiding the superiority-inferiority argument, the new racists could conceal their occupation of a structurally empowered position over and against the racial "others." Indeed, the new racism has become so normalized in the United States that a blatantly racist text such as *The Bell Curve*[14] that actually rests on assumptions of the biological superiority of whiteness is now accepted within mainstream political discourse as an objective factual report. The new racism is not contradictory to biologistic racist arguments; it can actually prepare the ground for their return.

For the new racist, the British, or, more precisely, the white Christian English, constituted a "race" just like the Asians, Africans, and Afro-Caribbeans; each culturally defined group had a distinct way of life that was *equally* vulnerable to disruption by other cultures. The fusion of each race-culture with an imaginary nation contributed further to the deracialization of the new racism. Each "race" had a natural "homeland" to which there corresponded an absolutely organic nationalist sentiment. With the fictitious concealment of the constitutive power relations between cultures, the erasure of differences within cultures, the naturalization of historical phenomena, and the spatialization of mythical race-cultures, the new racism preserved the xenophobic intolerance of the imperial racism, but recast it in suitably "tolerant" post-colonial terms. *Every* "race" had an *equal* interest in erecting strict immigration controls that would preserve the spatial and cultural "purity" of the race-nations. *Every* "race" had a naturally exclusionary culture in which racial otherness was always, by definition, alien. If white Britons resented the presence of those who, by their cultural otherness, constituted threats to the vulnerable (white) British nation, they should be allowed to express their naturally antagonistic sentiments. The new racism erects "thresholds of tolerance": the racial "others" could not be "digested" by the host race-nation if they arrived in large numbers and retained their dangerous alien identities.

For the new racist, then, it is simple common sense to state that the essence of Britishness is white Christianity, and that it is the patriotic duty of every politician to protect that essence from contamination by racial invaders. Consciousness of one's true racial-national identity translates directly into a natural interest in the fortification of that race-culture's national borders against racial aliens. The new racism transforms racist immigration policies into an entirely justifiable humanism. It recodes "intolerance" as a legitimate expression of natural beliefs; it liberates the racially intolerant from their post-colonial condition of guilt. Above all, the new racism provides a structure that allows the intolerant to misrecognize themselves as tolerant. Within the new racism, it is perfectly consistent to state that a blatantly racist immigration law has nothing to do with racial intolerance and, indeed, ought to be passed in the interests of the racial minorities themselves, for greater restrictions on racial immigration will by definition prepare the way for better "race relations." Since the white backlash was inevitable—and had nothing to do with political leadership—the racial minorities themselves *needed* racist immigration laws to ameliorate their condition within Britain.

Contemporary post-colonial racism cannot be analyzed solely in terms of nineteenth-century racial superiority frameworks. The new racism introduces a whole set of recodings that deracialize racism—euphemisms such as patriality in Britain's racist immigration laws are exemplary in this regard. (I will return to the patriality distinction in British legislation below.) The new racism teaches the racist that she has never been racist, that "the [white English] people" are fighting for their very survival, that the racial minorities themselves would pursue exactly the same policies in their own "homelands," and that the preservation of racial-cultural-national purity is the best defense against racial tensions. For the new racist, then, racist immigration legislation is the centerpiece of good race relations policies.

The new racism therefore constitutes a post-colonial departure from imperial racism. It rearticulates the imperial fusion of Britishness with white-Englishness, and racial otherness with anti-Britishness, but this articulation is now inserted into a matrix of representations that conceal and reverse relations of domination and resistance. The new racism resituates the dominant culture as the vulnerable defender who faces a devastating invasion by an overwhelming external force, namely foreign immigration and anti-British cultures. Racism becomes a natural and wholly legitimate resistance discourse—hence the numerous references by the new racists to Britain's resistance against the Nazis during World War II. These references are, of course, highly ironic since the new racism borrows heavily from fascist and anti-Semitic discourse.[15] In any event, with the naturalization of racial antagonisms, radically "intolerant" discourses are given a "tolerant" appearance. Repression and taboos that foreclose open discussion of the racist imperial tradition, combined with unworked-through resentment following from the loss of the colonies, and the displacement of that resentment and anxieties about socioeconomic dislocations onto the ethnic minority immigrant communities, contribute to the continual return of bitterly racist antagonisms in British politics through the 1960s to present. Only the thin veneer of racial euphemisms has shifted over this period, with blatantly racist discourse on immigration being recoded in discourse on criminality, inner-city decay and unrest, anti-Western terrorism, and multiculturalism. Indeed, the fundamentally cultural definition of race in the new racism allows for this mobile relocation of the racial-national borders to any number of sociopolitical sites.

New racist immigration discourse never took the simple form of the defense of the geographically fixed borders that protected one biologically defined group from the invasion by another biologically defined group, for it constructed white-Christian-Englishness as an imaginary cultural space. In addition to its simplistic invasion logic, it organized the immigration crisis around the highly mobile metaphors of leeching, contamination, and subversion. In this manner, the very logic of the new racism prepared the way for the redeployment of its immigration discourse to other sites of contestation around the boundaries of "normal" white Britishness. At the same time, the new racism has provided a compensatory framework for this continual return of racist intolerance; proponents of racial purification can take comfort in the myth that they are actually supporting multicultural "tolerance," for they can tell themselves that they are pursuing policies that serve the interests of both their own beleaguered racial group and that of the invading racially "other" group.

The Strategic Invocation of the "Good Homosexual" and the "Assimilable Immigrant"

The multiculturalism debate, then, did not take the form of an isolated demonization, for the anti-multiculturalists redeployed the new racist immigration discourse about foreign invaders and beleaguered patriots. The antipromotion of homosexuality campaign reiterated this appropriation of the new racism. When he presented the first bill that would have prohibited the promotion of homosexuality in the House of Lords in December 1986, Lord Halsbury stated,

> We have for several decades past been emancipating minorities who claimed that they were disadvantaged. Are they grateful? Not a bit. We emancipated races and got inverted racism. We emancipate homosexuals and they condemn heterosexism as chauvinist sexism, male oppression and so on. They will push us off the pavement [sidewalk] if we give them a chance.[16]

National self-determination and civil liberties were defined in this speech as privileges bestowed by a generous and "permissive" society. Entire histories of resistance against imperialist, capitalist, racist, homophobic, and sexist exploitation and oppression were erased from view. Decolonization and the "permissive" reforms around race and sexuality were combined together and described as an excessively tolerant mistake that had given birth to militant feminist, antiracist, and queer movements. Many of the so-called "permissive" reforms of the 1960s, such as race relations legislation and the decriminalization of homosexuality, actually have had highly ambiguous effects; black and Asian activists, as well as white racist extremists, have been charged with promoting racial hatred,[17] while the decriminalization of private sex acts between two consenting male adults has supported the intensification of the policing of an extremely broad range of public sex acts.[18] These minor and ambiguous reforms were nevertheless represented by Lord Halsbury as profoundly "emancipatory" measures. However, the paternalistic gifts of reform had been exploited by the "ungrateful" naughty children of the 1960s. The "tolerant" parent class—the dominant white-English-heterosexual culture—had become besieged by the very minorities that it had liberated. Like the new racism, Halsbury's homophobic discourse suggested that the only reasonable solution to this crisis was the reconstruction of the natural frontiers between the racial/sexual "foreigners" and the white-English familial nation.

The debates on Section 28 were saturated with similar reversals of power relations, such that the "normal" heterosexual population appeared as a besieged encampment that—because of the folly of excessive tolerance—was threatened with an invasion of homosexual "perversity." Grotesque distortions of the AIDS phenomenon were central to this reversal, and to the very construction of the endangered frontier between normalcy and perversity. Dame Jill Knight declared, "Some of that which is being taught to children in our schools would undoubtedly lead to a great spread of AIDS."[19] She also argued that Section 28 was necessary because "AIDS starts with and comes mainly from homosexuals" and only "spreads to others" later.[20]

Like the new racism, however, Thatcherite homophobic discourse was subtle and complex. Homosexuality was not simply represented as an illegitimate element and a dangerous invader. Thatcherite homophobia was articulated to the overall strategy of the Conservative Party—namely, the hegemonic redefinition of the entire political agenda in Britain. To achieve and to maintain a hegemonic position, the Thatcherites had to make their project appear to be the only possible solution to virtually every sociopolitical crisis. Because it was deployed within an overall hegemonic strategy, then, Thatcherite homophobia had to present itself to the British electorate as a centrist and rational response to the crisis around homosexuality and AIDS.

The extremism of homophobia seems to disappear as homophobia constructs an imaginary figure, the "good homosexual" and promises to grant this figure full inclusion within the "normal" social order. The "good homosexual" is defined as the "not-dangerous queer": the "good homosexual" is self-limiting, closeted, desexualized, and invisible, while the "dangerous queer" is an incorrigible pervert who pursues the sociopolitical infection of the general population at every opportunity. Where the new racism promotes the return of the non-white-Anglo immigrant to her "natural homeland," the pseudotolerant homophobia pretends to accept homosexuals as long as we remain closeted and "segregated" at a sanitary distance from heterosexual society. The Thatcherites implied that wherever homosexuals are not illegitimately politicized by socialist agitators, we tend to remain closeted, invisible, and relatively harmless. The closeted "good homosexual" space is therefore analogous to the new racism's "natural homelands," for this is the space that homosexuals are supposed to occupy in the absence of unnatural political intervention.

If the closet is for pseudotolerant homophobia our "natural homeland," we should note that this is not a neutral space: we can only return to the closet through self-annihilation. It need hardly be said that the "good homosexual" does not and cannot exist, for she is a contradiction in terms. Totally isolated from a lesbian and gay community, bereft of political solidarity, alienated from sexual relationships, and purified of every last fragment of "abnormal" sexual desires, the "good homosexual" would be the last homosexual. If we lesbians and gays ever did manage to squeeze ourselves into the total confines of this final position, we would, in effect, commit collective suicide, for we would destroy the conditions necessary to our survival as a viable alternative community and political movement. Thatcherism already knew this: it already knew that every social group's collective survival depends on the "promotion" of its specific sociocultural imaginary, for it had already seized on the idea that only the vigorous "promotion" of a "proper" (read: a heterosexist and racist) education would save the "authentic" (heterosexual white Christian English) British people from cultural extinction.

This contradiction—the fact that no one can actually occupy the position of the "good homosexual"—does not block the invocation of this figure in homophobic discourses that want to recode themselves as "tolerant." The "don't ask, don't tell, don't pursue" policy on homosexuality in the American military promises inclusion for lesbians and gays only to the extent that we conform to the rules of the "good homosexual." The policy states that "sexual orientation will not be a bar to [military] service unless manifested by homosexual conduct." Where the British measure, Section 28, prohibits the promotion of homosexuality, the American military policy bans the manifestation of homosexual conduct. In both cases, the utterly chaste, socially isolated, and politically inactive homosexual is supposedly tolerated as a legitimate member of "normal" society. This so-called "tolerance" therefore effectively takes the form of cultural genocide: if lesbians and gays could actually conform to the rules of inclusion and thereby pass as legitimate members of "normal" society, we would have to pay the price of self-destruction.

The supporters of Section 28 were almost perfectly consistent in their invocation of the "good homosexual" and their exclusive demonization of the "dangerous queer." Lord Halsbury, for example, argued that "responsible" homosexuals had to be set apart from their "exhibition[ist]," "promiscuous," and "proselytizing" counterparts.[21] Lord Monson stated that he recognized the "genuine" rights and freedoms of homosexuals, but emphasized that these rights pertained only to the "bedrooms of consenting adults" and not to "propaga[tion]."[22] Dickens, another Tory MP, argued that lesbians and gays who wanted support against the "queer-bashers" should accept the decriminalization of homosexuality "gently and steadily and not expect too much." Apparently unaware of his own double entendres, he concluded, "[homosexuals] are only likely to get that support [against violent attacks] if they stop continuing to flaunt their homosexuality and thrusting it down other people's throats."[23]

It is, of course, true that some of the supporters of Section 28 failed to invoke the "good homosexual": they described lesbians and gays in an utterly one-dimensional homophobic manner. Queer-bashers outside Parliament—whose violence was in effect sanctioned by the Thatcherite doublespeak—made no distinction between the "good homosexual" and the "dangerous queer." These discourses of singular bigotry were actually put to use by the Thatcherites. Contrasting themselves to the explicit bigots on the one side, and the "loony Left" on the other, the supporters of Section 28 were able to locate themselves as the centrist representatives of the moderate majority,[24] in a situation in which they would otherwise be recognized themselves as extremist reactionaries. Where Thatcher used the National Front to represent her stance on race as a moderate position that mediated between two extremes, the white fascists versus the black and Asian anarchists,[25] the pro-Section 28 discourse also "centered" itself between two extremes. The arguments of both the bigots and the opposers of Section 28 were represented in this context as equivalents, as equally disruptive extremisms—and the supporters' response to the crisis was represented as the only possible strategy for the restoration of order.

Again, the new racism argues that immigration policies that keep the majority of black and Asian migrants in their "natural homelands" would serve the true interests of both the racial minorities in question and the white-Anglo dominant bloc. Similarly, pseudotolerant homophobia represents the prohibition of the promotion of homosexuality as a policy that would keep homosexuals in our "natural state"—the closet—and would thereby serve the real interests of both the true homosexual community and the heterosexual "general population." Some of the supporters of Section 28 actually did express concern regarding the rise in homophobia against lesbians and gays, and argued that Section 28 was the best remedy in that it would "remove the source of the disquiet,"[26] namely the "unacceptable activities of a few extremist councils."[27] Some Section 28 supporters recognized that the lesbian and gay community faced rising discrimination and violence, but they attributed that backlash to the work of the dangerous queer, rather than to their own discourse. Conservative MP Wilshire stated that it is the "arrogan[ce], self-assertive[ness], aggressive boastfulness and self-glorification" of some homosexuals that has offended the "majority of people."[28] Homophobic violence was thereby naturalized, just as racist violence was depicted by Powell as the "natural" result of the "provocation" of nonwhite immigration. The "good homosexual" was therefore represented by the Thatcherites as the innocent victim of militant queer activism or as the pawn in a socialist plot. The Thatcherites concealed their homophobia by claiming that their real enemy was the socialist agitator in local authorities; indeed, it was implied that the Thatcherites who passed Section 28 into law were the true representatives of the real homosexual—the closeted majority who disowned lesbian and gay activism. Like the new racism, pseudotolerant homophobia argues that segregation serves the true interests of the persecuted minority in question.

The Incitement of Self-Disciplinary Assimilation

In the British case, the imaginary inclusion of the "good homosexual" within "normal society" reproduces a representational strategy that is central to the new racism. Again, the imaginary inclusion of the "assimilable [black or Asian] immigrant" gives the extremist new racism discourse a centrist appearance. Making racism "respectable" and "official" was one of Powell's most important achievements. Like all new racists, he recoded his extremism as a patriotic, common-sense humanism through his pseudoinclusion of the "assimilable" black or Asian immigrant. Concealing Britain's powerful anti-Semitic tradition, Powell claimed that the Conservative Party wanted

> to see the coloured immigrants no less integrated into the life and society of what is now their homeland than any other group, such as the Jewish community or the thousands of Poles living in Britain today. No other prospect is tolerable.

He also pledged to oppose anyone who claimed that there is "any difference between one citizen of this country and another on the grounds of his origin." These comments were included in Powell's contribution to a feature on "the immigrant problem" in the *Wolverhampton Express and Star* in 1964. Powell's own article was entitled, "Integration is the Only Way—Over Many Years." Powell's exclusion of any black or Asian immigrant who failed his impossible test of total assimilation was revealed in other passages in the article. He directly linked the "excessive" rate of black and Asian immigration with a whole range of "undesirable social problems." He also insisted that the "idea of immigrants as an unassimilated element in our society, living apart in certain districts and following only certain occupations, is insupportable." For Powell, the failure of assimilation was not a problem because black and Asian Britons would be denied full equality, but because it left this naturally alien population concentrated in undisciplined centers of otherness: "Any substantial addition to the immigrant population would defer assimilation indefinitely and entail upon Britain the evils of a deeply divided nation and society."

The rate of black and Asian immigration operated as a metaphor for the unspeakable racist anxieties around eugenics. In a discussion of the alleged racial difference in the birth rates of the white English and black and Asian communities in Britain, Powell argued that racial minorities will only achieve the same birth rate as whites when the "immigrant element [becomes] thoroughly absorbed into a host population." "Thorough absorption," however, cannot proceed because the rate of black and Asian immigration was already "excessive"; consequently, the racial aliens had already constructed separatist encampments that served as powerful bulwarks against assimilation. For Powell, the presence of distinct communities of Afro-Caribbeans and Asians in Britain constituted a lethal threat to the entire (white Christian English) nation.

> To suppose that the habits of the great mass of [black and Asian] immigrants, living in their own communities, speaking their own languages and maintaining their native customs, will change appreciably in the next two or three decades is a supposition so grotesque that only those could make it who are determined not to admit what they know to be true or not to see what they fear.[29]

The viral cycle of the enemy population is therefore self-perpetuating: as blacks and Asians arrive in larger numbers, they are less likely to become assimilated, more likely to reproduce at a higher rate, and more likely to resist integration in the future. The preservation of any degree of cultural difference, against the extremely violent pressures of "total absorption," on the part of the British racial minorities amounts to nothing less than a declaration of civil war. By calling for "total absorption" and the lowering of birth rates among Afro-Caribbeans and Asians, Powell made his promise of inclusion for racial minorities conditional upon their voluntary collective suicide as culturally distinct peoples. The only "tolerable" black or Asian difference, then, is the difference that promotes its own cultural extinction. It is in this sense that the Thatcherite prohibition of the promotion of homosexuality reproduced the assimilatory logic and the genocidal fantasies of the new racism.

The cultural violence in Powell's message was nevertheless concealed for his white supporters who misidentified as "tolerant" insofar as he reiterated his imaginary inclusion of assimilable racial otherness within the "normal" social order. Powell even claimed that his proposed program of racial purification was supported by many black and Asian Britons. In his article, "Integration the Only Way—Over Many Years," Powell stated that black and Asian immigration controls would contribute to "the interests of everyone, and most of all the immigrants themselves." Referring to his regular meetings with his constituents, he pointed out that many Afro-Caribbean and

Asian Britons had sought his aid as their MP, and that he had been "glad to serve them."[30] He continued to speak in the name of the assimilated black or Asian citizen throughout his most explicitly racist period in the late 1960s and early 1970s. In a 1968 speech at Eastbourne, he attacked race relations legislation as "reverse discrimination" and called for an official "repatriation" program for black and Asian Britons (in which all Britons of Afro-Caribbean, African, and south Asian descent would be encouraged or even forced to return to their "original homelands"). In the very same speech, he claimed that demands for increased black and Asian immigration controls had "come as much from my [black and Asian] immigrant constituents as from the rest, if not, more so; in this matter I was convinced of speaking for and in the interest of all my constituents." Here, as elsewhere, Powell strategically "deracialized" his racist attack on black and Asian immigrants by constructing a racially inclusive image of his supporters, and by stating that his real enemy was the "tiny minority" in control of the "channels of communication." Their crime was the promotion of censorship and disinformation; he charged that they would "resort to any device or extremity to blind both themselves and others" on the question of black and Asian immigration.[31] Powell therefore used the image of his black and Asian supporters to represent his discourse as a moderate and objective exercise in counterdisinformation.

The notion that the construction of sanitizing frontiers between the "normal" social order and the excluded actually serves the interests of the assimilable members of a demonized minority reemerges in Thatcherite homophobic discourse. In the parliamentary debates on Section 28, Lord Halsbury read a letter that he said was from a "male homosexual."

> I want to say how fed up I am with my fellow homosexuals. They have brought it upon themselves, their unpopularity. They are too promiscuous, too aggressive and exhibitionist. I cannot stand the sight of them. I wish they would keep themselves to themselves.[32]

The question of the document's authenticity is of course irrelevant. Through his quotation of this letter, Lord Halsbury attempted to position himself as the spokesperson for the "good homosexual," thereby reproducing Powell's invocation of the assimilable black or Asian immigrant who supports racist immigration legislation. By constructing an imaginary self-hating homosexual community that is totally opposed to the promotion of homosexuality— and who would therefore welcome the elimination of the lesbian and gay community as we now know it—Lord Halsbury positioned himself as a democratic hero who had rescued the "good homosexual" from the tyranny of the activists.

Again, these imaginary gestures of inclusion and democratic representation are chiefly targeted at the intolerant bigot who wants both to enjoy the Thatcherites' liberation of his bigotry and to retain his self-identification as a "tolerant" centrist. The invocation of the "good homosexual" by homophobic forces nevertheless raises serious strategic issues for the lesbian and gay movements. Although no lesbian or gay man can fully occupy the position of the "good homosexual," there is no shortage of volunteers for the "good homosexual"'s self-disciplining campaign. Deep divisions already exist within the lesbian and gay community regarding the legitimacy of militant activism, gender nonconformity, and sexual perversion.

Marshall Kirk and Hunter Madsen's notorious book *After the Ball*[33] is a classic expression of homophobic self-hatred. The authors blame the rise in homophobia on the "excessive" militancy of the "abnormal" members of the lesbian and gay communities. Not hesitating to use the highly subjective categories of "health," "morality," and "gender norms," and not hesitating to perpetuate myths about the abusive character of queer sexuality, they argue that the proper response of lesbians and gays to homophobia is a thorough self-sanitization.

> [The lesbian and gay community is represented as] *disgustingly* different and incapable of ever fitting in with the mentally healthy and morally upright. We're assumed to consist entirely of extreme stereotypes: men ultraswishy and ultraviolet, Frankensteinian thug-women with bolts in their necks, moustachio'd Dolly Parton wanna-bes, leather-men in boots and whips, ombudsmen of pederasty squiring their ombudsboys—all ridiculous, deranged, or criminal. And when we are *finally* allowed to rally and march, to lay our cast before the cameras of the straight American public, what do we do? We call out of the woodwork as our ambassadors of bad all the screamers, stompers, genderbenders, sadomasochists, and pederasts and confirm America's worst fears and hates.[34]

The authors even go so far as to include a "Self-Policing Social Code" for lesbians and gay men that formally summarizes the authors' call for self-discipline.[35] A thorough critique of homophobia, misogyny, and racism is, of course, entirely absent from their text. Bruce Bawer reproduces Kirk and Madsen's misrepresentation of homophobia as a mere public relations problem. His text effectively constructs an analogy between homophobic bigots and radical queer activists such that they become equivalent extremists and Bawer's own right-wing discourse appears as centrist common sense.[36] David Brock, an openly gay man and the author of a sensationalistic book against Anita Hill,[37] has also emerged as a prominent neoconservative intellectual.[38]

It should be noted here that there is nothing *inauthentic* about a conservative lesbian or gay man; there is no natural relation between progressive politics and the embrace of a homosexual identity. This antiessentialist point can be made, however, without abandoning all attempts to construct lesbian and gay politics as a fundamentally antiracist, feminist, and leftist project. Lesbian and gay activism should not become a single-issue movement that pretends to ignore the differences between conservatives, liberals, and radicals. Kirk, Madsen, Bawer, and Brock should be rejected by lesbians and gays not because they are gay and conservative—and as such occupy a pathological or traitorous category—but simply because they are conservative.

In any event, American neoconservative homosexuals will find themselves in an increasingly untenable situation. The British New Right has not been substantially defined by a religious agenda. The sociocultural elements that the British New Right adds to the monetarist and antistatist moments of neoconservatism chiefly consist of a moralistic exclusion of welfare "scroungers," a demonization of anything even remotely related to socialism, a racist patriotism, and an AIDS-era homophobia. The attacks on feminism and abortion rights that have been so prominent in American New Right have been relatively minor in its British counterpart. The British New Right's campaign to prohibit the promotion of homosexuality was a fairly isolated exception to its general avoidance of sex, gender, and morality.[39] Where the British New Right did launch a vociferous campaign against lesbian and gay rights, it made a consistent attempt to appear to include the "good homosexual."

In the United States, the neoconservative right tends either to avoid homophobic discourse altogether or to code its homophobic policies in pseudotolerant language and to engage in the pseudoinclusions of the "good homosexual" that are typical of the British New Right. The American religious right, however, is increasingly defining the American right as a whole. Ralph Reed has attempted to "mainstream" Pat Robertson's extremist Christian Coalition as a liberal democratic movement by calling for new coalitions between the religious right and African-Americans and by denouncing the KKK, George Wallace, and anti-Semitism.[40] In actuality, the religious right, like the neoconservatives, only pretends to champion liberal democratic rights and freedoms in order to defend traditional class, race, gender, and sexual inequalities. The moral authoritarianism of the American religious right is so profound that its hegemonic strategies—its attempts to pass its basically fascist agenda off as a liberal democratic project—reach a limit with homophobia; its pseudoinclusions extend only as far as right-wing women, blacks, and Jews. Unlike the neoconservatives, the religious right does not practice even a tokenistic or imaginary inclusion of homosexuality; it is engaged in nothing less than a total war against the entire lesbian and gay community.[41] No lesbian or gay man—not even the most fervent supporter of neoconservative politics—will be able to earn special dispensation in the religious right's holy war on America.

As lesbians and gays mobilized against Section 28 in Britain, voices of conservative reaction from within the community were raised against militant queers. These voices became a small but organized force during the campaign against homophobia that was led by the direct action group OutRage! in the 1990s. These conservative homosexuals basically agreed with the letter writer quoted by Lord Halsbury: queer militancy and its linkages with socialism, feminism, and antiracism were to blame for the rise in homophobia. They accepted the Thatcherite argument that the best remedy for homophobia is the censorship of progressive queer politics.[42] John Marshall, the editor of *Gay Times*, declared in an interview with a national daily newspaper, "The biggest enemies of our movement are those gay people who have decided that we should be called queer."[43] Radical queer groups such as OutRage! have won tremendous support from the British lesbian and gay community, but conservative homosexuals continue to attack all those who fail to observe the self-disciplining regulations of the "good homosexual." Wherever homophobic intolerance is recoded as "tolerant centrism," debates on assimilation, cooptation, and erasure will remain prominent within the lesbian and gay communities.

The Postcolonial Context of Queer Activism

The articulation of the struggle against homophobia with the struggle against racism is an urgent priority, and yet our understanding about the connection between homophobia and racism within specific political contexts is insufficient. In the United States, for example, lesbian and gay male leaders seem to be rushing headlong to embrace demands for gay marriage and gay spousal benefits without thinking through the implications of their campaign in the current political climate. Marital status is being used in an unprecedented manner in welfare "reforms" to penalize unmarried women, especially young single mothers on welfare. We need only examine the speeches of David Duke[44] to see that much of this campaign against young single mothers on welfare is motivated by racist arguments about the excessive fertility of the mythical black and Latino/a urban underclass. In actual fact, the majority of women on welfare are white, 50 percent of welfare mothers apply for benefits because of divorce, 30 percent of the fathers of babies born to girls under sixteen are men in their twenties or older, and childbirths among young black women have decreased since the 1970s.[45] Women of color nevertheless remain symbolically overrepresented in the official discourse on welfare reform. It is utterly unacceptable that the leaders of the lesbian and gay communities are failing to take this broader political context into account. This is not to say that demands for the extension of marital status to lesbians and gays should be altogether abandoned. However, our leaderships should be carefully constructing coalitions with welfare rights and antiracist groups in the pursuit of radical social change that would wholly transform the state's entire disciplinary stance vis-à-vis domestic relationships and parenting arrangements. To the extent that they pursue a narrow demand for the extension of marital status as it is currently defined in official discourse, the lesbian and gay leaderships risk adding our voice to that of the conservative, racist, and misogynist champions of the moralistic state.

In the case of Britain, it is particularly crucial that we recognize the specifically postcolonial context of official homophobic discourse. As racist colonialism isolated the Europeanizable "native" and set her against her

recalcitrant brothers and sisters, contemporary new racism invents the mythical figure of the assimilated black or Asian citizen and speaks its anti-non-
white-Anglo immigration and antiaffirmative action policies in her name,
and contemporary homophobia constructs the mythical figure of the "good
homosexual" and promises to include her within the "normal" social order
in return for her denunciation of her fellow queers.

The immigration legislation of the 1960s and 1970s that redefined
Britain's national borders after decolonization actually laid part of the
groundwork for the articulation of race and sexuality in the 1980s. As a
result of Britain's peculiar racial history—its central role in the slave trade, its
banishment and "resettlement" of Africans, and its economic hegemony
over the imperial colonies—very few Africans, Afro-Caribbeans, and south
Asians were permanently settled in the British Isles before World War II. The
migration of Afro-Caribbeans and Asians to Britain during the postwar
period was widely regarded as a racial invasion, even though these peoples
were descendants of the workers, indentured labourers, and slaves who had
virtually built the British Empire, and even though there was not supposed
to be an actual border between the "mother country" and her colonies. As
the process of decolonization progressed, and popular anxieties about black
and Asian immigration escalated, this border was in fact invented. Both the
Conservative and Labour Parties ultimately supported racist immigration
laws that specifically controlled black and Asian migration. Before these laws
were passed, there were no official distinctions between British passport
holders; citizens of the colonies were supposed to enjoy the same rights of
travel and settlement throughout the Empire as those who had been born in
Britain. Legislators could not respond to the "threat" of black and Asian
immigration by simply banning the entry of all people born in the former
colonies, for they wanted to leave the national door open to the families of
the white Britons who had worked abroad as colonial administrators, military officials, religious missionaries, and private entrepreneurs. The new
frontier in the postcolonial nation therefore had to operate in a complex
manner: it had to repel blacks and Asians and to allow whites safe passage,
and it had to conceal its racist operation from view.

The new laws achieved this goal by introducing a whole set of spatial,
temporal, and kinship distinctions. The 1971 Immigration Act is a case in
point. It restricted the "right of abode" in the United Kingdom to "patrials":
persons who were born in the U.K.; persons who obtained British citizenship
through adoption, registration, or naturalization; U.K. citizens who had
immigrated from another country and settled in the U.K. for a continuous
period of five years; and Commonwealth citizens who had a parent or grand-
parent born in the United Kingdom. It established a voluntary "repatriation"
payment scheme, whereby the government would pay for the travelling
expenses of any "nonpatrials" who wished to settle permanently in another
country. Because large-scale black and Asian migration to Britain only began

in the postwar period, legislators in the 1960s and 1970s were virtually assured that the foreign-born applicants for patrial status who had parents or grandparents born in Britain were white. Dilip Hiro estimates that because the 1971 law created a new "loophole" for the white descendants of Britons in Australia, New Zealand, and Canada—if their parents or grandparents had been born in the U.K., they could apply for "patrial" status—it allowed for a possible increase in total immigration.[46] When the 1971 Immigration Act went into effect in 1973, it virtually brought an end to primary black and Asian immigration.

The concept of "patriality" in this law was taken directly from the 1968 Commonwealth Immigrants Act that the Labour government had passed to exclude Kenyan and Asian immigrants. For our purposes, it should be noted that the 1971 act officially constructed the nation as a racial space that was defined in terms of familial blood ties. Home Secretary Reginald Maudling declared:

> It is said that most of the people with patrial status will be white. Most of us are white, and it is completely turning racial discrimination on its head to say that it is wrong for any country to accord those with a family relationship to it a special position in the law of that country.[47]

The centrality of the familial metaphor in distinguishing between the "true" British and the pretenders would be proved once again in the 1987–88 parliamentary debates on the prohibition of homosexuality. Just as the very peoples whose labor had given Britain its prominence in the developed world were disowned as unwanted foreigners, so too would an entire British gay male and lesbian population be characterized as an un-British invasion from the immoral outside. Where the racist privileging of white familial ties resulted in legislation that tore black and Asian families apart, right-wing concerns about protecting children from sexual corruption led to the forced separation of hundreds, perhaps even thousands, of lesbian and gay parents from their children. The familial definition of the British frontier that was deployed in the 1980s attack on the lesbian and gay community therefore had an important precedent in the racist closure of the nation in the postcolonial 1960s. In retrospect, we should not be surprised that the most venomous homophobic representations in Thatcherite discourse were reserved for the black lesbian. According to the New Right calculus, she was placed at the furthest possible distance outside the white familial nation.

Toward a Progressive Response to the Centrist Accommodation of Racism and Homophobia

Given the extensive advance of authoritarian populism in both Britain and the United States, only a fool or a sell-out could suggest a happy conclusion to a study of contemporary racism and homophobia. It may nevertheless be strategically useful to issue a warning: the accommodation of authoritarian populism by centrists and liberals will almost inevitably lead to a further shift to the right in British and American politics. Racist colonizing cultures, such as the formations that have been predominant in Britain and the United States, are wholly unprepared to cope with the current restructuring of the global economy and the decline in wealth and quality of life that is affecting virtually everyone except the very rich.[48] A racist colonizing culture incites the construction of pathological superiority complexes among white Europeans and white Anglo-Americans.[49] Since white cultures have been virtually saturated with megalomaniacal fantasies of the natural superiority of whiteness for centuries, whites who have not worked through their racist heritage tend to respond to the increasingly obvious signs of socioeconomic decline with nothing less than racist rage. Whiteness—and male whiteness in particular—has been trained to expect natural supremacy; now it cannot accept its lack, its inability to realize its racial promise. Instead of working through these failures and grasping the role of corporate greed in global restructuring, racist whiteness pursues self-splitting and projection. Locked in the individualistic ideology that the neoconservatives have normalized as common sense, racist whiteness secretly blames itself for its failure, but because it retains undigested aspects of its pathological superiority complex, it cannot openly avow its own shortcomings. Whiteness instead projects that unbearable part of itself—the part that appears to prevent whiteness from arriving at its true destiny as a master race—onto the demonized "other."[50]

It should be noted that although this relation appears to be a simple scapegoating formation, it is actually narcissistic in nature,[51] and as such, is relatively immune to superficial rational arguments. Racists appear to blame the Latino immigrant, the woman of color hired through an affirmative action program, or even the worker in a foreign country for the loss of their jobs or the decline in their wealth. Underneath this scapegoating appearance, however, the racists merely use the racial other as a site for the acting out of their own self-loathing. Racist whites are so thoroughly caught up in their superiority complex that whiteness consistently remains the chief object of their interest; as consistent segregationists, racist whites do not step outside their white-only imaginary even in their demonization of racial otherness. By the very structure of this narcissistic discourse, then, the racists' image of racial otherness has very little to do with actual blacks, Latinos, and Asians. The racists' racial otherness is largely the product of the racist whites' projection of their own hated selves onto the demonized figures of the day. As such, racism cannot be defeated by merely demonstrating that it misrepresents actual blacks, Latinos, and Asians for, by its very structure, it never promised to do so in the first place. Racist whites could be shown time and time again that racial others were not actually to blame for their socioeconomic conditions, and they would nevertheless stubbornly cling to their racism.

Like racist culture, heterosexist culture incites the formation of pathological superiority complexes. Heterosexuals who have not worked through their debt to homophobia often position themselves as omniscient with respect to homosexuals. Homophobic bigots, for example, often act as if they were able to "read the minds" of homosexuals.[52] Indeed, I have sometimes found myself in truly surreal arguments with homophobic bigots who have told me that my lesbianism was just a "phase," that my lover was not really my lover, and that they knew more about lesbian culture than I did. Homophobia can also take the form of self-splitting and projection. The scandal about gays in the American military, for example, offers imperialist patriotic Americans an attractive site for the acting out of their anxieties about the general decline of American hegemony. They secretly sense that there is something fundamentally lacking at the core of their own American heterosexual culture that is to blame for the American decline. Unable to confront their own shortcomings, however, they project the "evil within" onto the homosexual. The pervert wearing the military uniform of the once omnipotent nation becomes an external symbolization of their own unbearable rotten core. As such, the bigots who oppose the presence of gays in the military will not change their views simply because they have been exposed to studies that show that lesbians and gay men do not actually have a negative effect on military discipline, for their discourse actually has very little to do with lesbians and gays ourselves. Again, homophobic bigots are not classically "phobic." While they know little about our worlds and indeed celebrate their ignorance about homosexuality, they do not avoid homosexuality altogether. More precisely, they do not avoid their version of homosexuality; they are instead obsessed with their demonized images of homosexuality. Their obsession is in a sense structurally necessary, for the demonization of homosexuality is part of the discursive "glue" that holds their otherwise hopelessly self-contradictory discourse together.[53]

Barricaded behind impenetrable walls of superiority complexes, racist and homophobic bigots never actually have a relation with racial and sexual "others" as such. The bigots' obsession with themselves and their fantasies of power is such that even their hatred remains to a significant extent a relation of themselves with themselves—they tend to use racial and sexual "others" as empty screens upon which they can project and act out their self-hatred. They do not even respect the racial or sexual other enough to construct their hatred in response to actual black, Asian, Latina, and lesbian and gay discourses.

This narcissistic aspect of racist and homophobic discourse must be taken into consideration in the construction of resistance strategies. First, from the point of view of the success of authoritarian populism, it simply does not matter that this right-wing discourse offers "pretend inclusions" and insincere promises of "tolerance." It does not matter that many blacks, Latinos, Asians, lesbians, gays, and women are not convinced by the right-wing promises of inclusion, for these pseudoinclusions are not being performed for us. Authoritarian populist pseudoinclusions are performed for the most part so that the British New Right and the American neoconservative and religious right can position themselves as liberal democratic discourses. Thus positioned, authoritarian populism then thoroughly hollows out the most progressive moments of the liberal democratic tradition, and reinfuses those moments with utterly right-wing meanings. Thus gender and racial equality is redefined as "gender neutrality" and "colorblindness," such that white men can construct themselves as victims of affirmative action; "self-determination" becomes a legitimation for racist immigration policies or the defence of segregated schools; and the demand for the protection of democracy against a tyrannical minority is used to dismiss lesbian and gay rights as an authoritarian imposition of "special rights" onto an otherwise "egalitarian" society.

It hardly need be said that because authoritarian populism attempts to distance itself from its fascist origins and to burrow deep within the liberal democratic tradition through subversive parody and appropriation, leftist antiracist and antihomophobic resistance discourses must wage an all-out war to seize the liberal democratic tradition back from the right. It would, of course, be highly insufficient to stop there—if we could fantasize for even a moment that such a victory would be possible in our lifetimes—for the liberal democratic tradition has always been intertwined with possessive individualism, inequality, and the dictates of the capitalist market.[54] Nevertheless, it would be naive in the extreme to ignore the fact that in order to win the radical democratic war, we must first win the liberal democratic battle.

However, centrist and liberal leaderships have not launched an all-out war to win back even the few liberal democratic gains that have been made in the postcolonial, post-civil rights era. They are, instead, all too willing to accommodate the authoritarian populist right. Just as the Labour Party capitulated on several occasions to the Conservatives' call for increasingly racist immigration legislation in Britain,[55] many Democrats are now consistently abandoning the urban poor, blacks, Latinos, immigrants, women, lesbians, and gays in order to chase after the rightward-drifting political center. As the White House submits federal affirmative action programs to a review process, President Clinton has offered "sympathy and understanding" to white men who resent affirmative action. One administration official not only expected black criticisms of the policy review but welcomed them as politically valuable evidence of Clinton's "centrism": "We want black businessmen to scream enough to let angry white males understand that we've done something for them."[56] Feminist and antiracist critiques of this putatively "natural" white male resentment are almost entirely absent from Democratic discourse.

Instead of hopping on this accommodationist bandwagon, progressive activists must recognize the value of anti-assimilationist politics and explore new forms of political organizing. Right-wingers, centrists, and liberals alike will dismiss progressives as excessive militants in an increasingly hysterical manner. The 1995 bombing of a federal government building in Oklahoma was initially blamed—without a shred of evidence—on foreign Muslim fundamentalists. When the media could not ignore that the terrorism in the midwestern heartland was indeed the work of an American—a white male army veteran—the media made the American character of the terrorist attack bearable by giving it leftist and black origins. Leftists of the 1960s are being blamed for nothing less than the rise of the fascist militias; it is alleged that the lawless anarchists (read: blacks, communists, and black communists) of the 1960s paved the way for today's fascists by promoting a disrespect for the state.[57] The entire network of groups that make up the real heartland of this country—the lynch mobs, the Ku Klux Klan, the White Citizens' Councils, anti-Semitic and racist Aryan groups, the murderous thugs who have terrorized abortion clinics, racist law enforcement officers, fascist militias, and, at the unorganized "grassroots" level, gay bashers, "Paki bashers," "nigger hunters," wife beaters, rapists, and child abusers—are concealed from view. Those of us who remain committed to progressive social change need to find the courage to survive these most dangerous times and to dig in for the very bitter wars of position ahead. This would be a good time indeed to learn from the wisdom of the uncompromising anti-assimilationist politics that developed within the most progressive moments of the antiimperialist, civil rights, black power, sexual liberation, socialist feminist, lesbian feminist, and women of color feminist movements.

Notes

1. Roger Jowell, Lindsay Brook, and Bridget Taylor, with Gillian Prior, eds., *British Social Attitudes: The Eighth Report* (Aldershot: Gower, 1991); Roger Jowell, Sharon Witherspoon, Lindsay Brook, eds., *British Social Attitudes: The Fifth Report* (Aldershot: Gower, 1988).

2. Simon Watney, *Policing Desire: Pornography, AIDS, and the Media* (London: Methuen, 1987).

3. Stuart Hall, "Blue Election, Election Blues," in *The Hard Road to Renewal* (London: Verso, 1988), 259–67.

4. Slavoj Zizek, *The Sublime Object of Ideology* (London: Verso, 1989).

5. Zillah Eisenstein, *Feminism and Sexual Equality: Crisis in Liberal America* (New York: Monthly Review Press, 1984).

6. Jeffrey Weeks, *Sex, Politics, and Society: The Regulation of Sexuality Since 1800* (New York: Longman, 1981).

7. *Capital Gay*, 30 October 1987, 1.

8. Beverly Bryan, Stella Dadzie, and Suzanne Scafe, *The Heart of the Race: Black Women's Lives in Britain* (London: Virago, 1985), 74, 80.

9. Etienne Balibar, "Is There A Neo-Racism?" in Etienne Balibar and Immanuel Wallerstein, *Race, Nation, Class* (London: Verso, 1991), 21–3.

10. Because of the specifically post-colonial character of racism in contemporary Britain, racist discourse is chiefly organized around the figures of the Indian, Pakistani, Afro-Caribbean, and African immigrant.

11. Frantz Fanon, *The Wretched of the Earth* (New York: Grove Press, 1963), 41.

12. Stuart Hall, "Racism and Reaction," in John Rex et al., *Five Views of Multi-racial Britain* (London: Commission for Racial Equality, 1978), 25; Christopher Fyfe, "Race, Empire, and the Historians," *Race and Class*, 33.4 (1992), 15–30.

13. Quoted in Martin Barker, *The New Racism: Conservatives and the Ideology of the Tribe* (London: Junction Books, 1981), 40.

14. Richard Herrnstein and Charles Murray, *The Bell Curve: Intelligence and Class Structure in American Life* (New York: The Free Press, 1994).

15. Anna Marie Smith, *New Right Discourse on Race and Sexuality: Britain, 1968–1990* (Cambridge: Cambridge University Press, 1994), 169–71.

16. *Official Report*, House of Lords, 18 December 1986, col. 310.

17. Sona Osman, "Should It Be Unlawful to Incite Sexual Violence," in Gail Chester and Julienne Dickey, eds., *Feminism and Censorship* (Bridport: Prism Press, 1988), 156; A. Sivanandan, *A Different Hunger: Writings on Black Resistance* (London: Pluto, 1982), 17–18.

18. Weeks, *Sex, Politics, and Society*, 249–72.

19. Quoted in Martin Durham, *Sex and Politics: The Family and Morality in the Thatcher Years* (London: Macmillan, 1991), 122.

20. *Official Report*, House of Commons, 8 March 1987, col. 999.

21. *Official Report*, House of Lords, 18 December 1988, col. 310.

22. *Official Report*, House of Lords, 16 February 1988, col. 594.

23. *Official Report*, House of Commons, 9 March 1988, col. 406, 417.

24. *Official Report*, Wilshire, House of Commons, 9 March 1988, col. 404; Lord Ritchie, House of Lords, 16 February 1988, col. 604.

25. Barker, *The New Racism*, 1.

26. *Official Report*, Howard, House of Commons, 9 March 1988, col. 421.

27. *Official Report*, Earl of Caithness, House of Lords, 16 February 1988, col. 643.

28. *Official Report*, House of Commons, 9 March 1988, col. 406–7.

29. Enoch Powell, *Freedom and Reality* (Kingswood: Paperfront, 1969), 232.

30. Enoch Powell, "Integration is the Only Way—Over Many Years," *Wolverhampton Express and Star,* 10 October 1964, reproduced in Kobena Mercer, "Powellism: Race, Politics, and Discourse," unpublished Ph.D. thesis, Goldsmith's College, University of London, 1990, 242.

31. Powell, *Freedom and Reality,* 227.

32. *Official Report,* House of Lords, 1 February 1988, col. 874–5.

33. Marshall Kirk and Hunter Madsen, *After the Ball: How America Will Conquer Its Fear and Hatred of Gays in the '90s* (New York: Doubleday, 1989).

34. Ibid., 143, emphasis in original.

35. Ibid., 360.

36. Bruce Bawer, *A Place at the Table* (New York: Poseidon Press, 1993).

37. David Brock, *The Real Anita Hill: The Untold Story* (New York: Free Press, 1993).

38. James Atlas, "The Counter Counterculture," *New York Times Magazine,* 12 February 1995.

39. Smith, *New Right Discourse,* 29–31, 50–4.

40. Phil Gailey, "Mainstreaming Godliness," *New York Times Book Review,* 5 March 1995; Gustav Niebuhr, "Olive Branch to Jews From Conservative Christians," *New York Times,* 4 April 1995.

41. Chip Berlet, "The Rise of the Religious Right," address to the Brecht Forum, New York, 28 September 1994.

42. Smith, *New Right Discourse,* 227–36.

43. *The Independent,* 18 July 1991, 8.

44. Douglas D. Rose, *The Emergence of David Duke and the Politics of Race* (Chapel Hill: University of North Carolina Press, 1992).

45. Katha Pollitt, "Subject to Debate," *Nation,* 30 January 1995, 120; Adolph Reed, Jr., "The Underclass as Myth and Symbol: The Poverty of Discourse About Poverty," *Radical America* 24.1 (1990), 35.

46. Dilip Hiro, *Black British, White British* (London: Eyre and Spottiswoode, 1971), 362–63.

47. Quoted in Frank Reeves, *British Racial Discourse* (Cambridge: Cambridge University Press, 1983), 208.

48. Rhonda M. Williams, "Accumulation as Evisceration: Urban Rebellion and the New Growth Dynamics," in *Reading Rodney King, Reading*

Urban Uprising, edited by Robert Gooding-Williams (New York: Routledge, 1993), 82–96; Steven Holmes, "Income Gap Persists for Blacks and Whites," *New York Times,* 23 February 1995; Keith Bradsher, "Gap in Wealth in U.S. Called Widest in West," *New York Times,* 17 April 1995; Keith Bradsher, "America's Opportunity Gap," *New York Times,* 4 June 1995.

49. Frantz Fanon, *Black Skin, White Masks* (London: Pluto Press, 1986).

50. Etienne Balibar, "Class Racism," in Balibar and Wallerstein, *Race, Nation, Class,* 214.

51. Abdul JanMohamed, "The Economy of Manichean Allegory: The Function of Racial Difference in Colonialist Literature," in *"Race," Writing and Difference,* edited by Henry Louis Gates, Jr., (Chicago: University of Chicago Press, 1986), 85–6.

52. Eve Kosofsky Sedgwick, *Epistemology of the Closet* (Berkeley: University of California Press, 1990), 7.

53. Antonio Gramsci, *Selections From the Prison Notebooks,* Quintin Hoare and Geoffrey Nowell Smith, trans. and eds. (London: Lawrence and Wishart, 1971); Zizek, *The Sublime Object of Ideology.*

54. C.B. Macpherson, *The Political Theory of Possessive Individualism: Hobbes to Locke* (London: Oxford University Press, 1962).

55. Smith, *New Right Discourse,* 96–7, 144, 152, 162.

56. Steven Holmes, "White House Signals as Easing on Affirmative Action," *New York Times,* 25 February 1995; Robert Pear, "Report to Clinton Faults Programs to Aid Minorities," *New York Times,* 31 May 1995.

57. Katha Pollitt, "Subject to Debate," *The Nation,* 5 June 1995, 784.

7

Community, Rights Talk, and the Communitarian Dissent in *Bowers v. Hardwick*

Gordon A. Babst

Of late liberal political theory has come under sustained attack by communitarian critics for its emphasis on individual rights and civil liberties rather than community rights and civic duties or responsibilities.[1] This debate is relevant for political and legal theorists interested in how to balance those two sets of concerns within a sound framework that serves everyone, and in a political notion of community. In addition, clarifying some important issues in this debate can help political theory to cope with new voices demanding inclusion into the political community, and to understand aspirations and controversies heretofore not well anticipated. One such recent debate concerns the status of homosexuals in the United States and the value of citizenship for them.[2] This discussion focuses attention on the communitarian alternative argument on behalf of gay people put forth by Michael Sandel in the context of the Supreme Court's decision in *Bowers*.[3] Sandel, then, is taken to represent communitarianism on the sodomy issue; of course, other communitarians may here differ with him. Still, Sandel's argument illustrates well the course communitarian thought will most likely take in controversial issues. Marshalled against Georgia's sodomy statute, Sandel's community talk would cast aside argument based in liberal tolerance and urge that the dissent in *Bowers* adopt a communitarian strategy in order to persuade the majority of the moral intrinsic worth of homosexual unions and their closeness to heterosexual marriage commitments and intimacy in realizing important human goods.

It is unfortunate for the communitarian strategy that the majority in *Bowers* also relied on community talk, here a standard morals discourse tying homosexuality—and so homosexuals—to notions of sin. The majority cited the criminal law's traditional condemnation of sodomy and homosexuality; the Judeo-Christian basis of American moral standards and the need for the law to reflect this moral sense; existing anti-sodomy statutes in many states; personal and generalized revulsion at sodomy and homosexuality; and the lack of a constitutional right to privacy encompassing the act in question. By contrast, the dissent argued in the language of rights, encompassed intimate sexual relations between consenting adults within the right to privacy, and suggested that here the state had no compelling interest and no rational basis for its sodomy statute.

Here I will argue that the communitarian alternative on behalf of gay people, as articulated in Sandel's argument, fails to persuade. Contrary to Sandel's claims, this approach perversely makes possible the demeaning of gay people by the reigning community, with adverse and injurious political consequences. My argument will proceed as follows: First, I will present and critique Sandel's argument. Then I will review an especially strong criticism of Sandel's argument that focuses on his move to assimilate homosexual to heterosexual intimacies.[4] Bonnie Honig's critique is used to launch a further investigation into the communitarian alternative and the representability of gay people in it. In the final section I will argue that it is with good reason that the political interests of gay people are not advanced in community talk: here, gays & lesbians do not appear as themselves, but are rendered into the very discourse that debases them. In at least this area communitarianism is unreliable compared with what advantages rights talk is able to secure. The contortions communitarianism displays in its attempts to encompass or represent difference disable its efforts on behalf of gay persons. This conclusion tentatively suggests that a rights talk-based, constitutionally ordered, liberal democratic society espousing tolerance—such as envisioned by the dissent in *Bowers*—holds the best prospects for fairness to all Americans who, in all their diversity, share living among the many communities that have always existed in the United States, but have yet to feel included in the national political community for one reason or another.

Sandel's Alternative Communitarian Argument

The *Bowers* case concerned whether Georgia's "sodomy statute violates the fundamental rights of homosexuals," which the majority opinion took to present "whether the Federal Constitution confers a fundamental right upon homosexuals to engage in sodomy," a proposition they rejected.[5] In reversing a Court of Appeals ruling, the Court in *Bowers* reattached the U.S. Constitution to a preferred social system and its complement of traditional attitudes of hostility toward those disfavored by it, as well as its attendant and often vicious effects on gay Americans who are disapproved of by the dominant community. Owing to its deference to community standards, the

Court in *Bowers* showed itself unwilling to recognize the sexuality of some citizens, and to protect the liberty interests that for other citizens flow more freely from this recognition.

Although Sandel sides with the dissent, he thoroughly criticizes their arguments and implicates an ailing liberalism in their failure to persuade the Court to strike down Georgia's sodomy statute.[6] In opposition to the rights-based, "sophisticated" argument used by the dissent, Sandel recommends the "naive" style of argument, which holds that "the justice of laws depends on the moral worth of the conduct they prohibit or protect."[7] His aim is "to bring out the truth in the naive view . . . the truth in the naive way of arguing," that the "justice (or injustice) of laws against abortion and homosexual sodomy depends, at least in part, on the morality (or immorality) of those practices." (521, 522) Noting the "difficulty of bracketing moral judgments for purposes of law," Sandel opposes the view of politics as neutral among competing visions of the good life, where "those who want permissive laws because they approve of abortion and homosexuality often argue in the name of liberal toleration" and affirm the "voluntarist view" of persons so as to respect each person's autonomous ability to make life's important choices shielded from the value preferences of the majority.(522, 523) To ward off wrong impressions, Sandel writes that "although much of my argument criticizes leading theories of liberal toleration, I do not think it offers any comfort to majoritarianism. The cure for liberalism is not majoritarianism, but a keener appreciation of the role of substantive moral discourse in political and constitutional argument."(522) Sandel does not make clear what he means by "majoritarianism," however, nor does he describe what a "keener appreciation" entails.

The thrust of Sandel's argument is that the dissent in *Bowers* was wrong to argue privacy—that is, the "new" privacy, which uses "the language of autonomy to describe the interest privacy protects."(528)[8] This "new" privacy marks a shift from the "old" privacy of *Griswold v. Connecticut*,[9] where "it remained tied to the traditional notion . . . of keeping intimate affairs from public view" and its justification was "unabashedly teleological"(526, 527), to the "new" privacy of *Eisenstadt v. Baird*,[10] which

> involved two innovations, one explicit, the other unacknowledged. The explicit innovation redescribed the bearers of privacy rights from persons *qua* participants in the social institution of marriage to persons *qua* individuals, independent of their roles or attachments. . . . The subtler, though no less fateful change . . . found that the right to privacy now protected the freedom to engage in certain activities without governmental restriction. . . . The Court protected privacy in *Eisenstadt* not for the social practices it promoted but for the individual choice it secured. . . . the right of privacy had become the right to make certain sorts of choices free from interference by the state.(527, 528)[11]

For Sandel, the dissent in *Bowers*, relying on the newer, flawed right to privacy, "would have extended privacy protection to consensual homosexual activity on the grounds that," [quoting from Blackmun's dissent in *Bowers*] "much of the richness of a relationship will come from the freedom an individual has to *choose* the form and nature of these intensely personal bonds."(524) The naive view conceives the right to privacy differently; not identified with autonomy, privacy "need not presuppose a voluntarist conception of the person" and so is free to rely on its proper justification "in the name of the intrinsic value or social importance of the practice it protects." (524) Sandel neither mentions how the "intrinsic value or social importance" of a practice is ascertained, nor the possibility of conflict with nonconformists; presumably, disagreement in these matters would be resolved without recourse to majoritarian sentiment.

In *Bowers* the Court refused to extend privacy protection to cover consensual sexual activity between homosexual persons, thus ending the reaches of the "new" privacy's extension away from the marital, familial setting and toward the liberal conception of the person.[12] According to Sandel, the flaw in the liberal conception, which views the individual as the basic unit of society, became apparent when the Court sought to accommodate homosexual sodomy to its "concern for conventional family ties"—the site of the "old" privacy—through individualist terms.(530) Simply put, the family is a social institution that cannot be defended in the individualist terms of the "new" privacy.

In addition, the dissent's barring of religious condemnations of homosexuality from the range of acceptable rationales available to Georgia for justifying its sodomy statute merely reflected an all-too- liberal penchant for bracketing controversial moral issues away from the concern of the neutral liberal state.(530) The "voluntarist case for toleration," Sandel argues, is exemplified by the dissent in *Bowers* that proved unable to articulate a substantive argument for protecting the human goods realized in the practices of homosexual relationships, and so could not have succeeded.(533–38) Sandel draws a sharp distinction between the "voluntarist" and "substantive" cases for homosexual unions, overlooking the possibility that there is much that is substantive in the voluntarist case, and overestimating the persuasiveness of the analogy to conventional marriage. Contrariwise, Sandel does not confront the possibility that there may be much that is substantive but unwholesome in conventional relationships, and understimates the value of constitutional protections of the individual even to partners in conventional marriages.[13]

Sandel's moral argument draws "on the teleological dimension of *Griswold*" and "grounds the right to privacy on the good of the practice it would protect"; thus "protecting the human goods realized in marriage" and highlighting "the virtues homosexual intimacy may share with heterosexual intimacy, along with any distinctive virtues of its own." (535–36, 534)

Sandel does not reveal whereby these goods are determined, or the authority involved or invoked in making a (nonarbitrary) list of them, or of the accepted social practices or virtues looked to, if the latter is the route taken. Clearly, leaving these matters for individuals to decide is not what Sandel has in mind; presumably, neither does he have in mind a majoritarian approach to these substantive moral judgments.[14]

Sandel would articulate a tolerance for homosexual intimacy notable for "the quality of respect it secures" because the value and approval of the activity it is analogized to (intimacy in heterosexual marriage) are automatically conferred to it.(537) Sandel declines to mention that the obvious way to confer this respect would be to allow same-sex couples the *right* to marry, thus encouraging in a socially approved fashion faithfulness, security, commitment, and an aura of sinlessness in their relationships as well.[15]

By contrast, the tolerance individualist rights discourse secures demeans homosexual intimacy if grounded in an analogy to *Stanley v. Georgia,* which upheld the right to possess obscene materials in the privacy of one's home, or so Sandel argues.[16] Sandel states that "the analogy with *Stanley* tolerates homosexuality at the price of demeaning it; it puts homosexual intimacy on a par with obscenity—a base thing."(537)   The communitarian strategy would instead challenge the adverse views of homosexuality in an attempt to "win for homosexuals more than a thin and fragile toleration."(537)[17] By tying tolerance "to the merits of the conduct privacy protects," Sandel hopes to win for gay persons a greater measure of respect than can be accorded a relationship analogized to that in *Stanley,* "between a man and his pornography."(538, 537) Sandel concludes his argument by disdaining the practice of bracketing moral questions, which to his view suggests "the truth in the 'naive' view that the justice or injustice of laws against abortion and homosexual sodomy may have something to do with the morality or immorality of these practices after all."(538)   The majority in *Bowers* exemplified Sandel's preference for giving moral questions a determinative role in constitutional decision making. Finding the practice of sodomy immoral, the majority declared: "No connection between family, marriage, or procreation on the one hand and homosexual activity on the other has been demonstrated."[18]

Seemingly unconcerned with any problems that might adhere in making the required determinations of morality and immorality, Sandel may believe that these matters are easily grasped and entered into moral argument and courtroom proceedings. Unless Sandel's essay is a purely academic exercise, it should be interpreted as urging on the dissent in *Bowers* an actual argument that substitutes his community talk for their rights talk emphasis on a privacy right couched in autonomy.[19] The communitarian alternative on behalf of gays & lesbians likely would not work in a nonliberal society, and its application in western-style liberal democracies such as the United States would be fortuitous at best.[20] But would this approach succeed even here?

Honig's Criticism of Sandel's Communitarian Dissent

Honig's critique focuses on the political implications of the identity project she sees as central to Sandel's politics of friendship, which, as regards
gay people, relies on an assimilation of homosexual to heterosexual intimacy, the already erected standard. This politics will not succeed, for "his
mere assertion of likeness between heterosexual and homosexual intimacy
cannot by itself reverse existing patterns of heterosexist discrimination (or
substitute for an investigation of them)."[21] Honig is relying on Sandel's
description of the self as nested in the community's traditions and shared
understandings, from which the communitarian self derives its identity,
which it seeks to further along specifiable paths, and apart from which it
cannot imagine itself:

> living by them [our loyalties and convictions, aims and attachments] is
> *inseparable from understanding ourselves as the particular persons we are—*
> as members of this family or nation or people, as bearers of this history,
> as sons and daughters of that revolution, as citizens of this republic.
> Allegiances such as these are more than values I happen to have or aims
> "I espouse at any given time.". They go beyond the obligations I volun-
> tarily incur and the "natural duties" I owe to human beings as such. . . .[22]
> [emphasis added]

> . . . we cannot justify political arrangements without reference to com-
> mon purposes and ends, . . . *we cannot conceive of ourselves without refer-*
> *ence to our role* as citizens, as participants in a common life. . . .
> Open-ended though it be, the story of my life is always embedded in the
> story of those communities from which I derive my identity—whether
> family or city, tribe or nation, party or cause.[23] [emphasis added]

Following Sandel, in order for "us" to imagine ourselves gay or lesbian, or at
least committed to the rights of our fellow Americans who happen to be gay
or lesbian, "we" must first translate that aspect of ourselves—the sexual orientation or the commitment—into the community talk of marital goods.
But, should not one be concerned with the "remainders" that aren't constituted, or aren't yet constituted through such translation, and the measure of
autonomous choice granted a person to craft oneself?

Sandel's identity project rests on a core, essentialized identity that "exteri-
orizes" the voluntarism of unsanctified imposters to the community (e.g.,
abject gays & lesbians whose sexuality has not yet been likened to the standard) so that the heterosexual inhabitant's subjectivity lives on undisturbed.(189) In Sandel's drive to closure, he submits that the subject's
apparent multiplicity "is illusory. Beneath it lies a real unity, an authentic
(constative) self that . . . eschews the performativity of self-fashioning in
favor of the reassurance of constative self-discovery."(182) Sandel

implicitly assumes that the multiple ends and identity formations of the intrasubjective conception [of the self] are susceptible to harmonization and ordering in the right setting, given the right hothouse politics. The mongrel has a purebreed within it.(180)[24]

Honig critically examines Sandel's contention of assimilable hetero/ homosexual intimacies to expose the justificatory role of unassimilable sameness at work in garnering tolerance and respect for the gay person:

> Either the other is like "us" or he is "other." Either-or. If he is like us, he gets to share in the goods of our community, which include the right to privacy. If he cannot be *likened* to "us," *made like* "us," then he is rightly the object of ridicule. . . . What Sandel does not say is that, since the lives led by homosexuals are as heterogenous as those led by heterosexuals, this fuller respect could be accorded only to some, to those whose homosexual relationships are intimate in ways that are recognizable to "us" and can be likened to those "we" value as a culture. . . . Sandel's new economy of toleration and respect has a serious, structural inequality at its core: it includes some homosexuals on the basis of their likeness to a standard set by a dominant heterosexual and heterosexist culture. . . . the object of respect is not difference but sameness.(190)

Helping "us" to achieve or maintain closure of our identities—for who among "us" has other tendencies?—this *unidirectional* motion ("we" aren't under scrutiny, much less are "we" being assimilated) of standardizing destabilizes difference not just in the "other," who is thereby disempowered to be truly other, but in "our" selves as well, whose power and fictive center are thereby preserved, or so "we" believe.[25]

Gay people enter into this relationship when they are no longer "other" in any relevant respect; "in short, the price of Sandel's broader and deeper toleration is a broader and deeper intolerance. Its insistence on sameness *produces* the repugnance for difference and otherness it seeks to overcome."(191)[26] This repugnance properly is directed against pornography and any thing or person as yet undecidedly like "us":

> And ridicule, apparently, is the only voice with which members of Sandel's community speak to the truly other. It seems that the Court's mistake in *Bowers* was to treat homosexuality as other. It made *no* mistake in addressing the other sarcastically and dismissively. It made *no* mistake in thinking that it was within its provenance to regulate and define sexual pleasure.(191–92)

In a long footnote Honig takes issue with Sandel's apparent agreement with the majority in *Bowers* that a right to sodomy is absurd:

> Sandel's position presupposes a false analogy between (or a false attribution of likeness to) heterosexual and homosexual intercourse. In a heterosexist culture, a right to heterosexual intercourse might appear to be

absurd. But in that same culture, against a background of long-standing, violent, patterned, institutional and juridical discrimination against homosexuals, a right to sodomy is not absurd, no more absurd surely than the laws that outlaw the act. A right to sodomy can be made to appear absurd, though, if we assume that sexuality is a voluntaristically chosen, freely practiced, leisure activity instead of something more akin to a form of life or if we think of the state as the unquestionably legitimate regulator of sexuality. Sandel's agreement with the Court's ridicule of a right to sodomy follows from both assumptions, the first of which commits him to a voluntarism he otherwise rejects, the second, to a statism that he never really examines critically.(260, n. 53)

Remarking that the dissonance produced by the "other" is in reality within ourselves, revealing our contingencies and threatening the decidability of our catgories, Honig helps Sandel give otherness its due by interrogating the challenge of the "excess, the ill-fitted, the remainder, that which escapes and resists the standard frame of political subjectivities."(194) Absent the other's challenge, "politics goes well," Sandel assures us, "we may know a good in common that we cannot know alone."[27] But, Honig remarks,

> [w]hen politics goes that well . . . it is because the other, among us and in us, is being converted, suppressed, recognized, ejected, punished, or reintegrated into the fold. When politics goes that well it is because it is no longer political, it has been converted into a juridical, administrative practice that oversees (and is produced by) an economy of identification whose currency is that of a relentlessly categorizing friendship and enmity.(193)

Honig would encourage on us the good of living life politically "with undecidability and proliferation" of subjects, of according others real respect, and of "an enhanced appreciation of the contingency and multivocality that mark every being."(195)

Sandel's substantive approach to privacy seems not to notice the really curious analogical reasoning he defends on the majority's behalf. The privacy right, if grounded solely in sexual intimacy and the human goods realized in (heterosexual) marriage, itself is an abstraction that Sandel noted had proved itself elastic enough to stretch from countenancing a married couple's decision to use contraceptives, to protecting the individual in decisions of whether to marry, whom to marry, whether to procreate, and whether to carry a pregnancy to term. In practical terms, then, the voluntarist/substantive distinction means little, and we are unable to affirm or deny Sandel's claims that it is possible to appropriate homosexual to heterosexual and make real the analogy.[28]

Contra Sandel, the privacy right protects not just some possibly gay-friendly goods of marriage, but a decidedly not gay-friendly normative order for which it provides the bedrock. "Same-sex marriage," Hannah

Schwarzschild argues, is "profoundly threatening to the very institution in whose name 'privacy' was originally enshrined."[29] In summary, "Sandel allows Hardwick to surface so that we might decide *through him* whether homosexuality is the same or other. Is he to be tolerated or ridiculed? We need to know."(194)[30]

Honig offers us a politics that commits us to "the project of denaturalizing and deconstructing concretized identities," to "rouse enmity toward the orders that vouchsafe them, and to expose the power, violence, cruelty, and arrogance in their resolutions."(195) Such a politics will not finesse difference through a demeaning assimilation to the very order that produced this sick-making gesture in the first place, one that insists that "we" tolerate real differences. Communitarianism, by implication, is faulted for not seeing difference as difference, and for offering false community to those who truly are different, but no less eligible for full inclusion into the nation's political community.

The Representability of Gay People in Sandel's Communitarian Alternative

The problematization of gay people as subjects, and their lack of fit with heterosexual marriage, presented in the previous section's discussion of Honig's critique of Sandel, paves the way for our present investigation, which begins with the subjection of gays & lesbians to the law, which is predicated on the establishment of a distinct identity for "the homosexual," a fairly recent phenomenon.[31] The persons "homosexuality" identifies became categorizable as a distinct sort of human being in the nineteenth century, and were perceived as fundamentally different from "normal people," identified by heterosexuality. This deviation rendered them ineligible for equal legal standing and rights in the political community (should their secret become public knowledge). Homosexuality, manifested in homosexual acts or desires, indicates a homosexual person. Homosexuality in men is then identified with sodomy, the criminalization of which criminalizes a state of being. Notice in the following passage from *Padula v. Webster* how the Court reasons, classifies, and affirms state-sponsored discrimination through conflating acts and identities:

> If the Court was unwilling to object to state laws that criminalize the behavior that defines the class, it is hardly open to a lower court to conclude that state sponsored discrimination against the class is invidious. After all, there can hardly be more palpable discrimination against a class than making the behavior that defines the class criminal.[32]

And so, Janet Halley observes,

> the class of "homosexuals" is inherently sodomitical and thus intrinsically felonious; discrimination against it therefore merits no special judicial

solicitude. Statutes that expose homosexual sodomy, no matter how clandestine, to public scrutiny and punishment, also define the class of homosexuals and justify its exclusion from public benefits and responsibilities.[33]

Recent interesting work in the deconstruction of "heterosexuality" examines how we get from *felony* sodomy to *homosexual* sodomy, tuck away the former from judicial scrutiny, and confuse the issues before the Court.[34] Looking at equal protection analyses, or the lack thereof, in cases such as *Bowers* and *Padula,* this line of inquiry examines the judicial propensity to base rulings on definitions and categories or dichotomies, rather than on the processes whereby categorization occurs. Halley describes this phenomenon thus:

> a class of nonhomosexuals is diacritically constituted in practices of homosexual definition. . . . the deviance definition purports to found a class of homosexuals upon discrete bodily acts, without regard to the definition of any counterpart class. That counterpart class, purportedly having nothing to do with the foundation of a class of homosexuals and discernible only by rather ferocious tactics of unsympathetic reading, remains silent and invisible. Thus judges working with the deviance definition persistently fail to acknowledge the dichotomy they imply or their own agency and embeddedness within it. . . . This position is a class of *nonhomosexuals* who know what a homosexual is; who are at the same time exempt from the definitional clarity to which homosexuals are subject; and who because of both of these features are exempt from the discrimination to which "known homosexuals" are exposed. Both their epistemological privilege and their exemptions are contingent, however, on their continued silence about the heterogeneity and fabricatedness of their class. . . .[35]

Heterosexuality, then, is a default class—like nonmurderer—normalized by contrast to sexual practices and social identities othered by, firstly, making sodomitical practices and identities implicate each other, and implicating all that is good in the repro-narrativity of marital fecundity.[36] It is heteronormativity, of course, that imbues that sense of meaningfulness as both supreme and exclusively heterosexual, regardless of a lack of empirical data to impugn gay people's normal-functioning embeddedness in families as couples and as daughters, mothers, brothers, aunts, and so on.

It is no accident that Sandel looks to compare sodomy, a sexual practice of some gay and nongay persons, with marital intimacies, for this maneuver brings gays & lesbians, some of whom may not engage in sodomy, into the fold of *heteronormative* society. This failure to acknowledge is all-pervasive, for it hides the underlying structures and indeterminacy of a perspective that presumes a comprehensiveness and from which knowledge of the "crime not fit to be named," the "love that dare not speak its name," "the unmentionable vice," is both immediately known and made sensible to anyone familiar with what's "natural." Simply put, supposing Sandel's analogizing of intimacies were to convince the Court, it "would represent an act of interpretive adultery, whose shameful outcome can only be the birth of a bastard right" should gay people be represented as themselves (e.g., as persons who actually do engage in furtive sodomitical activity) in any way in the Court's natural discourse.[37]

Being unmindful of marriage as the keystone of heteronormativity, and the latter as the dialect of the *Bowers* decision, permits Kenneth Karst, in an otherwise highly perceptive analysis, to conclude wrongly that the discrimination of an antimiscegnation law is amplified beyond those characteristics it shares with sodomy laws: "What makes a miscegenation law invalid, after all, is not merely that it classifies on the basis of race, but that it is designed to promote white supremacy."[38] Karst errs in not realizing that sodomy laws too are "designed to promote" something, namely, heterosexual supremacy. And this despite Karst's own admonition:

> *A concern for stigma must be part of the analysis*, however, because a major reason for state refusal to provide homosexuals with any institutional alternative to marriage is that it is state policy to stigmatize homosexual conduct. . . . homosexuals are now denied the opportunity to formalize their commitment to each other through *the symbolism of marriage*.[39] [emphasis added]

It is a testament to the ubiquity of the masquerade heteronormativity puts on and to its ability to authorize even when performing in drag as "intimate association" that it is so overlooked.

The following passage is in keeping with the state of Georgia's and the Court's perspective on homosexuality and with their masked contempt for gay people;[40] moreover, it renders the unassimilability of homosexual sodomy to heterosexual marriage and reveals the false hope of Sandel's communitarian alternative:

> For the *negative* prohibitions of homosexual practices in Scripture make sense only in the light of its positive teaching in Genesis 1 and 2 about human sexuality and heterosexual marriage. Without the wholesome positive teaching of the Bible on sex and marriage, our perspective on the homosexual question is bound to be skewed. . . . modern loving homosexual partnerships must also be condemned . . . [for] they are incompatible with God's created order. And since that order was established by Creation, not culture, its validity is both permanent and universal. . . . [homosexual relationships'] love quality is not sufficient to justify them. Indeed, I have to add that they are incompatible with God's law.[41]

Although the same view is not held by all Christians, none would doubt its reign and influence—certainly not the majority in *Bowers*, who seemed enthralled by this law.[42] Wedded to the State's power to reinforce it, marriage as given above cannot but mean denouncing (as in *Bowers*) "modern loving homosexual relationships" and gay people for their horrid transgressions of God's plan.[43]

Occluded from view by the heteronormative image of the natural are the legal, political, and economic processes that maintain it, and the material effects of these on gay people. Sandel's "naive" view truly is naive in not addressing the role of these processes in shaping the contours of the familial goods discourse he valorizes and suggests can be made to accommodate homosexual intimacies.[44] These processes implicate relations of power, and are seen differently by gays & lesbians:

> Every person who comes to a queer self-understanding knows in one way or another that her stigmatization is intricated with gender, with the family, with notions of individual freedom, the state, public speech, consumption and desire, nature and culture, maturation, reproductive politics, racial and national fantasy, class identity, truth and trust, censorship, intimate life and social display, terror and violence, health care, and deep cultural norms about the bearing of the body. Being queer means fighting about these issues all the time, locally and piecemeal but always with consequences.[45]

As with other minorities, the phenomenon of "being at the wrong place at the wrong time" covers a lot more ground if you happen to be gay:

> Repeal of California's sodomy laws and selected local anti-discrimination laws have made this state a haven for gays from all over the country. But this kind of tolerance—the live and let live spirit that makes California a refuge—does not exist everywhere in the state. In some rural communities, California can be a lonely, hostile place. . . . In some California towns, being open . . . can result in discrimination in housing or employment, ostracism from professional peers, or a blunt instrument to the back of the head.[46]

Small-town America is home to communitarian sentimentality for a mythically pleasant past; the unreality of the preharmonized community is revealed in ever-recurring stories about the fate of those deemed "other" who wander, or move into the neighborhood.[47] Besides, the United States is no small town, nor should it be thought of as a big one.[48]

Sodomy laws regulate both behavior and identity primarily by marking out in the law unacceptable persons, and so maintaining the social opprobrium directed against them and diminishing their capacity for autonomous choice.[49] As with other subjects, the subjectivity of gays & lesbians is in part an effect of social power relations, the overall structure of which is given through law.[50] The concepts of "self" and "subjectivity" are far more complicated than communitarianism, at first glance, seems to acknowledge in its descriptions of rather crude, sometimes one-to-one correspondences between roles, persons, context, and community. William Connolly shows identity's complexity:

> Identity involves naming cultural formations that have become natural-
> ized and interiorized, and naturalized dispositions always contain a set of
> operational beliefs and judgments that help to constitute them. This slip-
> pery territory forms another site of conjunction and disjunction in the
> politics of identity, where cultural constitution and contingent disposi-
> tions inscribed into the body enter into relations of consonance and dis-
> sonance unsusceptible to independent specification through a culturally
> neutral vocabulary. . . . The body forms an indispensable basis of dis-
> course about identity and an insufficient and unreliable basis from which
> to draw culturally unmediated representations.[51]

The impact of sodomy laws is felt through social castigation, rather than through, say, police effectiveness at implementing them, and may pierce ordinary personal armor:

> It is no answer to say that an individual . . . might simply remain celibate.
> The living force of the law is at issue, not its logical form, and the real
> force of anti-homosexual laws, if obeyed, is that they enlist and redirect
> physical and emotional desires we do not expect people to suppress.
> Indeed, it is precisely the propensity of such prohibitions to operate on
> and put to use an individual's most elemental bodily faculties that gives
> the exertion of power in this area such formative force. We tend to ana-
> lyze these proscriptions today in terms of the propriety of punishing peo-
> ple for homosexual conduct. We tend, in measuring their morality, to
> form an image of either the homosexual imprisoned or . . . forced to give
> up his sexual acts. We ought, however, to give up the image of "the
> homosexual" in the first place and measure the law instead in terms of its
> creation of heterosexuals (and, in a different way, of homosexuals too)
> within the standardized parameters of a state-regulated identity. . . . say-
> ing that *homosexuals* remain free to exercise their suffrage in an attempt
> to overturn anti-homosexual laws begs the question.[52]

All this is to say that the Court's conclusion in *Bowers* preceded its analysis by its very use of a term (homosexual sodomy) that to the majority,
Powell's disposable Eighth Amendment concerns notwithstanding, called to
mind "an offense of 'deeper malignity' than rape, a heinous act 'the very
mention of which' . . ."[53] Communitarian concerns with maintaining a community's cultural traditions, its way of life, its moral sense, and its conception of the social-natural order which sanctifies and through the law permits
and prohibits certain self-constitutions all come together in Burger's concurring opinion. Burger at once acknowledged neither the constitutional issues

at hand, the citing and inspection of which are among his duties, nor the personal nature of the beliefs he was expounding.[54] The majority's discursive disclaimers undermine and "ultimately overtake" its "putatively detached and disinterested logic"; its "passion [for "proscriptions" that have "ancient roots" and for "majority sentiments about the morality of homosexuality"[55]] eclipses the cool constitutional reason by which the Supreme Court claims to be bound"; and its "denominated" reading of the claim brought before it as one of "a Constitutional right to engage in homosexual sodomy" betrays its ardous effort at preventing the "slippage of sexual identities" and at reinforcing a heteronormativity against homosexuality (and homosexual persons), which are necessarily labeled "deviant" to ensure the former's survival.[56] Simply put,

> [t]hese gestures create the character of the official knower, a man whose "common sense and common experience" render him unexceptionably a member of a stable, common majority that knows without having to find out. . . . The doctrinal result of such a dynamic has been judicial endorsement of definitions of homosexuality that are not definitions at all.[57]

It is for good reason that the cluster of interests important to gay Americans is not advanced in community talk, the first language of speakers of traditional morality for whom gay people are one-dimensional symbols of moral depravity.[58] I certainly would not rely on communitarian argument to secure gay rights (e.g., repeal of sodomy statutes, favorable child custody and partnership laws). Why abandon rights talk for any heretofore acknowledged community talk, for what community, tradition, or accepted values orientation prevalent somewhere in this country can be pointed to to ground the appeal? There are such communities, but these are the ones in question, currently seeking acceptance into, or at least peaceful coexistence with mainstream America.[59]

These communities exist in areas mainstream society has set apart by virtue of who lives there, what life projects are undertaken there, and other aspects deemed different from the wider community.[60] To advocate before the Supreme Court that the values embraced by these communities, which are presumed different from the mainstream, reflect "our" values is to beg the question, no matter how supplemental such an argument might be, for identification with these communities carries with it onerous and undesirable significations.[61] Communitarians notoriously obscure the origins of the standards they valorize, often ideologize "community," and certainly do not have in mind communities such as Camp Sister Spirit in Ovett, Mississippi, or the gay resorts of the Russian River Valley.[62] The communitarian alternative ignores ugly aspects of social reality and the fact that community talk has always been one instrument of repression, contrary to Sandel's illusions.

Gays and lesbians, and other marginalized persons, should not take up the community talk of the traditions or shared understandings repressive majorities historically have used to exclude them so as to maintain an arrogant monopoly on the presumptively unified meaning of what it means to be "American."[63] Built on silences and absences, the primarily religious tradition relied on by the majority in *Bowers* all but ignored the American rights tradition appealed to by the dissent, a tradition rooted in shared experience yet forward-looking all the same.

In the final analysis, the communitarian alternative argument on behalf of gay persons, as articulated by Sandel's argument for the dissent in *Bowers*, is substantively in the same class as the arguments advanced by the majority, but in disguise. To succeed on this footing implies that Sandel be entrusted to better his fellows at their own game, and relied on to convince other community talkers of their shortsightedness, lack of imagination, or incomplete grasp of their own traditions, so as to persuade them that members of the gay community are just like them in ways relevant to their thinking. Cautious suspicion is warranted, for in Sandel's alternative dissent gay people do not at all appear as themselves, but are rendered as no longer different, having been assimilated into a discourse of repro-narrativity that may not even bring all heterosexual marriage practices in its train. Judith Butler makes the point:

> Here it becomes important to recognize that oppression works not merely through acts of overt prohibition, but covertly, through the constitution of viable subjects and through the corollary constitution of a domain of unviable (un)subjects—*abjects*, we might call them. . . . Here oppression works through the production of a domain of unthinkability and unnameability. . . . To be prohibited explicitly is to occupy a discursive site from which something like a reverse-discourse can be articulated; to be implicitly proscribed is not even to qualify as an object of prohibition. . . . It is one thing to be erased from discourse, and yet another to be present within discourse as a falsehood.[64]

The act of persuading the majority in *Bowers* contemplated by Sandel involves him in two peculiar operations, neither of which communitarianism can comfortably accommodate. First, the entire gay and lesbian community may not wish to be constructed in the ways necessary to persuade the majority; it may not wish to be represented in the majority's terms of choice. Overriding this wish would involve an instrumental use or reconstruction of community, rather than appeal to an already validated community as final grounds, or an arbitrary determination of who is in, who is out, and so exteriorizing the remainder as Honig suggests occurs. Thus, at a minimum, this first sort of operation may violate a substantial portion of the gay community's and gay and lesbian persons' sense of self and would involve a use of force dubious by even communitarian standards.[65]

Alternatively, Sandel may wish to reconstruct for the majority its community talk so as to include gay people in it more favorably.[66] Here, there are questions of subjectivity and representation. How Sandel, regardless of whether he is a member of the gay community, could speak for it would point to a communitarian theory of representation that, perhaps, Sandel is laying the groundwork for. If so, it has a familiar look. Representation "is extended only to what can be acknowledged as a subject. . . . the qualifications for being a subject must first be met before representation can be extended."[67] In *Bowers* the majority's constitution of the gay person as a subject precludes direct appeal to the gay community, for gay people likely do not describe themselves that way (e.g., as volitional sinners, rather than as citizens pressing claims of wrongful discrimination). And Sandel restricts the gay subject, identified by the practice of sodomy, to heterosexual married intimacy. This counterfeits the gay person; as Honig points out, this move to sameness is predicated upon a denial of the reality of difference (e.g., some gay people really do engage in sodomy, and have a very different view and perhaps experience of it than did the majority in *Bowers*).[68] Here, the supposed difference lies not in juridical or political status, but in life experiences, worldview, and, perhaps, sexual practices.

The law in question in *Bowers*, Georgia's sodomy statute, was construed so as to apply only to homosexuals; moreover, this act was said to define them.[69] It seems there's an identity problem here. The Court wishes to identify gay people in a manner that the latter know to implicate them in a normative order that is the root cause of their oppression, while Sandel wishes to represent them before this Court through connecting their interests in privacy and intimacy to heterosexual, married intimacy. What kind of representation is this in which the representative's familiarity with the represented is questionable, and the commonality of interests used to base the (nonelected) claim to represent seems far-fetched? The issue is *not* the sexual orientation of the putative representative of gay people's interests, but that of the grounds in communitarian theory whereby a member of one community may represent another, or translate its perspectives and concerns into the discourse of another. Neither of those operations makes sense, given Sandel's communitarian understanding of communities. This points to a problem of knowledge, agency, and authority—a speaking *for* rather than the communitarian speaking *from*.

Sandel is assuming that gay people are representable by his value of intimacy, that it is really them in there as worthy human subjects. But, we have seen, gay people do not appear in this discourse in that way, and are preempted from doing so. In fact, as gay people appeared in *Bowers*, they may actually have increased their disempowerment:

> The effect was not only to deny homosexuals recognition of the personal value of their sexuality, but, in a real sense, to threaten their political opportunities to alter the public mind about its legitimacy and thus to

gain repeal of the proscriptions that authorize its prosecution and punishment.[70]

The sort of representation Sandel is offering to the gay community resembles that sort rejected by the British colonists in America, *virtual representation*, which came to be regarded as no representation at all. Were gays & lesbians to be granted representation in the discourse of marital intimacy, it would wreak havoc, much as would have actual representation of the American colonies in the British Parliament.[71]

Communitarianism offers gays & lesbians the opportunity to consent vicariously to representation by an outsider (one who would not follow the majority in *Bowers* and view gay people simply as promiscuous sexual deviants, moral delinquents, or as criminals by definition), in another discourse (such as the majority used in *Bowers*), with the aim of securing the full blessings of citizenship (as they are enjoyed by others). This restricts gay people to a discursive game that ensures the interests of the more powerful players, interests in *Bowers* that were not identified with gay people's constitutional guarantees or rights. This is a mere (re)presentation of what already was in no need of representation:

> If, in order to be heard, I must speak in ways that you have proposed, then I can be heard only if I speak like you, not like me. Rather than being an equal contributor, I remain enclosed in a discursive game that ensures your continuing advantage. . . . Although voice in this accommodative, add-on sense may appear to be a real advance over having no representation at all, it fails to satisfy in that it offers a representation of self in the terms defined by the dominant groups and so only advances their interests, not those of the less dominant. . . .[72]

Like the colonists before them, gays & lesbians should be skeptical of this presumption of shared interests, should look more closely at the unequal burden placed on them to conform to laws they had no part in making, no matter how facially neutral the laws may appear, and should thus hesitate before accepting the aid of communitarians in advancing their interests.

Gay Americans are not in fact represented in Sandel's communitarian alternative argument; only heterosexual, married couples need apply. It is this unrepresentability in Sandel's substantive moral discourse that makes possible the stabilization of an uncriticized standard that Honig elaborates; it is a refusal to see gays & lesbians as subjects on their own terms (e.g., subject to other desires), not objects of a stealthy juridical and moralizing discourse that occupies the site of normativity, which makes citizenship less valuable for them. A liberalism of rights, encompassing a privacy right, is more likely to secure fairness for them, which is why Blackmun's dissent focused on the privacy right of the individual, regardless of how the individual may realize herself to be constituted, or however she is held by others to be constituted.[73]

Conclusion

The very idea that the civil rights and liberties accorded to and reasonably presumed by all Americans as theirs should be subject to enactment per the whims of a local "moral majority," or to justification on the bar of one or other exclusionary discourse is repugnant and unassuaged by Sandel's countermajoritarianist impulses. For gay people, communitarianism mitigates against the potential of an America without caste, of an inclusive society where each individual is respectfully accorded full equality before the law, and where government is about securing the rights of *every* citizen subject to rational constraints.[74] People may seem accepted in Sandel's communitarian argument, but that does not mean that they belong. And it is the political and legal dimension to belonging that is foreshortened, if not precluded for Americans who happen to be gay or lesbian.[75]

Rights talk, beyond the protections it offers when things go badly, lays the inclusive political order's foundation for respect and dignity—perhaps one reason why rights talk has been our nation's traditional public talk. Here I call to mind the realism of Martha Minow's argument, which expresses concern for Honig's "remainders" who have yet to be fully present in the community, but just the same will not succumb to acquiesence in its oppressions:

> Rights can be understood as a kind of communal discourse that reconfirms the difficult commitment to live together even while engaging in conflicts and struggles. The struggle to make meaning of human existence may well demand our separation into groups away from, even antagonistic to, the larger community. If this is the case, then the discourse of rights may be all the more important as a medium for speaking across conflicting affiliations, about the separations and connections among individuals, groups, and the state. . . . We can listen to rights as a language that contains meaning but does not engender it, as sounds that demonstrate our sociability even while exposing the uniqueness of the speaker. Legal language, like a song, can be hummed by someone who did not write it and chanted by those for whom it was not intended.[76]

This essay has argued that communitarianism as revealed herein would have pernicious effects in practice, despite its warm-feeling appeal and any well-meaning intentions on the part of its promoters. Although Sandel's work on the constituted nature of the liberal self has important things to say, as regards sodomy laws and the greater inclusion into society of persons who happen to be gay or lesbian, Sandel could not have named his "naive view" better.

Notes

The author wishes to thank Bonnie Honig for helpful comments on the original draft of this essay, and Shane Phelan for guiding it through to its final form.

1. The two sets of concerns should not be assumed mutually exclusive, although they are usefully considered opposing poles and may be cast in terms perhaps more extreme than some of their cooler-headed supporters would allow. Accessible treatments of this debate are in Michael J. Sandel, "Morality and the Liberal Ideal," *New Republic* 190, no. 18(May 7, 1984): 15–17; Amy Gutmann, "Communitarian Critics of Liberalism," *Philosophy & Public Affairs* 14, no. 3(Summer 1985): 308–22; and Steven Lukes, "Five Fables About Human Rights," *Dissent* 40, no. 4(Fall 1993): 427–37. Although the argument presented here is meant to have implications for this broader debate, considerations of space prevent more than cursory references to it. For our purposes, rights talk is taken to emphasize personal choice and the constitutionally recognized rights and civil liberties of a modern liberal democratic society such as the United States; the language of rights often will appeal beyond legal rights to universalist conceptions of human rights— rights that adhere in any human being as such. Community talk emphasizes civic virtues, local values, and the social roles and practices individuals are identified by, with persons viewed as thickly constituted or encumbered by tradition and/or the predominant view of "the Good."

2. This paper uses *gays and lesbians*, or *gay people*. Here I will assume of the reader familiarity with traditional depictions of gay and lesbian persons. Homosexuality, unlike heterosexuality *per se*, has been well researched. For an elaboration of characteristics of people in both categories, as well as of the categories themselves, see the fine volume by David P. McWhirter, Stephanie A. Sanders, and June Machover Reinisch, eds., *Homosexuality/Heterosexuality: Concepts of Sexual Orientation* (New York: Oxford University Press, 1990), and James D. Weinrich, *Sexual Landscapes: Why We Are What We Are, Why We Love Whom We Love* (New York: Charles Scribner's Sons, 1987).

3. *Bowers v. Hardwick,* 478 U.S. 186 (1986). Michael J. Sandel, "Moral Argument and Liberal Toleration: Abortion and Homosexuality," *California Law Review* 77, no. 3(May 1989): 521–38. In this essay Sandel attacks the contemporary notion of privacy, and by implication liberal political theory in general, which is taken to give primacy to the

individual. Sandel does not in this essay proclaim communitarianism; however, the relation of his "substantive moral discourse" to liberal notions of choice and autonomy mark this as a communitarian argument. Sandel is the only theorist regarded by most scholars as a communitarian who puts forth a sustained argument incorporating relevant strands of communitarian thought, disparaging of rights talk, on the topics of homosexuality and same-sex relationships.

4. This criticism is found in Bonnie Honig, *Political Theory and the Displacement of Politics* (Ithaca: Cornell University Press, 1993), 186–95.

5. 478 U.S. 189, 190 (1986) (White, J., majority opinion).

6. Georgia Code Annotated Section 16-6-2 (1984) provides as follows:

> (a) A person commits the offense of sodomy when he performs or submits to any sexual act involving the sex organs of one person and the mouth or anus of another. A person commits the offense of aggravated sodomy when he commits sodomy with force and against the will of the other person.

> (b) A person convicted of the offense of sodomy shall be punished by imprisonment for not less than one nor more than 20 years. A person convicted of the offense of aggravated sodomy shall be punished by imprisonment for life or by imprisonment for not less than one nor more than 20 years.

> "[T]he Georgia statute does not single out homosexuals as a separate class meriting special disfavored treatment." *Bowers v. Hardwick,* 478 U.S. 219 (1986) (Stevens, J., dissenting). This is a facially neutral statute; note the gender neutrality of the wording, the unspecified sexual orientation of a perpetrator, the universal applicability to married and single persons, and the stiff punishment possible for a single act of sodomy (an act of passive or active oral or anal sex). Justice White noted that "today 24 states and the District of Columbia continue to provide criminal penalties for sodomy in private and between consenting adults." *Bowers v. Hardwick,* 478 U.S. 193 (1986) (majority opinion). Twenty-three states and the District of Columbia have decriminalized the crime of sodomy, and four states never had this law; seven states still prohibit same-sex sodomy; 16 still prohibit both same- and opposite-sex sodomy. See Los Angeles Gay & Lesbian Police Advisory Task Force, *Gay & Lesbian Cultural Awareness Training for Law Enforcement,* Appendix (1992), Topic 11, pp. 3–8, and David E. Newton, *Gay and Lesbian Rights: A Reference Handbook* (Santa Barbara: ABC-CLIO, 1994), 107–109.

7. Sandel, "Moral Argument and Liberal Toleration," 521—hereinafter in this section cited parenthetically.

8. This approach to *Bowers* is taken in Mary Ann Glendon, *Rights Talk: The Impoverishment of Political Discourse* (New York: Free Press, 1991), 61–75. She indicates that her discussion of privacy benefited from Sandel's earlier book *Liberalism and the Limits of Justice* (Cambridge: Cambridge University Press, 1982). Her discussion of *Bowers* is by way of comparison to a British case, *Dudgeon v. United Kingdom*, in the European Court of Human Rights in 1981. For a contrasting interpretation, see Jennifer F. Kimble, "A Comparative Analysis of *Dudgeon v. United Kingdom* and *Bowers v. Hardwick*," in Wayne R. Dynes and Stephen Donaldson, eds., *Homosexuality: Discrimination, Criminology, and the Law*, vol. VI, Studies in Homosexuality, (New York: Garland, 1992), 310–21. David J. Garrow, *Liberty and Sexuality: The Right to Privacy and the Making of* Roe v. Wade (New York: Macmillan, 1994), 616, takes issue with Glendon's sense of history and offers the contextually richest legal history of *Bowers*. See Ibid., 644–88.

9. 381 U.S. 479 (1965) (establishing a right to privacy and affirming a married couple's right to use contraceptives). Also see *Skinner v. Oklahoma,* 316 U.S. 535 (1942) (affirming the right to marriage and procreation).

10. 405 U.S. 438 (1972) (affirming unmarried persons' right to use contraceptives). Also see *Carey v. Population Services International,* 431 U.S. 678 (1977) (affirming that decisions concerning sexual relations are constitutionally protected).

11. Sandel draws the distinction too sharply, paying too little attention to the fact that this is but one interpretation of a long legal history. In connection with the "traditional notion of privacy" conceived as "freedom from surveillance or disclosure of intimate affairs," Sandel approvingly cites Justice Douglas, writing for the Court in *Griswold*: "The very idea [of obnoxious police intrusions into the marital bedroom] is repulsive to the *notions of privacy* surrounding the marriage relationship."(527, emphasis added) Shortly thereafter Sandel notes that "the privacy right [*Griswold*] proclaimed was consistent with traditional *notions of privacy* going back to the turn of the century."(527, emphasis added) Even as traditionally conceived, then, privacy is not a single entity, or even two; rather, there are notions of it. Conceived this way, one could argue, against Sandel's interpretation, that all along privacy may have at any time encompassed any of a number of possible notions, some articulated sooner, some later, but none fundamentally different and each adhering the right in the individual, with differing emphases placed on the right's purpose and context. This tack allows us to map the "new" privacy on the same grid as the "old," coordinating individuals and their contexts along with the judicial articulations of purpose the right to privacy is said to serve. Through new cases

brought before it, the Court simply has been exploring the concept of privacy and articulating the family resemblances it finds. This interpretation is entirely in keeping with the first exposition of the right to privacy, even though there the issue at hand was protecting the famous from media exposure. See Samuel D. Warren and Louis D. Brandeis, "The Right to Privacy," *Harvard Law Review* IV, no. 5(December 15, 1890): 193, 220. Also see the discussion of the right of privacy, *Bowers*, and the Ninth Amendment in Calvin R. Massey, "Federalism and Fundamental Rights: The Ninth Amendment," in Randy E. Barnett, ed., *The Rights Retained by the People: The History and Meaning of the Ninth Amendment* (Fairfax: George Mason University Press, 1989), 321–34, which sorts through the "unnecessarily muddled" legal history of the privacy cases.

12. It is commonly held that *Bowers* arrested the progress of the right to privacy, certainly since *Roe v. Wade,* 410 U.S. 113 (1973). The abrupt interruption of the expansion of privacy law was the spin given *Bowers* by the *New York Times* in its front-page coverage on July 1, 1986. One Comment, noting the "Black Line" *Bowers* cuts, found the majority's opinion "rooted in language strongly condemning homosexuality," which was not, nor could be, on trial, and relates that decision to *Roe*:

> If Ms. Roe's claim in *Roe v. Wade* were analyzed under the *Hardwick* framework, the Court would first determine if abortion fits under either definition of fundamental rights. To declare that the right to an abortion is "implicit in the concept of ordered liberty" would be stretching the meaning of the words beyond their breaking point. Given the longevity of abortion statutes, under Justice White's analysis, the right to an abortion is not "rooted in this Nation's history and tradition." If, however, abortion were to be considered a part of the right to personal autonomy, and *personal autonomy* is plugged into the fundamental rights equation, a more plausible argument is created that the limited right to personal autonomy is a fundamental right. On the other hand, *Hardwick* does not explain why homosexual sodomy is not a part of the right to personal autonomy. One is left with Justice Steven's conclusion that the majority excludes homosexuals from the Constitution's protection simply because it dislikes them.

See Julia K. Sullens, "Thus Far and No Further: The Supreme Court Draws the Outer Boundary of the Right to Privacy," *Tulane Law Review* 61 (March 1987): 929, 922 [reference notes omitted]. Also see Angelina Marie Massari, "The Supreme Court Gives States a Free Rein with Sodomy Statutes: *Bowers v. Hardwick*," *Washington University Journal of Urban and Contemporary Law* 31 (Winter 1987): 403–17.

13. The language of rights often is unfairly accused of lacking substantive moral features, when it, instead, easily is conceived of as securing

human dignity in the constitutional framework of a modern democratic society. See the essays by Alan Gewirth, William A. Parent, David A. J. Richards, and Louis Henkin, in Michael J. Meyer and William A. Parent, eds., *The Constitution of Rights: Human Dignity and American Values* (Ithaca: Cornell University Press, 1992).

14. In one analysis of same-sex marriage, the author explicitly relies on what he takes to be majoritarian sentiment and its religious roots—much as did the majority in *Bowers*—to assert the rightfulness of denying marriage to gay persons, even though "[t]o define a heritage is not an easy task when talking about something as broad and amorphous as the Judeo-Christian heritage. . . . While it is difficult to articulate a nonfaith rationale for the distinction made by the Judeo-Christian heritage between same-sex and opposite-sex mariage, the task is not impossible." See G. Sidney Buchanan, "Same-Sex Marriage: The Linchpin Issue," *University of Dayton Law Review* 10, no. 3(Spring 1985): 546, 549. The majoritarian argument he makes surely is greatly assisted by the belief that "[u]nprovable assumptions have their own legitimate role to play in advancing the 'compelling' interests of society." Ibid., 570.

15. Had Sandel pursued that thought in explicit argument, it might have resembled the major argument in Kenneth J. Karst, "The Freedom of Intimate Association," *Yale Law Journal* 87, no. 4(March 1980): 682–86, which nonetheless concludes for choice:

Nor is [the freedom of intimate association] an invitation to moral chaos. To say in a given case that the sovereign must keep its hands off an individual's associational choice is merely to reaffirm that moral responsibility lives in the only place it can live, the individual conscience. It is meaningless to speak of morality when there is no choice.

See ibid., 692. Also see Lindsy Van Gelder, "Marriage as a Restricted Club," *MS* 12, no. 8(February 1984): 59–60. Marriage was denied a homosexual couple in a Minnesota case; in his opinion Justice Peterson wrote: "[T]he institution of marriage as a union of man and woman, uniquely involving the procreation and rearing of children within a family, is as old as the book of Genesis." *Baker v. Nelson,* (191 N.W. 2d. 185, 1971), cited and discussed as an example of "pejorative misconceptions," "American cultural prejudice" in Jill Norgren and Serena Nanda, *American Cultural Pluralism and Law* (New York: Praeger, 1988), 152–53.

16. 394 U.S. 557 (1969). Sandel does not mention the majority opinion's inability to draw a distinction between consensual sexual activity in the home and possession of illegal goods, or its unquestioning acceptance of sodomy as a crime of legitimate state interest alongside, for example, incest. See *Bowers v. Hardwick,* 478 U.S. 193 (1986).

17. Sandel does not indicate that there may be a relationship between the traditional sense he valorizes and finds in analogies to the "old" privacy (e.g., marital privacy, given in *Griswold* as "intimate to the degree of being sacred . . . a harmony in living . . . a bilateral loyalty . . . an association for a noble purpose"[534]), and adverse views of homosexuality. Nor does Sandel note that the "thin and fragile toleration" rights discourse provides would become embedded in a precedent-setting Court decision, thus affecting subsequent decisions and possibly affecting change in the public at large. See Note, "The Constitutionality of Laws Forbidding Private Homosexual Conduct," *Michigan Law Review* 72, no. 8(August 1974): 1613–37 (arguing that the privacy argument is "clearly" the best argument given the controversial topic).

18. 478 U.S. 191 (1986). Justice White's failure to find any conceivable link here and its implication for legal status is discussed in Morris B. Kaplan, in this volume. That the majority, contra Sandel, did not see any resemblances between the intimate sexual activities of married or single heterosexuals, and homosexuals, prompted the label "the most willful blindness." 478 U.S. 205 (1986) (Blackmun, J., dissenting). For a history of the Court's recent attempts to come to grips with the challenges of a changing society and its difficulties in detecting long-recognized constitutional principles when they appear in new guises, see "'The Most Willful Blindness': The Supreme Court and Social Facts," in H.N. Hirsh, *A Theory of Liberty: The Constitution and Minorities* (New York: Routledge, 1992), 115–93.

19. The latter is a very different conception, for privacy, as interpreted in liberal constitutionalism, protects "moral and political heretics [in] their claim of simple justice for the space—free of criminal penalty and its stigma—in which to define a moral identity adequate to give value and dignity to their lives." See David A. J. Richards, "Liberalism, Public Morality, and Constitutional Law: Prolegomenon to a Theory of the Constitutional Right to Privacy," *Law and Contemporary Problems* 51, no. 1(Winter 1988): 150.

20. By "nonliberal," I have in mind places where gay people's lives are short, and none too sweet, such as Islamic societies of the Near and Middle East, and undemocratic states in South America. See Jairo A. Marin, "In Some Societies, to Be Gay Is to Be Dead," *Los Angeles Times* (October 18, 1991): B–7; John Gallager, "Gimme Shelter: Persecuted foreign gays and lesbians push for U.S. asylum," *Advocate*, no. 631(June 15, 1993): 31; and the edited volume, *The Third Pink Book: A Global View of Lesbian and Gay Oppression* (Buffalo: Prometheus, 1993), *en passim*.

21. Honig, *Political Theory and the Displacement of Politics*, 192—hereinafter in this section cited parenthetically.

22. Sandel, *Liberalism and the Limits of Justice*, 179. By way of sharp comparison, liberalism may well describe odious violators of human rights in much the same language:

> For everything turns on who counts as a fellow human being, as a rational agent in the only relevant sense—the sense in which rational agency is synonomous with membership in *our* moral community. . . . It is heartfelt. The identity of these people . . . is bound up with their sense of who they are *not*. Most people—especially people relatively untouched by the European Enlightenment—simply do not think of themselves as, first and foremost, a human being. Instead, they think of themselves as being a certain *good* sort of human being—a sort defined by explicit opposition to a particularly bad sort. It is crucial for their sense of who they are that they are not an infidel, *not* a queer, *not* a woman, *not* an untouchable.

See Richard Rorty, "Human Rights, Rationality, and Sentimentality," in Stephen Shute and Susan Hurley, eds., *On Human Rights: The Oxford Amnesty Lectures 1993* (New York: Basic Books, 1993), 124, 126.

23. Sandel, "Morality and the Liberal Ideal," 17.

24. For Sandel and communitarians generally, the self is discovered, not produced, and "constituted only by friends and not by enemies," nurtured on the "support provided by those who are, or imagine themselves to be, like oneself," who cooperate in maintaining thoroughly constituted subjects.(176, 172, 173)

25. This is preserved in a fairly lasting way, but not permanently, even given the state's enforcement powers, for "no way of life can constitute itself so exhaustively that all remnants of the other are expelled. . . ." (194) Others continue to intrude and disrupt "our" close-knit community. The dangers of the "gentle rhetoric of harmonization" and doubts about the harmlessness of the project of identity closure are discussed in William E. Connolly, *Identity/Difference: Democratic Negotiations of Political Paradox* (Ithaca: Cornell University Press, 1991), 90–91, 171–81. Describing heterosexuality as a "branded or entrenched contingency," a "category culturally preselected for you," Connolly urges us to "question the tendency to ethicize [or "universalize"] this disposition," to regard heterosexuality and aversion to homosexuality as given in nature. Failure to interrogate the us/them dichotomy, especially within oneself, risks repression of difference, self-contempt, a moralizing self-referential legitimization, and self-loathing. See ibid., 175–179.

26. . . . not always successfully: "obscenity—a base thing"—and perhaps consumers of pornography are irredeemable, for their essential natures can't be valorized and they must remain "other." Honig speculates that mere erotic behavior loses out in Sandel's economy of worthy goods,

so that the unity of "our" account of intimacy isn't challenged or threatened with being destabilized.(191, 192).

27. Sandel, *Liberalism and the Limits of Justice*, 183, quoting from the concluding sentence.

28. See the discussion of this analogy in Ali Khan, "The Invasion of Sexual Privacy," *San Diego Law Review* 23, no. 5(1986): 958–64.

29. Hannah Schwarzschild, "Same-Sex Marriage and Constitutional Privacy: Moral Threat and Legal Anomaly," *Berkeley Women's Law Journal* 4 (1988–89): 99, 127. Also see Buchanan, "Same-Sex Marriage," arguing that same-sex marriage would destroy the exclusiveness and intensity of heterosexuality's moral appeal, and J. Harvie Wilkinson, III, and G. Edward White, "Constitutional Protection for Personal Lifestyles," *Cornell Law Review* 62, no. 3(March, 1977): 563–625, where they argue against same-sex marriage because it threatens to become a viable alternative to heterosexual intimacy and would produce greater public exposure to homosexuality.

30. "Otherwise," Honig continues, "we risk destabilization of the same, a way of life that is maintained through eternally recurrent patterns of identification" that are relentless and unforgiving.(194)

31. See Michel Foucault, *The History of Sexuality, Volume I: Introduction*, translated by Robert Hurley (New York: Pantheon, 1978), 42–3, and the fine discussion of Foucault's contribution to understanding sexuality and law in Jed Rubenfeld, "The Right of Privacy," *Harvard Law Review* 102, no. 4(February 1989): 770–77, 783.

32. 822 F.2d. 97, 103 (D.C. Cir. 1987) (affirming FBI's refusal to hire a lesbian applicant for a special agent position).

33. Janet E. Halley, "Misreading Sodomy: A Critique of the Classification of 'Homosexuals' in Federal Equal Protection Law," in Julia Epstein and Kristina Straub, eds., *Body Guards: The Politics of Gender Ambiguity* (New York: Routledge, 1991), 354.

34. "The critical constitutional question in *Hardwick* was not what Michael Hardwick was doing in his bedroom, but what the state of Georgia was doing there." See Thomas B. Stoddard, "*Bowers v. Hardwick*: Precedent by Personal Predilection," *University of Chicago Law Review* 54, no. 2(Spring 1987): 655. Also see Joseph Robert Thornton, "*Bowers v. Hardwick*: An Incomplete Constitutional Analysis," *North Carolina Law Review* 65, no. 5(June 1987): 1100–23 (discussing the Court's "nontreatment" of any of the real issues before it in *Bowers*), and Paul Brest, "Supreme Court Proscribes a View of Privacy," *Los Angeles Times* (July 13, 1986): V-2 ("Nothing required the Supreme Court to focus on the statute's application to homosexuals, rather than

address the law on its own broad terms.... The court in this decision preempted the legislative judgment").

35. Janet E. Halley, "The Construction of Heterosexuality," in Michael Warner, ed., *Fear of a Queer Planet: Queer Politics and Social Theory* (Minneapolis: University of Minnesota Press, 1993), 95, 96. Also see her essay "The Politics of the Closet: Towards Equal Protection for Gay, Lesbian, and Bisexual Idenity," *UCLA Law Review* 36, no. 5(June 1989): 915–76, where she elaborates the constitutionally significant effects of the noun "homosexual" as used to indicate an essence or state of being, and the contention that sodomy is the behavior that defines the class of gay persons.

36. See Michael Warner, "Introduction: Fear of a Queer Planet," *Social Text* 29 (1991): 3–17, who defines "repro-narrativity" as "the notion that our lives are somehow made more meaningful by being embedded in a narrative of generational succession." Ibid., 7. The utterly heterosexual nature of marriage is discussed in Edward Veitch, "The Essence of Marriage—A Comment on the Homosexual Challenge," *Anglo-American Law Review* 5 (1976): 41–9.

37. See Kendall Thomas, "Corpus Juris (Hetero)sexualis: Doctrine, Discourse, and Desire in *Bowers v. Hardwick*," *GLQ* 1, no. 1(1993): 41. Perhaps the Court's natural discourse is devoid of empathic imagination and so is unable to render into human form the juridical subjects before it. One legal scholar sees *Bowers* as "an example of the complete failure of empathy in legal discourse"—on the part of the majority, who traded in stereotypy, "not hearing," and a "retreat to formalism"—"an illustration of the effect of absence of empathic understanding. . . . Blackmun was speaking for humans and for the positive values of a liberal state—respect for human freedom from oppression and tyranny." See Lynne N. Henderson, "Legality and Empathy," *Michigan Law Review* 85, no. 7(June 1987): 1577, 1590–91, 1592, 1649.

38. Karst, "The Freedom of Intimate Association," 683. Karst here is distinguishing issues involved with the analogy to *Loving v. Virginia.*

39. Ibid., 684, n. 270.

40. It should not be forgotten that Georgia's preferred justification for its sodomy statute was to "enhance the Georgia populace's sense of Judeo-Christian morality"; "to guide the public morals towards traditional Judeo-Christian values." See Rahel E. Kent, "An Imposition of the Justices' Own Moral Choices," *Whittier Law Review* 9, no.1(1987): 136. Consider that even the tradition referred to in *Bowers* famously fell under pressure of judicial scrutiny in *Loving v. Virginia,* 388 U.S. 1 (1967) (invidious racism of Virginia's antimiscegenation law, defended in strongly Christian language, violates equal protection and due

process clauses). In *Bowers*, Blackmun commented: "The parallel between *Loving* and this case is uncanny. There, too, the State relied on a religious justification for its law." *Bowers v. Hardwick*, 478 U.S. 210, n. 5 (1986) (Blackmun, J., dissenting). The *Loving-Bowers* nexus is explored in Andrew Koppelman, "The Miscegenation Analogy: Sodomy Law as Sex Discrimination," *Yale Law Journal* 98, no. 1 (November 1988): 145–64, who argues that by branding all gays as criminals, sodomy laws provide a justification for other forms of discrimination; miscegenation and sodomy laws have the same purpose—to support a regime of caste that locks some people into inferior social positions.

41. John R. W. Stott, "Homosexual Marriage: Why same-sex partnerships are not a Christian option," *Christianity Today* 29, no. 17(November 22, 1985): 24, 26.

42. See Ellen M. Barrett, "Legal Homophobia and the Christian Church," *Hastings Law Journal* 30, no. 4(March 1979): 1019–27.

43. "Of all social specters, however, the most terrifying to the Christian conservatives is homosexuality. In and of itself, homosexuality is an abomination to them. . . . [quoting a well-known, notorious Texas evangelist] It is perversion of the highest order. It is against God, against God's Word, against society, against nature. It is almost too repulsive to imagine and describe. It is filth." See Michael Lienesch, *Redeeming America: Piety & Politics in the New Christian Right* (Chapel Hill: University of North Carolina Press, 1993), 84. "Most churchgoers would probably be very surprised—if not upset—if they knew that monies they contribute during Sunday services are diverted to homosexual organizations. . . . After all, the nearly universal belief of people who attend church services . . . is that homosexual practices are an abomination, that homosexuality is a perversion of human nature, and that the Scriptures of all religions reject homosexuality." See Enrique Rueda, *The Homosexual Network: Private Lives and Public Policy* (Old Greenwich: Devin Adair, 1982), 504. The investigation in this 680-page tome was financed by Paul Weyrich's Free Congress Research and Education Foundation as a reference work for conservative political actors.

44. "Those who have never been allowed in any community or tradition in the first place may reasonably be even more doubtful" than others of this accommodation. See Shane Phelan, *Identity Politics: Lesbian Feminism and the Limits of Community* (Philadelphia: Temple University Press, 1989), 146. Phelan links the project of deconstruction of communitarianism's "common understandings" that, after all, are "not simply *there* but have been produced" to the project of finding lesbian-

feminist ground finally to be free "in a world where we are not yet safe from those who would have us tattoooed or sterilized or incarcerated." See ibid., 150–51.

45. Warner, "Introduction: Fear of a Queer Planet," 6.

46. J.S. Taub, "A Clash of Cultures . . . ," *California Journal* 24, no. 11 (November 1993): 17.

47. See Jack Levin and Jack McDevitt, *Hate Crimes: The Rising Tide of Bigotry and Bloodshed* (New York: Plenum, 1993), and Robert J. Kelly, ed., *Bias Crime: American Law Enforcement and Legal Responses* (Chicago: Office of International Criminal Justice/University of Illinois, 1993). One reviewer argues that the decision in *Bowers* harkens back to some people's version of the good old days. See Daniel R. Gordon, "The Ugly Mirror: *Bowers, Plessy,* and the Reemergence of the Constitutionalism of Social Stratification and Historical Reinforcement," *Journal of Contemporary Law* 19, no. 1(1993): 21–50. Also see *Watkins v. U.S. Army,* 847 F.2d. 1329, 1358 (1988) ("I believe that history will view *Hardwick* much as it views *Plessy* . . . and I am confident that, in the long run, *Hardwick*, like *Plessy*, will be overruled by a wiser and more enlightened Court") (Reinhardt, dissenting). Traditions themselves aren't simply given; sometimes they are made up, and the way in which they are shared may reflect and serve unequal relations of power. See Eric Hobsbawn and Terence Ranger, eds., *The Invention of Tradition* (Cambridge: Cambridge University Press, 1983), and Lyle A. Downing and Robert B. Thigpen, "Beyond Shared Understandings," *Political Theory* 14, no. 3(August 1986): 451–72.

48. See the essay by Christopher J. Berry, "Shared Understanding and the Democratic Way of Life," in John W. Chapman and Ian Shapiro, eds., *Nomos XXXV. Democratic Community* (New York: New York University Press, 1993), 67–87, which subjects communitarian concepts of democratic community and shared understandings to critical scrutiny, defending pluralist liberalism and rights in their stead.

49. See Paul Benson, "Autonomy and Oppressive Socialization," *Social Theory and Practice* 17, no. 3(Fall 1991): 385–408.

50. A particularly worthwhile investigation into the "body politics" of the relationship of law to the exercise of social power is in Kendall Thomas, "Beyond the Privacy Principle," *Columbia Law Review* 92, no. 6(October 1992): 1436–43. Using Foucault's analysis, Thomas argues against sodomy laws not from a basis in the privacy right, rather, from Eighth Amendment rights against "cruel and unusual punishments." Seeing political power implicated in patterns that resemble both racism and terrorism in the homophobic violence perpetrated by "private citizens," Thomas finds here "coordinate," not causal connec-

tions with sodomy laws; all this as well implicates government's dere-
liction of one of its primary duties to protect its citizens. The connection between sodomy laws and antigay discrimination and violence is
discussed in "Brief Amicus Curiae for . . . ," *New York University
Review of Law and Social Change* 14 (1986): 967–70.

51. Connolly, *Identity/Difference*, 175. Also see Adrian Coyle, "'My Own
Special Creation'? The Construction of Gay Identity," in Glynis M.
Breakwell, ed., *Social Psychology of Identity and the Self Concept*
(London: Surrey UK, 1992), 187–220.

52. Rubenfeld, "The Right of Privacy," 800–801, 806.

53. *Bowers v. Hardwick,* 478 U.S. 198 (Burger, C.J., concurring opinion,
quoting from Blackstone). Agreeing with the majority that there is "no
substantive right under the Due Process Clause" to homosexual
sodomy, Powell allayed his considerable Eighth Amendment concerns
principally by noting that Hardwick "has not been tried, much less con-
victed and sentenced." Ibid., 198 (Powell, J., concurring opinion).
Powell didn't take into proper account Georgia's willingness to enforce
the sodomy statute, the validity of which it argued all the way up to the
Supreme Court, and the injury suffered by Hardwick, who was
arrested, and injuries in store for prospective others. "By pointing out
the statute's inherent unfairness and then voting in favor of the statute's
validity with the majority, Justice Powell's opinion neither lent credibil-
ity to the statute challenged, nor to the majority of the Court." See
Kent, "An Imposition," 144.

54. The majority sought to distance itself and the Supreme Court from permitting the influence of personal beliefs: "This case does not require
a judgment on whether laws against sodomy between consenting
adults in general, or between homosexuals in particular, are wise or
desirable. . . Striving to assure itself and the public that announcing
rights not readily identifiable in the Constitution's text involves much
more than the imposition of the Justices' own choice of values on the
States and the Federal Government, . . ." *Bowers v. Hardwick,* 478 U.S.
190, 191 (1986) (White, J., majority opinion).

55. Ibid., 192, 196.

56. See Thomas, "Corpus Juris (Hetero)sexualis," 45, 34, 43. Also see
Brest, "Supreme Court Proscribes," V-2 ("The majority's opinion in
Hardwick, while written by a skilled jurist, is so lacking in legal craft
that it makes one wonder what was going on").

57. Halley, "Misreading Sodomy," 367, 366. For more on the fantastic
ability to know without investigating past the venerable old duffer on
the "Clapham omnibus," see H.L.A. Hart, "Social Solidarity and the

Enforcement of Morals," *University of Chicago Law Review* 35, no. 1(Autumn 1967): 1–13.

58. Traditional moral condemnations of sodomitical conduct are given in David A. J. Richards, "Constitutional Legitimacy and Constitutional Privacy," *New York University Law Review* 61, no. 5(November 1986): 858, n. 334. "These images [of incompetence, immaturity, licentiousness, and animalistic immorality] are themselves the cultural artifacts of a long history of uncritical common sense about proper sexuality, a common sense that required sex to be procreational, or to follow the pattern of masculine domination and feminine submission." Ibid., 854 (reference notes omitted). Others have used such images of gay persons to deny them "lifestyle rights" or "constitutional protection for secluded homosexual acts." Also see Wilkinson and White, "Constitutional Protection for Personal Lifestyles," 594–96, who rely not on empirical evidence, but on popular conceptions of gays & lesbians as recruiters and so a threat to youth—who, by way of example, can lead or turn persons toward homosexuality—to argue for restricting their appearance in public.

59. By this I mean communities of concentrated gay and lesbian populations, such as Greenwich Village in New York City, the Castro District of San Francisco, and West Hollywood, California. Persons in these communities and (needless to say) elsewhere are frequent victims of "hate crimes" which often are motivated by a righteous sense of traditional or religious values, considered enforced through this violence, and on occasion even a preference that these communities be ontologically dislocated. See Gary David Comstock, *Violence Against Lesbians and Gay Men* (New York: Columbia University Press, 1991). Also see the "Special Double Issue: Homophobia: An Overview," *Journal of Homosexuality* 10, nos. 1/2(Fall 1984); "Special Issue: Violence Against Lesbians and Gay Men: Issues for Research, Practice, and Policy," *Journal of Interpersonal Violence* 5, no. 3(September 1990); Peter N. Nardi and Ralph Bolton, "Gay-Bashing: Violence and Aggression Against Gay Men and Lesbians," in R. Baenniger, ed., *Targets of Violence and Aggression* (Elsevier: North Holland, 1991), 349–400; and, Gregory M. Herek and Kevin T. Berrill, eds., *Hate Crimes: Confronting the Violence Against Lesbians and Gay Men* (Newbury Park: SAGE, 1992).

60. An early discussion of these areas as "communities" is given in Stephen O. Murray, "The Institutional Elaboration of a Quasi-Ethnic Community," *International Review of Modern Sociology* 9 (July-December, 1979): 165–77.

61. See Joshua Dressler, "Judicial Homophobia: Gay Rights' Biggest Roadblock," *Civil Liberties* 5, no. 4(January/February 1979): 19–27. In a heteronormative culture the Court may forget that gay people's claims to equal treatment aren't statistically based, nor is their validity tied to the numbers of gay persons in the population. See the essay by Robert Dawidoff, "1% or 10%—the Law Isn't Counting," *Los Angeles Times* (April 16, 1993): B-7.

62. When not openly avowing a telos, communitarianism strains for principle in its accounts of origins and in its attempts to extend privileges to outsiders. For example, "Sandel thinks that continuity with tradition is the only thing that could justify extending rights in novel ways. He offers the example of homosexual relationships. . . . Note how Rousseauian the argument is—it appeals to what is accepted, solely on the grounds that it is so accepted; were another content accepted, it would equally well have a claim." See Arthur Ripstein, "Universal and General Wills: Hegel and Rousseau," *Political Theory* 22, no. 3(August 1994): 462.

63. It has been suggested that bald prejudice, negative stereotyped perceptions, and other traditional, cultural characterizations of groups have a deletory influence in public policy, serving to reinforce group members' disadvantages and to devalue their citizenship. See Anne Schneider and Helen Ingram, "Social Construction of Target Populations: Implications for Politics and Policy," *American Political Science Review* 87, no. 2(June 1993): 334–47. The literature on stigma and its wide-ranging pernicious effects is vast; for starters, see the "Moral Exclusion and Injustice" issue of *Journal of Social Issues* 46, no. 1(1990).

64. Judith Butler, "Imitation and Gender Insubordination," in Diana Fuss, ed., *Inside/Out: Lesbian Theories, Gay Theories* (New York: Routledge, 1991), 20.

65. The presumption here is that communitarian standards would respect the gay community and gay and lesbian persons' sense of self, and so not wish to force it or them to fit a mold not wished upon themselves.

66. But, the twentieth century "is so powerfully under the spell of the relatively recent dichotomy between hetero- and homosexuality that it is hard to imagine sodomy as anything but a charged signifier of deviance from the heterosexual norm." See Christopher Newfield, "Democracy and Homoeroticism," *Yale Journal of Criticism* 6, no. 2(Fall 1993): 34.

67. Judith Butler, *Gender Trouble: Feminism and the Subversion of Identity* (New York: Routledge, 1990), 1–2. Butler, a critic of universal rationality and foundationalist reasoning, urges us to reconceive identity and community as effects, as "produced or generated" and "misdescribed as foundations." See ibid., 147.

68. Butler points out the destabilizing effects of a move such as Sandel's on its heteronormative understanding of subjectivity: "the very notion of 'the person' is called into question by the cultural emergence of those 'incoherent' or 'discontinuous' gendered beings who appear to be persons but who fail to conform to the gendered norms of cultural intelligibility by which persons are defined." See ibid., 17.

69. A later court decision repudiated this identification: "It is an error of massive proportions to define the entire class of homosexuals by sodomy." *High Tech Gays v. Defense Ind. Clearance Office,* 909 F.2d. 375, 380 (9th Cir. 1990). *High Tech Gays* repudiated a long tradition of community reasoning and bigotry. This tradition in law and its persistent, pernicious consequences for gay persons are well-described in Robert Douglas Chesler, "Imagery of Community, Ideology of Authority: The Moral Reasoning of Chief Justice Burger," *Harvard Civil Rights-Civil Liberties Law Review* 18, no. 2(Summer 1983): 457–82 ("The power to exclude is implicit in the concept of the moral community"), and Anne B. Goldstein, "History, Homosexuality, and Political Values: Searching for the Hidden Determinants of *Bowers v. Hardwick,*" *Yale Law Journal* 97, no. 6(May 1988): 1073–1103 ("The majority opinion is written as if the term 'homosexual' solved, rather than confused, the problem of evaluating Hardwick's actions in terms of his constitutional rights").

70. Annamay T. Sheppard, "Private Passion, Public Outrage: Thoughts on *Bowers v. Hardwick,*" *Rutgers Law Review* 40, no. 2(Winter 1988): 545. Sheppard's essay directs attention toward the religious elements in anti-gay statutes.

71. For example, ". . . the preservation of traditional society and the values most Americans cherish does require the denial of the homosexual ideology. It is impossible to predict whether or not the homosexual movement will be successful. Were it to succeed, however, the nation as we have known it would cease to exist." See Rueda, *The Homosexual Network*, 140–41.

72. Edward E. Sampson, "Identity Politics: Challenges to Psychology's Understanding," *American Psychologist* 48, no. 12(December 1993): 1220, 1226.

73. "[T]he concept of privacy embodies the 'moral fact that a person belongs to himself and not others nor to society as a whole'" [reference notes omitted]. *Bowers v. Hardwick,* 478 U.S. 204 (1986) (Blackmun, J., dissenting). Kaplan takes issue with Sandel's interpretation of Blackmun's invocation of privacy. See Kaplan, "Intimacy and Equality," 359, n. 66.

74. The law, however, has on painful occasion proved a useful instrument for this or that community's "like-minded people" attempting to limit their community through, for example, zoning and planning. See "Folks Like Us; Lives Like Ours: Spatial Communities and the Law," in Norgren and Nanda, *American Cultural Pluralism and the Law*, 200–21.

75. This important issue in *Bowers* was not missed in another case:

    Thus, many of us, including many elected officials, are likely to have difficulty understanding or empathizing with homo-sexuals. . . . members of this group are particularly powerless to pursue their rights openly in the political process. . . . Even when gays overcome this prejudice enough to participate openly in politics, the general animus towards homosexuality may render this participation wholly ineffective. [*Watkins v. U.S. Army*, 847 F.2d. 1329, 1348 (9th Cir. 1988).]

76. Martha Minow, "Interpreting Rights: An Essay for Robert Cover," *Yale Law Journal* 96, no. 8(July 1987): 1911, 1912. Minow defends rights discourse as an appropriate *communal* language for American society.

8

Essentialism and the Political Articulation of Identity

Gary Lehring

> There is a specter haunting homosexuality: the specter of gay libera-
> tion. For to the extent that the aims of the gay liberation movement are
> attained, the homosexual, as he presently defines himself, will disappear.
> The conditions which, for example, place him outside his society and
> furnish a basis for critical detachment, will have been washed away in
> the flood tide of a new order.
>
> Jean Bethke Elshtain, "The Paradox of Gay Liberation"

So begins Jean Bethke Elshtain's 1981 *Salmagundi* article, one of her only
forays into the area of gay politics. Recently, while teaching a course in
gender and politics, I became reacquainted with this article, in which
Elshtain explores the paradoxes inherent in the goals of a gay "liberation"
movement which seeks to destroy the very society which has given gay politics birth. Elshtain makes many interesting claims which I will examine
below, but the basis for my renewed interest stemmed as much from student reaction to the article, as from the article itself. With amazing unanim-
ity the students, many of them gay and lesbian, vilified the article and its
author, dismissing many of the subtle and complicated arguments as
"homophobic," despite Elshtain's repeated endorsement of equality, civil
rights, and protection against discrimination for gays and lesbians. But
strangely, the students also rejected the liberationist arguments, bringing
them much closer to Elshtain than they realized, or cared to admit, making

me ask why the "liberationist" voice presents such a challenge to "hetero-sexuals" and "homosexuals" alike? In this paper I will reexamine Elshtain's arguments against gay liberation, demonstrate why I believe her arguments are flawed, and argue why I believe both she and contemporary gays and les-bians would do well to listen anew to the voices of gay liberation and pursue more cautiously the essentialist-centered equal rights strategy that is domi-nant in the lesbian and gay political movements today.

Paradox and Perversity in Gay Liberation

Elshtain's arguments against gay liberation have a familiar ring. The phan-tom haunting homosexuality has relatives haunting other political move-ments as well. In 1991 a specter haunted feminism: "the specter of difference constructed as a principle designed to trump all other principles, pops up everywhere these days."[1] Indeed, if one accepts Elshtain's account of things, all movements for social change seem to be plagued by wraiths and apparitions out to change the world. The interesting thing is not that Elshtain has been seeing ghosts for over a decade; rather it is how she con-jures up these spirits to frighten us all about the world we will inhabit should society change to reflect the goals of these social movements. Her rhetorical excess is always provocative, often disturbing, and in the specific case of gay liberation, sometimes distorted, but these distortions have the effect of demonizing any efforts to question or challenge the traditional institutions of heterosexuality, marriage, and family.

Elshtain's exploration is based upon a number of liberationist texts writ-ten mostly by gay men, including Dennis Altman,[2] Richard Goldstein,[3] John Murphy,[4] Edward Delph,[5] Carl Wittman,[6] Stuart Byron,[7] and Allen Young.[8] Yet her attempt to yield a single gay liberationist voice from many often mis-represents many of the authors' ideas about what gay liberation means. Like the zealous and hasty construction of the Frankenstein monster, Elshtain's straw gay liberationist is assembled from bits and pieces of many different intellectual and theoretical works, yielding a nightmarish vision that more accurately represents her fears about gay liberation than the liberationists' own dreams of how to change an oppressive society. The guiding thread of gay liberation was a rejection of enforced heterosexuality, marriage, tradi-tional gender roles and family arrangements, and sexual privacy all built upon an understanding of sexual identity as something other than fixed.

For example, Allen Young argued that enforced heterosexuality was an evil caused by a sexist culture "to protect the power of straight men . . . homosexuality becomes prohibited behavior."[9] Carl Wittman was less philosophical than Young, but more stridently to the point in his claim that "exclusive heterosexuality is fucked up." He added that "it reflects a fear of people of the same sex, it's anti-homosexual, and it is fraught with frustra-tion."[10] A lesbian-feminist group called the Radicalesbians articulated how this enforced heterosexuality affected a typical lesbian, who often finds herself in "painful conflict with people, situations, the accepted ways of thinking, feeling and behaving, until she is in a state of continual war with everything around her, and usually with herself." This turmoil "tends to induce guilt proportional to the degree to which she feels she is not meeting social expectations, and/or eventually drives her to question and analyze what the rest of her society more or less accepts."[11]

The rejection of heterosexuality was tied to similar disavowals of marriage, family, and sex roles. Martha Shelley argued that gay liberationists are "women and men who from the time of our earliest memories have been in revolt against the sex role-structure and the nuclear family structure." She asked other gays and lesbians to get in touch with "the reasons that made you reject straight society as a kid," remembering that for herself it was vowing never to be like the "vacant women drifting in and out of supermarkets." She concluded that "straight roles stink" and wondered, "Is love possible between heterosexuals?"[12]

Attacks on the sex roles and the social institutions of marriage and family are common in liberationist literature. Wittman writes, "Traditional marriage is a rotten, oppressive institution . . . a contract which smothers both people, denies needs and places impossible demands on both people."[13] Allen Young continues this criticism:

> The nuclear family, with its man-woman model built in by the presence of parents, is the primary means by which this restricted sexuality is created and enforced. Gays experience rejection by the family in a society where familial love is considered important. The family oppresses women and children as well as gays. The phenomena of runaway teenagers and increasing divorce rates are signs of the erosion of the nuclear family. Gay liberation is another sign. We attack the nuclear family when we refuse to get married and have a family. We are committed to building communal situations where children can grow strong and free.[14]

For the gay liberationists, the social institutions of marriage and family were suspect, in need of redefinition if not total elimination, because like heterosexuality, they were part and parcel of the very fabric of society that helped oppress lesbians and gays by rendering their lives and loves invisible. The enforced privacy surrounding all discussions of homosexuality made "getting the facts" impossible for an adolescent in the 1950s. In newspapers, magazines, on radio and TV, and in the movies, there "wasn't the slightest affirmation of homosexuality" if the "subject ever made an appearance."[15] Mostly, Young tells us, there was nothing. He also criticizes the liberal, "straight" notion that sexuality is "essentially a private matter" arguing that this perpetuated "male supremacy and patterns of dominance which are basically sexist and which are in the end anti-homosexual."[16] The

Radicalesbians too complained that a lesbian, "often at an extremely early age . . . [was] forced to evolve her own life pattern, often living much of her life alone, learning usually much earlier than her straight (heterosexual) sisters about the essential loneliness of life (which the myth of marriage obscures).[17] Stuart Byron, in a passage Elshtain criticizes, summed up best what many lesbians and gays experience as a result of the rigid enforcement of a privatized sexuality. He wrote:

> One is, after all, oppressed as a homosexual every minute of every day, inasmuch as one is restrained from acting in ways that would seem normal to a heterosexual. Every time one refrains from an act of public affection with a lover where a straight couple would not—in the park, on the movie line—one dies a little. . . . *Everything* in society—every movie, every billboard, everything done as second nature in public—reminds the gay person that what he or she is is unnatural.[18]

Although perhaps somewhat utopian in their outlook, the liberationists merged their personal insights and experiences of oppression with a rapidly expanding body of feminist and Marxist-feminist theory creating powerful criticisms of the institutions of heterosexuality, marriage, family, and privacy. These criticisms are still relevant as many young lesbians and gays continue to face oppressive home environments and abusive families when their sexual identity is discovered, but at least today this sad fact is widely acknowledged as a problem by straights and gays. What continues to be as radical today as it was in the 1970s is the liberationists' understanding of what it means to be "gay," of what constitutes lesbian or gay *being*. Allen Young wrote that "the artificial categories 'heterosexual' and 'homosexual' have been laid on us by a sexist society" and that "every straight man is a target for gay liberation."[19] The Radicalesbians argued that "lesbianism, like male homosexuality, is a category . . . possible only in a sexist society characterized by rigid roles and dominated by male supremacy,"[20] and Martha Shelley claimed that the "function of a homosexual is to make [heterosexuals] uneasy." Demanding understanding from "straights," she argued that they could only give this "by becoming one of us." One of the goals of gay liberation then was "to reach the homosexuals entombed in [heterosexuals], to liberate our brothers and sisters,"[21] to "free the homosexual in everyone."[22] This belief that sexuality was the product of a sexist society, and that heterosexuality and homosexuality were two equally oppressive social roles, was a sophisticated theoretical argument then and now, and many of the liberationist ideas are contained in the contemporary social constructivist understanding of sexuality. However, there is an important difference between the gay liberationists of the 1970s and the social constructivists of the 1990s: the issue of choice. While it is impossible to find a social constructivist who would equate social construction with choice, the liberationists did indeed argue that gays and straights alike needed only to *choose* to be gay to make it so. Far from simplistic, this position seemed carefully developed to help create anxiety and provoke reflection among the heterosexual majority that never had to give a second thought to their sexuality and the social institutions that support it. If Jean Elshtain's response to the liberationists is any indication, they were successful in this goal.

Elshtain begins her analysis of gay liberation with the worried claim that "the idea that homosexuality can and should become the basis from which present social institutions are assaulted and through which a new, liberated social order will arise is heady brew on which the organized gay movement appears to be drunk."[23] She attacks this liberationist vision on a number of fronts. In an effort to discredit their ideas she calls gay liberation the nightmarish fantasy of oversexed *men*, who wish to make "anonymous sex our individual and social anodyne."[24] No self-respecting woman—lesbian or straight— would accept the politics of gay liberation. But more importantly, she argues that the gay liberation agenda is bad for "us" (read straights) and bad for "them" (read gay liberationists, and at times, all gays and lesbians). It is bad for "us" because the liberationists have "no vision of a democratic politics, or a participatory commonweal, no sense of social goods or purposes" leading to an "over-personalized politics and an over-politicized personal identity being fused to create a situation where everything is grist for the public mill."[25] For gay liberationists themselves, liberation is bad, she suggests, because if successful, it would "culminate in the withering away of the group in whose behalf its efforts are being mounted."[26] These are complex and complicated arguments that need elaboration in greater detail.

In a footnote to the opening salvo cited above, Elshtain tells us that she refers to "the homosexual as 'he' advisedly," as most of the authors she targets for criticism are gay *men*. Elshtain's claim that gay liberation is really a front for other, more pernicious causes is perhaps the most interesting and the most revealing criticism offered. Despite her disagreement with lesbian feminists elsewhere,[27] here they are posited as defenders of hearth and home, and traditional values. She writes:

> There are many fewer lesbian liberationists who accept the promise of a future society in which all distinctions have been eliminated, long term relationships repudiated, and polymorphous perversity on demand legislated into existence—utopia according to the Marquis de Sade. (Though some believe that groovy goodness will reign and all nastiness will have been eliminated.) Lesbian feminists have, with some exceptions, been quick to recognize the Playboy "philosophy" lurking behind much male gay liberation. One also finds in lesbian discussions not only acceptance but endorsement of long term ties, of coupling and creating homes.[28]

Contrary to this portrayal, not all lesbians took issue with the liberationist attack on traditional structures of marriage and family; there were many lesbians who argued against the very values and institutions she credits them with defending. As witnessed above, writers like Martha Shelley and groups like the Radicalesbians developed far-reaching criticisms of traditional social practices and institutions. So too did Karla Jay, one of the editors of *Out of the Closets: Voices of Gay Liberation*, a text that Elshtain cites often in this article. Jay writes that lesbians and gays are "the negation of heterosexuality and of the nuclear family structure."[29] Conversely, many male liberationists who believed that heterosexual marriage and family were problematic concepts did not think sex on demand was the answer. The liberationists were more diverse and more sophisticated than Elshtain's analysis would indicate. For example, Allen Young's rejection of heterosexuality does include the declaration that to be gay means to be "sexually free," but he explicitly rejects Elshtain's characterization of the male liberationist position as one driven by sex, revealing that since becoming a liberationist he "has sex less often but finds it infinitely more satisfying."[30] He advises that this "sexual freedom is not some kind of groovy lifestyle with lots of sex, doing what feels good irrespective of others. It is sexual freedom premised upon the notion of pleasure through equality, no pleasure where there is no equality."[31]

The ideas for gay liberation described by these authors, all of whom Elshtain includes in her analysis, may indeed sound frightening to those invested in traditional relationships of marriage and family, but they are hardly utopia according to the Marquis de Sade; in fact, Elshtain's alarm notwithstanding, the liberationist vision of politics often sounds both democratic and egalitarian.

Elshtain's remaining objections center on two major points: the importance of a clear boundary between the public and the private, and the necessity of these sex roles and social institutions. Elshtain's attack on the way gay liberation's political agenda will adversely impact "us" is in significant part an attack on *all* politics that violate her belief in the necessity of maintaining a separation between what we think of as public and private. Ever mindful of the liberal commitment to privacy, she writes: "pseudopolitics of the sort I have in mind, and of which gay liberation is but one example, begins and ends in a stance in which private preferences get couched as public imperatives *simpliciter*."[32]

This violates one of her fundamental principles, and so she begins this critique of gay liberation, as she always begins, "by affirming some distinction between public and private activities and identities."[33] Her rigorous regulation of this buffer between the public and private spheres is meant to save politics itself, as well as to save each of us from ourselves, and from one another. In *Public Man, Private Woman* she writes:

> If a thinker incorporates the private realm of family into a total politicized structure of explanation, and flattens out all distinctions between what is public and what is private, the following dilemma necessarily emerges: if all relationships and activities, including our most intimate ones, are

political in their essence, if politics is everything and everywhere, then no genuine political action and purpose is possible, as we can never distinguish the political from anything else.[34]

The major dilemma presented by gay liberation is that its "key imperative . . . is the erosion of any distinction between the personal and the political."[35] This erosion opens the floodgates to greater state control, public regulation, and social coercion. According to Elshtain, the liberationists imagine themselves "a revolutionary vanguard" out to alter human nature itself, leading to a politics that would unleash a "terrible engine of social control." "This quest for absolute freedom" she tells us, "ends in absolute terror."[36] This Jacobin terror is the bogeyman that always awaits those taken in by political movements haunted by Elshtain's specters,[37] but gay liberation's terror is uniquely perverse, ending ultimately with the public sanctioning of the sexual abuse of children. Including members of the North American Man/Boy Love Association in her nightmarish vision of who the gay liberationists are, she claims that these "maximal liberationists" seek to end the existence of "laws governing the age of consent . . . or *any* constraints at all on sexual acting out," asserting that gays will claim that they face oppression "within this frame of reference, until society provides both the opportunity and the assurance of safety for adult gays—and one must assume heterosexuals—who wish to take young people under sixteen, with no limits, for their sexual partners."[38]

Elshtain's second concern about gay liberation is related to the first. The social and personal redefinition that she imagines will occur as the boundary between public and private is blurred leads to a paradoxical set of circumstances where gays desire to destroy the very society that gave birth to their identity. This is a paradox, Elshtain argues, because gay liberation turns out to be bad for the very group in whose name liberation is sought. This paradox is one inherent in the liberationist ontology. She writes that among gay liberationists there is a tacit recognition that homosexuality "exists as an internal margin or boundary in contemporary American society and is called into being *by* that society." Comparing homosexuality to adultery—the allure of which, at least partly, rests upon its status as "forbidden fruit"—Elshtain writes that "homosexuality remains an existential choice, a distinctive identity, *only* within a wider social system in which gays provide an identity for themselves and their group by 'negating' the norms, standards, and way of life of the culture's heterosexual majority." Heterosexuality then, "provides homosexuality with its dialectic opposite and gives homosexuality its special fascination and claims to uniqueness."[39]

The thrust of Elshtain's criticism is that *if* homosexuality is a choice made possible by a certain historical alignment of social institutions and traditional familial arrangements as is claimed by the liberationists, then an attack on the society that has helped define it, and has made their organization as a political group possible, is an attack on homosexuality itself; a kind of collective, unconscious, masochistic cry of *mea culpa* that renders their political goals and objectives untenable if not nonsensical. Of course, Elshtain believes this is a big *if*, suggesting that sexual identity, and gender identity, "are not only imbedded in ordinary language, they are constitutive of ordinary life";[40] she thus reveals her own discomfort with gendered or sexual identities that are anything other than fixed.[41]

Privacy and the Liberal Closet

Elshtain's warning concerning the danger of an ever-encroaching state regulatory apparatus that threatens any distinction between public and private is a concern worth heeding. Increasing state involvement in all areas of our life could well be dangerous to the democratic form of government. With this I have no objection, and indeed I have always found Elshtain persuasive on this point. But no matter how persuasive this insight, her larger argument must be rejected. Not only does she offer little evidence that gay liberation is likely to bring about the Jacobin terror she describes, but her attack on gay liberation is part and parcel of a larger conservative agenda in which lesbians and gays are demonized and liberal privacy—the privacy of the closet—is offered as the only viable political position for queers seeking political change. This, of course, was exactly the course rejected by the gay liberationists, who were "tired of waiting around for the liberals to repeal the sodomy laws."[42] So repulsed by gay liberation that she sees danger everywhere and overstates it, Elshtain is even willing to call upon the oldest argument of all to discredit it: What queers really want is to have sex with your kids. Conflating pedophilia and homosexuality is a tired, cheap trick but it serves her well, effectively halting all consideration of the many insights and proposals offered by the gay liberationists.

Most seriously, Elshtain misses many of gay liberation's concerns about privacy in a number of important respects. First, she ignores the central implication suggested by the liberationist critique—that the private institutions of marriage and family are actually publicly supported, defined, maintained, legitimated, and regulated, suggesting that there always has been significantly more overlap in the categories of "public" and "private" than she concedes, and that access to these institutions has less to do with a "natural order" that constitutes everyday life, than with the awarding of sociopolitical privileges granted to some at the expense of others.

Privacy, then, has never been a value that everyone shares in equally despite Elshtain's declaration that "the right to privacy, the right for gays to practice their sexual preference without fear of harassment, has been widely acknowledged as part of a protected right to privacy in American Society."[43] Five years after Elshtain's article was published the U.S. Supreme Court declared that there was no such constitutional privacy that protected the *practice* of gay sexual *preference*. In *Bowers v. Hardwick*, the Court made explicit what gays and lesbians had always known implicitly, that they could not expect to be included in the rights and privileges "widely acknowledged" as existing for heterosexuals.

Second, despite Elshtain's assertion that "gays or any other group of citizens have the civil right to be protected from life threatening intrusion of simple harassment under the right to privacy, as well as the right to be free from discrimination in employment, housing, and other areas [as] an ongoing imperative of our constitutional system,"[44] her understanding of *what* gays and lesbians *are* travels the same path as that of the Supreme Court in *Bowers*, a decision that denied these very same rights. When discussing the so-called "widely acknowledged right to privacy" above, Elshtain claims that this right protects gays in "the practice of their *sexual preference.*" Elsewhere in the same article she objects to the liberationist claim that gays are an oppressed class, rejecting this belief because she does not believe that "private *sexual preferences* are sufficient to constitute an oppressed class of persons." She does grant that "one's *sexual preference*—unless they do violence to others—should not affect assessments of one's rights and worth as an employee, a home-owner, and so on."[45] For Elshtain, the definition of gay and lesbian is embedded in what one does in bed. She extends to gays a right of privacy in which to shield all sexual activities—something the Supreme Court refused to do—but in doing so defines gays by and through those sexual activities. The sum of the difference between Elshtain and the Court is that one does not protect gays' right to have sex in private while the other does, but neither believes that being gay or lesbian is about anything more.[46]

President Clinton's "compromise" that allows gays in the military to serve as long as they are silent about their sexuality is another example of the way that privacy may be used to impose different sets of expectations upon gays and lesbians than those used to evaluate their heterosexual counterparts. In the name of privacy homosexual behavior, or any declarations of speech that acknowledge one's gay or lesbian identity, still result in one's dismissal from the military, transforming privacy into an enforced silence in which gays and lesbians do the work of self-policing, closeting themselves willingly if they wish to continue to serve. To be sure this does change the military's longstanding policy, but in a manner that employs privacy to further the interests of the military at the expense of those to whom this right is supposedly granted. It achieves this by enabling the military to abandon the ridiculous policy claim often cited by high-ranking military officials that there were "no homosexuals in the military," and to create a more realistic and seemingly more liberal policy position in which the presence of lesbians and gays is acknowledged, but tolerated only so long as no one knows for sure if any single individual is lesbian or gay. Under this understanding of sexual identity and the right of privacy, lesbians and gays are made invisible.

This "invisibilization" need not be only the result of official public policies; we often are asked to participate in this process in the way we are expected

to police our interactions with colleagues and friends. For example, during a
year I spent teaching at a small, prestigious liberal arts college, a supportive
and empathetic senior colleague once told me that there was "a certain kind
of gay person that does well at this college." This kind of gay person turned
out to be one who appeared to be in a long-term, monogamous relationship,
who never uttered the word "gay," and who for all intents and purposes was
"just like everyone else." The implication was clear. With books and posters
about lesbian and gays all over my office, announcements for the lesbian and
gay studies program posted on my door, and pictures of my latest boyfriend
on my desk, *I was not the kind of gay person* he had in mind. Certainly, I was
free to be gay—they were all good liberals in this department—but this freedom was to be bought with my complicity in my own invisibilization, a price
I was unwilling to pay. By imposing privacy and silence on what we would
never want made public in any case, this liberal privacy invisibilizes *all* parts
of lesbian and gay life. So threatening to the gender order is the idea that
being gay or lesbian may be more than simple sexual preference, that liberal
notions of privacy and civility must be called upon to help invisibilize the
possibility.

This invisibilization occurs too in the media treatment of lesbian and gay
issues. As Michelangelo Signorile has argued persuasively, if the media pries
into the private and intimate "lifestyles of the rich and famous" who are
straight, to do less when lesbians or gays are involved is a double standard
that screams of the hypocritical uses to which this right to privacy is put.[47]
The media does this and more, often reporting on the supposed heterosexual *tête-à-têtes* of people they know to be lesbian or gay. This is not to say
that I agree with the invasive and demeaning intrusions of the tabloid press.
It is simply that what rests behind the media's difference in treatment is not a
more expansive application of the liberal right to privacy to include gays and
lesbians, but rather a more polite and politically correct way to exclude gays
and lesbians from media coverage. It is another closet, and a closet lined
with liberal good intentions is still a closet.

Much of Elshtain's dismissal of liberationist criticism of traditional child-
rearing practices and sex role arrangements builds upon her defense of privacy. Both stem from her uneasiness with any attempts to rethink the
sacrosanct family, an institution she believes is the archetypal private/social
institution.[48] The gay liberationists argued persuasively that these central
elements of family contribute to the making of a gender order that many of
us find oppressive. The heterosexist assumption that *all* children are straight
and will grow up to desire to live in exactly the same model of heterosexual
marriage and family is a coercive power for which even the most oppressive
State can only hunger. The high rate of teenage suicide among sexual
minorities is testimony to the desperation many gays and lesbians feel when
confronted with the possibility of even having to tell their parents that they
are gay.[49] The privatized institution of family as presently arranged simply

fails those many children who would rather face death than disappoint their families. Feminists too have criticized the conjunction of marriage, family, and privacy as a site of gender subordination and a location in which wife and child abuse historically escape notice by police and state authorities.[50]

Sadly, it is within the very institution of family that the sexual abuse Elshtain decries most frequently takes place, and the sanctity of privacy surrounding family serves to prolong the abuse. In fact, it is our cultural shame surrounding sexuality—a value transmitted through the institution of family in most cases—that keeps children from reporting sexual molestation, making an unqualified celebration of privacy such as the one Elshtain undertakes somewhat difficult to understand.

Equally perplexing is Elshtain's second claim that if the liberationists succeed, then homosexual identity will disappear. Upon closer examination, the paradox of gay liberation seems not so paradoxical. Putting an end to the way that queers are treated by an oppressive society was exactly what the liberationists argued was necessary. If ending that social discrimination meant that both homosexuality and heterosexuality would cease to play the central role in our collective theorizing of who we are, if sexual identity would no longer be the way we tell the truth of our soul,[51] most of us would say so much the better. Giving up the privileged status of "forbidden fruit" seems a more than fair trade for winning a new social order where kids need not fear coming out to their parents or adults can live freely with the person of their choice without fear of the physical and economic violence and social ostracization that continues to be commonplace for many sexual minorities.

Elshtain's fear that this new society will end in a razing of all other social practices and social meanings seems similarly overstated. If institutions like compulsory heterosexuality, marriage, and family were somehow to be smashed, would this result in a blank slate, a kind of social tabula rasa from which all social meaning and identity would have to be fashioned anew? This seems doubtful at best.

Still, it is at this point that Elshtain's arguments provide insight into her greatest anxiety and fears about gay liberation. Should gay liberation succeed, not only would homosexuality disappear; its heterosexual counterpart would vanish as well. In the closing paragraphs of her article, Elshtain declares that "a viable liberationist project" would be one in which "homosexuals and heterosexuals . . . recognize and accept one another as brothers and sisters. Neither would be driven to deny their respective doubles, or set them up as hostile Others, to be repudiated, overcome, or in the language of open tyranny, 'reeducated' or 'reconstructed.'"[52] Heterosexuality then, requires a homosexual sibling—or more to the point, a homosexual step-sibling—in order to have meaning as a distinct category. As Judith Butler has argued, "if it were not for the notion of a homosexual *as* copy, there would be no construct of heterosexuality *as* origin."[53] Once heterosexuality is

184 / Queer Critiques

revealed to be no more "original" than homosexuality, having no greater claim to being "natural" than the other, then much more energy must be expended to make heterosexuality compulsory, to *appear* natural, to *become* original. It is this process of essentialization that one sees at work in Elshtain's critique of Allen Young's claim that both homosexuality and heterosexuality are the product of a sexist society. Her response is that these categories, like categories of gender, are "constitutive of ordinary life." Elshtain believes that the distinction between the sexes is the "primary social distinction" and that, like gender differentiation, the "distinction between homo- and heterosexuality is, if not so primary, nonetheless vital and important."[54] Ultimately Elshtain would like to fold sexual identity nicely into the primary social distinctions like male and female, allowing her to eschew the liberationist's lack of a fixed and firm sexual identity. This lack of fixity constitutes the core of the liberationists' theory and rhetoric and it is what proves so threatening to Elshtain. It is also what is missing from the gay equal rights approach that she so profusely endorses.

Interestingly, today the fixity of sexual identity, its permanence, and the lack of individual choice in the determination of this identity have become the shared territory of both sides of the constructivist/essentialist debate over sexuality. As Daniel Ortiz has argued, the question asked by essentialists ("What causes one to be gay?") is independent of the question "How is gay identity given meaning?" One is etiological, the other, epistemological, but both kinds of explanations about queer identity posit gays and lesbians who have little or no choice in the constitution of their own sexuality.[55] In theoretical discussions of sexual difference, as well as in the rough and tumble world of sexual politics, Ortiz's two questions are more difficult to keep separate than his analysis suggests. As Michel Foucault, Ann Fausto-Sterling, and Cheshire Calhoun make evident through the example of the hermaphrodite, legal and societal interpretations of what constitutes biological categories help to blur the line between etiology and epistemological categories of identity.[56] In our own struggles to gain lesbian and gay liberation, etiological arguments over what constitutes gay *being* are often used to constitute a public, social, or even official or legal identity for gays and lesbians. These arguments then contribute to the way identity categories are maintained and regulated, making a simple severing of ontological and episte-Jmological concerns difficult at best, and simplistic at worst. But these constructivist accounts join essentialist ones in their efforts to remove all element of choice from the explanation of one's sexuality. The radical element of gay liberation's ontological debates that caused social conservatives like Elshtain such anxiety, the element of choice, has simply disappeared. It was not only Elshtain that the gay liberationists' fluid understanding of sexuality had made uneasy, as witnessed in my students' reaction to her article.

The response of my students to Elshtain's arguments was a collective dismissal. They labeled Elshtain a homophobe whose argument need not be taken seriously. It was their feeling that she was, after all, engaging in the heterosexist practice of speaking *for* the gay community, telling the gay community its mind, without the slightest understanding of the issues involved. While I have some sympathy with this position (as indicated above), I was troubled by the *way* they dismissed Elshtain. They did not dismiss Elshtain simply because she was a conservative heterosexual who did not comprehend what the liberationists were on about. They dismissed her because they thought she had invented the liberationist arguments as a way to discredit gays and lesbians. This, in spite of the fact that Elshtain's critique draws extensively on the voices of gay and lesbian authors from the 1970s. It quickly became evident that the source of their discomfort continued to be the gay voices of "liberation" upon which Elshtain had based her criticism. In these students' opinion, Elshtain simply could not be telling the truth. They accused her instead of having invented the voices of the liberationists, as no one would really have made those claims about destroying marriage, traditional family, and heterosexuality.

These students retreated into the superiority of the "present" from which vantage point they could cast aspersions on the past. Throwing out the proverbial baby with the bath water, they dismissed both Elshtain and the liberationists, calling the liberationists simplistic, utopian, and dangerously radical. They found it difficult to believe that anyone would ever have had such strange and antisocial ideas. This seemed to me a bigger paradox than the one that Elshtain had described.

To today's young gay men and lesbians who (through no fault of their own) find themselves ignorant of much of lesbian and gay history, Elshtain's article and the liberationists themselves seemed hopelessly dated. Smarter, more sophisticated, better informed than all who had come before, these students, in their modest self-assessment, stood at the end of history, the teleological result of a historical process of sexual "liberation." The liberationist agenda which sought to change the social order, challenge the institutions of heterosexuality, and confront the cultural and social practices that make participation in these institutions almost "compulsory,"[57] was dismissed by my students as the radical rhetoric of an "immature" political movement.

Dismissing the claims of the liberationists so completely, they dismissed Elshtain as well; as the messenger who had carried the coarse message to their ears, she too was declared profane. But in their haste to distance themselves from the liberationists' radical agenda, they revealed another interesting fact: to a person they also understood their sexuality and its expression as a natural, unchangeable "truth."

Rejecting any understanding of their sexuality that was other than "essential," they scoffed at the liberationists' claim that homosexuality and heterosexuality were "artificial categories . . . laid on us by sexist society" as much as had Elshtain. They, and arguably, most of the gay and lesbian political movement today, seek integration, not (dis)integration, and assimilation with cultural institutions, not their obliteration.

These young gays and lesbians are interesting because they are representative of a larger contemporary "truth." Today, the bold claims of choice have disappeared, replaced by a "growing inclination in the gay movement in the United States to understand itself and project an image of itself in ever more 'essentialist' terms."[58]

The connection between an essentialist understanding of sexuality and the quest for equal rights came into sharp contrast with the liberationist agenda, an agenda that was premised on a more malleable construction of sexuality. As I pondered the shift in attitudes among gays and lesbians separated by less than a generation, I was led to ask some difficult questions: For example, if sexuality were really natural, essential, and "constitutive of everyday life" then why must the liberationists' voices be silenced, dismissed, or subjected to such vehement attack by straights and gays alike? What threat could the voice of gay liberation possibly represent if their assumptions about sexuality as a choice are so wrong-headed? What social and political forces have led to the greater essentialization of sexuality among gays and lesbians over the last decade, and how has this understanding of gay and lesbian "self" been related to the gay movement's new equal rights political strategy? Finally, what kind of limits do we impose on the possibilities for political change when we accept "essentialist" understandings of homosexuality? In the rest of this essay I will attempt to address these questions in the hope of demonstrating why I believe the essentialization is dangerous and ill advised, and why despite their utopian principles, the gay liberationist critique remains a powerful but neglected weapon in the arsenal of queers working toward social and political change.

(En)forcing the Essentialist Moment

Jean Elshtain was not the only one expressing reservations about the advances of gays and lesbians throughout the 1970s. Only months before the publication of Elshtain's article, the Pentagon issued the now well-known Department of Defense Directive 1332.14, which made homosexuality officially "incompatible with military service" as its presence undermined "discipline, good order and morale," adversely affected the "integrity of rank and command," and made it more difficult for the armed forces "to foster mutual trust and confidence among the members."[59]

Less than five years after this decision, in the 1986 *Bowers* decision, the Supreme Court went well beyond the question of the constitutionality of the Georgia sodomy law, ruling instead that the Constitution did not provide a right to privacy to gay and lesbian people, defined as those who engage in homosexual sex. In the five years following Elshtain's article, gay and lesbian identity was deployed not as a means of "assaulting the institutions of society" but by that society as a way to deny gays and lesbians rights that are taken for granted by *citizens* of the United States. These decisions set the tone and the direction for gay and lesbian political activism in the 1980s. The struggle became less one of gay liberation and more one which sought access to those things from which the law excluded them: equality in employment, privacy, and military service.

Coterminous with this greater emphasis on equal rights was an ever greater essentialization of homosexuality. The argument that gays and lesbians are born, not made, was first developed by medical practitioners in nineteenth-century Europe and the United States who hoped to challenge social and legal condemnations of sodomy. Beyond the fact that this position represents the way many gays and lesbians experience their own sexuality, it is also seen as the most viable position upon which to rest appeals for civil rights. It follows that if homosexuality is biologically or genetically determined, then it rests outside the sphere of individual control, and therefore should rest outside the realm of condemnation and discrimination. For many gays and lesbians who have had their sexual identity declared immature, or have been asked or pressured to change and become heterosexual, an essentialist claim to having always been gay provides more protection against bigotry and oppression than does the constructivist claim that "gay" and "lesbian" are textual, historical, or discursive productions.

To the extent that persecution, harassment, and discrimination do exist, biologistic explanations for sexual orientation allow gays and lesbians to seek and perhaps receive equal or even preferential treatment as members of a "protected class." For many, essentialist explanations for homosexuality allow gays and lesbians to challenge orthodox condemnations of homosexual feelings, acts, and identity. If sexual orientation does not depend upon human choice, then homosexuals can claim to be the creation of God as much as can heterosexuals, making the way in which they engage in sexual pleasure less problematic. If gays are born and not made, then a gay elementary school teacher serving as a role model for, or in a position of authority over, children, need present no threat to the child and no legitimate concern for the child's parents, as the teacher's sexual identity will not influence the sexual development of their students. Similarly, those suffering from AIDS can escape the charge that they are deserving of the illness, or worse, that their illness is the result of God's condemnation.

Gays and lesbians have benefited in some significant ways, politically and socially, as the result of this reconstitution of sexuality in terms of fixed, unchanging identities rather than behaviors, or more fluid constitutions of identities. For example, in recent years, major corporations such as Microsoft and the Levi Strauss Company, as well as esteemed colleges and universities like Stanford, Harvard, Wellesley, and Smith have granted spousal benefits for partners of gay and lesbian employees. Still greater numbers of employers, universities, and city and state governments have included sexual orientation in their nondiscrimination clauses. In 1992, even the staid American Political Science Association created a permanent standing committee on the status of gays and lesbians in the discipline.

But the 1980s also witnessed a battle over arts funding deemed homo-erotic, sadomasochistic, and antireligious; art, it was argued, which appealed to a depraved minority and threatened the nation's belief in traditional "family values." National Endowment for the Arts director John Frohnmayer was fired and replaced with a "gay unfriendly" lesbian, continuing the cynical game of identity politics that made possible the nomination of Clarence Thomas to the Supreme Court.[60] And in May of 1992, it was revealed that a top official at the Federal Emergency Management Association (FEMA) had demanded that a gay employee of FEMA help him create a list of all the FEMA employees who were gay, under threat of job loss if he refused to cooperate.[61] The reason for the existence of the list was never explained, and it was subsequently destroyed, but with increasing frequency gays and lesbians have become the subject of political and legislative discourse.

With gays figuring so prominently in the debates of the 1980s, it was no surprise that 1992 was called by some the "Year of the Queer,"[62] and the emphasis on equal rights led still others to conclude that the gay political movement had gone "mainstream."[63] The 1992 elections demonstrate both why an equal rights approach by the organized gay political movement is necessary and why it has become, potentially, so dangerous.

In the rhetoric of the 1992 presidential campaign, gays and lesbians were both courted for their support and vilified for their perversion. Democrats made promises to the gay community while Republicans made threats against it. Both parties helped make them "targets." Whether targets of political rhetoric designed to attract their votes, or of abuse and ridicule designed to create a category of "otherness," both strategies helped put gays and lesbians into the public and political discourse, creating the contested territory of struggle for the gay rights movement.

Furthermore, their reason for the denial of these rights rested on the idea (shared by gay liberationists) that "homosexuality" was a choice. While heterosexuality represents the only "authentic" and essential "truth," homosexuality was a perverted option. For example, in September Vice President Dan Quayle, speaking on a national news program, argued that homosexuality "was more of a choice than a biological situation." When pressed on where he stood, Quayle said, "I think it is a wrong choice. It is a wrong; it is a wrong choice. I do believe in most cases it certainly is a choice."[64] The Republican Party platform echoed this emphasis on "choice" when addressing the AIDS crisis. It declared, "a large part of our health care costs is caused by behavior."[65] The platform continued further to say that AIDS "prevention is linked to personal responsibility and moral behavior."[66]

Equal rights for gays and lesbians was a recurrent theme in the 1992 national elections. Homosexuality was described as an immoral choice, an anathematized behavior, and a perverted activity, in attempts to justify queers' exclusion from "equal rights," as well as to scapegoat them as the "population" responsible for AIDS. Gays and lesbians were portrayed as perverted demons seeking to undermine the cultural institutions of family and heterosexuality, and equal rights and equality of treatment under law was transformed into "preferential treatment."

At best, gays are represented as just another interest group seeking "special treatment" by bleeding-heart liberals, another lost cause that helps fragment the Democratic Party and its platform. Acknowledging the cultural, legal, and social inferiority and oppression directed toward gays and lesbians becomes the "progressive" alternative to hate mongering. But in order to be accepted as "just another interest group," their sexuality must be transformed into a fixed identity—both a personal one and a political one.

These examples of how sexual identity has been deployed as a way to distinguish between the two national political parties mark only the tip of the iceberg. Homosexuals have been "identified" with AIDS in this country. They have been targeted in the debate over National Endowment for the Arts funding of "homoerotic" art as immoral subverters of public morality and sensibility. More recently, they have had their fate, their future, their very *being* subjected to the whims of the majority in the referenda process in states like Oregon and Colorado and cities like Portland, Maine and Tampa, Florida. The politics of the 1980s and 1990s have made a public, legal, and official understanding of sexuality that was anything other than essential all but impossible. Despite the fact that many now claim that this approach in *Bowers* helped desexualize lesbians and gays,[67] it is still accepted as the perspective most likely to help advance lesbian and gay equality.

Essentialism and the Limits of Equal Rights

Today we celebrate the increasing political clout of a gay community whose political struggle in the United States has achieved a new level of recognition, attention, and understanding. Nonprofit organizations such as the National Gay and Lesbian Task Force and the Human Rights Campaign Fund lobby Congress, while Lambda Legal Defense Fund, the National Center for Lesbian Rights, and the National Gay Rights Advocates press for reform in the nation's courts. Openly gay and lesbian candidates have won election to local city councils, state legislatures, and to the United States Congress, and the treatment of gays and lesbians was a major difference between the two major political parties in the 1992 Presidential campaign.

Despite their diversity, what the gay political groups of the 1990s have in common is their equal rights approach to political change. That which Elshtain takes as a given—that "gays or any other group of citizens have the civil right to be protected from life threatening intrusion or simple harassment under the right to privacy, as well as the right to be free from discrimination in employment, housing, and other areas"[68] has become the

contested territory, the social and political battleground for the gay and lesbian struggle. For example, in *Baehr v. Lewin* the Supreme Court of the
State of Hawaii decided that the state marriage laws must be subjected to
the highest level of scrutiny under that state's constitution, because the
exclusion of members of the same sex from marriage may violate the ban
against sex discrimination.[69]

The claim made in this decision was that the prohibition against same-sex
marriage preserves the subordination of women in a way similar to the way
that laws against interracial marriage maintained white dominance over
African Americans in the South until a 1967 U.S. Supreme Court decision
declared them unconstitutional.[70] This has led Morris Kaplan to argue that
gay marriage might well be transformative of the entire institution of marriage as "whether lesbian and gay families conform to the normalizing
regimes of compulsory heterosexuality or act to subvert and challenge its
gendered forms remains an open and contested question."[71] But according
to this same scholar, the pursuit of gay marriage "provides a perhaps surprising locus for potential reconciliation with the defenders of traditional community norms" and shifts the ground of the lesbian and gay agenda away
from "sexual freedom and [toward] the recognition of lesbian and gay partnerships and families." The appeal of this approach is that it "asserts a commonality with the professed aspirations of the heterosexual majority and
undercuts the construction of queers as sexual subversives."[72] Kaplan's
objection to the sexual subversives is that he thinks they delude themselves.
He writes:

> To the extent that opposition to lesbian and gay domesticity invokes an
> image of sexual outlaws inventing radically alternative forms of life, it
> underestimates the extent to which even our most intimate activities are
> implicated in forms of social life, even through their interdiction. After
> all, outlaws, especially, are defined by the law.[73]

So too, it should be remembered, are those who simply seek assimilation
into these same legally constituted practices and institutions. I believe this
to be the wrong approach, as it does nothing to significantly alter the way in
which oppression is articulated in our society as a minoritizing identity politics and how the avenues for freedom from this oppression are determined
by this articulation. For lesbians and gays acting like good heterosexuals will
not change the majority's essentializing views of our "difference." Jean
Elshtain remains a case in point. In an article entitled "Against Gay
Marriage," she writes that she has "long favored domestic partnership possibilities" but does not think marriage should be extended to queers because
"marriage has never been primarily about two people—it is and always has
been about the possibility of generativity.[74] Putting aside the fact that
Elshtain must construe generativity narrowly or many lesbian couples would
qualify, partnership benefits then come to have a specific but quite restricted

function. They exist as "ways to regularize and stabilize commitments and relationships,"[75] while leaving in place all of the institutions and social practices that have been used to create sexual difference and oppress us all along.

Almost as if following Elshtain's script, today's gay political movement, and many of today's gay and lesbian youth, have "sobered up." The "heady brew" of liberation upon which their radical predecessors were drunk, has been abandoned in favor of "Liberation-Lite"—a less filling equal rights alternative made more palatable to the bland taste of the 1990s queer—for whom "We're Here, We're Queer, Get Used to It" constitutes a revolutionary agenda.

The gay political agenda today includes spousal benefits, privacy and employment rights, legitimation of gay and lesbian marriages, and the right of military service. Nothing on this agenda seeks to challenge, to disrupt, nor even to alter fundamentally the central institutions of society. Instead, this agenda seeks integration with these institutions. The voices of rupture— the liberationists—have fallen silent. Raising issues that made the struggle for equal rights more problematic, liberationists with their "radical" alternative that sexuality might be informed by society *and* by personal choice have become inconvenient, an excess the new legitimate gay and lesbian movement can no longer afford. The answer, of course, has been to declare sexuality "essential," an intractable aspect of a person's *being*, determined by genetics, biology, or some other "deep property" over which the individual has no control. In order to free "homosexuality" from the stigma associated with problematized sexual behavior, a flight into a fixed identity is required. As one's identity, sexuality is inexorable, unchangeable, and not the responsibility of the individuals involved. The fact of my homosexuality, *like heterosexuality*, is simply "beyond my control."

We have created gay teen groups to assist questioning teens in the "discovery" of their authentic sexuality. Adults, through therapy and self-exploration, reinterpret events in their life within the framework of this powerful new truth. The *truth* of sexuality has become so obvious to those possessing this knowledge that many gay people "will often remark of someone that he does not yet 'realize' he is gay—a clear indication that the category is not necessarily a self-conscious one in their view."[76] Choice has been removed from this debate. Similarly, in the nineteenth century, the freedom given to hermaphrodites to choose their sexuality when they became adults was stripped from them and reinvested in the site that brought together medical science (truth) and the state (power). Michel Foucault describes the consequences of this shift:

> From the legal point of view, this obviously implied the disappearance of free choice. It was no longer up to the individual to decide which sex he wished to belong to, juridically or socially. Rather it was up to the experts to say which sex nature had chosen for him and to which society must consequently ask him to adhere. The law, if it was necessary to

appeal to it (as when, for example, someone was suspected of not living under his true sex or of having improperly married), had to establish or reestablish the legitimacy of a sexual constitution that had not been sufficiently well recognized. But if nature, through its fantasies or accidents, might "deceive" the observer and hide their true sex for a time, individuals might also very well be suspected of hiding their inmost knowledge of their true sex and of profiting from certain anatomical oddities in order to make use of their bodies as if they belonged to the other sex. In short, the phantasmagorias of nature might be of service to licentious behavior, hence the *moral* interest that inhered in the *medical* diagnosis of the true sex.[77]

Today sexuality has gone the way of the hermaphrodite. As Foucault makes clear, there is a state interest and a moral interest in ensuring the fixity of identity, of guaranteeing that we all are who, and what, we claim to be. Having the freedom to choose a sexual identity creates anxiety in all of us. It is the same anxiety that Elshtain manifested toward the gay liberationists. She writes:

to declare homosexuals a class by virtue of their behavior . . . to insist that what makes homosexuals a class is the imposition of social control on a minority; yet simultaneously, to admit, that "homosexual members of the *dominant class* by and large manage very well, moving quite freely between the gay and straight worlds," seems unacceptably tendentious.[78]

We expect our sexualities to be clearly marked and easily read, lest lesbians and gays have the freedom to move between worlds, spies infiltrating the halls of privilege. Many gays and lesbians manifest this desire for fixity in their hostility directed at bisexuality, rejecting bisexuals' claims to be sexually and emotionally attracted to both men and women as similarly "unacceptably tendentious." We attribute to bisexuals everything from untrustworthiness to immaturity, as we internalize the state's desire that we have our identity papers ever in order, and take up the work of policing our own conceptions of what constitutes a legitimate sexual minority.

In 1951, writing in the *Origins of Totalitarianism*, political theorist Hannah Arendt documented the rise of racism directed at Jews in nineteenth-century Europe. Integral to this racism was the identification of Jews as a "race," as those *born* to a certain inescapable identity. She writes,

As far as the Jews were concerned, the transformation of the "crime" of Judaism into the fashionable "vice" of Jewishness was dangerous in the extreme. Jews had been able to escape from Judaism into conversion; from Jewishness there was no escape. A crime, moreover, is met with punishment; a vice can only be exterminated. The interpretation given by society to the fact of Jewish birth and the role played by Jews in the frame work of social life are intimately connected with the catastrophic thoroughness with which anti-Semitic devices could be put to work. The Nazi brand of anti-Semitism had its roots in these social conditions. . . .[79]

Arendt was one who realized the same transformation was taking place in the arena of sexuality, arguing that "the 'vice' of Jewishness and the 'vice' of homosexuality . . . became very much alike indeed."[80] The medical transformation of criminal *acts* of sodomy into sexual *vice* and *identities* parallels the transformation described by Arendt. Replacing the terms "Judaism" and "Jewishness" with "sodomy" and "homosexual" in the quote above makes clear the danger of this parallel transformation to all sexual minorities today.

Until quite recently, nongay historians have overlooked that the Nazis included gays and lesbians among those to be purged from society in the most apocalyptic use of identity politics by the modern state—the Holocaust. And while many today, even in the gay and lesbian community, remain convinced that "it can't happen here," the political success of candidates like Pat Buchanan and David Duke and of initiatives like those passed in Colorado should give us all pause.

The dilemma of a gay equal rights movement is that in accepting the essentialization of personal identity, they also accept the inferior status that this identity assigns them in the heterosexual/homosexual dichotomy. The fact that they seek state protection is evidence of their present social and political inferiority however unjust the discrimination they face. But in the struggle for equal rights, equality is defined by the superior partner in the dichotomy; in short, equality means "sameness." Gays and lesbians must struggle and fight to gain access to the *same* rights held by heterosexuals. They must take their demands to the state, seeking definition and protection and, after a long, often bitter struggle, they, no doubt, will be granted the same formal rights that the state provides for heterosexuals.

The danger of this drive to conform, this equal rights agenda, is that it adversely affects our desire to combine "what we regard as the better parts of the alternative; we want equality without its compelling us to accept identity; but also difference without its degenerating into superiority and inferiority."[81] By simply demanding the same rights as heterosexuals, in requesting integration into the social institutions of marriage and family, nothing is done to change the process by which difference was constructed in the first place, leaving intact the cultural and social institutions which produce "otherness." Within the equal rights ethos, the goal becomes integration with that which we do not have. Demands for change become pleas for admission to the privileges held by the dichotomous "self" from which we have been estranged in the process of "otherness" creation.

Even when successful, the guarantee of equal rights and integration will leave the same bias and hatred toward gays and lesbians operating within the straight/gay dichotomy. In order to fundamentally alter this, a rupture is required in the process of difference formulation. This may well require a rethinking and rejection of many of the social institutions and practices of our society along the lines that the '70s liberationists undertook.

While no small feat, one thing is clear: no voice of rupture is likely to be discovered among those seeking "equal rights." By accepting essentialism as our ontology and its corresponding goal of "equal rights," we limit our ability to change, to reconstitute ourselves and the process of differentiation which produced the heterosexual/homosexual dichotomy in the first place. Many of the insights of the liberationists were important. From the vantage point of the '70s liberationists, compulsory heterosexuality, traditional sex roles, and the oppression that is too often a part of traditional marriage and family all needed to be changed. Although significant changes have been achieved in these areas, more is needed. Gay liberation asked us to look beyond lesbian and gay mimicking of heterosexual relationships and to imagine different kinds of personal, family, and social arrangements that were less oppressive, more egalitarian, and more inspired. If we reject this message, if we buy wholesale into the idea that an equal rights ethos is the *only* legitimate progressive path, then we simply limit our ability to imagine ourselves differently, and differentiate ourselves imaginatively.

Notes

1. Jean Bethke Elshtain, "Battered Reason," *New Republic*, October 5, 1992, 25.

2. Dennis Altman, *Coming Out in the Seventies* (Boston: Alyson Publications, 1981).

3. Richard Goldstein, "Sex on Parole," *Village Voice*, August 20–26, 1980, 20–23.

4. John Murphy, *Homosexual Liberation* (New York: Praeger, 1971)

5. Edward William Delph, *The Silent Homosexual Community: Public Homosexual Encounters* (Beverly Hills, California: Age Publications, 1978).

6. Carl Wittman, "A Gay Manifesto," in Karfa Jay and Allen Young, *Out of the Closets: Voices of Gay Liberation*, (New York: Douglas Books, 1972), 330–41.

7. Stuart Byron, "The Closet Syndrome," in Jay and Young, *Out of the Closets*, 58–65.

8. Allen Young, "Out of the Closets, Into the Streets," in Jay and Young, *Out of the Closets*, 6–30.

9. Ibid., 9.

10. Wittman, "A Gay Manifesto," 331.

11. Radicalesbians, "The Woman-Identified Woman," in Jay and Young, *Out of the Closets*, 172.

12. Martha Shelley, "Gay is Good," in Jay and Young, *Out of the Closets*, 31–34.

13. Wittman, "A Gay Manifesto," 331.

14. Young, "Out of the Closets," 29.

15. Ibid., 17.

16. Ibid., 17.

17. Radicalesbians, "The Woman-Identified Woman," 172.

18. Byron, "The Closet Syndrome," 59.

19. Young, "Out of the Closets," 8.

20. Radicalesbians, "The Woman-Identified Woman," 172.

21. Shelley, "Gay is Good," 34.

22. Wittman, "A Gay Manifesto," 341.

23. Jean Bethke Elshtain, "Homosexual Politics: The Paradox of Gay Liberation," *Salmagundi*, vol. 58–59, 255.

24. Ibid., 276.

25. Ibid., 253.

26. Ibid., 253.

27. For example see Jean Bethke Elshtain, *Public Man, Private Woman: Women in Social and Political Thought* (Princeton: Princeton University Press, 1981), especially 87, 104, 202–203, 226, 256–84, 344.

28. Elshtain, "The Paradox of Gay Liberation," 252.

29. Jay, "Introduction," in Jay and Young, *Out of the Closets,* lxi.

30. Young, "Out of the Closets," 30.

31. Ibid., 28.

32. Elshtain, "The Paradox of Gay Liberation," 254.

33. Ibid., 253-254. In *Public Man, Private Woman,* Elshtain argues this same imperative is at work among "feminist analysts who urge that 'the personal is political' totally and simpliciter." 104.

34. Elshtain, *Public Man, Private Woman*, 104.

35. Elshtain, "The Paradox of Gay Liberation," 267.

36. Ibid., 254.

37. This Jacobin terror surfaces again in Elshtain's recent article "Stories and Political Life" in *PS* , vol. XXVIII, no. 2, June 1995.

38. Elshtain, "The Paradox of Gay Liberation," 262.

39. Ibid., 253.

40. Ibid., 275.

41. Elshtain's anxiety about a more fluid understanding of gender is manifested again in her article "Against Androgyny," *Telos*, Spring 1981.

42. Shelley, "Gay is Good," 32.

43. Elshtain, "The Paradox of Gay Liberation," 256–57.

44. Ibid., 254.

45. Ibid., 256. Emphasis mine.

46. Justice Harry Blackmun's dissent does make it clear that *Bowers* was indeed about more than the majority had indicated, writing in his dissent that "This case is no more about 'a fundamental right to engage in homosexual sodomy' . . . than [a leading obscenity case] was about a fundamental right to watch obscene movies. This case is about the most comprehensive of rights and the right most valued by civilized men, namely, 'the right to be let alone.'" 478 U.S. 199 (Blackmun, J., dissenting).

47. Michelangelo Signorile, *Queer in America: Sex, the Media, and the Closets of Power* (New York: Random House, 1993).

48. See for example, Jean Bethke Elshtain, "The Family in Trouble," *National Forum*, vol. 75, no. 1, Winter 1995; "The Ties that Bind," *Chronicles: A Magazine of American Culture*, vol. 13, no. 10, October 1, 1989; and "Feminism and Politics," *Partisan Review*, vol. 57, no. 2, Spring 1990.

49. A 1989 federal study indicated that 30 percent of the youth who kill themselves each year are gay and lesbian—a rate two to three times higher than for straight youths. See United States Department of Health and Human Services, "Report of the Secretary's Task Force on Youth Teen Suicide," 1989.

50. Catherine MacKinnon, *Feminism Unmodified* (Cambridge, MA: Harvard University Press, 1987), chapter 8. For an extension of this argument to include lesbian and gay rights, see Kendall Thomas, "Beyond the Privacy Principle," *Columbia Law Review*, October 1992. For a rebuttal of this position see Morris Kaplan, "Intimacy and Equality: The Question of Lesbian and Gay Marriage," *Philosophical Forum*, vol. XXV, no. 4, Summer 1994.

51. Michel Foucault, *The History of Sexuality Volume I* (New York: Random House, 1980).

52. Elshtain, "The Paradox of Gay Liberation," 280.

53. Judith Butler, "Imitation and Gender Subordination," in Henry Abelove, Michele Dina Barale, and David M. Halperin, *The Lesbian and Gay Studies Reader* (New York: Routledge, 1993), 307–20.

54. Elshtain, "The Paradox of Gay Liberation," 254.

55. Daniel Ortiz, "Creating Controversy: Essentialism and Constructivism and the Politics of Gay Identity," *Virginia Law Review*, vol. 79, 1993, 1833.

56. Michel Foucault, *Herculine Barbin: On the Recently Discovered Diaries of a 19th Century French Hermaphrodite* (New York: Pantheon Books, 1980); Ann Fausto-Sterling, *Myths of Gender: Biological Theories About Women and Men* (New York: Basic Books, 1985); and Cheshire Calhoun, "Denaturalizing and Desexualizing Lesbian and Gay Identity," *Virginia Law Review*, vol. 79, 1993, 1859.

57. Adrienne Rich argues that heterosexuality, rather than a "natural outcome," is an institution which depends on a great amount of power, energy, and violence in order to be maintained. See "Compulsory Heterosexuality and Lesbian Existence," *Signs*, vol. 5, no. 4, 1980, 631–60.

58. Stephen Epstein, "Gay Politics, Ethnic Identity: The Limits of Social Constructionism," *Socialist Review 93/94,* 1987, 12.

59. Department of Defense Directive 1332.14, dated January 16, 1981.

60. In a June 16, 1992, editorial, *The Advocate* called NEA Acting Chair Anne-Imelda Radice "a new doormat homosexual who could give [Bush's] administration's self hating blacks and male identified women a serious run for their money." The former chair of the Human Rights Campaign Fund, Vivian Shapiro, called Radice "a lesbian from hell."

61. Warren Leary, "U.S. Agency Shreds List of Gay Workers and Plans Inquiry," *New York Times*, May 19, 1992, A–17.

62. The Year of the Queer was the cover of the last edition of *The Advocate* for the year 1992.

63. Jeffrey Schmalz, "Gay Politics Goes Mainstream," *New York Times Magazine*, October, 11, 1992, 18.

64. Karen De Witt, "Quayle Contends Homosexuality Is a Matter of Choice, Not Biology," *New York Times*, September 14, 1992, A–17.

65. The 1992 Republican Party Platform, 13.

66. Ibid., 14.

67. Daniel Ortiz, "Creating Controversy: Essentialism and Constructivism and the Politics of Gay Identity"; Kendall Thomas, "Beyond the Privacy Principle"; Morris Kaplan, "Intimacy and Equality: The Question of Lesbian and Gay Marriage"; and Cheshire Calhoun, "Denaturalizing and Desexualizing Lesbian and Gay Identity."

68. Elshtain, "The Paradox of Gay Liberation," 254.

69. *Baehr v. Lewin*, 853 P.2d 44 (Hawaii 1993).

70. *Loving v. Virginia,* 388 U.S. 1 (1967).

71. Morris Kaplan, "Intimacy and Equality: The Question of Lesbian and Gay Marriage," 337.

72. Ibid., 336.

73. Ibid., 353.

74. Jean Bethke Elshtain, "Against Gay Marriage," *Commonweal*, vol. 118, no. 20, Nov. 22, 1991.

75. Ibid.

76. John Boswell, "Concepts, Experience, and Sexuality" in Edward Stein, *Forms of Desire: Sexual Orientation and the Social Constructionist Controversy* (New York: Garland Publishing, Inc., 1990), 147.

77. Michel Foucault, *Herculine Barbin*, ix.

78. Elshtain, "The Paradox of Gay Liberation," 259–60. The quote within Elshtain's quote is from Altman, *Coming Out,* 36.

79. Hannah Arendt, *The Origins of Totalitarianism* (New York: Harcourt Brace Jovanovich, 1973), 87.

80. Ibid., 80.

81. Tzvetan Todorov, *The Conquest of America: The Question of the Other* (New York: Harper Torchbooks, 1987), 249.

III. Queer Agendas

9

Intimacy and Equality:
The Question of Lesbian and
Gay Marriage

Morris B. Kaplan

"Intimacy and Equality," like *Sexual Justice*,[1] the larger project of which it is a part, juxtaposes terms that do not sit easily together within liberal political discourse; the sense of incongruity is heightened by proximity to "lesbian and gay marriage." If not quite oxymorons, these phrases suggest a conflation of categories of private and public, at the very least a blurring of boundaries that many modern thinkers have been concerned clearly to delineate and protect. It is the aim of this paper to contest the ways in which these boundaries have been drawn in relation to controversies over lesbian and gay rights. In one sense, this paper explores the ramifications for queer politics of the feminist insight that the personal is the political, a juxtaposition that requires revision of both terms.

The paper proceeds along two tracks: an interrogation of recent claims by proponents of lesbian and gay rights to a right to marry or otherwise establish legally recognized domestic partnerships (and to bear and raise children)[2] and a critical examination of the constitutional right of privacy as a resource for movements of homosexual liberation. A primary objective of the paper is to demonstrate the extent to which even the most intimate associations between individuals are situated within a matrix of social relations and legal arrangements that both constrain and support them. Given the critical importance of interpersonal relationships in defining individual identities and in contributing to human happiness, full equality for lesbian and gay citizens requires access to the legal and social recognition of our intimate associations. This demand for recognition of

202 / Queer Agendas

lesbian and gay personal relationships has appeared, and could appear, only within the context of a political and social movement by which queer citizens have rejected the confines of the closet and emerged to insist on full democratic equality.

The essay begins with an interrogation of the increasing demand by lesbian and gay citizens for a right to marry or otherwise to establish legally and socially recognized domestic partnerships. In modern democratic societies marriage provides one of the few instrumentalities by which individuals may join together to form associations that impose obligations on third parties. The desire to establish institutions to sustain shared lives and to have one's intimate commitments socially recognized expresses the extent of human needs for affiliation and domesticity. The critical point, I will argue, is that the need for intimate human connection runs very deep and across differing modes of sexuality and that social recognition and legal support is needed to maintain the always precarious associations through which such needs are met. No doubt under the anomic conditions of modernity, couples and families are under enormous strain; these fragile relations are often made to bear the full weight of individual needs for community. The emergence of claims for the recognition of lesbian and gay families is itself inconceivable without the background of an increasingly visible queer community within which such social choices become feasible. In this sense the political overcoming of the closet has provided the historical and social conditions for reconstructing lesbian and gay intimate associations. Whether these aspirations may best be fulfilled through securing access on equal terms to the already troubled institution of marriage or through the creation of new forms of socially recognized intimate relations and family life remains an open and contested question.

Much of this text is concerned to revisit the history and controversy around the constitutional right of privacy. My purpose is to argue that constitutional privacy rights remain a resource for movements of homosexual emancipation, especially as refigured in terms of the "freedom of intimate association" invoked by Justice Harry Blackmun in his dissenting opinion in *Bowers v. Hardwick*.[3] Blackmun claims that the right of privacy protects sexual activity between free and equal citizens as part of their ongoing efforts to define themselves in close relation to others and to construct shared institutions for the conduct of life. My defense of privacy rights is sensitive to the sustained critique of the very conception of privacy-based arguments by some feminist thinkers and shares their concerns about the invocation of privacy rights to defend the traditional nuclear family as a site of gender subordination.[4] Despite the historical force of these objections, I will argue that the concept of privacy as a right of intimate association has continuing importance in both feminist and queer politics, so long as privacy rights are defined in close connection with democratic conceptions of equality and the claims of each citizen to control important decisions affecting her life. In its brief history, the constitutional right of privacy has been the site of vacillating and sometimes inconsistent efforts by the Supreme Court both to promote the nuclear family as a locus of social value and to protect individual autonomy in crucial areas of personal life. The potential conflict between these aims surfaced most dramatically in the decisions and ensuing controversies regarding a woman's right to abortion. In this context, the insistence by the Court in *Hardwick* on reiterating the connection between privacy and family rights must be seen as a retrograde moment in the struggle over women's sexual and reproductive freedom as well as a setback in the effort to obtain lesbian and gay equality.

This paper comprises four sections: 1) an introduction that focuses on intimate association by interrogating the institution of marriage in the context of lesbian and gay rights; 2) an argument about the unstable linkage between sexual freedom and familial institutions in the articulation of a constitutional right of privacy; 3) a critical discussion of the decision in *Bowers v. Hardwick*; and 4) a conclusion developing some of the ethical and political concerns bearing on lesbian and gay intimate associations and the place of domestic institutions in modern democratic societies.

Why Lesbian and Gay Marriage?

Historically, claims of lesbian and gay rights have focused primarily on two distinct areas defining the relations between queer citizens and the state: 1) decriminalization of homosexual activities between consenting adults; and 2) the prohibition of discrimination against lesbians and gays in employment, housing, and public accommodations. In recent years there has emerged an increasing insistence on the legal and social recognition of lesbian and gay relationships and community institutions. The emphasis on lesbian and gay associations and families presents a more complex conception of the relations among sexuality, citizenship, and domesticity than that implied by arguments for decriminalization or for protection against discrimination. Moral and political opposition to the criminalization of intimate sexual behavior has been generally articulated in terms of the principles of John Stuart Mill's classic essay *On Liberty*. These arguments define privacy rights in terms of negative liberty, an individual "right to be let alone," limiting the state's authority over private behavior between consenting adults in which no one is harmed.[5] A different range of concerns has informed opposition to discrimination against lesbians and gays. The movement for lesbian and gay rights joins those of African-Americans, women, religious and ethnic minorities, and the disabled in seeking the protections of the civil rights laws. When couched in constitutional terms, these claims invoke the "equal protection clause" of the Fourteenth Amendment, whereas privacy claims depend upon the "due process" clause.[6] Antidiscrimination claims envision a more positive role for the state than do arguments supporting decriminalization: civil rights laws prohibit private citizens from exercising their prejudices against designated groups in specified areas of commercial life.

Richard Mohr has described this role of the state as that of "a civil shield"; he has argued importantly that such protections are necessary if lesbians and gays are not to be penalized for exercising their full rights of political participation.[7]

A related but distinct class of claims emerges when we turn to the growing demand for recognition of lesbian and gay relationships, families, and institutions. Among the practical issues addressed here are the right of lesbians and gays to marry or otherwise establish "domestic partnerships"; the demands of lesbian and gay organizations for official status in public schools, universities, or professional associations; the status of lesbian and gay institutions in the AIDS crisis; the claims of lesbian mothers and gay fathers to the custody of their own children and of lesbians and gays more generally to be considered as foster or adoptive parents; the demand to end the ban on openly gay and lesbian participation in the military.[8] The state functions in these claims not only as a "civil shield" protecting lesbian and gay citizens against discrimination, but also as a positive agency for realizing their aspirations to lead full lives. Although these claims appeal to fundamental conceptions of political equality, they go beyond antidiscrimination arguments by asserting the positive status of lesbian and gay citizenship. This development emphasizes human interdependence and situates individual efforts to attain a good life within a context of personal, familial, and civic relations and responsibilities. Moreover, the rights at issue pertain not only to individuals, but to couples, families, and voluntary associations. The personal contexts from which such claims emerge matter enormously to the people affected; they are at the heart of the efforts of many to find meaning and satisfaction in their lives. At the same time, many citizens not otherwise unfriendly to lesbian and gay rights stop short of endorsing the demands of queer families to enjoy equal social and legal status with their straight counterparts. Ultimately what is at stake is acceptance of the moral legitimacy and ethical validity of the shared ways of life of lesbian and gay citizens.[9]

Resistance to these claims is almost certainly increased by the perception that the traditional family is already in trouble and may not be able to tolerate any additional strain. These issues provide a focal point for comprehending the resistance to lesbian and gay rights generally: lesbians and gays are construed as posing a threat to "family values" already under siege in contemporary society. For many conservatives, queer families are simply the last straw. And yet, the seriousness with which lesbians and gays urge their capacities to share in the responsibilities of family life (and military service) also provides a surprising locus for potential reconciliation with the defenders of traditional community norms.[10] Shifting ground from sexual freedom to the recognition of lesbian and gay partnerships and families asserts a commonality with the professed aspirations of the heterosexual majority and undercuts the construction of queers as sexual subversives.

So much is this the case that some queer theorists fear that lesbian and gay marriage may mark the cultural triumph of compulsory heterosexuality, and feminist critics remind us of the historical role of marriage in maintaining the subordination of women.[11] With regard to these feminist objections to same-sex marriage as reinforcing gender hierarchy, we must take note of an important counterargument that will be examined further in a later section. In *Baehr v. Lewin*,[12] the Supreme Court of the State of Hawaii determined that state laws restricting marriage to members of different sexes must be subjected to the highest level of scrutiny under their state's constitution as potentially violating its ban on sex discrimination.   The claim advanced there, which has been developed by several legal scholars,[13] is that the prohibition of same-sex marriages serves to maintain the subordination of women in much the same way that laws against interracial marriage upheld white supremacy in the southern United States until the Supreme Court ruled them unconstitutional in 1967 in *Loving v. Virginia*.[14] The point here is that a serious case has been advanced that permitting same-sex marriages is itself an important step toward gender equality. Whether lesbian and gay families conform to the normalizing regimes of compulsory heterosexuality or act to subvert and challenge its gendered forms remains an open and contested question.

What are we to make of the recent attention given to these issues? Especially when we remember that half the states continue to outlaw same-sex activities in some form or another and that only eight states protect lesbian and gay citizens against discrimination. Certainly, for those affected, the status of marriage or domestic partnership brings concrete financial and material benefits. In addition, recognition of a couple's status acts to legitimate them in the eyes of the community, their families, and even themselves. The conjunction of material and symbolic gains associated with marital or partnership status requires some untangling here to clarify the political and ethical issues involved.[15] Let me emphasize again: the institution of marriage in modern societies provides a distinctive opportunity for individuals to create by their own decision a new association that institutionalizes mutual obligations and imposes duties on third parties. Both legally and socially, spouses are entitled to consideration not available to those not so recognized. Coverage under employee-benefit plans is only one of the most obvious of these entitlements, which range from shared invitations to social events to rights under a lease or rent-control law, to access to hospital rooms and nursing homes, and participation in life-or-death decisions concerning one's partner. Generally, two persons may adopt a child together only if they are married; couples eager to share responsibility for bringing up the children produced during the recent and ongoing lesbian "baby boom" regularly encounter the legal stumbling blocks resulting from their nonmarital status. The experience of many gay men during the AIDS epidemic has forcefully and painfully brought home the extent to which involvement in the fate of another may be reserved to spouses and members of a "natural family." In late modern liberal societies, access to the status of marriage remains an important mode of personal empowerment.

Perhaps even more importantly, the assertion of lesbian and gay demands for recognition of the forms of our shared lives, with particular emphasis on intimacy and family, signals the emergence of queer politics from a defensive fight for mere survival toward an effort to secure the social conditions of human flourishing on equal terms with straight citizens. Lesbians and gays have been able to survive at all on the margins of society only through the creation of informal networks of sustenance and support. Individuals have struggled to maintain intimate personal ties against considerable odds, and they have been supported in their efforts by relations of friendship and community. In fact, queer social life has become the site of processes redefining kinship in modern society with implications for all sorts of folks whose needs are not met by prevailing models.[16] As communitarian thinkers have especially emphasized, human life is a social enterprise. We are born needy and dependent; our emergence as individuals results from interaction with others in the contexts of family and community. Our need for recognition by others and exchange with others are transformed as we mature, but we do not outgrow a fundamentally social condition. In modern liberal societies, the claims of community depend on individual choices to create and sustain common institutions. By turning to marriage, partnership, and family rights, the movement for lesbian and gay rights and liberation affirms deeply felt human needs to establish intimate relationships as part of the ongoing conduct of life, culminating for many in the desire to bear and raise children of their own or otherwise to share in the care of others.

Privacy Rights, Sexual Freedom, and Family Values

My concern in this section is to focus on one aspect of the ongoing controversy about the legal and political status of the constitutional right of privacy: the extent to which the articulation of privacy rights has implicated the judicial construction of marriage and the family in the recognition of individual rights. My argument delineates a dual structure at work. On the one hand, the identification of privacy rights with participation in marriage and the family is taken as the strongest possible indication that such rights have been historically acknowledged in the American political tradition and are entitled to enforcement by the Supreme Court. In tension with this linkage of personal rights to membership in marriage and family has been the dynamic of constitutional egalitarianism by which, once acknowledged as fundamental, privacy rights have been extended to include all persons recognized as citizens, regardless of their family or marital status. The construction of constitutional barriers against the intrusion of the state into marital privacy has resulted in a conception of the individual citizen as herself bearing rights that may be claimed not only against the state but also against competing claims of a spouse, parent, or other family members. These tensions within the privacy jurisprudence have become explosively manifest in the ongoing conflict about a woman's right to abortion. However, even without reference to the problematic status of the fetus, the earlier privacy cases already manifested an unstable relationship between a conception of rights belonging to the autonomous individual and one derived from marital status or family membership.[17]

Although not decisive in philosophical terms, the constitutional right of privacy enunciated in *Griswold v. Connecticut*[18] and subsequent cases has become problematic in relation to the jurisprudence and politics of the current Supreme Court. The great irony of the privacy jurisprudence is that it receives its most coherent and theoretically impressive formulation in Justice Blackmun's *dissenting* opinion in *Bowers v. Hardwick*.[19] In that case, the Court refused to invalidate Georgia's consensual sodomy law as a violation of constitutionally based privacy rights (at least insofar as the law applied to homosexuals). In first formulating the constitutional right of privacy in *Griswold*, the Court invalidated a state ban on the possession and use of contraceptive devices and substances and on any acts that assist, abet, counsel, or otherwise contribute to such possession or use. Although the result was supported by a majority of seven to two, the justices offered quite diverse statements of the decision's rationale. As a result, the constitutional right of privacy has been the subject of a vigorous and heated academic and political debate, most recently and dramatically in the hearings on the nomination of Judge Robert Bork to the Supreme Court. Nonetheless, since 1965 the right of privacy has been applied to invalidate state laws aimed at regulating a variety of activities: the enjoyment of "obscene" materials in the home in *Stanley v. Georgia*;[20] the availability of contraception to unmarried adults in *Eisenstadt v. Baird*,[21] and subsequently to minors; and, of course, the right of a woman to terminate her pregnancy by abortion in *Roe v. Wade*.[22]

In his dissenting opinion in *Olmstead v. United States*,[23] Justice Brandeis identified the right of privacy as "the most comprehensive of rights and the right most valued by civilized men"; he defined it as "the right to be left alone." Privacy rights as defined by common law or by particular state or federal legislation differ from a right of privacy guaranteed by the United States Constitution. The latter, first formulated in *Griswold*, comes into play when a litigant seeks to have federal courts invalidate state legislation as an infringement of the due process clause of the Fourteenth Amendment. Justice Douglas, who wrote the opinion of the Court in *Griswold*, found the right of privacy to be grounded in general principles or values that underlie the specific provisions of the Bill of Rights and that define elements of due process of law. His task of justification was somewhat complicated by the prior history of constitutional adjudication, which had often set liberal proponents of an expansive reading of individual rights based on a literal interpretation of the specific provisions of the Bill of Rights against conservative jurists who were willing to impose on the states only those constraints found to be deeply embedded in the traditions of American political practice. No literal textual authority exists for the right of privacy.[24]

In *Griswold*, Douglas identified privacy as the fundamental value underlying the First, Third, Fourth, Fifth, and Ninth Amendments, which include such specifics as the prohibition of unreasonable searches and seizures, the protection against compulsory self-incrimination, the guarantee of free exercise of religion, and the proscription of quartering soldiers in people's homes. Justice Goldberg, in a concurring opinion, placed particular emphasis on the Ninth Amendment, which states that the enumeration of "certain rights" in the Constitution should not be construed as to "disparage other rights which are retained by the People." This language stands as a continuing rebuke by the framers to subsequent efforts to narrow the range of constitutionally protected rights, in the name of "strict construction" and "original intent" to those enumerated literally in the *other* provisions of the Bill of Rights. Thus, the Court in *Griswold* held that among the unenumerated rights retained by the People under the United States Constitution, and implicit in many of its specific provisions, is the right of privacy. In applying this principle to the matter at hand, the Court found that the Connecticut statute's application to married couples sealed its constitutional fate: "This law . . . operates directly on an intimate relation of husband and wife and their physician's role in one aspect of that relationship."[25] (As we shall see below, the conservative Justice Harlan relied on this fact to reach a similar conclusion from quite different premises.) Douglas proceeds from this characterization to list other fundamental rights previously recognized by the Court despite their not being enumerated within specific provisions of the Constitution.[26] Importantly, he focuses on rights of *association*: the right of parents to send their children to a school of their choice[27] and of students to study foreign languages.[28] These cases, which emphasize the integrity of the family and protect parental decision making against state control, linked these rights to the *public* terms of First Amendment freedoms:

> The right of freedom of speech and press includes not only the right to utter or print, but the right to distribute, the right to receive, the right to read . . . and freedom of inquiry, freedom of thought, and freedom to teach . . . indeed the freedom of the entire university community. . . . Without these peripheral rights the specific rights would be less secure.[29]

Douglas further develops the dependence of privacy rights on rights of political association: "In *N.A.A.C.P. v. Alabama*[30]. . . we protected the '*freedom to associate and privacy in one's associations*' [emphasis added] noting that freedom of association was a peripheral First Amendment right."[31] In *N.A.A.C.P. v. Button*,[32] according to Douglas, the Court emphasized that forms of association protected under the First Amendment were not only political, but any which contributed to the "social, legal or economic benefit" of their members. Central to Douglas's analysis is the definition of privacy, not simply as a negative right to be left alone, but as a positive capacity to form certain kinds of associations with others.

This formulation places the right of privacy close to the center of the scheme of individual rights protected by the Constitution and charged with enforcement by the Supreme Court.[33] By insisting on its continuity with more obviously public modes of association, Douglas identifies the right of privacy as a critical component of democratic freedom rather than as a naturalized, prepolitical right linked to traditional family structures. Nonetheless, the agreement of seven justices from diverse constitutional perspectives on the result in *Griswold* depended importantly on the Connecticut law's intrusion into the marital relationship. The statute forbade without qualification the use of contraceptives: "Would we allow the police to search the sacred precincts of marital bedrooms for telltale signs of the use of contraceptives? The very idea is repulsive to the notions of privacy surrounding the marriage relationship," wrote Justice Douglas for the Court.[34] Given that his argument had already invoked the specific Fourth Amendment prohibition of "unreasonable searches and seizures," one must question the limitation of privacy to "marital bedrooms," now figured as "sacred precincts." After all, the Fourth Amendment provides in part that: "The right of the people to be secure in their persons, houses, papers, and effects, against unreasonable searches and seizures, shall not be violated. . . ." It would appear that the privacy of any person's bedroom, married or single, and not just her bedroom, is to be respected. In the crunch, Douglas was unwilling to forgo the rhetorical and political advantages of that "marital bedroom." Yet, in defining the constitutional status of marriage, he has expressed the destabilizing tendencies implicit in the *Griswold* decision:

> We deal with a right of privacy older than the Bill of Rights. . . . Marriage is a coming together for better or for worse, hopefully enduring, and intimate to the degree of being sacred. It is an association that promotes a way of life, not causes; a harmony in living, not political faiths; a bilateral loyalty, not commercial or social projects. Yet it is an association for as noble a purpose as any involved in our prior decisions.[35]

On the one hand, Douglas risks making privacy rights dependent on marital status; on the other hand, he explicates the constitutional status of marriage itself by analogy with rights of political association that pertain to individual persons as citizens. That the Fourteenth Amendment requires equality in the treatment of citizens or legal persons has had important consequences in the brief history of constitutional privacy rights.

The most important single precursor to the *Griswold* decision was Justice Harlan's dissenting opinion in *Poe v. Ullman*,[36] in which the Court had declined to rule on the Connecticut contraception law. The language of that dissent, which Harlan himself quotes in his concurring opinion in *Griswold*, is quite revealing of the conflicting notions of privacy that were partially obscured by the fact of a seven-justice majority in that case: ". . . a statute making it a criminal offense for married couples to use contraceptives is an intolerable and unjustifiable invasion of privacy in the conduct of the most intimate concerns of an individual's personal life." Harlan insisted that he "would not suggest that adultery, homosexuality, fornication, and incest are immune from criminal inquiry, however privately practiced," but

> the intimacy of husband and wife is necessarily an essential and accepted feature of the institution of marriage, an institution which the state not only must allow, but which always and in every age it has fostered and protected. It is one thing when the State exerts its power either to forbid extra-marital sexuality altogether, or to say who may marry, but it is quite another when, having acknowledged a marriage and the intimacies inherent in it, it undertakes to regulate by means of the criminal law the details of that intimacy.[37]

Justice Harlan could not have been clearer that the privacy he is concerned to protect as "inherent in the concept of ordered liberty" is derived from an individual's status within the socially defined and approved institution of marriage. Moreover, Harlan is at some pains to exclude from the right of privacy any conception of individual sexual freedom outside of marriage. Indeed, in Harlan's view, the state's interest in the promotion of marriage provides justification for a wide range of regulations of individual sexual conduct. Perhaps most importantly for present purposes, he recognizes the extent to which marriage itself is a legal and social construction: it is after all the State that "may forbid extra-marital sexuality altogether" and that determines "who may marry." The traditionalist, almost statist, terms of Harlan's analysis contrast sharply with Douglas's assimilation of marriage to associational freedom in *Griswold*.

By 1972, the Supreme Court was required to address the ambiguities and tensions inherent in *Griswold* as a result of actions taken in direct response to that decision. In *Eisenstadt v. Baird*,[38] the Court ruled on the constitutionality of a Massachusetts law, similar to that of Connecticut, that had been amended in light of the earlier ruling to prohibit the distribution of contraceptive material *except* in the case of registered physicians and pharmacists providing the materials to married persons. For the Massachusetts legislature, the privacy rights enunciated in *Griswold* were identified with the relations of marital partners and their healthcare providers. Not so for the Supreme Court. In an eight-to-one decision, the Court, by Justice Brennan, announced that "viewed as a prohibition on contraception per se," the statute ". . . violates the rights of single persons under the Equal Protection Clause. . . . whatever the rights of the individual to access to contraceptives may be, the rights must be the same for married and unmarried alike."[39] In terms of the contrast between Harlan's traditionalist analysis and Douglas's associational analysis of marriage, the Court comes out squarely on the side of the latter:

> the marital couple is not an independent entity with a mind and heart of its own, but an association of two individuals each with a separate intellectual and emotional make-up. If the right of privacy means anything, it is the right of the *individual*, married or single, to be free from unwarranted intrusion into matters so fundamentally affecting a person as the decision whether to bear or beget a child. . . . [emphasis in original][40]

So much for the exclusiveness of "the sacred precincts of marital bedrooms."[41] This decision squarely identifies privacy as an individual right. The marital bedroom has become "a room of one's own," and the emphasis shifts decisively from concerns for protecting the institutional integrity of the family to respect for individual autonomy in making certain kinds of decisions.

The logic of these developments within the jurisprudence of privacy rights culminated in 1973 with the Court's decision in *Roe v. Wade*.[42] The critical point for this analysis is that the Court relied on *Griswold* and its progeny to ground the assertion of the fundamental right of a woman to make such important decisions as whether to terminate or continue her pregnancy: "The right of privacy . . . is broad enough to encompass a woman's decision whether or not to terminate her pregnancy. . . . All of these factors the woman and her responsible physician will consider in consultation."[43] Under circumstances fraught with implications for marriage and the family, no mention is made of these institutions and the state's interest in preserving and maintaining them.[44] The woman's physician is given a consulting role; her husband, if any, does not appear. Even with the qualification and erosion of the rights articulated in *Roe* by subsequent decisions of the Court, the majority in the most recent abortion case, *Casey v. Planned Parenthood*,[45] nonetheless overturned the provision of the Pennsylvania law that required a woman to notify a spouse of her decision to have an abortion. Moreover, in justifying that decision, the Court explicitly referred to the danger that the spousal notification requirement might actually place women at risk of physical harm through battery by angry husbands. Although constitutional rights of privacy may not secure all that justice requires in terms of abortion rights, especially for poor women, in *Casey* privacy rights were effectively deployed to defend a woman's decisional autonomy from being subordinated to her marital status.

The Supreme Court's privacy doctrine has traveled a considerable distance from the family-centered traditionalism of Justice Harlan's dissent in *Poe v. Ullman*, which had been so important in preparing the way for *Griswold*. Protection of the traditional family unit has been superseded by the defense of individual autonomy rights. It is no accident that the privacy cases have concerned matters like contraception and abortion: the right of privacy expresses in normative constitutional terms the disarticulation of sexuality from reproductive imperatives that is implicit in the circulation of contemporary contraceptive technologies. But the Supreme Court has avoided formulating a constitutional right of sexual freedom, especially as it might affect homosexual citizens.

The Alleged Right to Commit Homosexual Sodomy

By 1986 many constitutional scholars agreed with civil libertarians and advocates of lesbian and gay rights that a challenge to state laws which criminalized acts of sodomy performed in private by consenting adults would state a powerful claim within the developed logic of the privacy cases. In a five-to-four decision in *Bowers v. Hardwick*,[46] Justice White, writing for the Court, not only rejected that claim, but characterized the very assertion of a "constitutional right to commit homosexual sodomy" as "facetious." By now a great deal of ink has been spilled analyzing and criticizing the decision of this case.[47] My concern is to track the interplay of conceptions of individual liberty and of marital or familial integrity in the logic and rhetoric deployed to justify the Court's decision. I shall then examine the argument of Justice Blackmun's dissent. My overall objective is to consider the implications of these competing analyses of the right of privacy for the question of lesbian and gay family rights.

The decision in *Hardwick* looms critically over all subsequent efforts to theorize and litigate lesbian and gay rights in the context of the U.S. Constitution. Although a clear setback in the struggle for lesbian and gay emancipation in the courts, it acted to mobilize queer organizing efforts which may have become complacent in the belief that the Supreme Court would soon vindicate basic rights to sexual freedom. Since that was not to be, the movement for lesbian and gay rights has gone on to articulate its goals in broader and more political terms. Political protest and personal coming out have been reinterpreted in terms of the assertion of individual and communal pride as both an intrinsic good and an instrument for transforming social attitudes. Although of undoubted legal authority, and thus a stumbling block on the road to constitutional vindication, *Bowers v. Hardwick* has not been accorded the kind of moral authority Americans sometimes bestow on the Supreme Court (most clearly in the matter of racial justice since *Brown v. Board of Education*).

Some of the reasons for this may be found in the text and history of the decision itself. Although also addressing a highly controversial issue in a deeply divided polity, the Court in *Brown* spoke with one voice: the decision was unanimous and was articulated in a single opinion. Even *Roe v. Wade* was decided by a seven-to-two majority, although this fact often has been obscured by subsequent political struggles over abortion rights. *Hardwick* is a close case: five to four. Recently disclosed information reveals even more fully the contingency of the outcome. In the papers of late Supreme Court Justice Thurgood Marshall, one learns that the original vote of the Court when the case was conferenced was five to four in favor of upholding the Court of Appeals decision and overturning the Georgia sodomy law. On April 8, 1986, Justice Lewis Powell circulated a memorandum to his colleagues explaining that, although he continued to entertain reservations as to the penalties in the law, which prescribed imprisonment for up to twenty years, he was changing his vote as to the bottom-line question regarding the constitutionality of the statute. As a result, Justice White was assigned to write the opinion of the Court rather than a dissenting opinion, and Justice Blackmun's analysis became a dissent rather than the law of the land. And that's not the end of it. In a press conference at the National Press Club in October 1990 after his retirement, Powell acknowledged that he now believed he had voted the wrong way in *Bowers v. Hardwick*.[48]

The Supreme Court's decision in *Bowers v. Hardwick* was precipitated by a series of events in August 1982, culminating in the arrest of Michael Hardwick and his being charged with violation of the Georgia sodomy law because of acts performed with another adult male in the privacy of his bedroom.[49] Although the district attorney indicated that he did not intend to prosecute Hardwick based on the evidence then available, Hardwick went to federal court to enjoin any prosecution under the sodomy law as unconstitutional. The district court dismissed his action, but the Court of Appeals for the Eleventh Circuit reversed that judgment, with a divided court holding that the statute violated Hardwick's fundamental rights because "his homosexual activity is a private and intimate association that is beyond the reach of state regulation by reason of the Ninth Amendment and the Due Process Clause of the Fourteenth Amendment."[50] The Supreme Court reversed the court of appeals ruling, holding that the constitutional right of privacy did not extend to "a right to commit homosexual sodomy." The terms of White's argument are quite important: First, the restriction of the Court's attention to *homosexual* sodomy. The Georgia statute defines the crime of sodomy as follows: "(a) A person commits the offense of sodomy when he performs or submits to any sexual act involving the sex organs of one person and the mouth or anus of another. . . ." The Georgia sodomy law applies to *everybody*—male, female, married, single, heterosexual, homosexual. There are state laws that forbid sodomitical acts only between members of the same sex. Georgia's law is not one of them. Yet, as Justice Blackmun points out in his dissent, the Court refuses to consider the explicit language of the statute, but effectively rewrites it to avoid considering the constitutionality of its application to heterosexual men and women including married couples:

> [the] Court's almost obsessive focus on homosexual activity is particularly hard to justify in light of the broad language. . . . the Georgia legislature has not proceeded on the assumption that homosexuals are so

different from other citizens that their lives may be controlled in a way that would not be tolerated if it limited the choices of those other citizens.[51]

In fact, the Georgia sodomy law intrudes as fully into the "sacred precincts of marital bedrooms" as did the Connecticut contraception law invalidated in *Griswold*. The *Eisenstadt* holding implies that exempting married couples from such a law would have violated the equal protection rights of the unmarried. The Court's refusal to consider the Georgia law's application to heterosexual sodomy itself discriminates between homosexuals and heterosexuals in violation of the principle of equal protection of the laws that it is charged to enforce against the states under the Fourteenth Amendment. Indeed, in his dissenting opinion in *Hardwick*, Justice Stevens argues that the Georgia law as applied to heterosexuals is unconstitutional and that any attempt to apply it solely to homosexuals is unjustifiable and violates equal protection constraints.

Having restricted the reach of the Georgia statute contrary to its plain language, Justice White goes on to reinterpret the line of cases comprising the modern jurisprudence of privacy rights. Discussing a list of cases, including *Griswold, Eisenstadt, Roe,* and five others, he describes them as "dealing with": "child rearing and education," "family relationships," "procreation," "marriage," "contraception," and "abortion." Without further ado, the Court concludes:

> Accepting the decisions in these cases and the above description of them, we think it evident that none of the rights announced in those cases bears any resemblance to the claimed constitutional right of homosexuals to engage in sodomy that is asserted in this case. No connection between family, marriage, or procreation on the one hand and homosexual activity on the other has been demonstrated. [Moreover,] any claim that these cases nevertheless stand for the proposition that any kind of private sexual conduct between consenting adults is insulated against constitutional proscription in unsupportable.[52]

This argument returns to Harlan's analysis in *Poe v. Ullman* with its emphasis on legal and social commitments to preserving the integrity of marriage and the traditional family. But this paradigm is inadequate to the insistence on equality that decided *Eisenstadt* and to the concern for individual autonomy made explicit in *Roe*.[53] White engages in considerable intellectual gymnastics to secure the privacy cases within his domestic circle, and few commentators have found his efforts persuasive.[54]

One point stands out: in White's opinion, there is no *conceivable* link between homosexual activity and procreation, marriage, or the family. The result is that, cast out of the "sacred precincts" of the traditional family circle, homosexuals find ourselves stripped of privacy rights altogether. By its silence regarding the reach of the Georgia law and its "almost obsessive concern with homosexual activity,"[55] the Court has implied that heterosexuals may well be protected against the intrusion of the state's criminal law, because of the putative link between heterosexuality as such and "marriage, procreation and the family." (It is hard to follow the strange logic of negation by which abortion and contraception are linked to procreation and the family but nonprocreative homosexual activity is not.) One result is that the same physical acts may be permissible when performed by heterosexuals and forbidden to homosexuals, creating a dual status of persons before the criminal law. Even more importantly, homosexuals are actually defined as a class by these self-same "criminal" acts that are permitted to heterosexuals. The circle of argument here is rather narrow, and certainly vicious.[56] Indeed, White revealingly overstates his case when writing that ". . . the proposition that any kind of private sexual conduct between consenting adults is constitutionally insulated from state proscription is unsupportable."[57] I suppose he means "every kind of private sexual conduct," since on his own account of previous cases private heterosexual conduct (even among the unmarried, with or without contraception) is so insulated. Interestingly, in an earlier draft of the opinion to be found in the Thurgood Marshall papers in the Library of Congress, the sentence just quoted reads: ". . . any claim that these cases nevertheless stand for the proposition that any kind of private sexual conduct is *not* insulated against constitutional proscription is unsupportable." The rhetoric of White's opinion is excessive throughout, starting with the assertion that Michael Hardwick's claim to constitutional protection, supported by the Court of Appeals and almost endorsed by a majority of the Supreme Court, "must be facetious."[58]

In the tendentious revision of the privacy jurisprudence quoted above, the language itself shows evidence of the strain. White claims to "accept" these decisions, at least under the descriptions he offers in *Hardwick*. Nonetheless, *Bowers v. Hardwick* has unsettled the jurisprudence of the constitutional right of privacy. Indeed, seeing this decision as an expression of homophobia may be an optimistic interpretation. It is quite possible that its primary significance lies in signaling that the constitutional right of privacy as such no longer enjoys the support of a majority on the current Court. Certainly, its recuperation of the traditionalism and family values at work in Justice Harlan's conception of privacy rights is at one with efforts of a number of justices to secure the agreement of a majority of the court to overturn *Roe v. Wade*. It is no accident that White dissented in *Roe* and that Blackmun is its author. Those concerned for the right of privacy and for women's abortion rights may be to that extent relieved by the reaffirmation of the *Roe* decision in *Casey*, however attenuated; by Justice White's subsequent retirement; and by his replacement with Justice Ruth Bader Ginsberg.

The Ethics and Politics of Intimate Association

The argument of this paper had been fully developed and presented in a variety of settings when Justice Harry Blackmun announced his retirement from the Supreme Court. Final revisions were in process when President Clinton nominated Judge Stephen Breyer to succeed to his place. Judge Breyer was confirmed quickly and easily by the Senate. It is not hyperbolic to see Justice Blackmun's retirement as signaling finally the end of an era. Somewhat ironically, his departure leaves the Supreme Court without a veteran spokesman for the Warren Court legacy that actively defined its role as the great defender of individual and minority rights. The irony, of course, derives from the fact that Harry Blackmun was not a member of the Court when Chief Justice Earl Warren presided, but rather was appointed by Richard Nixon. At the time of his appointment and for several years thereafter, he appeared indistinguishable from his Minnesota colleague and friend Warren Burger, whom Nixon had appointed Chief Justice; journalists referred to them as the "Minnesota twins." Burger wrote a concurring opinion in *Bowers v. Hardwick* that almost makes White's opinion for the Court look moderate.[59] However, the fact is that Justice Blackmun's tenure on the Court saw his development as a great spokesman for human rights—in his *Roe v. Wade* opinion, in his *Hardwick* dissent, and in his belated but passionate dissents on the death penalty. His moral and political progress should caution us against too quickly judging the merits of the successor generation. In the context of this paper, it is worth noting that Justice Breyer served as law clerk to Justice Arthur Goldberg during the term *Griswold* was decided. In that case, Goldberg wrote an eloquent concurring opinion drawing on the Ninth Amendment as authority for the Court's duty to consider rights other than those explicitly enumerated in the Bill of Rights. The Ninth Amendment has become an important component of arguments supporting the contention that the framers had an expansive conception of the rights of the people, which the Constitution was not intended to foreclose. The most important of these currently contested unenumerated rights may well be privacy.

The most comprehensive argument in support of the constitutional right of privacy appears in Justice Blackmun's dissent in *Bowers v. Hardwick*. Elsewhere I have argued that Blackmun not only summarizes and justifies the privacy jurisprudence in relation to doctrines of fundamental rights, but also sketches the terms of a "constitutional morality" in which concepts of autonomy, equality, and moral plurality are articulated.[60] For Blackmun, at issue is the right of individuals to pursue happiness through freely chosen intimate associations with other persons. This moral and legal principle lies at the heart of the scheme of constitutional protections of individual rights.[61] Moreover, by emphasizing the place of "intimate association" within a broader context of political neutrality and moral pluralism, Blackmun lays the groundwork for incorporating substantive ethical concerns into a liberal concern for the right and for human rights. In this section, I explore the specific implications of Blackmun's treatment of the relation between individual freedom and the social construction of domestic institutions. My reading of Blackmun's opinion will take it as the expression of seminal arguments in ethics and political philosophy that transcend the legal and institutional context of its writing. In constitutional terms, it has no legal authority, although it may come to join the dissents of the "great dissenter," the nineteenth-century Justice Harlan, whose "premature" dissenting opinions on racial justice were eventually vindicated by the decisions of later generations of justices.[62] My primary concern will be to spell out some of the ethical and political implications of the "freedom of intimate association" on which Blackmun grounds the constitutional right of privacy. Returning to the question of lesbian and gay marriage, I argue that privacy rights must be analyzed in close interconnection with constitutional norms of equality affecting both gender and the citizenship of sexual minorities.

In his *Hardwick* dissent, Blackmun summarizes the constitutional jurisprudence of privacy rights as providing protection for both certain decisions that are taken to belong primarily to the individuals affected and certain places that are insulated against social and legal intrusions. In responding to the Court's limitation of these protections to matters regarding marriage and the family, Blackmun warns against "closing our eyes to the basic reasons why certain rights associated with the family have been accorded shelter under the Fourteenth Amendment's Due Process Clause."[63] Blackmun concludes that these reasons have less to do with some calculus of social benefits to be derived from family institutions than "because they form so central a part of an individual's life." His argument focuses on the underlying ethical concerns expressed in claims to fundamental rights. Blackmun rejects the definition of "the alleged right to commit homosexual sodomy" as a configuration of body parts and characterizes sexual activity as an aspect of emotional and interpersonal relationships. In terms of recent identity politics, Blackmun sees the intersubjective domain of intimacy as a site of self-formation and personal identity as requiring expression through association with others.[64] Critically, he denaturalizes family values by interpreting them as various ways in which people come together to construct shared lives:

> a necessary corollary of giving individuals freedom to choose how to conduct their lives is acceptance of the fact that different persons will make different choices. [The] fact that different individuals define themselves in a significant way through their intimate sexual relationships with others suggests, in a Nation as diverse as ours, that there may be many "right" ways of conducting those relationships, and that much of the richness of a relationship will come from the freedom an individual has to choose the form and nature of these intensely personal bonds. . . . the Court really has refused to recognize . . . the fundamental interest all individuals have in controlling the nature of their intimate associations with others.[65]

This argument concentrates a number of important insights into both sexual freedom and the character of domestic institutions. For Justice Blackmun, individual freedom must be socially situated and expressed through affiliation with others. A society that truly values individual freedom must eventually recognize a diversity of shared forms of life, especially in the context of intimate association. Although voluntary choice is a necessary component in legitimizing common institutions within democratic societies, freedom requires embodiment in social practices and institutions if individuals are to flourish.[66]

Blackmun's point, central to any understanding of modern intimacy, is that consensual relations among adults are both expressions of the voluntary choices of individual participants and necessary elements in the construction of intersubjectively constituted personal identities. Freedom in the choice of partners and modes of relationship is one component of the good of intimate association that produces socially recognized shared forms of life. Intimate associations often find expression in sexual activity. Blackmun suggests that a plurality of forms of intimate association may itself be a good in a nation so large and diverse as the United States.[67] Thus, diversity of personal and sexual expression has an irreducibly political dimension requiring the social recognition of "experiments in living": the existence of different sexualities with their own modes of intimacy is itself a contribution to human flourishing. The critical importance of intimacy as a constituent in most persons' conceptions of themselves and of a good life leads to its protection as a fundamental right: "[It] is precisely because the issue raised in this case touches the heart of what makes individuals what they are that we should be especially sensitive to the rights of those whose choices upset the majority."[68]

Finally, Justice Blackmun's analysis of the freedom of intimate association reframes the question of marriage and the family in the privacy jurisprudence. The freedom of intimate association requires not just a negative right to be left alone, but rather the positive capacity to create intimate spaces and the social support of personal choices that enable individuals to establish and develop their relationships.[69] These intimate spaces are often figured as home. Domesticity is the metaphorical and actual space of intimacy: the privacy cases demonstrate the dependence of such a sphere on its recognition by legal and social authorities. These decisions have constructed a domain of intimacy through which mutual personal decisions are not only insulated against interference from government or society but also given a place in the world. In part, this construction results from recognition of tradition and established social practice; in part, it has required the Court to apply fundamental principles of liberty and equality to domains previously governed by majoritarian morality. Blackmun's analysis points toward the need for recognizing a plurality of intimate associations through which individuals may pursue their goals and within which they may establish their homes and together shape their personal identities.

Within the normative framework of democratic constitutionalism, the recognition of intimate associations requires their conformity to ideals of freedom and reciprocity. In the earlier privacy cases, traditional marriage and family arrangements were emphasized without acknowledging that they may conflict with overriding concerns for individual autonomy and civic equality. These intimate associations are entitled to constitutional protection as fundamental rights only when they comport with the requirements of equal liberty for all. Justice Blackmun's argument for a constitutional right of privacy grounded in a positive freedom of intimate association recognizes deep human needs for intimacy and the extent to which even the most personal relations require social and legal support. But why marriage? To what extent may the valorization of marriage implicit in demands for lesbian and gay equality of access be at odds with feminist theory and the aspirations of the women's movement to overcome gender subordination and the institutionalized abuse of women? Feminists have eloquently and persuasively demonstrated the ways in which the institution of marriage has historically reinforced male privilege and implemented the subjection of women. Recent scholarship has demonstrated that many of the recent reforms in divorce law, sometimes in the name of gender equality, have also functioned to disadvantage women both economically and socially. In ongoing relationships, marital privacy has been invoked to shield abusing men and perpetuate the vulnerability of women to sexual and physical abuse.

The decision of the Supreme Court of the State of Hawaii in *Baehr v. Lewin*, mentioned in the first section of this article, has called attention to a different feminist analysis of same-sex marriage. In deciding that the denial of marital status to same-sex couples must be scrutinized in the light of state constitutional prohibitions on sex discrimination, that court has given legal authority and political impetus to an argument that has been advanced by a number of scholars in recent years.[70] Before concluding my own analysis, I want to consider briefly the argument about gender equality and heterosexual marriage, as formulated by Cass Sunstein.[71] He develops the analogy between miscegenation laws that banned interracial marriage and the denial of marital status to same-sex couples. In terms of constitutional equality, both cases present instances of formal legal equality established against a background of social hierarchy. Bans on miscegenation applied equally to whites and blacks; the restrictions on marriage equally affect women who want to marry women and men who want to marry men. How then is the denial of marital status to same-sex couples a case of sex discrimination? In *Loving v. Virginia*, the Supreme Court held that the prohibition of interracial marriages was part of a system that maintained white supremacy. Sunstein argues that the institution of marriage works to maintain a caste system based on gender through its restriction to heterosexual couples. Drawing on feminist legal and social analysis,[72] he argues that gender hierarchy is supported by a definition of roles in which heterosexuality is employed to subordinate women to the men they love and marry. For women or men to refuse their place in this heterosexual matrix is to be cast out of central social institutions.[73] Heterosexual marriage has perpetuated a gendered division of labor within the household and social divisions between private and public that maintain women's subordination. Sunstein concludes that constitutional norms of sexual equality require access to marriage for lesbians and gays as part of an assault on the gender caste system. If Sunstein's view is correct, the establishment of lesbian and gay marriages should have transformative, or at least subversive, effects on the organization of gender relations.

This argument is not easily evaluated, in part because it requires complex historical judgments and predictions concerning the effects of legal and social innovation. At one level, the institution of same-sex marriages and households must pose a challenge and provide alternatives to the gendered divisions of labor still prevalent in so many places. Of course, lesbians and gays may replicate these patterns through the assumption of gender-stereotyped roles. But the evident disarticulation between social role and biological sex within such same-sex couples subverts social assumptions about the naturalness of gender. Moreover, to the extent that gender remains at work, even in same-sex relationships, it is hard to see that securing the legal recognition of lesbian and gay marriage will necessarily increase its power. Justice Blackmun's dissent points toward the desirability of legal and social recognition for a diversity of forms of intimate association and family life. However, focusing on a "right to marry" that has been denied to lesbian and gay citizens has distinct proximal advantages. As directed at a status currently available to heterosexual citizens, marriage claims can be formulated in terms of the denial of constitutionally protected "equal protection of the laws." The argument that this exclusion is a form of sex discrimination in particular strengthens that case given the current status of homosexuals in constitutional law. If Justice Blackmun provides ethical grounds for recognizing fundamental rights of intimate association, then political ideals of equal citizenship and legal norms of "equal protection" complete a constitutional case for recognizing lesbian and gay marriage. The ethical and social question remains: whether the identification of rights to intimate association with access to marriage might foreclose the diversity of forms of life that Blackmun so eloquently evokes.

I have several concerns about the argument for lesbian and gay marriage based on gender equality. First, the legal strategy must not be permitted to obscure the specificity of lesbian and gay oppression nor subordinate the claims of queer citizens to tactical moves in the struggle for gender equality. The equality of the sexes and equal citizenship for sexual minorities are related but distinct goals. In the United States today, pervasive legal disabilities define homosexuals as second-class citizens.[74] Consider the following: the criminalization of same-sex activities in one-half the states and the denial to homosexuals of constitutional privacy rights that are well established for heterosexual citizens; the failure of most states and the federal government to protect lesbian and gay citizens from retaliation for the exercise of political freedom in their efforts to attain full equality; the stigmatization as demands for "special rights" of efforts to attain constitutional equality; and the systematic denial of legal recognition to same-sex couples and queer families who want to establish lasting relationships. The legal status of homosexuals in the contemporary United States effectively relegates queer citizens to a second-class citizenship fundamentally at odds with the egalitarian aspirations of modern democracy. The claim of a right to marry derives ethical and political force by appealing to ideals of equal citizenship. In terms of other inequalities, tied to class difference and income, marital status makes available "off the rack" a package of rights otherwise available only through expensive "custom-made" legal arrangements. While continuing to hope for and celebrate a plurality of "experiments in living," I am reluctant to accept a legal condition where lesbian and gay citizens must find alternatives to marriage whether they wish to or not, whether they can afford it or not. Thus, the demand for recognition of lesbian and gay marriage or domestic partnership appears as a necessary corollary of equal citizenship in the domestic sphere. Although some advocates worry that success on this front would result in the assimilation of a distinct lesbian and gay ethos to the imitation of heterosexist models, this objection strikes me as both understating and exaggerating the importance of formal legal rights. It underestimates the practical consequences of legal recognition as a form of empowerment by which individuals may create institutions that third parties must acknowledge. On the other hand, it overstates the extent to which such recognition deprives individuals of the capacity to shape and revise the institutions they voluntarily create. To the extent that opposition to lesbian and gay domesticity invokes an image of sexual outlaws inventing radically alternative forms of life, it underestimates the extent to which even our most intimate activities are implicated in forms of social life, even through their interdiction. After all, outlaws, especially, are defined by the law.

No one can deny that marriage is already a troubled institution in modern liberal societies. The rate of divorce, the number of single-parent households with children, the increasing incidence of single-person or unmarried-combination living arrangements, the number of children growing up with connections to multiple families through remarriage, all these facts emphasize the extent to which the model of a nuclear family composed of husband, wife, and the children they have conceived together is already a fiction. The need to rethink the legal arrangements by which we secure our common lives and the rearing of our children seems obvious. I find it hard to believe that pressure for lesbian and gay marital and parental rights will actually operate to entrench further and to legitimate more fully these institutions as we know them. One of the merits of focusing on queer families as a political issue is its small-scale and associational character. In fact, lesbians and gays are "marrying," sharing commitment ceremonies, bearing and raising children, establishing households and families, in unprecedented numbers. What they seek from the state is the additional empowerment that derives from legal recognition. Moreover, this shifting pattern of homosexual intimacy is itself the product of decades of concerted activities through which more and more queer citizens have rejected the closet to create a movement of personal and political transformation. The proliferation of queer couples and families may help to redefine the social and legal conditions available to sustain intimate and domestic relationships more generally. In the meantime, the energies mobilized around the demands for recognition of lesbian and gay families already extend the discourse of "family values" beyond the terms of conservative lament and the scapegoating of single mothers. Lesbian and gay marriages, domestic partnerships, and the reconceiving of family institutions as modes of intimate association among free and equal citizens all are efforts to appropriate, extend, and transform the available possibilities.

Notes

This essay is dedicated to Ed Stein, whose critical engagement with these issues provoked, challenged, and sustained my own efforts through several drafts and countless conversations. The work was supported by grants from the Rockefeller Foundation, the American Council of Learned Societies, and the President's Junior Faculty Fellowship at Purchase College, SUNY. Earlier versions of this paper were presented to a Philosophy Department Colloquium at SUNY Stony Brook; at a panel in the normative political theory section of the American Political Science Association; and in lectures at the University of California, Santa Cruz; at a Political Science Colloquium at the University of Washington; at the Stanford Law School; and at Willamette University. I am grateful to all of those who engaged me on those occasions, including Robert J. Anderson, Kenneth Baynes, Wendy Brown, Judith Butler, Christine de Stefano, Janet Halley, Eva Kitay, Sally Markowitz, Jason Mayerfeld, Jerome Neu, Joan W. Scott, and especially Cheryl Hall and Marcos Bisticas-Cocoves, who were formal respondents. Many thanks to Cheshire Calhoun, Richard Eldridge, Don Gifford, Dan Ortiz, Alan Ryan, and Ed Stein for their comments on written drafts. I am especially grateful to the Stanford Humanities Center where I spent the academic year 1993–94 as the inaugural Rockefeller Foundation Fellow in Legal Humanities. Wanda Korn, Charles Junkerman, the staff, and Fellows provided a congenial and engaging scholarly environment.

1. *Sexual Justice* was published by Routledge in 1997.

2. This paper includes within its general construction of a right of intimate association the right of lesbian and gay citizens to raise their own

children and to be considered for foster care and adoption on the same terms as heterosexuals. However, the specific issues that emerge in decisions affecting children will be not be treated here.

3. 478 U.S. 186 (1986). J. Blackmun, dissenting, cited in Kenneth Karst, "The Freedom of Intimate Association," *Yale Law Journal* 89 (1980), 624.

4. These thinkers have argued that privacy rights have been traditionally exploited to insulate families from state investigation of offenses against women and children by the male figures who have been their primary beneficiary. They argue that appeals to privacy reinforce the isolation of the nuclear family as an arena insulated against the claims of social justice. Oddly, this feminist critique intersects in its conclusions at least with a line of conservative arguments which have attacked the constitutional right of privacy from its inception as an exercise in illegitimate judicial decision making unsupported by the text of the U.S. Constitution. A leading proponent of this view is Robert Bork, whose insistence that Americans do not enjoy a constitutionally based right of privacy may have cost him a seat on the Supreme Court. Of course, unlike conservatives who reject the right of privacy as an illicit extension of judicial power ungrounded in the text and history of the Constitution, feminist critics of privacy rights have been insistent that a woman's right to abortion can only be strengthened by grounding it in terms of gender equality under the equal protection clause of the Fourteenth Amendment. See, e.g., Catherine A. MacKinnon, *Feminism Unmodified* (Cambridge, MA: Harvard University Press, 1987), ch. 8. For a critique in the context of lesbian and gay rights, see Kendall Thomas, "Beyond the Privacy Principle," *Columbia Law Review,* October 1992.

5. Approximately one-half of the states still prohibit sodomy in some form, either between any "persons" or between persons of the same sex.

6. According to a survey published in the *Harvard Law Review* in 1989, over sixty jurisdictions included sexual orientation as a protected class under their civil rights laws. That list included only two states; subsequently, six other states have amended their civil rights laws to include sexual orientation, as have numerous other jurisdictions. However, some localities have rescinded the inclusion of lesbians and gays. This matter has been the subject of highly publicized statewide referenda in Oregon and Colorado. Cf. "Developments in the law—sexual orientation and the law," 62 *Harvard Law Review* 617 (January 1989).

7. Richard Mohr has effectively marshaled the arguments favoring the inclusion of sexual orientation in civil rights legislation, emphasizing the importance of such legislation as a guarantee that lesbian and gay

citizens exercising their fundamental political rights may not be subjected to certain kinds of retaliation. Richard Mohr, *Gays/Justice* (New York: Columbia University Press, 1990), especially chapters 5–7.

8. Although in part an argument against discrimination by the state, this claim depends importantly on the notion that lesbians and gays are entitled to equal citizenship as *lesbian and gay*, that is, without having to conceal or deny their sexual orientation.

9. Cf. Mark Blasius, "The Ethos of Lesbian and Gay Existence," *Political Theory* 20/4 (1992).

10. In an op-ed piece, Andrew Sullivan, former editor of the *New Republic*, has argued just such a case. The political argument seems to me to stand independently of the essentialism with which Sullivan partially defends it. Further, one can recognize the integrity of the position without endorsing its more general political stance. Andrew Sullivan, "Gay Values, Truly Conservative," *New York Times*, February 9, 1993, A21.

11. Paula Ettelbrick, "Since When Is Marriage a Path to Liberation," in William Rubenstein, *Lesbians, Gays, and the Law* (New York: The New Press, 1993), 401–405.

12. 852 P.2d 44 (Hawaii 1993).

13. Sylvia Law, "Homosexuality and the Social Meaning of Gender," 1988 *Wisconsin Law Review* 187; Andrew Koppelman, "The Miscegenation Analogy: Sodomy Law as Sex Discrimination," *Yale Law Journal* 98 (November 1988), 145–64; William Eskridge, "A History of Same-Sex Marriage, *Virginia Law Review*, 79 (October 1993), 1419–1511; Cass Sunstein, "Homosexuality and the Constitution," *Metaphilosophy*, forthcoming.

14. 388 U.S. 1 (1967).

15. In late December 1992, the *New York Times* reported that Stanford and Chicago Universities had extended health benefits to the unmarried domestic partners of their employees. Stanford restricted such coverage to same-sex couples on the ground that they are denied the choice of marriage. In January 1993, Mayor David Dinkins announced the creation of a registry for unmarried domestic partnerships in New York City and the extension of some limited benefits to city employees in such partnerships. Although the movement to recognize domestic partnerships is an important trend, most such efforts fall far short of conveying the range of rights and benefits associated with marital status.

16. Kath Weston, *Families We Choose* (New York: Columbia University Press, 1991); Ellen Lewin, *Lesbian Mothers* (Ithaca, NY: Cornell University Press, 1993).

17. This tension has been identified and amplified in the work of those feminist legal scholars and political theorists who have been profoundly suspicious of reliance on the right of privacy to secure a woman's right to abortion. They rightly insist on the importance of equality-based arguments which recognize the disparate impact of abortions rights on men and women. In addition, they have emphasized that privacy talk has been traditionally deployed to insulate patriarchal power relations within the family from scrutiny and intervention by the state. See, e.g., MacKinnon, supra. My point here is to acknowledge the force of these critiques but to underscore the historical instability of this deployment such that the recognition of privacy rights has also systematically undermined the independence of the familial institution they are invoked to support. See particularly the discussion of *Eisenstadt v. Baird*, below.

18. 381 U.S. 479 (1965).

19. 478 U.S. 186 (1986).

20. 394 U.S. 557 (1969).

21. 405 U.S. 438 (1972).

22. 410 U.S. 113 (1973).

23. 277 U.S. 438 (1928).

24. For a more detailed discussion of *Griswold* in the context of constitutional jurisprudence and political philosophy, see Morris B. Kaplan, "Autonomy, Equality, and Community," 11 *Praxis International* 195 (July 1991).

25. 381 U.S. 479 at 482.

26. The argument proceeds on two complementary fronts: Douglas's more general strategy is to establish that rights unenumerated in the Constitution have been recognized and enforced as necessary for the protection of, therefore peripheral to, specific rights that *are* enumerated in the Constitution; more particularly, he anchors privacy rights within the penumbra of specific enumerated rights. In addition to those linked to First Amendment freedoms of association, Douglas identifies zones of privacy generated by the Third Amendment prohibition of the quartering of soldiers in people's homes during peacetime without the consent of the owners, the Fourth Amendment prohibition of "unreasonable searches and seizures," the Fifth Amendment's protection against compulsory self-incrimination, and the Ninth Amendment.

27. *Pierce v. Society of Sisters*, 268 U.S. 510 (1925).

28. *Meyer v. Nebraska*, 262 U.S. 390 (1923).

29. 381 U.S. 479 at 482.

30. 357 U.S. 449 (1958).

31. 381 U.S. 479 at 483.

32. 371 U.S. 415 (1962).

33. What is at issue in the right of privacy is the theory of limited government which informs the constitutional framework. For the framers, this theory was critically linked to the conception of natural rights, possessed by persons as such, independently of any positive legal or constitutional enactments. As Senator Joseph Biden insisted in his exchanges with Judge Bork at the confirmation hearings, rights are something one is born with; they are not given to us by the government. Although such theories have been out of fashion, especially among academics, for over a century, they played an important role in the philosophical defense of the American Revolution and were institutionalized in the Bills of Rights enacted as parts of the constitutions of the newly independent states and eventually of the United States. What attention to the Ninth Amendment emphasizes is that the enumeration of rights to be protected against infringement by the new governments was understood as a *recognition* and *specification* rather than a positive creation of individual rights. Thus, the constitutional right of privacy appears as a belated formulation of a conception of the relation between individuals and their government which is central to the political philosophy of the Constitution. Indeed, the Federalists had initially opposed the adoption of an enumerated Bill of Rights as part of the Constitution on the grounds that it was unnecessary and potentially misleading. They feared that later generations might come to view such a list as exhaustive of constitutionally protected individual rights. In *The Federalist*, #84, Alexander Hamilton insisted that the Constitution created and defined the powers of a limited government whereas persons naturally possessed *rights* prior to the institution of government. When the Bill of Rights was adopted in the first Congress, the Ninth Amendment was adopted as a prophylaxis against the "strict construction" of personal rights.

34. 381 U.S. 479 at 485–86.

35. 381 U.S. 479 at 486.

36. 367 U.S. 497 (1961).

37. 367 U.S. 497 at 553.

38. 405 U.S. 438 (1972).

39. 405 U.S. 438 at 453.

40. Ibid.

41. That bedroom had already suffered some profanation in 1969 when the Court decided in *Stanley v. Georgia,* 394 U.S. 557 (1969) that privacy rights combined with the First Amendment to prevent the state from prosecuting a man for the possession of obscene material within his home. They recognized the individual's "right to satisfy his intellectual and emotional needs in the privacy of his own home." Not even the state's interest in regulating "obscenity," already acknowledged as exempt from First Amendment limitations, justifies such intrusion: "... a State has no business telling a man, sitting alone in his house, what books he may read or what films he may watch." 394 U.S. 557 at 565.

42. 410 U.S. 113 (1972).

43. 410 U.S. 113 at 153.

44. The Court goes on to establish a tripartite analysis of the state's interest in regulating these decisions from a minimal concern with defining conditions of medical safety in the first trimester through a more active concern for the mother's health in the second to an interest in the potential life of the fetus in the third trimester (or after viability). The weighting of competing interests focused on the mother's liberty and health and on the state's concern for the potential life of the affected fetus. Political controversy has combined with academic skepticism about the force of its arguments to undermine confidence in the quality of Blackmun's opinion in *Roe v. Wade,* even among those who support its outcome. I think that this view underestimates the statesmanship underlying its compromises: as a framework for working through the complex balancing that abortion requires, it has not been superseded.

45. —U.S.–(1992).

46. 478 U.S. 186 (1986).

47. See, e.g., Anne B. Goldstein, "History, Homosexuality, and Political Values: Searching for the Hidden Determinants of *Bowers v. Hardwick,*" 97 *Yale Law Journal* (1988), 1073, 1081–89; Janet E. Halley, "Reasoning About Sodomy: Act and Identity in and After *Bowers v. Hardwick,*" 79 *Virginia Law Review* (1993), 1721, 1750–67. The criticism extends across a broad spectrum of constitutional per-spectives from left-republican Frank Michelman, "Law's Republic," *Yale Law Journal,* to libertarian Richard A. Posner, *Sex and Reason* (Cambridge, MA: Harvard University Press, 1993).

48. See the *Washington Post* story quoted in William Rubenstein, *Lesbians, Gay Men, and the Law,* 148–49.

49. The official version of these events has emphasized that the police were at Mr. Hardwick's home to enforce a warrant that had been issued because of his nonappearance in court on an unrelated matter. Michael

Hardwick has offered a fuller and less benign picture of the events leading to his arrest. See Peter Irons, *The Courage of Their Convictions*
(1988), 394–96; Rubenstein, *Lesbians, Gays, and the Law,* 125–131.
Kendall Thomas has used this fuller and more convincing account of
the episode in developing an argument about the role of sodomy laws
in licensing homophobic violence. Kendall Thomas "Beyond the
Privacy Principle," *Columbia Law Journal,* (October 1992).

50. 478 U.S. 186 at 196.

51. 478 U.S. 186 at 200 (Blackmun, J., dissenting).

52. 487 U.S. 186 at 190–91.

53. As to the right "to satisfy his own intellectual and emotional needs in
    the privacy of one's home" enforced as to the solitary enjoyment of
    pornography in *Stanley,* even White saw that it could not be said to
    "deal with" procreation, marriage, and the family. He devotes a sepa-
    rate paragraph to arguing that this is really a First Amendment case and
    not a privacy case at all, despite the acknowledged fact that the First
    Amendment does not protect obscene material outside the home.

54. See note 47, supra.

55. 478 U.S. at 200 (Blackmun, J., dissenting).

56. Cf. Jonathan Goldberg, *Sodometries* (Stanford: Stanford University
    Press, 1992), Introduction, for an interesting historical and critical
    account of this and other anomalies of the sodomy laws.

57. 478 U.S. 186, at 194.

58. See Eve Kosofsky Sedgwick, *The Epistemology of the Closet* (Berkeley:
    University of California Press, 1990); Kendall Thomas, "Corpus Juris
    (Hetero)Sexualis," *GLQ: a journal of lesbian and gay studies,* vol. 1, no.
    1, 33–52.

59. "Condemnation of those practices [homosexual conduct] is firmly
    rooted in Judeo-Christian moral and ethical standards. Homosexual
    sodomy was a capital crime under Roman law. . . . Blackstone
    described 'the infamous *crime against nature* as an offense of deeper
    malignity' than rape, 'the very mention of which is a disgrace to human
    nature,' and 'a crime not fit to be named'. . . ." 487 U.S. at 185–86."
    Anne B. Goldstein, "History, Homosexuality," has discussed the prolif-
    eration of historical errors and distortions throughout this case.

60. For a more detailed exposition, see Morris B. Kaplan "Autonomy,
    Equality, and Community," *Praxis International* 11 (July 1991),
    204–209.

61. By calling attention to the relevance of the First Amendment to the pri-
    vacy issue, Blackmun develops both critical and positive aspects of con-

stitutional morality. His analysis links up fundamental conceptions of
political neutrality, moral community, and individual autonomy within
a constitutional framework. First, religious teaching alone cannot be
used to legitimate state action: the moral principles underlying the
criminal law require justification in secular terms acceptable to a community of diverse religious beliefs and varieties of unbelief as well.
Second, a constitutional morality must recognize the centrality of individual autonomy in moral matters. Recognition of the right of individuals to determine freely their conduct is itself an element in the
morality within which democratic politics is conducted. Restrictions
on such individual autonomy cannot be justified in majoritarian terms,
but rather in terms of the need to guarantee for all the right to make
such choices. The secular framework within which competing moral
claims and practices must be adjudicated is conjoined with a commitment to the equality of persons with regard to their rights. Third, the
rights to which each person is entitled under the dictates of constitutional morality will be expressed in their activities, often in association
with other individuals. That is, constitutional rights are not simply
individual but apply to concerted activities and to the institutions to
which they give rise.

62. The most famous of these was in *Plessy v. Ferguson*, which established
the constitutionality of segregation with the "separate but equal doctrine" finally rejected in *Brown v. Board of Education*.

63. 478 U.S. 186 at 204 (Blackmun, J., dissenting).

64. For differing interpretations of Blackmun's dissent in relation to
debates between essentialists and social constructivists about sexual
identities, see articles by Daniel R. Ortiz, Cheshire Calhoun, and Morris
B. Kaplan in *Virginia Law Review*, October 1993, devoted to "Sexual
Orientation and the Law."

65. 478 U.S. 186 at 205–06 (Blackmun, J., dissenting).

66. Michael Sandel has argued that the invocation of privacy on behalf of
lesbian and gay rights in the *Hardwick* dissent shares a generic liberal
proceduralism which avoids substantive ethical argumentation with its
necessary reference to conceptions of a good life. Sandel's claim seriously mistakes the force and direction of Justice Blackmun's argument.
The redefinition of private rights as protecting freedom of intimate
association does more than trigger the protections of the due process
clause. Michael Sandel, "Moral Argument and Liberal Toleration:
Abortion and Homosexuality," 77 *California Law Review* 521 (1989).

67. The notion that a plurality of forms of shared life represents a positive
good rather than simply a political retreat from substantive ethics has
been an important component of liberal thought from the *Federalist*
papers through J.S. Mill to Isaiah Berlin.

68. 478 U.S. 186 at 211 (Blackmun, J. dissenting).

69. Although the right to marry belongs to individuals and requires state action for its fulfillment, it distinctively depends on mutual and joint decision making for its realization. At the same time, the married couple enjoys a special status vis-à-vis both state and society. The family unit created by marriage comes to have independent status even in relation to those individuals who created it. Until the wave of reform in state divorce laws since the 1960s, and even today in some jurisdictions, state authority has made it quite difficult to dissolve a marriage once formed. Indeed, nowhere is it as easy to end as to initiate a marriage, and this remains true even where there are no children whose welfare may be at issue. One reader of this paper insisted that he would go along with the argument for lesbian and gay marriage so long as it was clear that there would also be a right of lesbian and gay divorce.

70. Andrew Koppelman, "The Misequation Analogy"; Sylvia Law, "Homosexuality and the Social Meaning of Gender," 1988 *Wisconsin Law Review* 187.

71. Cass Sunstein, "Homosexuality and the Constitution," *Metaphilosophy*, October 1994. I develop a more detailed critical response in "Why *Does* Sexuality Matter to Philosophy—and How? Mutual Interrogations" in the same issue, which include the papers and commentary from a symposium, "Why Sexuality Matters to Philosophy," sponsored in 1993 at the eastern division of the American Philosophical Association by the Society for Lesbian and Gay Philosophy, the Society for Women in Philosophy, and the Society for the Philosophy of Sex and Love.

72. Especially the work of Catherine MacKinnon.

73. The most forceful and influential articulation of this position is Adrienne Rich, "Compulsory Heterosexuality and Lesbian Existence," in Henry Abelove, David Halperin, and Michele Aina Barale, eds., *The Lesbian-Gay Studies Reader* (New York: Routledge, 1993).

74. An important exploration of the relations between gender and sexuality, feminism and queer politics, to which I am indebted, is Gayle Rubin, "Thinking Sex," in Abelove, Halperin, and Barale, eds., *The Lesbian and Gay Studies Reader* (New York: Routledge, 1993).

10

Politics, Practices, Publics: Identity and Queer Rights

Paisley Currah

[W]e don't oppose homosexuals having jobs, running for office, being involved in the civic process, owning and renting property and so forth. What we're against . . . it's not a matter of being against or hating homosexuals; it's a matter of what's good law—we're against sexual preference being included as a criteria for granting minority status for special rights and privileges under civil rights statutes. We think historically civil rights has been understood to mean protecting people based on age, race, national origin, gender, or disability, and that's the way we think it ought to stay.[1]

[A] contingent marching behind the [Irish-American Gay, Lesbian and Bisexual] organization's banner would at least bear witness to the fact that some Irish are gay, lesbian, or bisexual, and the presence of the organized marchers would suggest the view that people of their sexual orientations have as much claim to unqualified social acceptance as heterosexuals and indeed as members of parade units organized around other identifying characteristics.[2]

When the rhetoricians of the right label queer demands for equality as "special rights," they imply that homosexuality is produced by practices, rather than inhering in immutable essences. According to this logic, antidiscrimination laws must be restricted to cover only those groups whose identity is fixed and ascribed, not chosen; conferring rights on gay, lesbian, and bisexual people would endow us with the same extra rights that "minorities" now enjoy. The use of the adjective "special" to describe rights attaching to practices, or sets of practices, rather than to supposedly fixed and unitary identities has been a central strategy of the right's attack on lesbian, gay, bisexual, and transgendered people. In fact, the right wing's use of special rights rhetoric to argue against the equality demands of sexual minorities—lesbians, gays, bisexuals, and transgendered people, "queers" for the purposes of this article—actually reflects larger anxieties shared by more moderate critics outside the right wing, including communitarian critics. Although many agree that the public arena provides a vital venue for deliberation about contested values, communitarians and conservatives alike worry about the phenomena of previously marginalized groups expressing their claims in the form of identity politics. It is not so much the identity claim itself, but the notion that those claims can be, indeed must be, expressed in a public venue that so riles.[3]

The author of the first epigraph, the head of the newly empowered and deeply politicized Christian Coalition, might at first glance be pleased with the recent U.S. Supreme Court decision upholding the banning of an Irish-American gay, lesbian, and bisexual group from participating in Boston's St. Patrick's Day Parade (second epigraph). The Supreme Court decided that as a fundamentally private affair, the free speech rights of the homophobic parade organizers could not be restricted: the state could not force them to include within the parade a group whose views differed so drastically from their own. But in fact the outcome of the case hinged on the fact that both the group organizing the parade and the gay, lesbian, and bisexual group that wanted to march in it openly were sending content-based messages. Thus, the Supreme Court recognized that Irish-American queers marching openly in a parade is an expressive form of speech that would be protected were that contingent to organize a parade of its own. Moreover, construing coming out as lesbian, bisexual, or gay as a form of speech covered by the First Amendment implies that the act of identification is, at least in part, a public and potentially political process. Whether the homophobic elements of the right like it or not, the recent trend of increased protection for religious freedoms has had the unintended effect of moving our notions of citizenship away from the essentialism that underlies the attack on so-called "special rights" and toward a recognition that identity is constructed in and through practices, many of which take place in the public sphere.

The criticisms of "gay rights" as "special rights" are reflected back onto the issues and identities, including religious ones so dear to the right wing itself. Whether put forth by Irish-American queers, fundamentalist Christians, or the Ku Klux Klan, identity claims depend on public expression not only for recognition but also in part for their constitution. The coherence of the "special rights" attack depends on separating queer conduct from queer identities, on asserting in fact there are no such things as gay, lesbian, bisexual or transgendered identities, only choices that individuals make about their lifestyle and behavior. Whether queer practices are choices, the result of social construction, or even biologically determined to some degree, queer identities cannot be separated from the practices through which they are produced.[4] Similarly, the identities of fundamentalist Christians are also produced through practices, including practices in the familial, economic, and political realms which affirm the values of their particular Christian faith. The protection of public expressions of Christian identity can also be construed as a "special right." Special rights, then, are really free speech rights.

The special rights attack on queers, however, fits into the more general assault on the liberal regime, including the practice of putting individual, even group, rights ahead of the common good: in this sense, the gay, lesbian, and bisexual rights movement is yet another example of the identity politics reviled by so many on the left as well as the right. Communitarians tell us that identity politics soils the rarefied air of the *agora* with the interest-based demands of faction. This argument assumes that in the public sphere identity precedes "political deliberation." Identity, however, cannot be confined to the private sphere: identity is produced through practices that take place in the public sphere as well as the private, and we must understand identity as a "constitutively constrained"[5] political practice. For example, the first "gay liberation" movement in the United States was precipitated by the 1969 Stonewall police raid, an attempt to close off a public space vital to production of the identities of the bulldaggers, queens, and fairies who fabricated their queer selves there, among other places.[6]

Also, although the 1986 *Bowers v. Hardwick* Supreme Court decision was purportedly about the private sexual practice of "homosexual sodomy," many gays, lesbians, bisexuals, and transgendered people immediately understood that the actual effect of that decision would be to circumscribe even further many of the practices that go into the production of the identities of sexual minorities—including coming out as queer. Both these events show that, as Nancy Fraser suggests, "public spheres are not only arenas for the formation of discursive opinion; in addition they are arenas for the formation and enactment of social identities."[7] Thus, the notion of the self associated with both the rights tradition and the communitarian critiques of that tradition fail to acknowledge that it is the very indeterminacy and contingency of group identities, including agonistic contestations around the cultural production of identities, that produce politics.

Indeed, if we understand identity claims as fluid and negotiable, then we can understand the emergence of identity politics in the contemporary U.S. liberal regime as infusing public debate into civic life rather than foreclosing it. Furthermore, emphasizing contingent practices rather than fixed identities will release queer-identified folk from the encumbrance of having to prove the existence of an immutable "homosexual" identity before we can come out in public without the threat of being fired or refused housing (in all but the nine states and hundreds of municipalities in the United States that include sexual orientation in antidiscrimination laws). In fact, I suggest that liberalism, and the rights discourse it has generated, is particularly suited to the adjudication of competing identity claims if we modify the traditional liberal categories so that they are no longer based on the fictions about identity that have proved to be so inadequate.[8] My argument proceeds as follows: the first section of the article describes the impasse at which liberalism has apparently arrived and the response of communitarian critics to that impasse. That section ends with my suggestions for revising liberal notions about identity and rights. The second section moves to the debate around queer rights claims, discussing both the rhetoric of special rights and the case law on the antigay ballot initiatives. The final section returns to a discussion of the parameters of the new liberalism and queer rights.

From Liberalism to Identity Politics

If we are to believe liberalism's critics, from the fount of liberalism have sprung the problems of individualism gone awry, of the fragmented polity, of the politics of difference, of multiculturalism. The liberal individualist ethos that the United States was founded on and flourished under has given birth to a rights-based politics of identity; consequently, liberalism has mutated into a cruel parody of its original doctrine—an abomination that mimics, even clings to, liberalism's formal, proceduralist rigidity while permeating its epistemological rationalism and ontological atomism with theories of knowing and being that appear to constitute a stinging repudiation of the original doctrine. The final humiliation is that its mutated progeny, "my-group first" identity politics, while proliferating in the newly expanded public domain of the liberal welfare state, still remains true to the first principle of individualist liberalism—that the public good has no claim on any fundamental right. And in the discourse of identity politics, all identity-based rights claims are cast as fundamental.[9]

If one were to cast the degeneration of liberalism as a seamless narrative it might read as follows: in its inception the social contract theory of Locke, for purposes entirely consistent with the political exigencies of its time—including the struggle against the absolutist monarchical state—construed identity as prepolitical, as presocial. Construing identity as prepolitical is an essential element of social contract theory since a contract presupposes the prior existence of reasoning agents to consent to it. And the social contract narrative itself was introduced as an alternative cartography of power relations to that of the absolutist monarchy. Atomistic individuals enter the social contract with certain inviolable, nonnegotiable rights, rights that neither the monarch nor the contract's cosignatories can undermine.[10]

The narrative continues: Liberalism in practice, however, has not always lived up to the theory: distinctions made on the basis of group differences—gender, race, class—denied many the rights they would have enjoyed had liberalism *per se* been instituted at its inception in an egalitarian way, rather than the exclusionary way it was realized in liberal democratic states such as the United States. Eventually, however, disenfranchised groups persuaded the majority to make adjustments to include them in the liberal scheme, and guarantee all citizens the "equal protection of the laws." We now have the two elements that, when combined, result in the ascension of the divisive "politics of difference" from the ashes of pure liberal theory: the introduction of the concept of equality within a liberal regime in which rights trump and the recognition—by the courts, by elected representatives, by the people, and in the Constitution itself (explicitly in the Thirteenth, Fifteenth, and Nineteenth Amendments)[11]—of group identities, or more precisely, of differences between groups.

Thus, the liberal convention of separating the public and private spheres, of leaving our particular identities behind when we deliberate on the few matters of public concern, is partially transposed: identity itself now becomes a consideration in the affairs of the liberal state. The public/private dichotomy undergoes only a partial revisioning, however, because identity claims, although emerging in a now enlarged public sphere, remain non-negotiable; that is, they are phrased as fundamental rights that cannot, in accordance with the liberal rule, be subject to political deliberation and be adjudicated in accordance with the larger common good.

This group politics of identity is itself not stable, however, for its very logic engenders the proliferation of increasingly differentiated groups who perpetually make demands on the polity, demands phrased as fundamental rights. Finally, the much-maligned phenomenon of "identity politics" emerges as the logical conclusion to our seamless narrative of liberalism: we come into the public sphere—as women, as African-Americans, as Chicanos, as Latinas, as queers, in short, with our essential identities constituted prior to the social contract—and demand the fulfillment of the liberal promise on the basis of these identities.

According to many critics of liberalism—from both the left and the right—identity politics wreaks havoc on the polity because it forecloses political debate by reifying identitarian categories, by making the political claims of identity-based groups nonnegotiable. The pursuit of the common good is entirely overcome by particular groups' demands; the public sphere is overwhelmed by private interests. The American political landscape has been transformed into clusters of identity-based factions: women and racial minorities demanding affirmative action, homosexuals demanding the "special right" of toleration and acceptance, Latinos/as demanding the right to speak Spanish in the workplace, illegal and legal immigrants demanding the same privileges to which American citizens are entitled. Certainly, with the recent emergence in the United States of straight white men as a self-declared identity group, even the formerly universal subject of rights has thrust itself onto the domain of identity politics.[12]

A coherent and sustained critique of liberal theory and practice has developed in the last two decades as an attempt to find our way out of this liberal

236 / Queer Agendas

abyss. Responding to the 1971 publication of John Rawls's liberal manifesto, *A Theory of Justice*,[13] and to the increasingly unwieldy, besieged, and inefficient modern liberal welfare state, communitarian theory has captured the imaginations of the political theorists and policy people who have found traditional liberal theory an inadequate guide to a polity where resources are more scarce, where fragmentation is more abundant, and where alienation has displaced atomism as the more apt description of the current post-industrial landscape of the United States.[14]

The communitarian critique of liberalism, although by no means entirely homogenous, centers on its conception of identity. The narrative articulated by liberal theorists, such as Locke, Hobbes, and more recently, Rawls and Robert Nozick, sustains an atomistic theory in which "man" is construed not as a social animal, but rather as a self-sufficient, fully-formed, presocial or prepolitical individual who enters into a social contract with other men only for the purposes of better protecting his life, liberty, and property.[15] Although Locke did not attempt to cloak his notion of subjectivity behind a supposedly neutral veil—we understand his text quite clearly to distinguish women, "Indians," servants, and children from the rational agent of liberalism[16]—his twentieth-century successor, Rawls, has insisted on a "veil of ignorance" that purports to divorce any one preferred notion of subjectivity from the subject who, from an "original position" or Archimedean point, would create a political order. Michael Sandel, a communitarian thinker, finds this atomistic Archimedean agent untenable: "a self totally detached from its empirically-given features would seem no more than a kind of abstract consciousness ... a radically situated subject given way to a radically disembodied one."[17]

Communitarians, following Sandel's work, regard the liberal subject, supposedly "ontologically prior" to its social world, not just as a fiction, but as a dangerous fiction. And, of course, to attribute rights to a fiction would be to ignore the constitutive grounding of identity: the social. To the liberal fantasy of autonomy and atomistic individualism, then, communitarians respond with a conception of identity based on embeddedness.[18] Thus, the communitarian approach to identity has been developed as a corrective to the liberal fiction of the rational contracting agent, recognizing instead that identity is produced intersubjectively, and that humans are social animals.

Basing their programmatic approach on their critique of liberalism's presuppositions about identity, communitarian theorists, drawing on Aristotle, Machiavelli, and Rousseau, grant priority to the common good over individual rights, emphasize the inculcation of virtue in its citizens through both the state and the family, and bemoan the extent of contemporary American society's engagement with concerns, such as the market, consumerism, and the pursuit of pleasure, that are bracketed in liberal theory.[19]

In a typical communitarian formulation, then, identity, insofar as it represents a category that inevitably refers to particular, historical, contextualized identities, is construed as antipolitical: it separates citizens from each other, and tears them apart as identity-based groups battle over the spoils to be doled out by the newly expanded liberal state. This formulation rests on the unstated, and doubtful, assumption that any identity-based action in the public sphere is really about the zero-sum game of economic competition. The historical convergence of classical liberal theory with classical economic theory, however, does not necessarily mean that they are inevitably bound up together.

Although the communitarian theory of identity rejects Rawls, and emphasizes "radically situated" identity, its view of a citizen becomes remarkably abstract when it comes to envisioning political debate in the public sphere. Ignoring its own claims of embeddedness and socially constructed identity, in the public arena we suddenly assume the status of citizens; "group identities" drop out of the picture as aspects of our private selves. We subsume our selves to the public good and are thus able to deliberate without rancor. Suddenly we become Rawls's abstract subjects again, deciding on a vision of the common good without taking into account our own radically situated selves.

Note the rhetorical move communitarians make to accomplish this retreat and how their own conception of the public sphere shares the same abstract proceduralism of its target, liberalism. They assume a utopian public sphere, or "community," in which oppression has already ceased to exist, where differences between people do not lead to violence and domination, and where the ground rules of public discourse affect every citizen equally.[20] In fact, this impulse effectively bounds the public sphere by excluding consideration of particular identities. This very definition obviates political deliberation about the oppressive relations based on differences.[21] The communitarian assessment of liberalism, then, inevitably fails because the communitarian project is primarily motivated not by a desire to diagnose the maladies of liberalism, but rather by an urge to set up barricades against the onslaught of the "barbarians" of a "new dark age"—a dark age in which nontraditional identities, customs, and practices encroach upon the settled white supremacist, patriarchal order that both traditional liberalism and communitarian theory set out to uphold.[22]

The communitarian ontological critique of liberalism, then, fails not because it interrogates the liberal fiction of the autonomous self but because it does not question that fantasy thoroughly enough. It ignores the range of communities, practices, histories, cultures, traditions, and practices that constitute the social to retain a nostalgic version of the social. Consequently, the communitarian understanding of identity ends up propagating its own fictions.

Communitarian theory does more than take the social into its account of subjectivity: the communitarian impulse is to reify certain social networks of belonging, to protect them, to cherish them—and, as Alasdair MacIntyre states, to see them as "constraints" on our actions, our identity, in opposition to the liberal fantasy of autonomy and agency. However, for communitarians "the social" usually refers only to the "heteronormative" networks, practices, communities, political activities that meet with communitarian approbation.[23] "It is," in Stephen Holmes's words, "as if 'the dental' referred exclusively to healthy teeth."[24]

The principle of selecting which social networks to endorse is clearly bound up with the notion of identity as constraint. For example, Robert Bellah describes a community that sounds remarkably similar to an urban gay community in the United States as unauthentic precisely because the "contemporary lifestyle enclave is based on a degree of individual choice that largely frees it from traditional ethnic and religious boundaries."[25] Social networks that are assumed to result from individual agency, rather than from traditional, even premodern, static arrangements are thus deemed artificial. Not surprisingly, this principle results in the endorsement of traditional heterosexual families, and communities modeled after traditional New England towns, with their face-to-face democratic politics.[26]

The appearance of identitarian claims in the political arena must be understood not as nonnegotiable trumps, but as both a method of participation and the subject of political debate. Rights, identities, and publics must be conceptualized somewhat differently than in traditional communitarian and liberal political theory. First, many of the theoretical insights that fall under the rubric of postmodernism are consistent with a revised liberal project; instead of undermining a liberal emancipatory project, the fundamental indeterminacy that postmodern theory announces in fact makes possible a politics which centers on political deliberation in the public sphere. Indeed, rights can also be construed as practices. The problem with traditional liberal theory is not with rights per se, but with conceiving them as Archimedean procedures unaffected by the world, over which they apparently waft. Rights are not reified "things"; rather, their existence depends on their exercise in a specific historical, institutional, or discursive context. Thus, rights are not prepolitical or antipolitical. They are part and parcel of the complex negotiations that constitute the substance of politics. Liberalism, then, if its language is rightly understood, is not ahistorical, but is—in all its historical specificity—necessarily historical.[27]

Second, an emphasis on public, political deliberation does not have to be understood as antithetical to a revised liberalism. Not only is this rearrangement achievable, it is in fact essential that a blend of identitarian practices, liberal procedures (including the priority of the right over the good), and public, political deliberation be developed. The public sphere is the central venue of the agonistic substance of politics. But the "public sphere" is also much broader than the townhall meetings so often represented in the nostalgic communitarian fantasy. If the public sphere is to be taken seriously, as the communitarians would have it, then we must recognize that it comprises multiple publics, including what Nancy Fraser terms "subaltern counter-publics" and defines as "parallel discursive arenas where members of subordinated social groups invent and circulate counterdiscourses, so as to formulate oppositional interpretations of their identities, interests, and needs."[28]

Finally, if we understand identity not as essential, nonnegotiable, and pre-political but as both a subject and a method of political deliberation, then identitarian practices, including identity politics, can assume a legitimate standing in the political arena. Particular identities have no meaning apart from their historical circum-stances. One's identity, as a woman, for example, is dependent on the gender arrangements constructed in the cultural practices. As de Beauvoir wrote, "One is not born, but rather becomes, a woman."[29] Identity, and identity politics, must be understood as "constitutively constrained" political practices, rather than static, essentialist constructions.

Special Rights

> Frankly, the majority of society does not agree with the practices and the acts of homosexuality. Most people say if they want to practice it in their bedrooms, that's okay, but if they want to come out of the bedroom and say because of what we're doing in the bedroom we want special rights, we want special recognition, we want special protection, people in Colorado and people all over the nation—if they have an opportunity—will say, "That's not fair."[30]

Until recently, the outcome of queer rights claims in the United States has hinged on the question of how homosexual identity is produced. Gay, lesbian, and bisexual rights claims have most often taken the form of equal protection claims and, until recently, those claims involved arguing that sexual orientation constitutes a "suspect class"; the analogy of course, is to race, which the Supreme Court has deemed constitutes a suspect class.[31] Unfortunately, neither the Supreme Court nor any federal circuit court has definitively held that gays, lesbians, and bisexuals constitute a suspect or quasi-suspect class.[32] In fact the binaries generated around the notions of agency/immutability, conduct/orientation, and act/identity, operate to preclude the successful designation of suspect or quasi-suspect class status for gays, lesbians, and bisexuals. Overall, it is the first term (conduct/act/agency) of these binaries that has been deemed ultimately constitutive of homosexuality by the courts; when advocates for gay, lesbian, and bisexual rights attempt to invoke notions of immutability (homosexuality as a genetic, inherited characteristic) or a fixed "orientation" (homosexuality as unchangeable in adults) as being constitutive of homosexuality (even entirely distinct from homosexual conduct), the courts close the circle again, responding that the notion of a fixed identity is itself only a signifier of the more central phenomenon—homosexual conduct. The courts justify the decisions denying equal protection to gays, lesbians, and bisexuals by pointing out the fundamental incoherence that inheres in the strategy of asserting that a homosexual orientation is distinct from homosexual conduct. As a federal circuit court decided in 1987, "If the [Supreme] Court [in *Bowers v. Hardwick*] was unwilling to object to state laws that criminalize the behavior that defines the class, it is hardly open to a lower court to conclude that state-sponsored discrimination against the class is invidious."[33] And recently another federal circuit court reasoned that:

> [N]o law can successfully be drafted that is calculated to burden or penalize, or to benefit or protect, an unidentifiable group or class of individuals whose identity is defined by subjective and unapparent characteristics such as innate desires, drives, and thoughts. Those persons having a homosexual "orientation" simply do not, as such, comprise an identifiable class. Many homosexuals successfully conceal their orientation. Because homosexuals generally are not identifiable "on sight" unless they elect to be so identifiable by conduct (such as public displays of homosexual affection or self-proclamation of homosexual tendencies) they cannot constitute a suspect class or a quasi-suspect class because "they do not [necessarily] exhibit obvious, immutable, or distinguishing characteristics that define them as a discrete group." . . . Those persons who fall within the orbit of legislation concerning sexual orientation are so affected not because of their orientation but rather by their *conduct* [italics in original].[34]

According to the logic of the opinion, then, since homosexuals are not "easily identifiable" as such, the only thing that could identify us is our conduct—kissing or coming out, for example—and conduct is not protected. It is important to note, however, that even if homosexuals were designated a suspect class, practices that are associated with queer identity—gender crossing, for example—would not necessarily be protected: masculine "women" and feminine "men" (whether homosexual or heterosexual) could be fired from their jobs for transgressing traditional gender norms. Karl E. Klare has demonstrated the unwillingness of the courts to "acknowledge the communicative significance of appearance practices," including expressions of cultural identity such as "Afro" hair styles.[35] Laws that protect people on the basis of an immutable identity do not necessarily protect the practices through which that identity is produced.

Since sexual orientation has been denied suspect or quasi-suspect class status, queer rights advocates have begun following a different avenue, an avenue that does not require that sexual orientation be construed as immutable in order for these rights claims to succeed. Instead of asserting the existence of an unchangeable homosexual identity, as was the case in many of the equal protection challenges brought against the ban on gays in the military,[36] the new strategy involves claiming that the fundamental right of gays, lesbians, and bisexuals to participate equally in the political process cannot be abridged because certain forms of state-sanctioned discrimination against gays, lesbians, and bisexuals inhibit our ability to take part in the political process on an equal basis. Contending that gays and lesbians have a right to participate openly and equally in political and social life does not require establishing that homosexual identity is natural, genetic, ascribed, or prepolitical; to succeed, it requires only that gays, lesbians, and bisexuals constitute an "identifiable group." An identifiable group is defined not by an identifiable characteristic but by virtue of being singled out by the state and laden with special burdens. This new trend leaves room for a conception of identity as potentially political. Indeed, it is the open participation of gay, lesbian, and bisexual people that underlies the claim made here that identity can itself be a subject and a method of politics.

The new legal strategy was actually brought about by the intensified efforts of the Christian right to revoke statutory breakthroughs won by lesbian, bisexual, and gay communities in several municipalities and state agencies. During the 1992 elections, organizations of the Christian right in both Colorado and Oregon succeeded in placing on those states' ballots a voter-initiated referendum that would make it illegal to ban discrimination on the basis of sexual orientation. One of the slogans circulated by the proponents of the antigay voter referenda in Colorado and Oregon was: "No special rights for homosexuals." The power of this appeal lay in the statement's unstated yet implicit affirmation of the idea that homosexuals were after, or already had, "special rights" that did not apply to heterosexual American citizens. For example, according to the literature distributed by Colorado for Family Values, the organization that sponsored Amendment 2, the Colorado antigay voter initiative:

> What's fair about an affluent group gaining minority privileges simply for what they do in bed?... What's fair about people who enjoy all the rights and privileges of American citizenship asking for special status?... Special rights for homosexuals just isn't fair— especially to disadvantaged minorities in Colorado.[37]

Similarly, leaders of the Oregon Citizen's Alliance, the organization that sponsored the antigay Measure 9 in Oregon during the same 1992 elections, argued that since homosexuality was a behavior, rather than a genetically conferred identity like gender and race, it deserved no special rights or protections.[38]

Of course, the towns and municipalities and other state actors whose legislators had passed ordinances banning discrimination on the basis of sexual orientation in housing, services, and employment—usually with exemptions for religious organizations and landlords who rent rooms out of their own residences—had not given to their gay, lesbian, or bisexual residents any rights that other residents did not have; the ordinances merely added sexual orientation to the categories of race, gender, age, national origin, and ethnicity.

Nevertheless, the "No special rights" slogan was an integral part of the rhetoric of the Christian right's campaigns in Colorado and Oregon for antigay amendments to those states' constitutions. In fact, it may have been the most effective element of the antigay campaigns, if the different outcomes in Colorado and Oregon are taken into account. In Colorado, Amendment 2 was actually passed by the voters of Colorado on November 3, 1992, with 53.4 percent of voters in favor of the amendment and 46.6 percent against. The actual amendment reads:

> No Protected Status Based on Homosexual, Lesbian, or Bisexual Orientation. Neither the State of Colorado, through any of its branches or departments, nor any of its agencies, political subdivisions, municipalities or school districts, shall enact, adopt or enforce any statute, regulation, ordinance or policy whereby homosexual, lesbian, or bisexual orientation, conduct, practices or relationships shall constitute or otherwise be the basis of or entitle any person or class of persons to have or claim any minority status, quota preferences, protected status or claim of discrimination. This Section of the Constitution shall be in all respects self-executing.[39]

The relevant parts of Ballot Measure 9, the antigay amendment to Oregon's constitution voted on in the same election, differ markedly in tone from those in Colorado's Amendment 2. Among other things, this measure would have required all levels of government in the state of Oregon to "assist in setting a standard for Oregon's youth that recognizes homosexuality, pedophilia, sadism, or masochism as abnormal, wrong, unnatural, and perverse and that these behaviors are to be discouraged and avoided."[40] Unlike Colorado's Amendment 2, Oregon's proposed constitutional amendment was rejected by voters at the polls by a margin of 57 percent to 43 percent.[41] The more virulent homophobia exhibited by the language of Oregon's amendment undoubtedly played a role in its demise: perhaps the language associating homosexuality with pedophilia, sadism, and masochism jolted the gay, lesbian, and bisexual community into action, causing them to organize earlier and campaign harder than their counterparts in Colorado. Or it may be that the virulent language turned off the previously uncommitted yet all-important middle elements who were unwilling to commit themselves to such an extreme position. Or perhaps both factors played a role defeating the measure.

It is important to point out that the organized religious right wing in the United States took note of the differing results and concluded that future state-wide voter-initiated antigay referenda should be modeled on Colorado's Amendment 2. That is, extreme homophobia, while energizing and calling to action members of the religious right, does not succeed in winning over less homophobic segments of the population who might nonetheless agree that no group deserves "special rights." Consequently, throughout the United States, on both the national and state level, the religious right's strategists have vastly simplified their message to the mainstream from the jumble of messages promulgated in 1992: now it is simply, "No special rights for homosexuals." The notion of "special rights" nicely complements the argument that appears in the equal protection case law that homosexuality is fundamentally different from other axes of identity.

National leaders of the religious right have relied heavily on this rhetoric when they have addressed the issue of the homosexual agenda in the mainstream media. Senator Jesse Helms expresses the same reservations about "special rights" for homosexuals: "[A]ll I'm saying is I've got nothing to complain about if [homosexuals] do it privately. Heterosexuals don't use such conduct. They don't demand special rights. And that's what bothers me about the homosexuals and the lesbians."[42] And right-wing Christian broadcaster (and former Republican presidential contender) Pat Robertson succinctly states, "[P]eople who engage in homosexuality are not to be given special civil rights privileges."[43]

The "special rights" rhetoric is echoed incessantly by state and municipal leaders of antigay efforts. Will Perkins, founder of Colorado for Family Values, argues that the homosexual "agenda is to overhaul straight America ... to get total affirmation of their lifestyle, and the best and easiest way to do it is to get special class status."[44] According to Perkins, "Homosexuals have the same civil rights as everyone else, but what they were seeking was protective class status that made them equivalent of an ethnic minority."[45] Reverend Lou Sheldon, a California antigay activist, holds to the special rights theme as well: "Homosexuals are really asking for special rights. They don't qualify."[46] When Idaho state senator Stan Hawkins presented a bill that would deny homosexuals "special rights," he argued: "I don't think homosexuals should receive special privileges. I don't think anybody should, unless they earn them."[47] Phil Burress, a leader of the Ohio Pro-Family Forum, argues that homosexuals "are already protected by the Constitution and the Bill of Rights. . . . This is not a personal attack on homosexuals. We are anti-special rights. We are not anti-person."[48]

The extensive circulation of this slogan constitutes a rhetorical *coup* for the proponents of antigay ballot initiatives and the religious right: not only does it imply that gays and lesbians are attempting to win for themselves special rights that others do not have; for many voters it is intended to bring to mind the civil rights revolution of the 1960s and '70s. Clearly, the insidious appeal of "special rights" rhetoric cannot be easily dismissed by logical arguments because it so neatly plays into unresolved conflicts about the nature and scope of the civil rights movement in general. Lon Mabon, who also organized the antihomosexual ballot initiatives in Oregon, Idaho, and

Washington for the 1994 elections, argues against comparing homosexuality to race or ethnicity: "We are not going to recognize homosexuality as a minority classification, or allow any classification like sexual preference to be established in the law."[49]

It is, of course, a truism of the mainstream right wing (though not necessarily the Christian right, which includes fundamentalist African-American churches) that the civil rights revolution led to "unearned" political, social, and economic gains for women and people of color through the means of "affirmative action," "quotas," and "minority status." Thus, alongside the argument that queers do not constitute a legitimate "minority" because homosexuality is defined by behaviors that are chosen, rather than by identities that are given, lurks an implicit entreaty that voters not recognize, not legitimate, one more identity-based group demanding special protections against discrimination, one more special-interest group advancing itself not by merit, but by means of affirmative action and "quota" policies.[50] These elements came together in the language of "special rights" with repeated references to "minorities," "quotas," and "affirmative action" manifested by the text of Colorado's Amendment 2 and the Christian right's homophobic rhetoric.

The slippage that occurs in "special rights" rhetoric when protection against discrimination is associated with affirmative action policies which are, in turn, associated with the much-maligned quotas reveals how gay and lesbian rights claims collapse into a larger anxiety about identity politics and civil rights discourse in general. In fact, antidiscrimination laws and ordinances, which are the product of the majoritarian political process and which govern the private as well as the public sector, do not at all mandate affirmative action policies or quotas:[51] affirmative action policies and quotas are the results of decisions of a state entity—be it the federal government, state governments and agencies, or municipal governments—to take race and/or gender into account in its contract assignments and hiring policies.[52] What is interesting, however, is the conflation of banning discrimination on the basis of sexual orientation with "quotas" for "minorities." This anxiety plays into a larger anxiety about the proliferation of identity-based groups.

According to the arguments circulated by the right wing, in order to prevent the rise of more special interest groups, a line must be drawn—and that line should be drawn when homosexuality, defined as a practice rather than by an ascribed identity (like women or African-Americans), becomes a meaningful category in equal protection rights discourse.[53] Interestingly, then, the rhetoric of "special rights" alludes to the same identity-behavior binary that crops up in the case law that denies suspect or quasi-suspect class status to homosexuals. According to the religious right, "special rights" are all about homosexuals *qua* homosexuals enjoying civil rights in the public sphere—rights that would not be necessary if homosexuals were to keep our sexual orientation hidden. That is, homosexuals would not need special protections against being fired or being denied housing for being gay if we never disclosed our sexual orientation in a public, or quasi-public manner: the assumption is that there would be no discrimination if there were no identifiable gay, lesbian, bisexual, or transgendered people. The highly effective rhetoric of special rights depends for its coherence on a notion of identity as enacted, as avowed, as conduct, in other words—a reprise, then, of the identity/conduct distinction that turned out to be incoherent in both the old and the new regulations governing gays and lesbians in the military. The new regulations on homosexuals in the military, for example, explicitly define coming out speech as conduct.[54]

Amendment 2 would have radically transformed the way advocates for lesbian, bisexual, and gay rights participated in the legislative process because it outlawed, in one stroke, any part of the state government, any municipalities or school districts, or any political subdivisions from enacting any law or statute that would ban discrimination on the basis of sexual orientation. The only means of securing antidiscrimination laws that would benefit gays, lesbians, and bisexuals would be to initiate—and win—another statewide referendum. While other groups (landlords, tenants, physically disabled people, farmers, etc.) are able to approach the appropriate legislative body (town councils, the state agricultural department, school board districts, etc.) to argue for the enactment of certain laws, rulings, or statutes to further their cause, gays, lesbians, and bisexuals, would be denied this venue of democratic participation. Consider the hypothetical case of a lesbian being denied a ride on a city bus because the bus driver doesn't allow "dykes" on his bus. Normally, this lesbian could meet with other queers, find out if others had experienced the same discrimination, and approach the head of the transit authority or perhaps her city councilor to try to rectify the problem. As a result of traditional democratic lobbying, the transit authority might issue a directive to its drivers ordering them not to discriminate on the basis of sexual orientation, the city council might include sexual orientation in its antidiscrimination policy, or the state's legislators might include sexual orientation in state antidiscrimination law. None of these bodies would have to change its policy on the basis of the lobbying efforts of queers and their supporters. But if Amendment 2 had been put into effect none of these state entities could even consider whether to change their policy. Instead, the only means to rectify this type of discrimination would be for the state's sexual minorities to organize, get a referendum on the state's ballot, and win on election day. No other group would face such procedural obstacles in order simply to participate in the democratic process.[55]

Gay, lesbian, and bisexual rights advocates challenged Amendment 2 by using the concept of fundamental rights. This approach required convincing the courts to safeguard the fundamental right of gays, lesbians, and bisexuals merely to enter the political arena, to participate in the political process, in order to fight for substantive rights—such as serving openly in the armed services, or engaging in sodomy—within the majoritarian legislative process. As Justice Brennan once argued, "[b]ecause of the immediate and severe opprobrium often manifested against homosexuals once so identified publicly, members of this group are particularly powerless to pursue their rights openly in the political arena."[56] These types of equal protection claims, then, are limited to seeking protection for the rights of members of "identifiable" groups to take part in the political processes through which the society's substantive decisions are made. This is the approach that proved successful in challenging the constitutionality of Colorado's Amendment 2 before the Colorado Supreme Court.

That court decided that that "Amendment 2 alters the political process so that a targeted class is prohibited from obtaining legislative, executive, and judicial protection or redress from discrimination absent the consent of a majority of the electorate through the adoption of a constitutional amendment."[57] Extending the analysis of a series of U.S. Supreme Court cases about the ability of individuals to participate equally in the political process, the Colorado Supreme Court in *Evans v. Romer* found that "the Equal Protection Clause guarantees the fundamental right to participate equally in the political process and any attempt to infringe on an independently identifiable group's ability to exercise that right is subject to strict judicial scrutiny."[58] In contrast to the notion of "substantive due process" and the rights many believe are guaranteed by that notion,[59] the Colorado Supreme Court's reasoning in *Evans v. Romer* emphasizes the importance of fairness inhering in the process itself.[60] Procedural fairness requires that queers not be "fenced out" as an identifiable social group and prevented from participating in the political process alongside any other identifiable social group.

Evans v. Romer was heard by the U.S. Supreme Court in October 1995 and the Court's decision came down in May 1996. The majority affirmed the judgment of the lower court, but explicitly eschewed the fundamental rights reasoning of the Colorado Supreme Court. Instead, Justice Kennedy, the author of the six-three majority decision, applied the most lenient type of judicial scrunity and found that Amendment 2 did not even meet that test: "It is a status-based enactment divorced from any factual context from which we could discern a relationship to legitimate state interests; it is a classification of persons undertaken for its own sake, something the Equal Protection Clause does not permit."[61] The Supreme Court, then, did not follow the Colorado court in asserting the existence of a "fundamental right" to participate equally in the political process. Rather, the Court followed the simple reasoning presented by Laurence Tribe, in an *amici curiae* brief, that Amendment 2 constitutes a literal violation of the Equal Protection Clause of the Fourteenth Amendment—that no person shall be denied the equal protection of the laws.[62] Thus, the decision does suggest that a law that burdens the ability of a group to participate in civic life will not easily pass constitutional muster:

[W]e cannot accept the view that Amendment 2's prohibition on specific legal protections does no more than deprive homosexuals of special rights. To the contrary, the amendment imposes a special disability upon those persons alone. Homosexuals are forbidden the safeguards that others enjoy or may seek without constraint. They can obtain specific protection against discrimination only by enlisting the citizenry of Colorado to amend that state constitution or perhaps, on the State's view, by trying to pass helpful laws of general applicability. This is so no matter how local or discrete the harm, no matter how public and widespread the injury. We find nothing special in the protections Amendment 2 withholds. These are protections taken for granted by most people either because they already have them or do not need them; these are protections against exclusion from an almost limitless number of transactions and endeavors that constitute ordinary civic life in a free society.[63]

It is important to note that the decision mandates only that gays, lesbians, and bisexuals not be excluded at the outset from participating in the endeavors "that constitute ordinary civic life in a free society"; the decision does not, however, mandate that that participation be successful.

In this case, then, advocates for the gay, lesbian, and bisexual citizens of Colorado who worked to have Amendment 2 declared unconstitutional were successful not because gays, lesbians, and bisexuals constitute a suspect class with an immutable identity, not because equal political participation was deemed a fundamental right, but because the law excluded us from participating at the outset for no "legitimate" reason. As John Ely notes, in U.S. constitutional law the fairness of the procedure must take priority over the whims of the majority to restrict that fundamental fairness.[64] Similarly, the radical pluralist liberalism I am advocating requires that the rules setting out the bounds of political participation in the public sphere be fair. If the expressive conduct that goes into the production of identity is to be construed as a political practice, particular identities cannot be ruled out of bounds before the process begins.

Perhaps, as Shane Phelan has so cogently suggested, it is time for contemporary political theorists to move away from the Lockean and Rawlsian liberal tradition that has so dominated our scholarship in the last two decades.[65] It may be that that other liberal, John Stuart Mill, has more to offer to those who wish to examine how expressive activity can itself be a political activity. Similarly, for sexual minorities, perhaps it is time to move away from battles about the origins of homosexual identity. Instead of relying on the failed strategy of using the Fourteenth Amendment's promise of equally protecting persons, perhaps we might rely on the First Amendment to protect our expressive activity.[66]

It may be that the free speech clause of the First Amendment can provide the judiciary with the means to protect some or many of the practices that go into the construction of identity. The Court has also come out strongly in favor of the free speech clause of the First Amendment, when the right of free speech has been invoked in the name of religious freedom.[67] Whether the Court will consider the public identification of oneself as a gay, lesbian, or bisexual person as expressive activity protected by the First Amendment remains to be seen. The new Department of Defense policy which defines coming out as "homosexual conduct" and thus as reason for discharge is now being challenged in the courts and will soon work its way up to the Supreme Court.[68]

More importantly, how will the courts respond to challenges to the almost universally unprotected practice of transgressing traditional gender codes and arrangements, especially as these practices become disentangled in the popular imaginary from the supposedly stable categories of lesbian, gay, and bisexual? Recently, a few municipalities have begun amending their human rights codes to take transgender activity and identity into account. For example, Iowa City recently amended its code to include "gender identity," which is defined in the ordinance as a "person's various individual attributes, actual or perceived, in behavior, practice, or appearance, as they are understood to be masculine *and/or* feminine" [italics added].[69] The increasing fluidity of gender identity and the growth of open cross-gender practices and identifications poses a serious challenge to a discursive regime that depends for its coherence on a viable distinction between conduct and identity.

Public Speaking

Conceptions of identity premised on its supposed "prepolitical" character—whether prepolitical is taken to mean immutable (following the precedent of suspect classes), atomistic (following traditional liberal discourse), or a product of the private, familial sphere (following the organicist strains in contemporary communitarian thinking)—fail to recognize the central role that identity and the public, political production of identities play in the political process. A radical pluralist liberalism requires a conception of identity and identitarian practices as potentially political, as potentially central to the political process itself. Furthermore, not only is identity a political category, the production of identity must be construed as constituting, in part, the political process itself.

In the traditional liberal narrative, identity is conceived as "prepolitical," as antecedent to the social contract that creates the political regime.[70] Furthermore, traditional liberalism adjudicates conflicts between the common good and individual right in favor of the latter: the right of the individual trumps the good of all.[71] According to both conservative and communitarian critics, the combination of traditional rights discourse with its emphasis on the primacy of rights, and identitarian politics, with its emphasis on the prepolitical, essential basis of identity, has had and continues to have negative consequences on the smooth functioning of the polity.

At the end of three decades during which the political arrangement underwent a fundamental reorganization—a reorganization brought on by the civil rights movement of the 1960s, the women's liberation movement of the 1970s,[72] and the ever-increasing proliferation of diverse "new social movements" in the 1980s and 1990s—identity politics has supposedly brought the polity to the brink of collapse, if we are to believe its communitarian and conservative critics. By basing rights claims, which take precedence over the common good, and which are nonnegotiable, on identity, which is itself apparently not subject to negotiation in the political sphere, the political sphere has been emptied of any significance. For example, in the United States, the "rights revolution" has caused power to pass from the majoritarian political process to the counter-majoritarian, hermeneutic tradition of constitutional exegesis, vested in the hands of the life-tenured justices of the Supreme Court. Politics becomes merely the adjudication of rights claims; the "people" and the general will drop out of the picture entirely. For example, one communitarian critic, Mary Ann Glendon, argues that the expansion of rights associated with the proliferation of identities and practices severely hampers the search for a common meaning, and threatens to shut down public dialogue altogether.[73] Although these identitarian rights claims are made in the public sphere, they fail to transform that sphere into a domain of decision and action because they are articulated as prepolitical.

Communitarian thinkers would solve this dilemma by requiring that the majoritarian demands of the common good take precedence over the rights of the individual. Recognizing, rightly, that identity is produced through social relations,[74] communitarians contend that the impasse brought on by identity politics can be broken by repudiating the priority of individual right over the general good, since those rights are supposedly based on the antecedence of identity to the political. For example, Michael Sandel, following the work of Charles Taylor, dismisses the traditional liberal self (Rawls's version of it in particular) as "an antecedently individuated subject, standing always at a certain distance from the interests it has. One consequence of this distance is to put the self beyond the reach of experience, to make it invulnerable, to fix its identity once and for all."[75] This understanding of identity, according to Sandel, rules out any conception of the good of the community:

> [A] self so thoroughly independent ... rules out the possibility of any attachment (or obsession) able to reach beyond our values and sentiments to engage our identity itself. It rules out the possibility of a public life in which, for good or ill, the identity as well as the interests of the participants could be at stake.... More generally, Rawls' account rules out the possibility of what we might call "intersubjective" or "intrasubjective"

forms of self-understanding, ways of conceiving the subject that do not assume its bounds to be given in advance.[76]

Thus, the communitarian response to the conceptions of identity apparently promulgated in traditional liberal theory is to dispense with the priority of rights altogether.

The difficult with traditional liberal discourse, however, results not from the priority of the right over the good but from liberalism's conception of identity as antecedent to politics. It is entirely possible, and indeed preferable, to conceive of identity as produced in and through social relations and still advance a rights-based politics that does not negate the political. And indeed, the communitarian conception of identity, though recognizing the importance of the social in the constructing of identity, fails to take the social, and thus identity itself, seriously enough. Nostalgia for the rural, local, direct democracy represented in communitarian discussions about the nature of community manifests an anxiety about what "the social" has become in the predominantly urban, post-industrial landscape of the contemporary United States.[77] In fact, the recognition on the part of communitarians that identity is a product of the social leads communitarians to rearrange it according to their own historically and culturally based preferences—many of which center on the family and many of which, interestingly, constitute an implicit attack on both African-American and gay and lesbian family or living arrangements.[78] Christopher Lasch, for example, would outlaw divorce;[79] another communitarian policy advocate would severely limit state support for single mothers;[80] and Jean Bethke Elshtain would allocate resources to heterosexual families but not homosexual ones.[81] But, of course, "the social" cannot be radically restructured according to the nostalgic wishes of the critic: that would be to deny to the category of the social the importance that these same critics have championed.

There remain, however, some very persuasive aspects to Sandel's critique of traditional liberal theory's notion of the prepolitical self. In both communitarian and postmodern theory identity is understood to be produced intersubjectively or socially and any pluralist rights-based politics must take that into account. One might argue—and many have—that the story of the prepolitical, individuated liberal self is just that, a story, not a theory, one whose utility may have run its course. As Lisa Bower argues, "Transformation occurs not merely by exposing differences and arguing for their inclusion under the guise of liberal tolerance; rather, change occurs when the affiliations of 'ordinary people,' are reconstituted."[82] "Individuals" are constituted through discourses, institutions, and historical practices; individuals' interests and desires are transformed when they come together in the public sphere; identity is determined by identifications with, projections on, rejections of, the other.

The literature of traditional political science describes the political process as a give-and-take process between particular interest-based groups (farmers, welfare recipients, defense contractors, Southerners, etc.);[83] a radical pluralist revisioning of the rights tradition must similarly construe the new "politics of identity" as a give-and-take process in which identity is understood both as a subject and a method of political participation. That is, identity becomes both the means through which people decide to participate in the political process and also becomes itself subject to "negotiation" in the public sphere. Negotiation in this sense means not that any individual, or group, is required to "bargain away" fundamental aspects of itself, but that the adjudication of conflicts between competing identity claims determines the spheres in which the practices constituting a particular identity will come into play.

This argument for a rights-based pluralist politics of identity does not demand the transformation of all public, quasi-public, private, and quasi-private spaces into an all-encompassing public sphere. Traditional liberal theory, with its emphasis on privacy, the antecedent individual, and property, leaves little room for a viable public sphere; in fact, the priority of the right over the common good is an indication of the insignificance attributed to the public sphere in traditional liberal theory. Communitarian theory, on the other hand, with its focus on the intrasubjective nature of identity, leaves little room for a protected private sphere; for example, its policies actually call for the state to intrude into that most private of spheres, the family. Of course, the line that divides the public from the private sphere shifts depending on which model is used. Jeff Weintraub has identified four different models of the public-private distinction, which Bruce Robbins has summarized as follows:

> The first is a liberal-economistic model that defines the public as state administration and the private as the market economy. For the second or "republican virtue" model, which would include Habermas, the public means community and citizenship, as distinct both from state sovereignty on the one side and from the economy on the other. The third is a "sociability" model, as in Richard Sennett and Philippe Aries, which emphasizes symbolic display and theatrical self-representation but has little if anything to do with collective decision-making or state power. The fourth, a model shared by feminist and other historians, opposes a privacy defined largely as the domestic or familial to a publicness defined largely as the economy of wage earners.[84]

Rather than adopting one overarching distinction between the public and the private spheres, a radical, pluralist, identitarian liberal theory would conceptualize the private sphere and the public sphere as occupying the opposite ends of a continuum. The domestic sphere is firmly located within the private sphere; the market economy is understood as either semiprivate or semipublic, depending on the particular institution or practice under consideration (for example, large corporations would be placed in the semipublic realm while small businesses would be located in the semiprivate); and the agencies of the state, all types of media, and so-called cultural institutions would be located in the public sphere.

Rawls has recently developed a new definition of the public sphere, which he terms, following Kant, "the public uses of reason." Rawls would limit the public uses of reason in his well-ordered liberal society to

> presently accepted general beliefs and forms of reasoning found in common sense, and the methods and conclusions of science when these are not controversial. . . . As far as possible, the knowledge and ways of reasoning . . . are to rest on the plain truths widely accepted or available to citizens generally. Otherwise, the political conception would not provide a public basis of justification.[85]

The limitations that Rawls places on the public uses of reason manifests an anxiety about the effect of real disagreements that ensues when people with different outlooks, beliefs, and identities attempt to decide on the particular content of the common good. Rawls thus reduces the domain of the public sphere from the outset in order to preclude any such debates from taking place; however, while his approach may prevent ugly confrontations from taking place in the public sphere, by so severely circumscribing political participation, few real disagreements would ever be resolved—opponents would be left to fight them out in the war of all against all in Rawls's massive private sphere. Although liberalism has traditionally shied away from any commitment to the resolution of differences over the common good in the public sphere, it is essential that a radical revisioning of liberalism not avoid public discussions of differences, however those discussions are manifested. Furthermore, Rawls's decision to include within the realm of public reason only "widely accepted truths" or "accepted beliefs" resembles the communitarian tendency to assume in advance that a common ground exists where in fact none does; this tendency results in the bracketing of differences and implicitly hampers the ability of subordinated groups to participate in the public discourse on an equal footing with the dominant groups. However, a rights-based politics of identity seeks neither to disable the vitality of the public sphere nor to open completely the private sphere to the politics of identity. Instead, the adjudication of identity-based rights claims opens up the public sphere to the equal participation of all groups.

The reach of identity claims extends beyond the traditional list of "natural" identities (race, gender, ethnicity) to which homosexuality has attempted to be added. Religious identities, for example, and the claims based on those identities, also must be construed as a method and subject of political participation. For example, a landlord in California argued that her constitutional right to religious freedom had been restricted by a state civil rights law that did not allow her to discriminate against unmarried couples "living in sin."[86] In this case, then, the landlord, Evelyn Smith, argued that her right of religious expression—what to her was a fundamental aspect of her identity—conflicted with the rights of unmarried couples, which would presumably include lesbian and gay couples, and that her right should take precedence.

While an appellate court agreed with her argument, the highest court in California decided that the policy of not discriminating against unmarried couples did not substantially burden her right to practice her religion. There are three alternative means of adjudicating this conflict: the first approach would be to argue that housing arrangements, especially property rights, are matters that should be left to the private sphere, and should not be subject to state interference. This approach represents a pre-civil-rights type of liberalism, one in which the public sphere is truncated, the private is enlarged, and the state exerts little control over the economic realm.[87] Such an approach accepts Smith's religious beliefs as part of a prepolitical identity, not subject to the whims of the majority. The second approach would be simply to outlaw Smith's discriminatory practices. This approach illustrates the type of nonnegotiable identitarian rights claims that so worries the communitarians: the public sphere, in this case the economic realm, is construed as the realm in which nonnegotiable rights claims are enacted. In this particular case, it would be the identitarian equal protection claims of unmarried same-sex and opposite-sex couples that prevailed because those claims would be seen as nonnegotiable. Finally, the rights-based identitarian approach advocated here would dissect the problem somewhat differently, paying special attention to the boundaries between the private and the public spheres.[88] If the landlord refused to let out rooms in her own house to unmarried couples or to gays or lesbians, that would be allowed within her own zone of freedom. But if the landlord discriminated as a general policy in all the buildings she owned, that practice could be legitimately outlawed since it would fall in the semipublic domain that the elected legislators of the state of California had deemed open to antidiscrimination legislation. A radically pluralist identity-based revisioning of liberalism would adhere to traditional liberalism's preference for procedural fairness over substantively based versions of the good; that is, such a theory would keep the priority of the right over the good intact and would leave traditional standards of morality out of the picture entirely. When rights conflict, the adjudication of those rights claims depends on the determination of the sphere in which the claim is made. Certainly unmarried or queer couples do not have the right to live in the same abode as their landlord because the landlord's right to the free exercise of her religion cannot be abridged in the private sphere. Conversely, a person who rents out hundreds of units is operating in the semipublic sphere, and the people of the state of California have deemed it a public good to prohibit discrimination on the basis of marital status and sexual orientation. Thus, this theory does not understand identity as inhering exclusively in either the private or the public realm, not does it posit a stable distinction between those spheres.

The strategy of asserting that some types of antidiscrimination legislation, especially legislation protecting gays, lesbians, and bisexuals from discrimination, interferes with religious liberty was delineated in a recent *Notre Dame Law Review* article. The author, Richard Duncan, argues that discrimination against African-Americans differs fundamentally from discrimination against gays and lesbians, although not because of the immutability of race:

> Racial discrimination is wrong not because race is immutable and inherent, but rather because it is a morally neutral characteristic. Race tells us nothing about a person's character. Sexual behavior and orientation, however, tell us much about a person's character because they tell us what a person does (or what he is inclined to do).[89]

This argument is premised on asserting a fundamental difference between race and sexual orientation: race is cast not as an immutable characteristic but as a morally neutral one. Homosexuality, however, is not morally neutral, according to Duncan: "Sexual conduct and preferences are fraught with moral and religious significance."[90] Although he dismisses the argument that it is because homosexuality is not immutable that homosexuals are not a protected class, Duncan nevertheless resorts to the favorite weapon of conservatives, the conduct/identity distinction.

This argument appears to be a traditional liberal one: the state should not abrogate the right of individuals to the free exercise of their religion by forcing them not to discriminate against homosexuals. Duncan's argument becomes muddled, however, when he asserts that racial discrimination is wrong because race is a morally neutral category while homosexuality is not: here the argument slides from a liberal private-sphere, rights-based argument to a communitarian common good-based argument. That is, by arguing that antidiscrimination legislation should protect only morally "neutral" categories, Duncan is inserting something other than pure liberal proceduralism into the public sphere: definitions of morality. Morality is, of course, a substantive notion that traditional liberalism attempts to avoid defining. Instead, it focuses on procedural fairness. Thus, Duncan attempts to hide a content-based political vision behind a traditional rights-based argument. (Certainly slavery and segregation were justified by the dominant culture's notion of morality, sanctified by the Bible.) That he is unable to do so indicates the futility of using traditional rights-based liberalism to come to grips with the kind of disagreements between identitarian factions that are commonplace on today's political landscape.

The analogy between race and sexual orientation that many queer advocates attempt to make and many conservatives such as Duncan try to disprove may not be the most fitting one, however. Perhaps in many cases it would be more useful to compare sexual orientation with religious affiliation, or sexual practices with spiritual expression, or sex-radical queers with fundamentalist Christians. It seems clear that the queer rights advocates and the religious right would not be able to disagree so vehemently if there were no fundamental similarities between the way both identities are produced: both depend on communities, cultural networks, shared languages and norms, recognized holidays, even public spectacles such as parades. When homophobic fundamentalist Christians show up at the New York Gay and Lesbian Pride parade every year with signs saying "God hates fags" and "Homosexuality is a sin," the queers, gays, lesbians, bisexuals, transvestites, transsexuals, and homosexuals marching along Fifth Avenue and our detractors shout back, "Shame, shame, shame." That is political deliberation.[91]

Notes

1. Ralph Reed, interviewed on NBC, *Meet the Press,* 29 November 1992.

2. *Hurley v. Irish-American Gay, Lesbian, and Bisexual Group of Boston,* 63 U.S.L.W. 4630 (U.S., June 19, 1995) (No. 94-749).

3. For example, Jean Bethke Elshtain has suggested recently that "[m]ilitant liberationists . . . seek official, mandated protection and approval of their private identities and behaviors. . . . As a result, the demand for public validation of sexual preferences, by ignoring the distinction between the personal and the political, threatens to erode authentic civil rights, including the right to privacy." *Democracy on Trial* (New York: Basic Books, 1995), 57. While maintaining the importance of a strict separation between the public and private spheres—identity should be a strictly private matter—Elshtain has conveniently ignored the fact that the Supreme Court decided in its 1986 *Bowers v. Hardwick* decision that homosexuals have no right to privacy under the Constitution. Similarly, in *The De-Moralization of Society* (New York: Knopf, 1995) Gertrude Himmelfarb has lauded the ability of Victorian family values, including the role of shame, in policing aberrant behavior.

4. While the essentialism-constructionism debate about the origins of "homosexual"—whatever that terms means—identity continues to rage, the search for such "origins" has no effect on the attempt to protect queer practices in the public sphere.

5. Judith Butler's actual phrase is "construction as constitutive constraint," from *Bodies That Matter* (New York and London: Routledge, 1993), xi.

6. See Donn Teal, *The Gay Militants* (New York: Stein and Day, 1971) and Karla Jay and Allen Young, eds., *Out of the Closets* (New York: New York University Press, 1972).

7. Nancy Fraser, "Rethinking the Public Sphere," in *The Phantom Public Sphere,* edited by Bruce Robbins (London and Minneapolis: University of Minnesota Press, 1993), 16.

8. Other recent work by feminist and queer theorists that has argued in support of liberalism and rights in the face of the communitarian critique includes Didi Herman, *Rights of Passage* (Toronto: University of Toronto Press, 1994); Elizabeth Kiss, "Feminism and Rights," *Dissent* (Summer 1995): 342–47; and Kirstie McClure, "On the Subject of Rights: Pluralism, Plurality, and Political Identity," in *Dimensions of Radical Democracy*, edited by Chantal Mouffe (Verso: London, 1992), 108–127.

9. In *The End of Liberalism* (New York and London: W.W. Norton & Company, 1969), Theodore Lowi has shown how interest group politics have overwhelmed the liberal state since the Second World War. In *Habits of the Heart* (New York: Harper and Row, 1985) and *The Good Society* (New York: Alfred A. Knopf, 1991), Robert Bellah, Richard Madsen, William Sullivan, Ann Swidler, and Steven Tipton outline the failed promises of a liberal individualist procedural approach to today's problems. Identity politics have been identified as the cause of liberalism's dissolution. See Amitai Etzioni, *The Spirit of Community: Rights, Responsibilities, and the Communitarian Agenda* (New York: Crown Publishers, 1993); and Michael Sandel, "The Procedural Republic and the Unencumbered Self," *Political Theory* 12 (February 1984): 81–96.

10. This does not hold, of course, for Rousseau's social contract.

11. The Thirteenth Amendment (1865) explicitly prohibits slavery; the Fifteenth Amendment (1879) prohibits denying the right of citizens to vote on account of race, color, or previous condition of servitude; the Nineteenth Amendment (1920) prohibits denying citizens the right to vote on account of sex. U.S. Constitution.

12. Many commentators saw the 1994 U.S. congressional elections, in which white male voters supported the Republicans by a margin of 63 to 37 percent, as the marking the emergence of a powerful white, male voting bloc. See Thomas B. Edsall, "Revolt of the Discontented," 11 November 1994, *Washington Post*; and Susan Estrich, "The Last Victim," 18 December 1994, *New York Times Magazine*.

13. Rawls's *A Theory of Justice* (Cambridge, MA: Harvard University Press, 1971) obviously exemplifies the most extreme version of what Michael Sandel has termed "de-ontological liberalism"; Rawls has since attempted to base his liberal theory on politics rather than metaphysics, although some of his original critics do not appear satisfied. See Rawls, *Political Liberalism* (New York: Columbia University Press, 1993). Michael Sandel's communitarian evaluation of de-ontological liberalism, which I believe set the standard for the communitarian critique of liberalism's notions of identity, appears in *Liberalism and the Limits of Justice* (Cambridge: Cambridge University Press, 1982).

14. Important communitarian texts include: Michael Sandel, *Liberalism and the Limits of Justice*; Alasdair MacIntyre, *After Virtue* (South Bend, Indiana: University of Notre Dame Press, 1981); and Charles Taylor, "Cross-Purposes: The Liberal-Communitarian Debate," in *Liberalism and the Moral Life*, edited by Nancy Rosenblum (Cambridge, MA: Harvard University Press, 1989), 159–82 and *Sources of the Self* (Cambridge: Cambridge University Press, 1990). Other critics who could be identified with communitarian theory but who also develop and advocate antiliberal policy positions include Robert Bellah, Jean Bethke Elshtain, Amitai Etzioni, William Galston, and Mary Ann Glendon.

15. See John Locke, *Two Treatises of Government*, edited by Peter Laslett (Cambridge: Cambridge University Press, 1960); Thomas Hobbes, *Leviathan* (New York: Penguin, 1968); Rawls, *A Theory of Justice*; and Robert Nozick, *Anarchy, State, and Utopia* (Oxford: Blackwell, 1974). Charles Taylor lays out the liberal traditions view of identity very clearly in Taylor, "Atomism," in *Philosophy and the Human Sciences: Philosophical Papers 2* (Cambridge: Cambridge University Press, 1985), 187–210.

16. John Locke, *Two Treatises of Government*, 318, 330, 346.

17. Sandel, *Liberalism and the Limits of Justice*, 20.

18. For example, Alasdair MacIntyre contrasts modern individualism's version of identity with what he calls a "narrative" understanding of identity. He writes, "For the story of my life is always embedded in the story of those communities from which I derive my identity. I am born with a past; and to try to cut myself off from that past in an individualistic mode is to deform my present relationships." MacIntyre, *After Virtue*, 221.

19. See Bellah et al., *Habits of the Heart* and *The Good Society*.

20. This move is analogous to Habermas's much-maligned conception of the public sphere as a discursive arena where differences are already bracketed, though Habermas could not be cast as a communitarian. Iris Young, in *Justice and the Politics of Difference* (Princeton: Princeton University Press, 1990), has thoroughly examined the problematic implications of Habermas's conception of the public sphere and the kind of communicative ethics he envisions taking place there. Nancy Fraser also has a critique of Habermas's "bourgeois, masculinist" public sphere: "Rethinking the Public Sphere," in *The Phantom Public Sphere*, edited by Bruce Robbins (London and Minneapolis: University of Minnesota Press, 1993), 1–32.

21. In "Polity and Group Difference: A Critique of the Ideal of Universal Citizenship," *Ethics* 99 (January 1989): 252, 258, Iris Young notes,

"The ideal of the public realm of citizenship as expressing a general will, a point of view and interest that citizens have in common which transcends their differences, has operated in fact as a demand for homogeneity among citizens." Young asserts that the desire for unity expressed in communitarian theory "suppresses but does not eliminate differences and tends to exclude some perspectives from the public."

22. Alasdair MacIntyre ends his opus thus:

What matters at this stage is the construction of local forms of community within which civility and the intellectual and moral life can be sustained through the new dark ages which are already upon us. And if the tradition of the virtues was able to survive the horrors of the last dark ages, we are not entirely without grounds for hope. This time however the barbarians are not waiting beyond the frontiers; they have already been governing us for some time. And it is our lack of consciousness of this that constitutes part of our predicament. We are waiting not for a Godot, but for another—doubtless very different—St. Benedict.

After Virtue, 263.

23. Michael Warner has used the word "heteronormative" to refer to heterosexual ideology, "heterosexual culture's exclusive ability to interpret itself as society." See Warner's introduction to *Fear of a Queer Planet*, edited by Michael Warner (Minneapolis: University of Minnesota Press, 1993), xxi–xxv.

24. Stephen Holmes, "The Permanent Structure of Antiliberal Thought," in *Liberalism and the Moral Life*, edited by Nancy Rosenblum (Cambridge, MA: Harvard University Press, 1989), 232.

25. Bellah et al., *Habits of the Heart,* 72–74: "the lifestyle enclave is an expression of private life. It is linked most closely to leisure and consumption. . . . It brings together those who are socially, economically, or culturally similar, and one of its chief aims is the enjoyment of being with those who 'share one's lifestyle.' . . . Whereas a community attempts to be an inclusive whole, celebrating the interdependence of public and private life and of the different callings of all, lifestyle is fundamentally segmental and celebrates the narcissism of similarity. . . . The contemporary lifestyle enclave is based on a degree of individual choice that largely frees it from traditional ethnic and religious boundaries . . . most obvious in large cities."

26. The fact that communities are not free of oppression is obviously a fundamental aspect of any critique of communitarianism, but I am not pursuing that here because it has been pursued so thoroughly elsewhere. See, for example, Marilyn Friedman, "Feminism and Modern Friendship: Dislocating the Community," *Ethics* 99 (January 1989): 279.

Friedman has pointed out that "civic republican theory fails to acknowledge that many communities make illegitimate moral claims on their members, linked to hierarchies of domination and subordination." Similarly, in *Identity Politics: Lesbian Feminism and the Limits of Community* (Philadelphia: Temple University Press, 1989), Shane Phelan examined the communitarian impulse in lesbian feminist discourse of the 1970s and '80s. She found that as lesbians attempted to construct for themselves an identity that was not based on psychoanalytic pathologizing of their sexuality, "lesbian feminists did not deal with the problem of difference. . . . Any sense of the plurality of lesbian lives was lost in the construction of 'the' lesbian" (138). Amy Gutmann also finds the political implications of communitarianism ominous. Although, as she notes, many communitarian theorists adopt a rhetoric of openness and inclusion, the effects of a dependence on notions of tradition and family may not bear out the openness they promise. In fact, one of the leading communitarian theorists, Michael Sandel, in a rare discussion of communitarian policy preferences, admits that "communitarians would be more likely than liberals to allow a town to ban pornographic bookstores, on the grounds that pornography offends the way of life and values that sustain it." Arguing that communitarianism does not breed intolerance, Sandel writes, "intolerance flourishes most where forms of life are dislocated, roots unsettled, traditions undone." "Morality and the Liberal Ideal," *New Republic*, May 7, 1984, p. 17.

Given the above example of a communitarian policy preference, this hoped-for tolerance seems somewhat unlikely, as Gutmann suggests: "if Sandel is arguing that when members of a society have settled roots and established traditions, they will tolerate the speech, religion, sexual, and associational preferences of minorities, then history simply does not bear out his optimism." Gutmann, "Communitarian Critics of Liberalism," *Philosophy and Public Affairs* 14 (Summer 1985): 319.

27. See Cornel West, *Keeping Faith: Philosophy and Race in America* (New York: Routledge, 1993), 228.

28. Fraser, "Rethinking the Public Sphere," 14. Fraser uses late-twentieth-century U.S. feminism as an example of a counterpublic "with its variegated array of journals, bookstores, publishing companies, film and video distribution networks, lecture series, research centers, academic programs, conferences, conventions, festivals, and local meeting places."

29. Simone de Beauvoir, *The Second Sex*, translated by H.M. Parshley (New York: Vintage Books, 1989), 267.

30. Bill Perkins, chairman of Colorado for Family Values, quoted on CBS, "Bill Moyers' Journal," November 1993.

31. There are three criteria that must be met before suspect class status is achieved: first, the group in question must have suffered a history of discrimination; second, they must be relatively politically powerless to pursue their grievances through majoritarian processes; third, and most importantly for gays, lesbians, and bisexuals, the group in question must be characterized by an immutable characteristic. Once a category is designated a suspect class, any law that singles out the class, either directly or, more commonly, indirectly, is subject to "strict scrutiny" by the courts. If a law singles out a class of people that the Supreme Court has designated "quasi-suspect," then that law is subject to "heightened" scrutiny by the courts. For the law that fences out a suspect class to pass constitutional muster, the state must show that it supports a compelling state interest and that it is narrowly drawn to achieve that interest; in the case of a quasi-suspect class, the state must demonstrate that the law in question is substantially related to a legitimate government interest. Thus far race and national ancestry origin have been designated suspect categories by the Supreme Court; gender and illegitimacy have been deemed quasi-suspect categories. The suspect class designation has made it easier to declare unconstitutional statutes that indirectly discriminate against African-Americans, most notably housing laws. Cases challenging discrimination on the basis of gender, a quasi-suspect designation, have fared less well, although some challenges have been successful. Recently, the Supreme Court applied "skeptical scrutiny" to the Virginia Military Institute's refusal to admit women to its publicly funded program, finding that VMI's justification for excluding women was not "exceedingly persuasive." *U.S. v. Virginia*, 1996 WL 345786, 10, 11 (U.S.). If no suspect or quasi-suspect classes are involved in an equal protection challenge, the state must indicate only that the state action at issue is rationally related to a legitimate government interest. For a more sustained discussion of the gay, lesbian, and bisexual quest for suspect class status, see Paisley Currah, "Searching for Immutability: Homosexuality, Race, and Rights Discourse," in *A Simple Matter of Justice*, edited by Angelia R. Wilson (London: Cassell Press, 1995).

32. See, for example, *High Tech Gays v. Defense Indus. Sec. Clearance Office*, 895 F.2d 563, 571 (9th Cir. 1990); *Ben-Shalom v. Marsh*, 881 F.2d 454, 464 (7th Cir. 1989), cert. denied sub nom. *Ben-Shalom v. Stone*, 494 U.S. 1004 (1990); *Woodward v. United States*, 871 F.2d 1068, 1076 (Fed. Cir. 1989), cert. denied, 494 U.S. 1003 (1990); *Padula v. Webster*, 822 F.2d 97 103 (D.C. Cir. 1987).

33. *Padula v. Webster*, 822 F.2d 97, 103 (D.C. Cir. 1987).

34. This decision, on the constitutionality of Cincinnati's "Issue 3," which would have amended the Cincinnati's city charter to ban laws and poli-

cies prohibiting discrimination against gays, lesbians, and bisexuals, was vacated by the U.S. Supreme Court in light of *Evans v. Romer*. *Equality Foundation of Greater Cincinnati, Inc. v. City of Cincinnati*, 54 F.3rd 261, 267 (6th Cir. 1995), vacated and remanded 64 U.S.L.W. 3831 (U.S. June 17, 1996).

35. Karl E. Klare, "Power/Dressing: Regulation of Employee Appearance," 26 *New England Law Review* 1395, 1411 (Summer 1992).

36. See, for example, Richard Green's affidavit on homosexual orientation as an immutable characteristic, from *Steffan v. Cheney*, 780 F.Supp. 1 (D.D.C. 1991) and reprinted in *Gays in the Military: Joseph Steffan versus the United States*, edited by Kenneth Sherrill and Marc Wolinsky (Princeton: Princeton University Press, 1993), 56–83.

37. Colorado for Family Values pamphlet, cited in Donna Minkowitz, "The Christian Right's Anti-Gay Campaign," *Christianity and Crisis*, 12 April 1993.

38. "Doctors Dismiss OCA Argument," *Oregonian*, 1 October 1992, cited in Nicholas Strinkowski, "Oregon's Ballot Measure 9: Religious Fundamentalism, Gay Activism, and the Political Center," presented at the Annual Meeting of the American Political Science Association, September 2–5, 1993.

39. Cited in *Evans v. Romer*, 854 P.2d 1270, 1272 (Colo. 1993).

40. Oregon's Ballot Measure 9.

41. Cited in *Evans v. Romer*, 854 P.2d 1270, 1272 (Colo. 1993).

42. CNN, *Evans and Novak,* 12 February 1994.

43. "Christian Coalition," *Atlanta Constitution*, 4 June 1994.

44. "Colorado's Gay-Rights War Worries Some Christians," *Times-Picayune*, 2 May 1993.

45. "Gays See Growing Backlash," *Boston Globe*, 28 November 1993.

46. Ibid.

47. "Hawkins Backs Bill to Define Minority Status," *Idaho Falls Post Register*, 8 February 1994.

48. "Anti-Gay Group May Go Statewide," *UPI,* 16 February 1994. These are but a few of the myriad examples of the "special rights" rhetoric being utilized by the religious right wing. Indeed, a Nexus search of the national and regional news media from the period July 1, 1992 to November 1, 1994 that asked for any news article or transcript that contained the word "special" within five words of the words "homosexual" or "homosexuals" generated 1033 items.

49. "Gays See Growing Backlash," *Boston Globe*, 28 November 1993.

50. Many of Oregon's Ballot Measure 9 advocates interviewed by Heather MacDonald for her film "Ballot Measure 9" refer, directly or indirectly, to the costs of affirmative action to "ordinary Americans" in support of their arguments for the amendment. For powerful analysis of the Christian right's rhetoric around rights discourse, based on interviews with the Christian right activists behind these antigay amendments, see Didi Herman's *The AntiGay Agenda: Orthodox Vision and the Christian Right* (Chicago: University of Chicago Press, forthcoming in 1997).

51. Though it is true that statistics can be used as evidence in discrimination claims.

52. Though now it appears that affirmative action is under attack from many sides: The Supreme Court has recently severely restricted the scope of permissible affirmative action policies. *Adarand Constructors, Inc. v. Pena*, 115 S.Ct. 2097 (1995). And its decision not to review a Fifth Circuit decision finding a University of Texas affirmative action policy unconstitutional leaves the issue unresolved. *Texas v. Hopwood*, 84 F.3d 710 (5th Cir., 1996), cert. denied (U.S., July 1, 1996).

53. During the 1992 campaign for Ballot Measure 9 in Oregon, Lon Mabon argued that the measure was merely intended to prevent homosexuals from gaining legal status as a minority. "The Measure 9 campaign draws a line in the sand that says, 'No more.'" Cited in "Oregon Voters Weigh Anti-Homosexual Rights Ballot," *Orlando Sentinel Tribune*, 4 October 1992.

54. "Text of Pentagon's New Policy Guidelines on Homosexuals in the Military," *New York Times*, 20 July 1993.

55. I thank Suzanne Goldberg of Lambda Legal Defense and Education Fund for this example.

56. *Rowland v. Mad River Local School District, Montgomery County*, 470 U.S. 1004, 1009 (1985) (J. Brennan, dissenting from denial of cert.).

57. *Evans v. Romer*, 854 P.2d 1270, 1285 (Colo. 1993). The Colorado Supreme Court laid out its reasoning finding Amendment 2 unconstitutional when it upheld a temporary injunction prohibiting the enforcement of Amendment 2 by a lower court. Its actual decision on the case can be found in *Evans v. Romer*, 882 P.2d 1335 (Colo. 1994).

58. *Evans v. Romer*, 854 P.2d 1270 (Colo. 1993).

59. The decision upholding the constitutionality of state laws that criminalize homosexual sodomy in *Bowers v. Hardwick*, 478 U.S. 186 (1986) was based on the notion that there existed no substantive right to commit homosexual sodomy.

60. See John Ely, *Democracy and Distrust* (Cambridge, MA and London: Harvard University Press, 1980), 87.

61. *Evans v. Romer*, 116 S.Ct. 1620, 1628 (1996).

62. Brief of Laurence H. Tribe, John Hart Ely, Gerald Gunther, Philip B. Kurland, and Kathleen M. Sullivan, in support of respondents at 1, *Evans v. Romer,* 854 P.2d 1270 (Colo. 1993) (No. 94-1039). Justice Kennedy, in the majority opinion, writes that, "A law declaring that in general it shall be more difficult for one group of citizens than for all others to seek aid from the government is itself a denial of equal protection of the laws in the most literal sense." *Evans v. Romer*, 116 S.Ct. 1620, 1628 (U.S.).

63. *Evans v. Romer*, 116 S.Ct. 1620, 1626, 1627 (1996).

64. Ely, *Democracy and Distrust*, 87.

65. Shane Phelan made these remarks at the 1995 Meeting of the Western Political Science Association, Portland, Oregon, March 1995.

66. See, for example, Janet Halley, "The Construction of Heterosexuality," in *Fear of a Queer Planet*, edited by Michael Warner (Minneapolis: University of Minnesota Press, 1993).

67. See *Capitol Square Review and Advisory Board v. Pinette*, 115 S.Ct. 2440 (1995) and *Rosenberger v. Rector of the University of Virginia*, 115 S.Ct. 2510 (1995).

68. Recently, the Second Circuit indicated that the new policy might be constitutional. *Able v. USA*, 1996 U.S. App. LEXIS 15737 (2d Cir. July 1, 1996). And in another decision, the Fourth Circuit also recently found policy constitutional. *Thomason v. Perry*, 1996 WL 157451 (April 1996). The Ninth Circuit will soon rule on the issue in another case, *Philips v. Perry*, 883 F. Supp. 539 (W.D. Wash, 1995), cert. granted.

69. Iowa City Human Rights Code, ordinance number 95-3697, passed October 1995. And San Francisco altered its human rights code to include gender identity as well, defining gender identity as "a person's various individual attributes as they are understood to be masculine *and/or* feminine" [italics added]. San Francisco Civic Ordinance Number 433-94, passed December 1994. Minnesota's human rights act does not include gender identity, but it does define sexual orientation as "having or being perceived as having an emotional, physical, or sexual attachment to another person without regard to the sex of that person or having or being perceived as having an orientation for such an attachment, or *having or being perceived as having a self-image or identity not traditionally associated with one's biological maleness or femaleness*" [italics added]. Minnesota Statues 1992, section 363.01, subdivision 23.

70. This line of thinking can be (and has been) charted in the "state of nature" tradition, including the work of Thomas Hobbes, John Locke,

and, more recently, John Rawls. But it is important to avoid construing texts from the liberal state of nature tradition as hard and fast theories about the relation between identity and the political order; rather, examining their status as narratives, or counternarratives, to the prevailing organicist notions may result in more illuminating readings. C.B. Macpherson has argued, for example, that Hobbes's conception of man's essence (as an essentially desirous consumer of utility) in fact depends for its coherence on an understanding of men's interaction with each other in society. See *The Political Theory of Possessive Individualism* (Oxford: Oxford University Press, 1962), 17–46. Even Rawls has amended his initial theory in response to criticisms of the ahistorical Archimedean position of the rational subject of liberalism. See John Rawls, *Political Liberalism*, 22–28.

71. See Ronald Dworkin, "Rights as Trumps," in *Theories of Rights*, edited by Jeremy Waldron (Oxford: Oxford University Press, 1984), 153–67.

72. Sara Evans has described the birth of identity politics in the women's movement's splitting away from the male-dominated (yet supposedly universalist) new left movement of the 1960s. See *Personal Politics* (New York: Vintage, 1980).

73. Mary Ann Glendon, *Rights Talk* (New York: Free Press, 1992), 1–17.

74. See Charles Taylor, "Atomism," in *Philosophy and the Human Sciences*: Philosophical Paper 2, 187–210.

75. Sandel, *Liberalism and the Limits of Justice*, 62.

76. Ibid.

77. See Bellah et al., *Habits of the Heart*, 27–51

78. Though Amitai Etzioni, who often speaks for communitarians, generously refuses to rule out the participation of nondominant groups in the communitarian vision: "While of course it is true that the socioeconomic structure makes it easier for some people than others to follow a communitarian course, nobody should be written off just because they are in the wrong structural position." Amitai Etzioni, "On Communitarianism and Its Inclusive Agenda," *Tikkun* 8, 50.

79. Christopher Lasch, "Who Owes What To Whom," *Harper's*, February 1991, 48.

80. Margaret O'Brien Steinfels, "Rights and Responsibilities," *Dissent* (Spring 1994): 269–71.

81. For Elshtain, it is because certain social goods are at stake that, for example, society must distinguish between heterosexual families and homosexual "lifestyles":

No social order has ever existed that did not endorse certain activities and practices as preferable to others. Every social order forges terms of exclusion and inclusion. Ethically responsible challenges to our terms of exclusion and inclusion push towards a loosening but not a wholesale negation in our normative endorsement of intergenerational family life. In defining family authority, then, one acknowledges that one is *privileging* relations of a particular kind when and where certain social goods are at stake [emphasis in original].

Jean Bethke Elshtain, *Power Trips and Other Journeys* (Madison: University of Wisconsin Press, 1990), 60.

82. Lisa Bower, "Queer Acts and the Politics of 'Direct Address': Rethinking Law, Culture, and Community," 28 *Law and Society Review* 1009, 1030. See also Chantal Mouffe, "Democratic Citizenship and Political Community," in *Dimensions of Radical Democracy*, edited by Chantal Mouffe (London and New York: Verso, 1992).

83. See Arthur F. Bentley, *The Process of Government* (Cambridge, MA: Harvard University Press, 1908); David Truman, *The Governmental Process* (New York: Knopf, 1951); Earl Latham, *The Group Basis of Politics* (Ithaca, NY: Cornell University Press, 1952); Theodore Lowi, *The End of Liberalism* (New York and London: Oxford University Press, 1969); and William Connolly, "The Challenge to Pluralist Theory," in *The Bias of Pluralism*, edited by William Connolly (New York: Atherton Press, 1969), 3–34.

84. Bruce Robbins, Introduction to *The Phantom Public Sphere*, edited by Bruce Robbins (Minneapolis: University of Minnesota Press, 1993), xiii.

85. John Rawls, *Political Liberalism*, 224.

86. In this particular case, the Supreme Court of California reversed a lower court's ruling that held that the landlord's right to the free exercise of her religion had been violated. The landlord did not reside in the building in question. *Smith v. Commission of Fair Empl. & Hous.*, 12 Cal. 4th 1143 (1996). In another housing discrimination case involving an unmarried couple, an Alaska court found that a landlord's freedom of religion was outweighed by the state's interest in preventing discrimination against unmarried couples. *Swanner v. Anchorage Equal Rights Com'n.*, 874 P.2d 274 (Alaska 1994), cert. denied 115 S.Ct. 460 (1994).

87. This approach resembles the argument made by Andrew Sullivan, in *Virtually Normal* (New York: Knopf, 1995), 171. He limits his definition of the public realm to the state and suggests that this public-private distinction should be inviolable. Thus, while the state should not make any distinctions between heterosexuals and homosexuals, those in "culture and society at large" may make any distinctions they like.

88. Michael Walzer has also suggested flexibility in applying what he calls "pluralistic principles of justice." See his *Sphere of Justice* (New York: Basic Books, 1983).

89. Richard F. Duncan, "Who Wants to Stop the Church: Homosexual Rights Legislation, Public Policy, and Religious Freedom," 63 *Notre Dame Law Review* 393, 402–403 (1994).

90. Ibid., 403–404.

91. I would like to thank Monica Barrett, Susan Buck-Morss, Christine Di Stefano, Zillah Eisenstein, David Kahane, Isaac Kramnick, Shannon Minter, Debra Morris, and Shane Phelan for their comments and advice on various drafts of this article.

11
Queer Problems/Straight Solutions: The Limits of a Politics of "Offcial Recognition"

Lisa Bower

Scholarship mapping the terrain between law and the emerging field of "queer theory" attempts to move away from a reliance upon identity politics. At least through the 1970s, a cohesive lesbian or gay identity was embraced as part of an emancipatory strategy which could be used for political purposes, including positive legal change for gays and lesbians. The most significant events conspiring to create a crisis in and around this unproblematized conception of identity politics were: the AIDS crisis and the right-wing backlash which developed in response to it; the politicization of internal differences within gay communities over questions of race and "correct" sexual practices; and the pivotal 1986 Supreme Court decision in *Bowers v Hardwick*[1] and subsequent cases which insidiously deployed the trope of identity to establish that homosexuals do not have a "fundamental right" to engage in sodomy.

In the aftermath of these events, activists acknowledged the need for a "critical theory linking gay empowerment to broad institutional change."[2] Queer readings of law and legal doctrine are fairly recent contributions to this political project.[3] Practitioners of what could now be deemed queer legal theory such as Paisley Currah, Janet Halley, and Carl Stychin have brilliantly demonstrated how legal discourse creates norms which universalize particular modes of living, and specific identities and acts, while suppressing other practices and identities which appear deviant or abnormal. In light of the Supreme Court's opinion in *Hardwick,* these theorists have focused on

268 / Queer Agendas

the practices of categorization whereby juridical conceptions of homosexuality and heterosexuality are themselves produced. Not legal categories, but legal constructions of identity, should be the focal point, Halley writes: "The searching examination of cultural identity formation which has been underway in feminist criticism, critical race theory, and queer critique in recent years should now be involved in the development of legal strategy."[4] Exposing the juridical effort expended to maintain compulsory heterosexuality and the stability of the homosexual/heterosexual binary, their efforts to unsettle legal constructions of homosexual and heterosexual identities promise to extend the scope of queer theory.

In spite of their compelling deconstruction of the relationship between legal doctrine and sexual identities, and their recognition of how the ambiguities and the politics of juridical inclination bode poorly for the acknowledgement of transformative legal or political change, Currah, Halley, and Stychin ultimately resort to doctrinal solutions. They evade the implications of their own analyses, embracing instead a politics of "official recognition" that assumes the modern constitutional state is the privileged site of political action. A return to legal categories valorizes a conception of identity, requiring us to recognize the "other" as like "ourselves," and activating a view of community as constituted by shared affiliations.[5]

Rather than seeking a legal solution which would fit the queer "other" within some space already acknowledged by the liberal nation-state, I want to explore how destabilizing both law and identity categories might provide an alternative conception of the relationship between these terms and instigate a different kind of political practice. In comparison to a politics of "official recognition," this politics of "direct address," as Kirstie McClure has described it, redefines the political to include the "everyday enactment of social practices and the routine reiteration of cultural representations."[6] And it also invites a reconfiguration of community which does not depend on a logic of sameness, emphasizing the importance of identification as opposed to identity.

Since the 1986 Supreme Court decision in *Bowers v. Hardwick* is the legal case around which queer legal theory initially organized itself, I will first focus on queer legal theorists' response to *Hardwick*. At the most general level, my purpose is to describe briefly how this decision forced gay and lesbian rights activists to rethink their strategies for engaging with law, and how queer legal theorists have met this challenge. While Currah and Halley aptly demonstrate the doctrinal pecularities of the *Hardwick* opinion and subsequent cases, they miss an opportunity to explore the implications of the incoherence of *all sexual identities*. In other words, what potential might the legal field afford for the articulation of *nonidentity* when such articulations operate to explode legal categories and the taxonomies supporting dominant, unitary classifications of identity?

To explore answers to this question, I turn to a 1984 employment discrimination case, *Ulane v. Eastern Airlines,* in which Karen Ulane was fired by

Eastern Airlines after having sex reassignment surgery. Read together, the district court case (*Ulane v Eastern Airlines* 1984; hereafter "*Ulane I*")[7] and the court of appeals case (*Ulane v Eastern Airlines* 1984; hereafter "*Ulane II*")[8] offer a less strained reading of the dialectical interplay between subject positions and juridical power than queer legal theorists' interpretation of *Hardwick.* Unlike the latter decision, *Ulane I* provides a riveting narrative about the subversive deployment of identity that suggests the queer possibilities of articulating nonidentity. On the other hand, the *Hardwick* opinion and the appellate court decision in *Ulane II* invoke an "imagined [heterosexual] community,"[9] one corresponding to the definitions constructed in and by legal discourse. Queer legal theorists must interrogate the mutual constitution of community and identity. We must attend to how the language of community and its allied view of identity is used within the juridical field as "an authorizing force of exclusion."[10]

Finally, as I suggest below, if queers refuse the discursive subject positions and configurations of community embedded in a politics of "official recognition," then they might focus instead on the cultural contestations, and the transformation and shifting of identifications which legal decisions enable. In short, queer legal theory needs to take into account the new styles of politics—such as Queer Nation's cultural improvisations—which developed in response to *Hardwick* for, consequentially, the relationship between law and politics has been fundamentally altered.

Doctrinal Solutions to Queer Problems

In *Hardwick,* the Supreme Court found there was no "fundamental right" to engage in homosexual sodomy. While the Georgia statute specifically stated "[Any] *person* commits the offense of sodomy when he performs or submits to a sexual act involving the sex organs of one person and the mouth or anus of another . . . ,"[11] the Court found the statute applied only to homosexuals. Writing for the majority, Justice White found the right to privacy does not extend to homosexual sodomy (and this constituted his reason for the dismissal of the fundamental rights argument). He also found the statute constitutional under the rational basis test, noting the "majority of the electorate in Georgia [believe] homosexual sodomy is immoral and unacceptable."[12] Queer theorists, however, have argued that due to rhetorical slippage in the Court's opinion, the issue in *Hardwick* was framed as one of "homosexual sodomy." The Supreme Court decision thus enacted "a sodometry [by fixing] an identity based on acts."[13] This litigation interrupted lesbian and gay activists' identity-based engagement with law and forced them to face the limits of liberal tolerance.

Prior to *Hardwick,* gay rights advocates argued "that homosexual orientation is unitary, fundamental, irresistible and inalterable."[14] Homosexuality was viewed as immutable, that is, biologically determined.[15] Judicial acceptance of such an argument would situate gays and lesbians as a suspect class, which would lead to legal gains. One benefit of claiming a suspect class would be that homosexuality, like race, would be accorded "heightened scrutiny" under the Fourteenth Amendment equal protection clause. Sexual orientation discrimination would require that such action be justified by a "compelling state" interest. For example, an employer's alleged discriminatory practices against gays or lesbians would have to be justified by an overriding state interest and could not be based on mere administrative convenience.

The confusion engendered by the *Hardwick* decision, specifically the conflation of acts and identity as defining features of homosexuality, created a legal nightmare as later courts attempted to interpret the *Hardwick* holding. For the Supreme Court to reach the conclusion that homosexual sodomy was unconstitutional, they had to perform what Naomi Mezey has described as "wholesale rhetorical recategorization [thereby] wrenching heterosexual identity free from the act of sodomy while making sodomy the equivalent of homosexual identity."[16] For example, in *Padula v Webster*,[17] the plaintiff argued that the FBI violated her right to equal protection by refusing to hire her because she was homosexual, but the appellate court argued that "conduct" defines "identity":

> [B]ecause *Hardwick* allowed states to criminalize "the behavior that defines the class, it is hardly open to a lower court to conclude that state-sponsored discrimination against the class is invidious. After all there can hardly be more palpable discrimination against a class than making the conduct that defines the class criminal."[18]

In other words, the *Padula* court followed the logic of *Hardwick* and asserted that *Hardwick* permits states to criminalize same-sex sodomy, and such practices are "the behavior that defines the class." The use of the *Hardwick* precedent thus precluded the application of heightened scrutiny in future cases of apparent discrimination against gays and lesbians.[19]

Gay rights advocates responded to cases such as *Padula* by pursuing legal strategies that would convincingly demonstrate that the "class," gays, lesbians, and bisexuals, was not defined solely by the behavior or act of sodomy. As Halley notes, "litigators set out to constrain *Hardwick* by framing equal protection cases in which plaintiffs had been subjected to unfavorable treatment not because of any sexual conduct but because of their public and private identities as gay, lesbian or bisexual."[20] However, this strategy also proved ineffective. Many courts were unable to make the distinction between conduct and identity because they were operating within the terms set by the *Hardwick* precedent.[21] As a result, arguments that homosexuality can be defined either by sexual acts or as an immutable characteristic of identity have failed to attract the desired suspect classification for lesbians, gays, and bisexuals.

Accordingly, gay rights activists turned to the task of redefining legal definitions of homosexuality. In "The Politics of the Closet," which arguably represents the first article in a wave of queer legal scholarship addressing the doctrinal peculiarities of *Bowers v Hardwick,* Halley suggests it is necessary to ascertain "how the class of homosexuals is constituted."[22] Drawing on empirical research, she argues any emphasis on a fixed sexual orientation identity, whether by the court or by gay rights activists, is ill founded and empirically incorrect. Sexual identities are neither simply fixed nor constitutively unstable. For some, sexual orientation may be a question of choice, while for others this choice is foreclosed. As Halley elaborates, for most individuals sexual orientation is fundamentally mutable "not only in its practice but also in its manifestation."[23] Homosexual identities must be continually (re)constructed within a milieu defined by the dominance of heterosexuality. And when the cost of claiming a homosexual "identity" (or having it claimed for you) is loss of employment and other material benefits, there is pressure to engage the definitive expression of mutability, "passing." Conversely, when the assertion of one's sexual orientation identity activates the withdrawal of such benefits, the harms may be even more nefarious.

Developing the theoretical insights sketched out in "The Politics of the Closet," Halley refines them as she addresses the *Hardwick* opinion directly in "Misreading Sodomy" and "The Construction of Heterosexuality." In the former, Halley argues the *Hardwick* decision was a hegemonic move for putatively heterosexual America. To reduce homosexual identity to a unitary essence based upon a singular behavior stabilizes heterosexual identity. As she points out, it is "heterosexuality" that is implicitly, but insistently, called into question in the "sodomy" cases. To describe homosexuality as different is a means of displacing the anxieties and doubts which sustain the classification "heterosexual" as a cohesive class. Expanding this point, Halley claims the mutability of sexual orientation identity might be utilized to demonstrate the instability of heterosexuality by showing how heterosexuals, as a class, "predicate homosexual identity upon acts of sodomy in a constantly eroding effort to police [their] own coherence and referentiality."[24] Settling down to an admirable deconstruction of the hetero/homosexual binary, Halley shows how ultimately the *Hardwick* opinion was a desperate, covert attempt to (re)constitute heterosexuality as a stable category. At the same time, she glosses over the instability of homosexuality, thereby missing an opportunity to highlight the ambiguity of all sexual orientation identities, an argument she so carefully developed in "The Politics of the Closet."[25]

In this latter article, Halley returns to the constitutional context for a resolution to the dilemma she has identified. She suggests a doctrinal alternative which will avoid the mutability/immutability conundrum. Drawing on Justice Stone's famous "Footnote 4," which called for the protection of "discrete and insular minorities" particularly when discrimination against such groups curtails their access to the political arena,[27] Halley claims that antihomosexual discrimination and the hegemony of heterosexuality "interfere sharply, albeit indirectly, with the political process."[28] At a minimum, an important constituency—one available to contest sodomy laws, and the notion of a "sodomitical" essence as an accurate description of either homosexuality or homosexuals—is deterred from engaging in public debate. Doctrinally framed, lesbians, gays, and bisexuals are denied the fundamental right to claim protection for a public identity protected by the political process. Proof of such denial would activate the most stringent level of review under the Fourteenth Amendment equal protection clause, "heightened scrutiny."[29]

Why does Halley return to legal categories and classifications to "solve" the problem of juridical interpretations of homosexuality? One answer is intimated by Halley herself when she argues that the deconstruction of the homosexual/heterosexual binary might create "a problem unanticipated in purely textualist critical theory: the use of incoherent and multiple identities not to deconstruct a monolithic cultural binarism, but to enforce one."[30] Identifying a potential pitfall of deconstructive scholarship, Halley argues that exposing the instability of any category may have little effect on hegemonic power relations and, equally worrisome, such efforts will almost always be seized as discursive opportunities by both gay and antigay forces.[31] Applying this insight to the legal field, a problem familiar to socio-legal scholars emerges: rights have the capacity to "cut both ways," to activate social change, to reinforce hegemonic values, and to fix identity and enable its articulation.[32] If this instability is a feature of any discursive field, including law, might it be used to strategic advantage?

In an article that often parallels Halley's, Currah examines flaws in arguments privileging the immutability perspective. Like Halley, Currah shows how cases decided in light of *Hardwick* continue to conflate acts and identities; also like Halley, Currah points to the need for an alternative to the suspect classification approach. Arguing that "the identity-based approach to what used to be called 'gay liberation' must undergo a thorough interrogation,"[33] Currah proposes that the rational basis test might accommodate the complex relationship between law and culture, given that the judiciary "reflects and participates in the culture's construction of sexuality."[34] Noting *Hardwick* instigated the formation of a "new social movement" of gays, lesbians, and bisexuals, and that the "movement generated an oppositional discourse that provided an alternative to anti-homophobic narratives which in turn made the military's ban on gays, lesbians and bisexuals seem 'irrational' in some courts,"[35] she stresses the historically contingent nature of rationality, and the mutual interplay between law and culture. Currah can then "queer" the rational basis test and argue for the importance of "infus[ing] cultural constructions with counter-narratives" as a means of changing juridical discourse.[36] Opting for a solution that relies on a return to legal doctrine, the rational basis test, Currah stops short of developing her insights about the relationship among (and between) law, culture, and political change.

Stychin explores this relationship in *Law's Desire: Sexuality and the Limits of Justice,* the first book about queer legal theory to date. His discussion of a number of legal cases and controversies in Britain, Canada, and the United States is framed by an analysis of the postmodern, queer subject. Working the connections among cultural studies, poststructuralism, and law, he explores "how identities are formed and expressed in the cultural environment of the late 20th century," and how "new forms of political subjectivity [might be constructed] through cultural production and consumption."[37] Incorporating Rosemary Coombe's pathbreaking work.[38] Stychin argues that while law limits the articulation of homosexual identities, it cannot in every instance control the use of its own signifiers, particularly when such signifiers enter the public sphere where they may be appropriated and given new, potentially subversive meaning by marginalized others. Paradoxically, "identities can be forged within the very discourse through which one's subjectivity has been denied articulation." Such articulations may become the basis of a political program which law indirectly enables.

Less concerned with legal doctrine than Halley and Currah, Stychin explores how the destabilization of the hetero/homosexual binary may create "opportunities for resistance within the legal realm [by showing how] . . . the weakness in the system might be subverted and even queered."[39] In comparison to Halley, he suggests that the instability of homosexual identities, their capacity to expose how any sexual identity is always an "imitation of a copy," to paraphrase Judith Butler,[40] might be politically productive. In other words, if the articulation of homosexuality within a cultural and political arena reveals the false universalism of heterosexuality, then sexual identities and their expression may become a site of political contestation.[41] Like Halley, he recognizes that occupying the closet means access to the political process and public dialogue is denied. However, contrary to Halley, who argues for a return to legal categories to remedy this problem, Stychin implies that legal discourse may be most politically productive when it is reappropriated and transformed by marginalized others who seek to "disrupt [law's] discursive address" and "inscribe their own authorial signature on the official social text."[42] When attention is directed to the realm of cultural politics, then the aim is not merely to reconfigure legal doctrine. Investigating the discursive connections among social and cultural processes and law is necessary, but it is equally important to explore how such processes might transform affiliations and identifications.

Stychin does not develop this latter point. Moreover, in his conclusion, he retreats to a position which seems odd given the arguments preceding it. Recognizing the paradoxical nature of law, that it is "dynamic, unstable and unpredictable," and yet has the tendency to insidiously fix identities, he nevertheless argues that it is necessary to utilize "coherent categories as a strategy of political reform and transformation."[43] One reason Stychin argues for a return to legal categories lies in his conceptualization of queerness as a means to "undermine and destabilise sexual (and other identities) as the basis of both activism and theory," and *as an identity category,* one "potentially provid[ing] a point of unity across differences of gender, sexual practices and sexual orientation."[44] Queerness offers a focal point for coalitions to develop, and for differences within queerness to be recognized. On the other hand, the articulation of identity categories within law may "create a category that *matters* and that warrants legal protection."[45] However, Stychin has already demonstrated that law is most useful not when it simply recognizes an identity, but when those on the margins of juridical power rearticulate its meaning. Remaining within the logic of "official recognition," Stychin suppresses the cultural contestations he initially highlighted.

Having suggested both the indeterminacy of law and identity, and the relationship established between these two terms, Halley, Currah, and Stychin return to a politics of "official recognition." While Halley and Currah realize that the constitution of "homosexual" subjects is subject to the vagaries of legal interpretation, they remain wedded to a view of the political that premises legal standing as the quintessential expression of a political subject. Despite their compelling analysis of how legal categories consistently fail to represent political constituents adequately, they seek official recognition for a subject who, again despite their problematization of identity, becomes remarkably unambiguous when legal categories are called upon to represent that identity. Stychin presses further. Yet he, too, succumbs to the seduction of "official recognition" when he returns to law asking it to valorize and protect the "stigmatized" identity it has played an integral role in constituting.

There are several issues I have raised which I will explore as I take up a discussion of the *Ulane* case and return to the *Hardwick* decision. First, I want to compare the insidious construction of identity characterizing the *Hardwick* decision with a case suggesting the possibilities of articulating non-identity. A return to the legal field informed by an examination of cultural identity formation specific to queer theory reminds us that queer legal theorists' interpretation of *Hardwick* remains incomplete: specifically, it stops short of insisting on the instability of all sexual identities. Unlike the *Hardwick* decision, *Ulane I* intimates a profound difference between an insidious deployment of identity and the subversive undermining of fixed definitions of sexual identity. The district court case provides a clearer view of how sexual identities might be unsettled in light of the mutually constituted instability of law, sex, and gender.[46]

This case and the subsequent appellate court opinion, *Ulane II,* also demonstrate that subversive representations of identity in the legal field do not guarantee transformative social change. This might be a reason to dismiss the importance of articulating non-identity. As Butler puts it, attempts to subvert heterosexuality either through "denaturalizing parodies" or reversals of binary oppositions may merely "reidealize heterosexual norms."[47]

The district court decision does not effect such a reidealization, although it comes periously close. Judge Grady's close encounter with Karen Ulane's ambiguous sexual identity, coupled with his need to recognize her "officially," forced him to deconstruct sex and to wonder what it was about gender that kept him from doing the same.

Judge Grady, "What Did We Get When We Got Sex?"

In 1980, Karen Ulane was fired by Eastern Airlines after having sex reassignment surgery. Suing under Title VII of the Civil Rights Act of 1964, her case was first heard in the Federal District Court in Chicago and, subsequently, by the Court of Appeals for the Seventh Circuit.

In *Ulane I,* Judge Grady was called upon to determine whether Eastern Airlines had wrongfully discharged Karen Ulane. The central problem of the case lay in conclusively determining the meaning of sex. While the legal questions presented in the district court case suggest Judge Grady's task was merely to decide if Ulane was female (and therefore a member of a class protected by Title VII), Ulane's transsexuality confounded the determination of "sex" from the beginning. Once it became clear that there was no fixed definition of sex per se, it was necessary to distinguish this case from one in which Ulane was discharged simply because she was a woman. Rather, the question of how "sex" and "gender" *signify* within the boundaries of Title VII became crucial. Unlike the *Hardwick* case, which proposed categorical distinctions bound by a behavior/identity construct, Ulane's identity could not be confined to an essentialized category, precisely because she had no "essence." As Judge Grady described it, the plaintiff's transsexuality opened up "a can of worms,"[48] that is, the decidedly queer problem of questioning dominant social and legal classifications of identity posed either in terms of biological sex, gender, or sexual orientation.

In the cause of recognizing an ambiguously sexed subject, Grady asserted that sex should be reconceived as a question of "sexual identity" defined in social and relational terms, rather than as a discrete, essential category of being.[49] Judge Grady concluded that the greater weight of the evidence showed that sex was not a "cut and dried matter of chromosomes," rather the term "sex," as used in medical science, "can be and should be reasonably interpreted to include among its denotations the question of sexual identity." The medical testimony in this case was a key factor in Grady's affirmation that "transsexuals are protected by Title VII." In contrast to the defendant's witnesses who argued that sex was simply chromosomal, an expression of fixed biological categories (an argument paralleling the *Hardwick* Court's construction of a "sodomitical essence"), several members of the University of Chicago Medical School Gender Identity Board presented decisive evidence showing sex was an "unstable" category."[50] While some Board members considered sex reassignment surgery a success based on factors such as psychological stability and emotional health,[51] their testimony intimated Karen's successful performance as a gendered woman was equally important in evaluating the outcome of her surgery.

However, by claiming the articulation of appropriate performance in the gender of choice as the hallmark of a postoperative transsexual identity, witnesses for Ulane and Grady reinstated the fixity of sex based on a binary system of gender. Grady's opinion suggests that gender signifies psychological, social, and cultural stability because it demonstrates that sexual ambiguity has been erased. Aided paradoxically by medical testimony enabling him to recognize Ulane's ambiguous sex and to reestablish the fixity of gender roles, Grady reaches the discursive limits of his own deconstructive efforts.

Clearly, Grady is puzzled by Ulane because he wants to recognize her, but he can only do so by assuming the instability of her sexual identity. Desperate to find some stable category capturing Ulane's identity within legal parameters, Grady seized on gender. In so doing, he constructed Ulane as a "gendered woman" thereby revealing how gender is "not the product of a choice, but the forcible citation of a norm, one whose complex historicity is indissociable from relations of discipline, regulation, punishment."[52] Describing Ulane in terms of discrete gender roles allowed him to define her identity according to a familiar binary opposition and thus to recognize her "officially." To this end, Grady noted Karen Ulane's remarkable adjustment to her sex-change operation:

> She appears to (the various psychiatrists) to be a woman. She conducts herself as a woman. She dresses as a woman. There is nothing flamboyant, nothing freakish about the plaintiff. It would take an extremely practiced eye, it seems to me, to detect any difference between the plaintiff and the biological woman. . . . She appears (to me) to be a biological woman.[53]

And, most importantly, "there has been no reversion to any masculine behavior that we have any knowledge of."[54]

Grady could press no further without acknowledging that transsexuality *also* reveals the instability of gender and the biological and cultural instabilities built into the sex/gender system, thus releasing the tensions contained in the legal and social insistence on the fixity of "male" and "female." As Julia Epstein and Kristina Straub observe, definitions of gender and sex provide one of the "primary differentiating principles by which binary structures are socially initiated and maintained." In light of such differentiating principles, "ambiguous identities and erotic practices"[55] may provide a location for destabilizing the taxonomies underwriting the sex/gender system. When the possibilities for resignifying gender are opened up by virtue of the fact that a gendered subject must be discursively constituted "again and again" through the compulsory reiteration of norms,[56] then revealing the performativity of gender might prompt a reevaluation of the binary thinking informing legal categories of analysis and systems of heterosexist power.

Constrained by the limits imposed both by legal categories and the problems Ulane's ambiguous identity posed, Grady established Ulane was a transsexual because of her ability to enact a successful fixed gender identity. Subsequently, he considered the specific reasons for her discharge after the sex-change operation. Eastern expressed concern with a "transsexual in the cockpit" through their focus on the relationship between safety and psychological stability. Both Karen's biological lack and her successful acquisition of a female gender role generated anxiety. Since Ulane not only disrupts conventional notions of sex and gender, but also calls into question the heterosexual matrix which depends on discrete, oppositional, and immutable definitions of sex and gender, the anxiety generated by transsexuality is indeed related to "safety," just as Eastern argued. However, it may not be the safety of the public or crew members that is at stake here, but *the relative safety and security of the term "sex" and the comfort we take in assuming that gender categories fix identities unproblematically.*

The final difficulty Grady faced in deciding the case was his inability to recognize Ulane as a transsexual (Count II) without changing the law; that is, Ulane's identity couldn't be contained within legal categories. However, he couldn't argue that Ulane was discriminated against as a woman (Count I), which would allow him to decide the case within the boundaries of Title VII, because he thought the evidence showed that she was discriminated against as a transsexual. Faced with two contradictory theories, he found: "The evidence most clearly establishes that transsexuals are entitled to protection under the act than it does that an operated transsexual is now a woman. While I would not argue with the latter proposition, the former seems to me more strongly supported."[57] During a post-trial hearing, however, Grady expressed reservations about his decision, suggesting the certainty he had gained by finding gender to be a fixed marker of identity was decisive. Accordingly, judgement for Ulane was entered in favor of both Counts I and II: Karen Ulane was both a transsexual and a woman.

Mirroring the confusion which transsexuality generated, yet ultimately constrained by the need to maintain the legal fiction of a binary system of gender, Grady's opinion highlighted the ambiguity of "sex," thereby creating an opportunity for further contestation within the legal field. Grady presented his puzzlement in a public discursive space, subversively dismantling sex and extending the scope of Title VII, no small undertaking for a federal district court judge. In comparison, when Justice White announced the *Hardwick* decision, he claimed an authority and decisiveness that foreclosed any doubt about the meaning of the categories he employed. Judge Grady's efforts to write a coherent identity for Ulane in order, as Halley puts it, "to place legal burdens on it,"[58] cast light on the legal field as an interpretive field of practice by tacitly underscoring the radical undecideability of the term "sex," and the law's potential inability to contain the meaning of any sexual identity.

> Judge Wood, "Congress . . . never intended this 1964 legislation to apply to anything other than the traditional concept of sex."

> Justice White, "[T]he majority of the electorate of Georgia believes that homosexual sodomy is immoral and unacceptable."

In *Ulane II,* Grady's opinion was overruled, and the court of appeals found that sex was not defined as "sexual identity." The appeals court argued that what Congress had in mind when amending Title VII to include sex discrimination was "sex, in its plain meaning," suggesting that is "unlawful to discriminate against women because they are women and against men because they are men."[59] Once sex is redefined as merely a biological category, it is possible to rewrite transsexual identity: "Ulane is . . . a biological male . . ." and therefore not afforded protection by Title VII. Further dismantling the lower court opinion, Judge Wood decreed: "It is clear from the evidence that if Eastern did discriminate against Ulane, it was not because she is female, but because Ulane is a transsexual—a biological male who takes female hormones, cross-dresses, and has surgically altered parts of her body to make it appear to be female."[60]

The destabilization created by Grady's initial interpretation of sex is foreclosed, in part because, as the appellate court judges argued, Judge Grady failed to think "straight." The interpretive problem the court of appeals faced was to create a seemingly fixed ground which would enable the reduction of the complexities and incongruities surrounding Ulane's non-identity which, in their view, had lead Grady astray. Since this ground could not be reinstated simply by returning to fixed biological categories, the court of appeals sought to justify their reversal of the lower court decision by referring to the history of the Civil Rights Act of 1964:

> When Congress enacted the Civil Rights Act of 1964 . . . sex . . . was added as a floor amendment one day before the House approved Title VII without prior hearing or debate. . . . This sex amendment was the gambit of a congressman seeking to scuttle adoption of the Civil Rights Act. The ploy failed and sex discrimination was abruptly added. . . . The total lack of legislative history supporting the sex amendment coupled with the circumstances of the amendment's adoption clearly indicates that Congress never considered nor intended that this 1964 legislation apply to anything other than *the traditional concept of sex.*[61]

Congressional intent is invoked as a metaphor for a fictive community that is presumed to endorse the "traditional" meaning of sex ("men are men, and women are women"). This community is composed of individuals whose sexual identities are fixed and naturally ordered, and whose affiliations with others are implicitly confined to a heterosexual model. The juridical interpretation of sex appears to rest on an extra-legal foundation, a homogeneous community of unambiguously sexed individuals. However, this community, as in the court of appeals' decision, is both constituted and (re)created as an effect of legal discourse. Since legal classifications of "sex" are unstable, they may be validated by a fictive community whose sexual identity is ostensibly fixed. As a result, differently sexed subjects are theorized as marginal to this community and, accordingly, denied legal protection.

The opinions in both *Ulane II* and *Hardwick* testify to the power of legal discourse to constitute both sex and sexual identity. The legal actors in these cases rely on a conception of community peculiar to a politics of "official recognition," respectively, to justify the reduction of transsexuality to biological categories, and homosexuality to a singular act. Within the logic of "official recognition," community is conceived as stable and animated by universal, transhistorical values which are shared by like-minded community members. In the *Hardwick* decision, Justice White, writing for the majority, justified his construction of homosexuals and homosexuality by drawing on nascent views of community embedded in his peculiar reading of the history of sodomy, and his invocation of tradition and morality. The dissenters perform the same function by valorizing patriarchal family values, the institution of marriage, and reconstituting the public sphere defined by sanitized heterosexual behavior.

(Mis)reading the history of sodomy, Justice White first extends his description beyond the geographical and temporal boundaries of the contemporary United States to note that "prescriptions against [homosexual sodomy] have ancient roots."[62] Closer to home, he notes that "sodomy was a criminal offense at common law and was forbidden by the laws of 13 states when they ratified the Bill of Rights."[63] In two brief paragraphs, he sketches out an argument that is historically inaccurate, as several commentators have noted.[64] While Justice White's description "promotes formal sameness over radical historical discontinuity,"[65] constructing sodomy as a transhistorical practice peculiar to homosexuals, it also serves an additional purpose. Deploying a static conception of the history of sodomy allows him to show why homosexuality, conveniently defined as engagement in sodomy, is *not* "deeply rooted in this Nation's history and tradition."[66] In short, Justice White can avoid legislating from the bench by declaring that he is merely mirroring (rather than constructing) community values, norms, and traditions which have animated and continue to sustain an unproblematized conception of American "nationhood." More transparently, when he is called upon to address Hardwick's claim that the Georgia statute cannot be justified merely by "the presumed belief of the majority of the electorate in

Georgia that homosexual sodomy is immoral and unacceptable," he concludes otherwise, noting that "majority sentiments" are adequate to uphold
the constitutionality of the Georgia statute.[67]

The dissenters in *Hardwick* set out to criticize some of the more egregious
oversights effected by the majority opinion. However, they end up valorizing
individuals' rights to make decisions about the most "intimate aspects of
their lives" within the parameters of the private sphere. Noting that state
regulation does not extend to the regulation of "intimate behavior in intimate places," they simultaneously assert that nothing in their argument forecloses the state from policing expressions of "intimate behavior" in public.[68]
What emerges from the dissents is a description of the public arena which
mirrors Michael Warner's observation that the public sphere "has been structured . . . by a logic of abstraction that provides a privilege for unmarked
identities: the male, the white, the middle-class, and the normal."[69]

Unlike the opinion in *Ulane II,* the dissents do not constitute a community
of the "unambiguously sexed." Rather, they reinstate the familiar distinction
between the private and public spheres. In the former, individuals are free to
do as they like. Yet any "intimate" acts (or identities), except those defined
by the familiar tropes of marriage and reproductivity, are denied expression
in a public discursive space. Accordingly, such articulations can neither constitute this abstraction, the "public," nor enable the potential transformation
of citizens' affiliations and identifications.

When courts deploy the language of "community" or related concepts as
the basis for removing particular cultural expressions from circulation, they
are (re)presenting the "imagined community" of the liberal state. While
queer legal theorists have demonstrated how decisions such as *Hardwick*
construct individual and group identities and reinstate binary oppositions,
attention must also be directed to the intimate relationship between community and identity. In *Hardwick* and *Ulane II,* the former rests on notions
of sameness which "initiate a particular agenda with respect to the representation and positioning of difference. Differences are what this concept of
community is intended to overcome."[70] The particularity of identities is
thereby lost, and the political contestation which might arise from a recognition of the contingent and transitory character both of community, and of
the multiple, fractured nature of identities, is erased. Remaining within a politics of "official recognition" forecloses recognition of the proliferation of
new political spaces and identities that might unsettle reductive notions of
either identity or community. As Currah and Stychin intimate, without fully
developing the idea, such a disruption might also reveal the intimate relationship between (and among) law, community, identity.

Both the court of appeals' invocation of a community of unambiguously
sexed individuals and the *Hardwick* Court's reliance on specific configurations of public and private identities rest on a model of politics that assumes
individual interests are aggregated based on shared affiliations which can be

addressed to a sovereign state. In comparison, a queer politics of "direct address" suggests that identities are themselves contingent rather than fixed, and community is more forcefully articulated in the plural. Locating community in the realm of the social signals "a move beyond the territorially bounded juridical institutions of the state into the far more fluid and shifting domain of cultural representation."[71] For example, cultural transgressions, such as those enacted by Queer Nation, realize the potential of political identifications and the types of aspirational communities they might enable.

Queer Nation, "We're Here, We're Queer, Get Used to It."

Since *Bowers v Hardwick,* we have seen the development of different types of political practice which invoke political identities *that do not ask the law for recognition*. In other words, legal decisions, including those in which the plaintiff loses, may create a "cultural space for politicization."[x] Paradoxically, the aftermath of *Bowers v Hardwick* fostered the development of a new politics signified most forcefully by the group known as "Queer Nation."[72] Queers propose to make the articulation of identity a political project, to disaggregate legal definitions of homosexuality and to constitute a cultural politics as a political commitment. It is this politics of "direct address" which distinguishes these new styles of politics from a politics of "official recognition" embraced by most legal actors and also advanced by some queer legal theorists.

While the *Hardwick* decision forced gays and lesbians to rethink their strategies for implementing legal change, it also revitalized a new social movement of gays, lesbians, and bisexuals.[73] The classificatory and normalizing tendencies of legal discourse, which in *Hardwick* reduced homosexuality to a fixed "sodomitical essence,"[74] created the rhetorical conditions for queers to resist this representation of their identity and to turn to alternate forms of social activism.

Queer cultural improvisations, like those of other subordinate groups, can be used to "affirm emergent identities and communities."[75] Moreover, these cultural interventions suggest that political practice may be reconceived to include "the everyday enactment of social practices and the reiteration of cultural representations."[76] By invading straight bars, for example, queers broadcast the "ordinariness" of the queer body. As Lauren Berlant and Elizabeth Freeman point out, "Queer Nights Out" show a heterosexual culture that "gay sexual identity is no longer a reliable foil for straightness," and that what "looked like bounded gay subcultural activity has itself become restless and improvisatory, taking its pleasures in a theater near you."[77] Similarly, Queer Shopping Network uses the mall, print media, and advertising to take advantage of that quintessentially American institution, the "consumer's pleasure in vicarious identification." Queer Shopping Network's strategy is "to reveal to the consumer desires he/she didn't know he/she had, to make his/her identification with the product, homosexuality, both an unsettling and pleasurable experience [thereby making] consumer pleasure central to the transformation of public culture."[78] The staged mall spectacle of same-sex couples embracing, kissing, and holding hands incites the consumer's own "perverse desire to experience a different body" while offering itself as "the most stylish of the many attitudes on sale in the mall."[79] Unlike the other "displays" present in the mall setting, the queer body invites identification with a commodity that shoppers already possess: "a sexually inflected and explicitly desiring body."

If, as Berlant has suggested, American cultural legitimacy derives from "the privilege to suppress and protect the body," as both the opinions in *Hardwick* and *Ulane II* starkly demonstrate, then queers clearly unsettle a central feature of national identity.[80] Queer Nation rejects the dominant culture's categorization of homosexual bodies to assert the positivity of a queer sexuality which is public, political, and particular. Queers reject "right to privacy" arguments which are asserted to invalidate anti-sodomy laws; they reject their status as disembodied subjects of the public sphere; they refuse the historical, cultural, and legal terms used to frame sexuality; and they reconfigure the public sphere as a potential site for the articulation of multiply sexed subjects. Familiarizing mainstream America with "otherness" in all its varieties means that queers do not seek inclusion under the rubric of liberal tolerance; rather, they suggest that the processes whereby identities are constructed should become objects of criticism in their own right.

This politics has several features that distinguish it from traditional accounts of liberal citizenship or liberal legalism, that is, from a politics of "official recognition." First, the location of what counts as political practice is shifted to the enactment of social practices and cultural codes that become vehicles for affirming the identities of marginalized groups. Second, identity is refigured, as Chantal Mouffe puts it, "as the articulation of an ensemble of subject positions, constructed within specific discourses and . . . precariously sutured at the intersection of these subject positions."[81] In contrast to the unitary subject of liberal citizenship whose interests are projected "onto the screen of state policy,"[82] the creation of this subject's identity and agency is contingent on forms of identification that emerge from contesting differences without necessarily asserting similarity. Group interests are not aggregated based on sameness; rather the contestation which emerges from negotiating differences of race, class, ethnicity, sexual orientation, and gender may provide opportunities for the modification of available forms of identity and their embrace. Third, community is reconceived, not as a "final achievement,"[83] but as an historically contingent phenomenon which is enacted within, and limited by, the "historical realm of discourses and institutions."[84]

When a conception of the political is expanded to incorporate the everyday enactment of social practices and cultural significations, politics becomes a form of "signifying activity."[85] Marginalized groups may become active agents of change by drawing on historically available signifieds, including those which legal discourse puts into circulation. The (re)appropriation of legal signs and legal inscriptions of identity provides resources for the formation of identity and community. However, as Rosemary Coombe observes, these "tactics of appropriation" are not necessarily taken up to return to the legal field as a site of struggle.[86] Queers use legal descriptions of homosexuality to create contestation in the public sphere, to reimagine community and to transform the political field by challenging community members' own identifications.

Queers' response to the legal normalization of homosexual identity might be described as a means to get people to stop seeing "straight," for seeing straight is a form of "misrecognition"[87] of oneself, of others, and of the space we share. Marginalized groups may claim that their identities cannot be contained by the legal classifications which define them, and they may do so through tactics of familiarization that appropriate dominant consumer imagery. Public recognition of a norm may shift attention to the subordinate terms and identities which sustain it through processes that provoke identification by redefining the familiar landscape of the mall, for instance, while critically marking it as a site of difference.

A renewal of community and politics may occur through a politics of direct address enacted through cultural interventions and the reimagination of community. Transformation occurs not merely by exposing differences and arguing for their inclusion under the guise of a politics of official "recognition"; rather change occurs when the affiliations of "ordinary people" are reconstituted. Queers' engagement of tactics of cultural subversion such as those engendered by the decision in *Bowers v Hardwick* suggests that legal and social change may depend on the local and particularized interventions of agents whose actions are not merely defined by rights consciousness, but rather emerge in relation to the contradictions embodied in the relationships among (and between) "self," "other," and "community."

For example, within the logic of a politics of "direct address," identities are constituted in relation to each other, but they are also constituted through political identifications which constantly reconfigure those identities.[88] In other words, identities are constituted out of bits and pieces of experience, but in their articulation, they become more than just the sum of their original elements.[89] As Douglas Crimp illustrates:

[A] white, middle-class, HIV-negative lesbian might form an identification with a poor black mother with AIDS and through that identification might be inclined to work on pediatric health care issues; or, outraged by attention to the needs of babies at the expense of the needs of women who bear them, she might decide to fight against clinical trials whose sole purpose is to examine the effects of an antiviral drug on perinatal transmission and thus ignores effects on the mother's body. She might form an identification with a gay male friend with AIDS and work for faster testing of new treatments for opportunistic infections, but then, through her understanding that her friend would be able to afford such treatments while others would not, she might shift her attention to health care access issues.[90]

Political identifications may thus become vehicles for remaking identities. Fields of practice such as law might thereby be shaped and reshaped in relation to the shifting terrain of citizens' affiliations even as they are circumscribed by past struggles which define the possibilities of transformation.

Like the civil rights and feminist movements' use of cultural tactics to effect political, social, and legal change, queers aim to transform citizens' identifications as a means of rewriting the social text. Unlike these other movements, queers refuse an identity which is limited by dominant, unitary legal classifications. Queers destabilize fixed notions of sexual identity and argue for a reformulation of the conditions under which "further interventions into the juridical, policy, and popular practices of contemporary America" can occur.[91] Can sexual differences understood "not in terms of naturalized identities but as a form of dissent . . . as a constellation of nonconforming practices, expressions and beliefs" create a renewal of political practice?[92] Rather than regard the modern constitutional state as the privileged site of the political, queer legal theorists might refuse to accept the discursive subject positions that law provides, and focus instead on the cultural constestations and the transformation and shifting of identifications which legal decisions might enable. Refusing legal definitions of identity, highlighting the ambiguity peculiar to "sex" and any claim to a fixed "sexual" identity might challenge an unproblematized return to legal fora. Moreover, social transformations might lead to a reconfiguration of community thereby creating the conditions for the articulation of sexual identities, including "queerness."

More generally, what implications do such practices carry, not only for a queer agenda, but also for a renewal of community and politics? As David Carroll observes, it is not enough "to grant autonomy to and enfranchise, in the name of liberal pluralism, the plurality of groups and collectivities demanding to be recognized and legitimated as communities"; rather community must be conceived in terms of a "radical otherness."[93] Rather than conceive community in terms of what we have "in common" with others, how we are like others,[94] the interplay between community and its role in the construction of identities might be emphasized. By claiming that relationships among community members are based on "commonness," such a view of community overlooks "the radical lack threatening the identity of these agents."[95] As Ernesto Laclau suggests, if all identities are "founded" on a lack, mere claims to shared identity or a homogeneity of interests can not dispense with this constitutive failure. A belief in external referents such as law merely covers over the impossibility of founding a community based on shared affiliations. The particularity of identities and the social antagonisms they create render untenable such a view of community and suggest the importance of the partial and contingent nature of political and social identifications. In comparison, according to the logic of a politics of "direct address," community is not viewed as a source of support per se nor as a stable location where subjects with cohesive identities engage. Rather, as Jean-Luc Nancy describes it, "being in common" means "no longer having, in any form, in any empirical or ideal place, such a substantial identity and sharing this [narcissistic] lack of identity."[96]

Aspirational communities such as those developed by Queer Nation effect a critique of the vision of community peculiar to a politics of "official recognition" as articulated in both the *Hardwick* and *Ulane* cases. They do so by enjoining us to take seriously the role of identification, as compared to identity, in constituting citizens' affiliations. Unlike queer legal theorists' embrace of doctrinal solutions, a queer notion of community and law suggests that the processes whereby communities and identifications are transformed are integrally related to the manner in which both terms might be reconceived. In this sense, the outcome of neither *Bowers v Hardwick* nor the *Ulane* case is wholly negative. Granted both Ulane and Hardwick "lose" their cases, but the legal decisions can be interpreted to suggest the instability of sex and sexual identities and the capacity of ambiguous identities to create contestation in the legal field. At the same time, both cases suggest the bankruptcy of a conception of community which attempts to flee toward identity as the ground of its political aspirations.

Notes

Parts of this chapter appeared in *Law and Society Review* vol. 28, no. 5 (1994): 1009. I am grateful to Rosemary Coombe for her willingness to engage in extended conversations about the relationship between community and identity, and for her excellent editorial advice, and to Shane Phelan for her patience and encouragement. A number of people provided valuable insights, including the faithful members of my writing group at the University of Minnesota, Lisa Disch and Jennifer Pierce, and my colleagues at Arizona State University, Elizabeth Horan and Susan McCabe. All archival materials are from the National Archives & Record Administration, 7358 Pulaski Avenue, Chicago, IL.

1. *Bowers v Hardwick,* 478 U.S. 196 (1986).

2. Steven Seidman, "Symposium: Queer Theory/Sociology: A Dialogue," *Sociological Theory* 12 (1994): 166.

3. For examples (which are discussed below) see Janet Halley, "The Politics of the Closet: Towards Equal Protection for Gay, Lesbian, and Bisexual Identity," first published in *UCLA Law Review* 36 (1989): 915–976, and reprinted in Jonathan Goldberg, ed., *Reclaiming Sodom*

(New York: Routledge, 1994), 145–204, all citations from *Reclaiming Sodom;* "Misreading Sodomy: A Critique of the Classification of 'Homosexuals' in Federal Equal Protection Law," in *Body Guards: The Cultural Politics of Gender Ambiguity,* Julia Epstein and Kristina Straub, eds. (New York: Routledge, 1991), 351–378; "The Construction of Heterosexuality," in *Fear of a Queer Planet,* Michael Warner, ed. (Minneapolis: University of Minnesota Press, 1993), 82–104; "Reasoning About Sodomy: Act and Identity In and After *Bowers v. Hardwick,*" *Virginia Law Review* 79 (1993): 1721–1780; and "Sexual Orientation and the Politics of Biology: A Critique of the Argument from Immutability," *Stanford Law Review* 46 (1994): 503–568. Also see Paisley Currah, "Searching For Immutability: Homosexuality, Race, and Rights Discourse," in *A Simple Matter of Justice?,* A.R. Wilson, ed. (London: Cassell, 1995), 51–90; and Carl Stychin, *Law's Desire: Sexuality and the Limits of Justice* (London: Routledge, 1995) and "To Take Him 'At His Word': Theorizing Law, Sexuality, and the U.S. Military Exclusion Policy," forthcoming, *Social and Legal Studies* 5 (1996).

4. Halley, "The Construction of Heterosexuality," 83.

5. Linda Singer, "Recalling a Community at Loose Ends," in *Community at Loose Ends,* Miami Theory Collective, ed. (Minneapolis: University of Minnesota Press, 1991), 124.

6. Kristie McClure, "On the Subject of Rights: Pluralism, Plurality, and Political Identity," in *Dimensions of Radical Democracy: Pluralism, Citizenship, Community,* Chantal Mouffe, ed. (London: Verso, 1992), 123.

7. *Ulane v Eastern Airlines,* 581 F.Supp. 821, 35 F.E.P. 1332 (N.D. Ill. 1984).

8. *Ulane v Eastern Airlines,* 742 F.2d 1081, 35 F.E.P. 1348 (7th Cir. 1984).

9. See Benedict Anderson, *Imagined Communities: Reflections on the Origin and Spread of Nationalism* (London: Verso, 1994).

10. Singer, "Recalling a Community at Loose Ends," 124.

11. *Bowers v Hardwick,* 186; emphasis added.

12. Ibid., 196.

13. Jonathan Goldberg, *Sodometries: Renaissance Texts, Modern Sexualities* (Stanford: Stanford University Press, 1992), 24.

In his incisive analysis of sodomy and *Bowers v Hardwick,* Jonathan Goldberg sketches intriguing parallels among Renaissance texts, colonial American statutes, and the Supreme Court's decision in the *Hardwick* case. Each legitimizes an act (heterosexual sodomy) in one situation that it stigmatizes in another (homosexual sodomy). As

Goldberg puts it: "[T]o define an identity through an act that it also permits to those whose identities are not defined by the performance of the act, [the decision] leaves open the question of where heterosexual identity resides beyond the affirmation of a difference that has no content, an identity in other words that is defined by no specificity of acts but only claims to be an identity" (10). Sodomy, that "utterly confused category," continues to animate contemporary juridical regimes of power and "to perform the work of categorical confusion that is necessary to maintain the state" (11). The distinctions drawn between homosexual and heterosexual sodomy, and between identities and acts are productive in the Foucaultian sense because they (re)affirm the patriarchal family, the institution of marriage, and the hom(m)o-sociality of the public sphere that is covered over by "the thin veneer of family life as the sole domain of sexual behavior" (17).

14. Halley, "The Politics of the Closet," 148.

15. See Halley, "Sexual Orientation and the Politics of Biology," for a discussion of how the "immutability" argument, supported by recent scientific studies claiming sexual orientation is "genetically determined," has been extended in post-*Hardwick* cases.

16. Naomi Mezey, "Dismantling the Wall: Bisexuality and the Possibilities of Sexual Identity Classification Based on Acts," *Berkeley Women's Law Review* 10 (1995): 123.

17. *Paula v Webster,* 822 F.2d 97 (D.C. Cir., 1987).

18. Mezey, "Dismantling the Wall," 123.

19. Ibid.

20. Halley, "Sexual Orientation," 511.

21. For a discussion of relevant cases which suggest the courts' inability to grapple with this distinction, see Currah, "Searching for Immutability," 63–68; Halley, "The Construction of Heterosexuality"; and Stychin, "Inside and Out of the Military," in *Law's Desire,* 90–101 and "To Take Him 'At His Word.'"

22. Halley, "The Politics of the Closet," 148.

23. Ibid., 180.

24. Halley, "Misreading Sodomy," 352.

25. My thanks to Rosemary Coombe for bringing this argument to my attention, and insisting I develop it.

27. This footnote was appended to a rather unremarkable case dealing with adulterated milk products, *U.S. v Carolene Products,* which was decided in 1942. Justice Stone's footnote had little impact until the Warren

Court resurrected it and used it to create a number of fundamental rights associated with the civil rights era.

28. Halley, "The Politics of the Closet," 180.

29. Ibid., 188.

30. Halley, "The Construction of Heterosexuality," 98.

31. Ibid.

32. A number of socio-legal scholars have made this argument, including Kristin Bumiller, "Victims in the Shadow of the Law: A Critique of the Model of Legal Protection," *Signs* 12 (1987): 421–439; Sally Merry, *Getting Justice and Getting Even: Legal Consciousness Among Working Class Americans* (Chicago: University of Chicago Press, 1990); Michael McCann, *Rights at Work: Pay Equity Reform and the Politics of Legal Mobilization* (Chicago: University of Chicago Press, 1994); and Stuart Scheingold, "Constitutional Rights and Social Change: Civil Rights in Perspective," in *Judging the Constitution,* Michael McCann and Gerald Houseman, eds. (Glenview, Illinois: Scott Foresman, 1989): 73–91.

33. Currah, "Searching for Immutability," 53–4.

34. Ibid., 58.

35. Ibid., 78.

36. Ibid.

37. Stychin, *Law's Desire,* 12.

38. This argument is particularly well developed in the following articles by Rosemary Coombe: "Publicity Rights and Political Aspiration: Mass Culture, Gender Identity, and Democracy," *New England Law Review* 26 (1992):1221–80, and "Tactics of Appropriation and the Politics of Recognition in Late Modern Democracies," *Politcal Theory* 21 (1993): 411–433.

39. Stychin, *Law's Desire,* 140.

40. Judith Butler, "Imitation and Gender Insubordination," in *Inside/Out: Lesbian Theories, Gay Theories* (New York: Routledge, 1991), 21.

41. Ibid., 31.

42. Coombe, "Tactics of Appropriation," 427.

43. Stychin, *Law's Desire,* 31.

44. Ibid., 142.

45. Ibid., 155, emphasis original.

46. While there is clearly a difference between a gay or lesbian subject position and one occupied by transsexuals, for my purposes *Ulane I* shows how a politics of non-identity works within the legal field. For a discus-

sion of this point, see Janet Halley, introduction to "Intersections: Sexuality, Cultural Tradition, and the Law," *Yale Journal of Law & the Humanities* 8 (1996): 102–3.

47. Judith Butler, "Critically Queer," see page 21 this volume.

48. Transcript of Proceedings, 10 Jan. 1984, p. 15, Box 193001.

49. Dean Dickie (Karen Ulane's lawyer) and Dr. Tom Jones (an endocrinologist associated with the University of Chicago Gender Identity Board) described Grady as a rather conservative judge with a high regard for the medical profession. Their recollection is that Grady demonstrated a remarkable learning curve during the course of the trial (Interviews, 26 May 1993 and 2 June 1993). As Judge Grady notes in his oral memorandum, "Prior to my participation in this case, I would have had no doubt that the question of sex was a very straightforward matter of whether you are male or female. . . . After listening to the evidence in this case, it is clear to me that there is no settled definition in the medical community as to what we mean by sex." *Ulane I,* 823.

50. *Ulane I,* 825.

51. Dr. Tom Jones, Interview, 2 June 1993.

52. Butler, "Critically Queer," page 22 in this volume.

53. *Ulane I,* 827.

54. Ibid.

55. Julia Epstein and Kristina Straub, "Introduction: The Guarded Body," in *Body Guards: The Cultural Politics of Gender Ambiguity,* Julia Epstein and Kristina Straub, eds. (New York: Routledge, 1990), 6.

56. Judith Butler, "For A Careful Reading," in *Feminist Contentions: A Philosophical Exchange,* Seyla Benhabib, Judith Butler, Drucilla Cornell, and Nancy Fraser, eds. (New York: Routledge, 1995), 135.

57. *Ulane I,* 838.

58. Halley, "Misreading Sodomy," 363.

59. *Ulane II,* 1085.

60. *Ulane II,* 1087.

61. *Ulane II,* 1085, emphasis added.

62. *Bowers v Hardwick,* 192.

63. Ibid.

64. For further discussion of this point see Goldberg, *Reclaiming Sodom;* Halley, "Reasoning About Sodomy"; and sources cited in both.

65. Halley, "Reasoning About Sodomy," 1753.

66. *Bowers v Hardwick,* 194.

67. Ibid, 196.

68. Ibid., 212.

69. Michael Warner, "The Mass Public and the Mass Subject," in Bruce Robbins, ed., *The Phantom Public Sphere* (Minneapolis: University of Minnesota Press, 1993), 240.

70. Singer, "Recalling a Community at Loose Ends," 124.

71. McClure, "On the Subject of Rights," 123.

x. Scherngold, "Constitutional Rights," 86.

72. Although as Simon Watney observes in "AIDS and the Politics of Queer Diaspora," in *Negotiating Lesbian and Gay Subjects,* Monica Dorenkamp and Richard Henke, eds. (New York: Routledge, 1995) "much of the energy which accompanied the emergence of activist organizations such as Queer Nation in the U.S. and Outrage! in the U.K. have run out of steam" (52), for my purposes Queer Nation remains an important model of the cultural practices of subversion.

73. I am not suggesting that the decision in *Bowers v Hardwick* was the sole factor leading to this renewal of gay and lesbian activism. In 1990, Queer Nation emerged out of the ACT UP movement in response to a marked increase in violence against lesbians and gays.

74. Halley, "Misreading Sodomy," 354.

75. Coombe, "Publicity Rights and Political Aspiration," 1222–3.

76. McClure, "On the Subject of Rights," 123.

77. Lauren Berlant and Elizabeth Freeman, "Queer Nationality," *Boundary 2; and International Journal of Law and Literature* 19 (1992): 162.

78. Ibid., 164.

79. Ibid., 167.

80. Lauren Berlant, "National Brands/National Body: *Imitation of Life,*" in *Comparative American Identities: Race, Sex, and Nationality in the Modern Text,* Hortense Spillers, ed. (New York: Routledge, 1991).

81. Chantal Mouffe, "Democratic Citizenship and Political Community," in *Community at Loose Ends,* Miami Theory Collective, ed. (Minneapolis: University of Minnesota Press), 80.

82. McClure, "On the Subject of Rights," 1991, 120.

83. Mouffe, "Democratic Citizenship," 81.

84. Paul Smith, "Laclau and Mouffe's Secret Agent," in *Community at Loose Ends.*

85. Coombe, "Tactics of Appropriation," 412.

86. Ibid.

87. I use this term here to suggest that seeing "straight" is based on structural and linguistically produced misunderstandings about the nature of sexual categories.

88. See Douglas Crimp, "Right On, Girlfriend!" *Social Text* 33 (1992): 2–18.

89. See Jonathan Rutherford, "A Place Called Home: Identity and the Cultural Politics of Difference," in *Identity: Community, Culture, and Difference,* Jonathan Rutherford, ed. (London: Lawrence and Wishart, 1991).

90. Crimp, "Right On, Girlfriend!" 15–16.

91. Berlant and Freeman, "Queer Nationality," 154.

92. Lisa Duggan, "Queering the State," *Social Text* 39 (1994): 1.

93. David Carroll, "Community After Devastation," in *Politics, Theory and Contemporary Culture,* Mark Poster, ed. (New York: Columbia University Press, 1993), 183.

94. Phelan Shane, *Getting Specific: Postmodern Lesbian Politics* (Minneapolis: University of Minnesota Press, 1994), 82.

95. Ernesto Laclau, introduction in *The Making of Political Identities,* Ernesto Laclau, ed. (London: Verso, 1994), 2.

96. Quoted in Phelan, *Getting Specific,* 83